FRANCE IN THE WORLD

# France in the World

*The Career of André Siegfried*

SEAN M. KENNEDY

McGill-Queen's University Press
Montreal & Kingston · London · Chicago

© McGill-Queen's University Press 2023

ISBN 978-0-2280-1431-7 (cloth)
ISBN 978-0-2280-1533-8 (ePDF)
ISBN 978-0-2280-1534-5 (ePUB)

Legal deposit first quarter 2023
Bibliothèque nationale du Québec

Printed in Canada on acid-free paper that is 100% ancient forest free (100% post-consumer recycled), processed chlorine free

This book has been published with the help of a Harrison McCain Foundation Grant in Aid of Scholarly Publishing. Publication has also been supported by the Department of History and Faculty of Arts of the University of New Brunswick.

We acknowledge the support of the Canada Council for the Arts.

Nous remercions le Conseil des arts du Canada de son soutien.

---

Library and Archives Canada Cataloguing in Publication

Title: France in the world : the career of André Siegfried / Sean M. Kennedy.

Names: Kennedy, Sean, 1969- author.

Description: Includes bibliographical references and index.

Identifiers: Canadiana (print) 20220408270 | Canadiana (ebook) 20220408300 | ISBN 9780228014317 (cloth) | ISBN 9780228015338 (ePDF) | ISBN 9780228015345 (ePUB)

Subjects: LCSH: Siegfried, André, 1875-1959. | LCSH: Political scientists—France—Biography. | LCSH: Intellectuals—France—Biography. | LCSH: France—Intellectual life—20th century. | LCGFT: Biographies.

Classification: LCC JC261.S57 K46 2023 | DDC 320.092—dc23

---

This book was typeset by Marquis Interscript in 10.5/13 Sabon.

# Contents

Acknowledgments   vii

Abbreviations   xi

Introduction   3

1 An Extensive Education   24

2 Many Paths   48

3 France and the Anglo-Saxons   84

4 Horizons Old and New   118

5 War and Occupation   153

6 Facing the Postwar World   189

7 Final Years   224

Epilogue   256

Notes   269

Bibliography   309

Index   333

# Acknowledgments

Completing this work has been a long journey, and there are institutions and people without whose support, of various kinds, I would have never made it this far. For essential financial support, I am deeply grateful to the Social Sciences and Humanities Research Council of Canada for a Standard Research Grant. I am equally grateful for funding from the University of New Brunswick, in particular the Department of History's James K. Chapman Fund and the Busteed Fund of the Faculty of Arts, for publication support. I also wish to convey my sincere appreciation for a generous Scholarly Book Publishing Award from the Harrison McCain Foundation.

In France, many thanks to Odile Gaultier-Voituriez and Dominique Parcollet for helping me work through the papers of André Siegfried, and the records of Sciences Po, held at the Archives d'histoire contemporaine. Staff at the archives of the Collége de France, the Institut de France, the Bibliothèque de l'Institut de France, and the Musée social made possible efficient access to materials relating to Siegfried's career. Similarly, the personnel of the Bibliothèque nationale, Archives nationales, Archives du ministère des Affaires étrangères, Service historique de la défense, and the UK National Archives were invariably helpful. I am most grateful to the Archives départementales de la Seine-Maritime for sending me a copy of Siegfried's military record. Closer to home, the interlibrary loan staff of the Harriet Irving Library have, time and again, proven to be marvels of resourcefulness in tracking down elusive publications. In the earlier stages of this project, Leah Irvine was an admirably efficient and extremely insightful research assistant, who located many of Siegfried's articles, and helped me to understand how English-speaking reviewers responded to his work.

I would also like to thank the Canadian Historical Association for permission to reproduce material from my article "A Tocqueville for the North? André Siegfried and Canada," *Journal of the Canadian Historical Association* 14 (2003), 117–36, and to Berghahn Books for permission to reproduce material from the following articles: "Situating France: The Career of André Siegfried, 1900–1940," *Historical Reflections* 30, no. 2 (2004), 179–203, and "André Siegfried and the Complexities of French Anti-Americanism," *French Politics, Culture & Society* 27, no. 2 (2009), 1–22.

The Department of History at the University of New Brunswick has experienced many personnel changes in the years I have worked on this book, but my colleagues have always shown interest in my work; I am grateful to all of them. In particular, I would like to thank Gary Waite for taking time out of a very hectic schedule to read a draft manuscript in its entirety and provide thoughtful and helpful comments; David Frank for helping me to work out Siegfried's perspective on Canada; Jeff Brown and Steve Turner for encouraging me to dig deeper in his writings on the United States; and Lisa Todd and Funké Aladejebi (now of the University of Toronto), for suggestions and encouragement on the publishing process. Attendees at the Tri-Campus Colloquium of the UNB Fredericton, UNB Saint John, and St Thomas University provided helpful feedback during a discussion of a draft of chapter 3. Grant Peters, a very able and industrious undergraduate, encouraged me to give a lunchtime talk on Siegfried to our students, and helped convince me that this project remained worthwhile. Our administrative staff – Carole Hines (now retired), Elizabeth Arnold, and Misty Sullivan – are a pleasure to work with, and have been amazingly helpful.

In the broader community of scholars of modern France, over many years I have benefited from comments and suggestions about how to tackle this project at various conferences, notably from Seth Armus, Jackie Clarke, Hugh Clout, Bertram Gordon, John Hellman, Samuel Kalman, Richard Kuisel, Kevin Passmore, David Schalk, and Olivier Wieviorka. François Boulet, Gérard Fabre, and Nicolas Rousellier were kind enough to meet with me and to provide suggestions and comments. The anonymous readers, first for my research grant application, and then for the manuscript itself, recommended that I be more precise in my thinking; their comments were highly beneficial and much appreciated. Of course, I alone take full responsibility for any errors or oversights. At McGill-Queen's University Press, Kyla

Madden has shown great kindness, expert knowledge, and considerable forbearance. Production editor Alyssa Favreau gave detailed advice on preparing the final manuscript and managing editor Kathleen Fraser has provided excellent guidance during the publication process. I am most grateful to Gillian Scobie for skillful copyediting, saving me from errors and offering perceptive suggestions. I have also benefited from the collegial advice and support of Caroline Campbell, Norman Ingram, Laurent Kestel, Chris Millington, Kenneth Mouré, Geoff Read, and, before his sad passing, Michael Sibalis. Bill Irvine, a wonderful historian who continued to provide enthusiastic support and friendship long after I completed my doctorate, is terribly missed.

Finally, friends and family have shown generosity and support, especially at challenging times. My sincere thanks to Mary and David Charters, John Bingham and Barbara Clow, John FitzGerald, Kong Sun Lim, Kate Hayward and Gary Waite, Bobbi and Marc Milner, Joanne Minor and Stephen and Rowan Schryer, Kathryn Taglia and Ross Leckie. My sister Carolyn, brother-in-law Ed, and nephews Michael and Max have always been welcoming and fun during return visits to St John's, Newfoundland. My father Mike, sadly no longer with us, patiently listened to me talk about Siegfried. My mother Theresa amazes me with her resilience in the era of Covid, and has been enthusiastic and encouraging about this project throughout. As for Lisa, her strength, energy, and love have remained steadfast; I am so grateful that she has taken this and other journeys with me.

# Abbreviations

ACF    Archives du Collège de France
AHC    Archives d'histoire contemporaine, Centre d'histoire Sciences Po
AIF    Archives de l'Institut de France
AMS    Archives du Musée social
AN     Archives nationales
BIF    Bibliothèque de l'Institut de France
CNOF   Conseil national de l'organisation française
EDC    European Defense Community
ENA    École nationale d'administration
FNSP   Fondation nationale des sciences politiques
FRG    Federal Republic of Germany
IEP    Institut d'études politiques
ISTH   Institut sciences et techniques humains
MAE    Archives du ministère des Affaires étrangères
MRP    Mouvement républicain populaire
NATO   North Atlantic Treaty Organization
PCF    Parti communiste français
RIIA   Archives of the Royal Institute of International Affairs
RPF    Rassemblement du peuple français
SFIO   Section française de l'internationale ouvrière
SPD    Sozialdemokratische Partei Deutschlands
TNA    United Kingdom National Archives

FRANCE IN THE WORLD

# Introduction

André Siegfried (1875–1959) was a key figure in French intellectual and academic life during the first six decades of the twentieth century. From a socially prominent background, he was introduced to the workings of French politics under the Third Republic (1870–1940) very early in his youth; he was also increasingly acquainted with a rapidly changing world, travelling the globe as a young man. He began publishing his observations of foreign lands at an early stage, and soon sought to follow his father's lead into the fields of politics and social reform. In the years to come, Siegfried would embrace many roles – journalist, social reformer, political candidate, professor, soldier, government official, cultural diplomat – but his fascination with his country's politics, and in interpreting other cultures and international trends, persisted.

As he achieved growing status in France as well as international recognition, Siegfried wrote over thirty books, many of them translated into other languages, as well as countless newspaper, magazine, and journal articles. His subjects varied: among his later books were a study of how to speak in public and an analysis of how disease spreads across continents. But his key interests remained pre-eminent. Siegfried wrote extensively about French politics during a turbulent era that encompassed both world wars and vast social change. In the process, he pioneered research into electoral geography but also articulated a liberal vision for his country, evincing strong commitments to a moderate republic while seeking to blunt the appeal of socialism and, later, communism. He called for economic modernization, but in ways that would avoid what he saw as the perils of excessive state intervention and Americanization. Looking outward from France, his gaze at first focused most intensely on the British dominions of New Zealand and Canada, though his growing interest in the United States was also apparent. During the 1920s, he concentrated his efforts heavily on Britain and the United States; in the 1930s, his interests and writing broadened further as he travelled throughout Europe, the Americas, and the Mediterranean, including visits to Egypt, British-ruled Palestine, and Turkey. As the scope of his writings widened, his anxieties for the future intensifed; increasingly, he saw a Europe whose pre-eminence was threatened on the one hand by the growth of American economic power and cultural influence, and on the other by the rising challenge of non-white nationalism. Both trends remained acutely concerning to Siegfried through the upheavals of a second global war, the advent of the Cold War, and the onset of decolonization. In France, too, he saw plenty of cause for worry, as, first, Charles de Gaulle's provisional government, and then the new Fourth Republic, experienced calls for more radical reform amid ongoing political instability.

Diverse though Siegfried's interests and writings were, this book contends that in significant ways they were interconnected. Broadly speaking, Siegfried's work can be seen as an effort to situate France – politically, economically, culturally, and most contentiously, racially – in a rapidly changing world. Through in-depth studies as well as extensive political commentary, Siegfried advocated for a classically liberal, republican France where authority and democracy were reconciled, where clerical nationalism was held in check, where the power of the left was contained, and where the influence of immigrants and Jews was limited. On the international stage, France was part of Europe and, more broadly, "the West" – entities that had dominated the globe for centuries, but whose pre-eminence was now under threat. Europe had to confront its own internal divisions and come to terms with the growing power of the United States while preserving its values. More generally, Siegfried observed, Western civilization, itself the work of "the white race," faced the rise of non-white peoples' greater assertiveness, itself inspired partly by American influence; to respond, it had to reaffirm its unity and self-confidence, and reassert its unique qualifications for global leadership. For, despite the challenge posed by a United States increasingly divorced from traditional Western values, Siegfried believed that the European branch of Western civilization possessed enduring strengths – a commitment to individual liberty, a genius for innovation and

Introduction 5

organization, and a more balanced way of life that was respectful of humanist traditions – that he hoped might yet preserve its privileged status. These qualities were ones that his own country notably embodied. Though not without its faults and limitations, for Siegfried France was utterly indispensable to ensuring the distinctiveness of European and Western identity.

Siegfried was well positioned to achieve prominence, though his path was not always a smooth one. His father, Jules Siegfried (1837–1922), came from an Alsatian family; he had become wealthy in the cotton trade, relocated to the Atlantic port of Le Havre, and went on to enjoy a long and prominent career in municipal and then national politics. André's mother, Julie (née Puaux, 1848–1922), had been born in Normandy, though her family's roots were in southern France; she played a leading role in women's social reform and suffragist movements. On both sides, the family was Protestant: in earlier times this might have been a disadvantage in public life, but Protestants played a critical role in establishing the Third Republic during the late nineteenth century. André and his three brothers thus grew up in a privileged household, though certainly one in which expectations of future achievement were high.

When Jules Siegfried was elected to the Chamber of Deputies in 1885, the family relocated to Paris; André would complete his education at elite institutions, first the Lycée Condorcet, and then at the Sorbonne and the École libre des sciences politiques. Established in the early years of the Third Republic with the goal of building a new elite following France's disastrous defeat in the Franco-Prussian War of 1870–71, the École libre, or Sciences Po as it became known, was created with the financial support of various notables, including Jules Siegfried and his brother Jacques, a successful financier. Sciences Po proved to be the anchor of André's career; he became arguably the most prominent faculty member at an institution that played an integral role in shaping the French establishment, and that also attracted prominent foreign students. But that path lay years in the future; first, Siegfried completed his education, while also engaging in wide-ranging travel. This included a global tour beginning in 1898 that took him to the Americas, Australasia, and Asia. The tour left a lasting impression and stimulated Siegfried's writing, both as a contributor to newspapers and reviews as well as more academic works. His doctoral dissertation, published as his first book in 1904, was a study of New Zealand.

Developments in France remained crucial to him during these years, though. Siegfried participated in various social reform initiatives, most prominently through his affiliation with the Musée social, a private think tank intended to study social problems and promote reforms that would leave capitalist structures intact, to counter the rise of socialism. Here again, Jules Siegfried had played a major role in establishing an institution with which his son developed a lifelong connection, though one that has not received much attention from scholars. Jules also strongly encouraged his son to seek election to the Chamber of Deputies, which André attempted in 1902–03, 1906, and 1910. In the first attempt, Siegfried *fils* failed to unseat a well-established conservative, even though the initial result was invalidated because of electoral irregularities. A re-run was held in 1903, to no avail for Siegfried. In 1906 and 1910, he ran in the more congenial environment of his native city of Le Havre but lost again, first to the right and then to the left; his liberal republican platform and family connections had not been enough.

By this time, Siegfried was changing course. In 1907, he had married Paule Laroche; this relationship provided a powerful support in all facets of his life. Though the available sources have unfortunately left only a few traces of Paule's ideas and activities, she was constantly by his side, attending his lectures, accompanying him on many of his journeys, assisting him in his research, and establishing an environment in which he could pursue professional success. By the eve of the Great War, Siegfried's focus had settled on academia and writing. After his work on New Zealand, he had further consolidated his status as an authority on the British Empire with a second book, a study of Canada, which appeared in 1906. This was followed by a faculty appointment to Sciences Po in 1910, where Siegfried began introducing elite students to his interpretation of global affairs, even as he continued to travel and write for broader audiences. French politics remained a matter of intense interest to him, however. Influenced by the approach of his doctoral supervisor and other mentors, as well as his experiences as a candidate, after years of research he published an ambitious regional analysis of French electoral geography, the *Tableau politique de la France de l'Ouest*, in 1913. Though not an immediate commercial success, the book's analysis framed much of Siegfried's later commentary on French politics, and in time it came to be regarded as a pioneering study of electoral geography.

Siegfried's professional path was coming into focus, but then the Great War intervened. Fulfilling his military commitments, he served at the front as an interpreter for over two years; in 1917, he transferred to the staff of the blockade effort against the Central Powers. As the war ended, this position was followed by an appointment to the French section of the nascent League of Nations. For a relatively brief but crucial period, Siegfried was an economic adviser helping to shape French policy at several international conferences seeking to promote international stability after the Paris peace settlement. However, in 1922–23 – following the death of both his parents, as well as the loss of his brother Robert to suicide – Siegfried recommitted himself to a life of writing, teaching, and public engagement.

He soon became the star lecturer at Sciences Po while also helping to train officials at the French Foreign Ministry. His renewed involvement with the Musée social also proved very fruitful; it supported travel to Britain and the United States, which soon led to the publication of two prominent books, *L'Angleterre d'aujourd'hui* in 1924 and *Les États-Unis d'aujourd'hui* in 1927. The latter in particular was a great publishing success and Siegfried became a widely sought-after commentator, continuing his journeys and writing for an impressive variety of French- and English-language publications. He was elected to the Académie des sciences morales et politiques in 1932 and joined the faculty at the prestigious Collège de France the following year. During the 1930s, he returned to the study of French political geography at a regional level while continuing to travel widely and expanding the scope of his commentary on international affairs, now explicitly through the lens of a crisis of European hegemony.

With the coming of the Second World War, Siegfried undertook to support the domestic war effort, strengthen the Anglo-French alliance, and encourage American intervention. But after the defeat of 1940, though international travel was no longer possible, he otherwise resumed many of his traditional activities at Sciences Po and the Collège de France, later assuming the presidency of the Musée social. He also wrote for the daily press until the Germans occupied Vichy territory in 1942, and he continued to publish and lecture in other venues. Though he evinced cautious skepticism about aspects of the National Revolution, some of his wartime writings promoted racist ideas and exclusionary values that dismayed some contemporaries and have become a source of controversy. Nevertheless, Siegfried emerged from the war with his reputation broadly intact, having avoided deep entanglement with Vichy and endorsed republican values at key junctures. Indeed, in the autumn of 1944 he was elected to the Académie française, the country's most prestigious cultural institution, as part of an effort to reinvigorate its republican credentials.

As the war ended, Siegfried quickly resumed extensive travel, ranging across the Americas, Africa, and South Asia. Having become a regular contributor to the influential conservative daily *Le Figaro*, his column enabled him to advance his views on French politics, international affairs, and the transformation of modern society to a significant audience. Some of his convictions, especially his continuing focus on ethnicity – indeed, hierarchies of race – were increasingly contested, however, especially in the United States. Meanwhile, in France, he was drawn into debates about postwar reconstruction and the evolution of the new Fourth Republic. Siegfried was disappointed by several trends in postwar French politics, and the intensification of decolonization and the decline of European global leadership unnerved him. Nevertheless, he continued to believe that there were hopeful signs of renewed French dynamism and ways for Europe and potentially the West to be reinvigorated. After his death in 1959, tributes poured in, identifying him as one of his country's widest-ranging, most incisive minds.

### INTERPRETING SIEGFRIED

Siegfried has been the subject of a growing body of scholarship; it includes tributes from former colleagues and students, as well as studies of particular aspects of his career or writings. He certainly had enemies in his lifetime – in 1957, the Catholic ultranationalist Xavier Vallat referred to him as a "Huguenot" who was hostile to the papacy.[1] But he also had a great many admirers. Roger Seydoux, who had been one of Siegfried's students at Sciences Po, then secretary general and subsequently director of that institution, and later a prominent diplomat, offered the following remarks in a 1947 address, which are suggestive: "Your reputation as a scholar and a teacher does not end at our borders: it extends to all of the nations of the world, thanks not only to your foreign students but to your frequent travels to all continents, which allows you to retain in your teaching the youthfulness which is one of the most striking aspects of your personality."[2] Pierre Brisson, editor of *Le Figaro*, who worked with Siegfried for years, observed of his writing that "Innumerable questions are

Introduction

addressed ... with clarity, precision, and sometimes humour, with this spirit of connection which, like your global travels, shifts from one aspect of a problem to another and one moment to another in history, all with an ease that never ceases to amaze."[3]

Early posthumous writings about Siegfried continued in a broadly similar vein. The essayist Jean Pommier, Siegfried's successor at the Académie des sciences morales et politiques, gave an address in 1961 providing an overview of his life and work in which he described his subject as being "in Tocqueville's lineage."[4] This was a recurring theme in commentary on Siegfried's work and was not restricted to French writers; the Australian scholar Fred Alexander had made the same point in 1960.[5] Thereafter, some of Siegfried's early works were republished, notably the *Tableau politique de la France de l'Ouest* in 1964; and an English translation of his 1906 study, *Le Canada: Les deux races* two years later, with a foreword by the well-known Canadian historian Frank Underhill, who also likened Siegfried to de Tocqueville.[6] Abel Miroglio, whom Siegfried had supported in setting up a centre for the study of the psychology of peoples in his home city of Le Havre, also praised the breadth and depth of his mentor's analyses of various cultures, stressing the extent to which Siegfried's work transcended conventional disciplinary boundaries.[7]

In 1975, the centenary of his birth, Siegfried's former student and colleague François Goguel, now president of the Fondation national des sciences politiques (FNSP), penned a concise overview of his scholarship, as well as a more personal portrait of an inquisitive man deeply shaped by his Protestant background, which Goguel shared. In the context of early-twentieth-century French life, when the secular Third Republic still confronted powerful Catholic influences, this minority background could still lead to controversy. Goguel noted that in the 1930s, Siegfried's name had come up as a candidate to join the supervisory committee for the prominent Parisian newspaper *Le Temps*, only to be rejected on account of his "overly strict Protestantism." Siegfried reportedly chose to regard this ostensible outsider status as an advantage in some respects, as it gave him perspective; his faith also informed his commitment to liberty, which guided him through an often-troubled era.[8]

The centenary of Siegfried's birth was also the occasion for an exhibition at the FNSP devoted to his life and work, and the issuing of a postage stamp bearing his likeness. A colloquium was held at the Collège de France in March 1975 where various aspects of Siegfried's career – including his writing on political geography, French politics, and the United States – were assessed by a prominent group of scholars. Most of them were French, but the group also included the political scientist Stanley Hoffmann and the anthropologist Laurence Wylie, who were among the leading American specialists in French politics and society of the time. The proceedings, published in 1977, noted some lacunae in Siegfried's work and acknowledged that some of his views, notably regarding the role of what he called "ethnic temperaments" in shaping political behaviour, now seemed essentialist and had become controversial. But the dominant impression was that Siegfried still warranted, as Goguel reiterated, recognition as a thinker in the tradition of de Tocqueville, "which begins with Montesquieu and has continued in this generation, in particular through Raymond Aron, a distinctive profile of men who are simultaneously anti-reactionary, anti-plebiscitary, anti-collectivist, and above all concerned with intellectual and individual liberty."[9]

Another commemorative conference was held at the Sorbonne in 1988, this time to mark the seventy-fifth anniversary of the publication of Siegfried's *Tableau politique de la France de l'Ouest*. On this occasion, participants focused more specifically on Siegfried's status as a geographer. This was the discipline with which he most closely identified over the course of his career, though he has also been labelled at various times as an economist, political scientist, sociologist, and even historian. Ranging widely, as their predecessors had done in 1975, the contributors assessed Siegfried's writings on other lands as well as his interest in topics such as international trade and the diffusion of disease. It was also noted that although it had become a highly influential work, the *Tableau politique* had not been a commercial success when it first appeared. Only with the passage of time and through the efforts of individuals like Goguel was the book's significance as a foundational work of political science recognized.[10] In 2013, a colloquium was held at Cerisy-la-Salle to mark the centenary of the *Tableau*'s publication, with contributions from geographers, sociologists, historians, and political scientists. The proceedings, which appeared in 2016, contextualized the *Tableau* in relation to Siegfried's career and the broader intellectual environment in which it was produced; they also considered Siegfried's legacies and revisited his findings after a century of political and social change in western France. The contributors noted shortcomings in Siegfried's approach and pointed out that his works were sometimes marred by racist assertions;

but the overall image of the *Tableau* that emerges is still one of a perceptive and pioneering work, whose author's insights merit careful consideration and further engagement.[11]

While the *Tableau* has become a subject of study in its own right, interest in Siegfried himself has also continued, with most scholars concentrating on specific facets of his career and work. In France, the focus remained, initially, on his role in the evolution of political science. Pierre Favre's *Naissances de la science politique en France* discussed the genesis and effect of the *Tableau politique* in depth, providing a contextual analysis of Siegfried's activities during that era.[12] Across the Atlantic, Gérard Bergeron compared Siegfried's writings on post-Confederation Canada with Alexis de Tocqueville's earlier, more fragmented analyses of the colonial era.[13] Siegfried's writings about the United States featured regularly in studies of French and European attitudes toward the United States, with scholars such as Richard Kuisel, Victoria de Grazia, and David Ellwood regarding him as as a telling example of Gallic anxieties about growing American economic and cultural influence.[14]

In 1993, Pierre Birnbaum provided a wider-ranging, and highly critical, portrait of Siegfried in his book *"La France aux Français": Histoire des haines nationalistes*. Making use of Siegfried's personal papers, Birnbaum contended that racism was at the core of the prominent scholar's thinking. Profoundly fearful that the West was declining, Siegfried despaired at the growing assertiveness of non-whites, frequently deploying racist language and stereotypes when discussing Asians and Africans. When it came to France itself, Birnbaum stressed the extent to which Siegfried was influenced by the nationalist writer Maurice Barrès and adopted an essentialist and exclusionary view of French identity as far as various immigrants, particularly Jews, were concerned. As a result, over the course of his career Siegfried gave credence to long-standing anti-Semitic stereotypes, lending his prestige to the cause of xenophobia. Birnbaum also criticized Siegfried's conduct between 1940 and 1944, concluding that he accommodated Vichy and became even more explicit in aspects of his racism.[15]

Birnbaum's critique echoed in other publications. In the introduction to the third edition of his influential work *Ni droite ni gauche: L'idéologie fasciste en France*, which appeared in 2000, Zeev Sternhell also highlighted Siegfried's proclivity for ethnic determinism as a powerful example of how French elites could succumb to ideologies of exclusion. Sternhell was particularly distressed that Siegfried's ideas could be endorsed for decades by prominent members of the French establishment. "Despite the fact that Siegfried was inclined towards superficial and dangerous generalizations, he became nearly untouchable due to his social status and notoriety."[16] Other scholars, commenting on Siegfried in the context of wider-ranging studies, are more cautious but concur that his racism was troubling. In his thought-provoking *Les origines républicaines de Vichy*, Gérard Noiriel suggested that Siegfried, though a sincere republican, had, during the interwar years, abandoned his earlier, less determinist approach and published work that legitimized xenophobia.[17] The entry for Siegfried in the *Dictionnaire des intellectuels français*, authored by Nicolas Roussellier, noted the racist element of his writings.[18] In his work on Dreyfusards who later embraced elements of Vichy's National Revolution, Simon Epstein agreed that Siegfried displayed a worrisome ambivalence about Jews, though adding that this did not make him a promoter of hatred.[19] In a 2005 article, Carole Reynaud Paligot identified Siegfried as a key practitioner of "the psychology of peoples," whose French proponents often proclaimed their commitment to the republican values of liberty and fraternity but also incorporated racist precepts into their outlook.[20]

Other scholars have been less critical. In his preface to the 1995 edition of the *Tableau politique*, historian Pierre Milza responded directly to Birnbaum, conceding that today Siegfried's use of racial language would be "indefensible," but adding that it must be situated in its proper intellectual context. Siegfried's "penchant for ethnic determinism," Milza stressed, was widely shared: the term "race" was a commonly used manner of conceptualizing human difference throughout this period, "whether in 1900, 1942, or 1950."[21] In a 2001 study, François Boulet emphasized Siegfried's cosmopolitan outlook; with specific reference to the latter's writings during the Second World War, Boulet concludes that there is little evidence that Siegfried accepted Vichy's reactionary outlook and notes that that Siegfried also refused to serve on the regime's Conseil national. Regarding his attitudes toward Jews, Boulet contends that Siegfried cited racist language to illustrate contemporary attitudes rather than expressing his own convictions; indeed, Boulet suggests, as a member of a religious minority himself, Siegfried discerned affinities between French Jews and Protestants.[22] Focusing on Siegfried's studies of North America, especially Canada, Gérard Fabre concedes that his work is sometimes marred by essentialism and Eurocentrism; nevertheless, his interdisciplinary and non-dogmatic approach to the study of other cultures could display nuance and depth.[23] Hugh Clout, concentrating upon Siegfried's contributions to geography, similarly notes that his subject made extensive use of racial language, but closes by observing that "[m]any of the questions he addressed are still close to the top of the political agenda for people in different parts of the world."[24]

André-Louis Sanguin's 2010 biography of Siegfried, the most in-depth published study to date, offers a broadly favourable view of its subject. A geographer himself, Sanguin is particularly interested in exploring Siegfried's significance for that discipline. But his book goes well beyond this theme, discussing his subject's activities at Sciences Po and the Collège de France, as well as his writings on a wide variety of topics. Sanguin acknowledges that Siegfried was anxious about the decline of Europe as a force in global politics and concerned about the fragmentation of "the West" as a cohesive civilization, as American power expanded vis-à-vis Europe. But he sees his subject as first and foremost an urbane and cosmopolitan humanist with a broad perspective and keen powers of observation. Rejecting the views of critics such as Birnbaum, Sanguin concludes that it is unfair to depict Siegfried as a racist or an anti-Semite. "The criticisms, expressed more than a half-century after his death, seem to derive from a decoupling between the current context in which these criticisms have been conceived, and the personal, scientific, and political context in which Siegfried lived." Instead, Sanguin contends, Siegfried should be regarded primarily as a perceptive witness to a complex and troubled era, whose notion of a West in crisis is still pertinent, albeit in a very different context.[25]

Serge Tillmann's 2018 doctoral thesis offers a different view. In over 400 pages of text, Tillmann argues that Siegfried's writings can be seen as an ongoing effort to delineate and uphold a vision of "the West" as the most advanced of the world's civilizations. With his own family deeply involved in imperial expansion – Jules Siegfried was a prominent member of the colonial group in the Chamber of Deputies – from his earliest studies of New Zealand and Canada, André celebrated the accomplishments of white European imperialists while glossing over the violence of colonization. Western civilization, defined by Siegfried in geographic, cultural, and racial terms, faced various threats, ranging from Asian immigration at the turn of the century, to growing differences between its American and European branches, to anti-colonial nationalism in later years.[26] Throughout his influential career, Siegfried defined and advocated for the defence of boundaries between supposedly civilized whites and other peoples, even though other, more humane attitudes existed at the time: "Siegfried neither wanted nor was able to conceive of the world other than in the form of an organized and hierarchical [system of] domination that would, under Western guidance, participate in the progress of civilization."[27]

### SITUATING SIEGFRIED

While gratefully acknowledging and drawing on the contributions of other scholars, the present work contends that a particular vision of French identity and politics lies at the heart of Siegfried's wide-ranging oeuvre and should occupy a more prominent place when analyzing it. To be sure, it is often acknowledged that he devoted considerable effort to mapping French regional voting patterns and political cultures in the West and later the Midi, even though in the latter case his efforts did not result in a comprehensive study. But less attention has been devoted to Siegfried's articulation of a political, economic, and social vision for his country, one that invoked what he defined as the liberal heritage of 1789 in opposition to the forces of reaction, but also to the more egalitarian implications of the French revolutionary tradition. His idealized vision of France was arguably elitist and exclusionary, but to his mind one that would allow his country to face the challenges of the modern world and sustain its unique role. This vision of France heavily informed Siegfried's analyses of international politics. When discussing the latter, he employed conceptions of various supranational entities – Europe, Latinity, the Mediterranean, and the West – at different points in his career. But when he defined these terms, the values that he depicted as most dear to them – the preservation of high culture, a balanced economy that respected tradition and quality as well as innovation, and a commitment to individual freedom – were ones that he believed France embodied to a singular degree.

Siegfried also defined these supranational entities and values in opposition to various threats. At different times, these included Imperial Germany, the Soviet Union, and the Third Reich. But in his interpretation of global affairs, the most consistent challenges came first from the United States, which he believed was growing more distant from Europe both in terms of its shifting ethnicity and increasingly materialist values, and later from the intensifying desires of the peoples of Africa, Asia, and Latin America to overcome

Introduction

imperialism. Ultimately, American materialism and ostensible anti-colonialism meant that these challenges intersected, increasingly undermining a global system of Europe's making, which featured a distinctive French imprint. This book thus explores the evolution of Siegfried's vision of France and its status in a turbulent global order, in the process seeking to offer a more rounded and integrated account of an influential career.

In the process, the book explores four interconnected themes. The first of these highlights the diversity of Siegfried's activities and affiliations. Though first and foremost an academic, exploring his involvement in politics, social reform, and journalism is essential to understanding the evolution of his career. Secondly, this study draws attention to the significance and promotion of Siegfried's liberal republican views, suggesting that this dimension of his thought and work merit closer attention. It emphasizes Siegfried's attachment to what he defined as the liberal heritage of the French Revolution, as well as the exclusionary aspects of his views on national identity. The book's third theme examines Siegfried's ambivalent responses to changing economic and social trends over the course of his lifetime. Though often impressed by technological innovation and capable of subtle commentary on cultural trends, as a classical liberal and cultural elitist Siegfried was deeply perplexed by the evolution of mass consumer societies and the growth of state intervention. Finally, as its fourth theme, the book traces the formation and evolution of Siegfried's views on other cultures and international relations. It underscores his desire to preserve a "Western Civilization" in which European, and, most specifically, French values were preserved despite the growing influence of the United States and the rise of anti-colonial nationalism.

In considering Siegfried's institutional affiliations and diverse activities, Sciences Po was, as previous scholarship has shown, at the heart of his professional life. The present study builds on that work by drawing on the institution's own records and other sources to further explore his administrative and teaching activies. By contrast, Siegfried's activities at the Musée social have hitherto received little attention. This study breaks new ground by making use of its archival records pertaining to Siegfried, reconstructing a long-standing affiliation that reveals the depth of his commitment to liberal-inspired social reform in France, as well as his evolving views on other cultures.[28] The present work also places greater emphasis on Siegfried's journalism, making use of materials preserved in his extensive personal archives held at Sciences Po.[29] While these archives have been consulted by other scholars, their utility in providing insight into his journalism, especially from the earlier stages of his career, deserves greater recognition. Siegfried's early journalistic forays also provided a foundation for his subsequent contributions to national papers such as *Le Temps* and, above all, *Le Figaro*. This study also provides a more detailed analysis of his later journalism than other works, shedding light on his outlook during the Second World War and his interventions in postwar French politics.

Siegfried's personal archives from his military service and time as a public servant are of limited use. However, records from France's Ministries of National Defense and Foreign Affairs, as well as previously unexploited published sources, allow for a reconstruction of his experiences during the Great War, his participation in the French mission to Australia in 1918, his work with the French section of the League of Nations, and his activities as a member of the French delegation to the 1945 San Francisco Conference.[30] Diplomatic archives in the UK have also been used to retrace Siegfried's activities and significance as a cultural ambassador for his country.[31] In all, these records have made it possible to better understand key episodes of Siegfried's multifaceted career, which in turn informed his thinking and writing.

As his growing prominence translated into his being elected to elite institutions, Siegfried cemented his status as a member of the academic establishment. His dossier from the Collège de France, which has been used by other scholars, is essential to interpreting his activities there; I have also employed the relevant minutes of the Collège's Assembly of Professors to retrace Siegfried's interventions in their deliberations. In addition, I have drawn on materials from the Archives de l'Institut de France, which help to detail his elections to and activities as a member, first of the Académie des sciences morales et politiques, and then the Académie française.[32]

Assessed as a whole, Siegfried's highly variegated activities and affiliations provide a revealing example of how a scion of the Third Republic's establishment achieved enduring intellectual and cultural prominence. Indeed, his career arguably provides an alternative model for conceptualizing French intellectual engagement in the twentieth century. Many studies of French intellectual history understandably draw attention to the significance of explicit political engagement in times of crises as expressed through manifestos, petitions, and protests;

Siegfried tended to avoid such activities, preferring to adopt a more detached tone. Yet for all that, he advanced his views in various media, sometimes to considerable effect.[33]

This brings us to the character and significance of Siegfried's political views. His attachment to liberal republicanism – opposed to France's absolutist traditions but also the prospect of violent revolution, advocating individual rights but suspicious of the masses, accepting limited state intervention but committed to the free market – has often been acknowledged, but not been examined systematically. To be sure, Siegfried's unsuccessful efforts to become a deputy have been documented, and his 1913 *Tableau politique de la France de l'Ouest* receives ongoing attention, but the extent to which he continued to promote his political vision in subsequent years warrants further examination. In his writings on French politics, he contended that a liberal republic was the best option for a paradoxical country with a history of political turbulence but whose citizens, he believed, tended to be conservative in their private lives. Siegfried endorsed what he regarded as a pragmatic, constructive approach to politics, which he depicted as being perpetually threatened by the nationalist, clerical right as well as the socialist and, later, communist left. This dynamic, he claimed, had distorting effects, resulting in a political culture that rhetorically leaned to the left while hindering the emergence of a moderate two-party system that would provide much-needed stability.

Following the Great War, Siegfried's political views grew somewhat more conservative; he now judged the prewar years (1871–1914) of the Third Republic as very promising, but discerned elements of a decline during the 1920s and 1930s. However, he praised politicians such as Raymond Poincaré and remained committed to representative institutions; thus, he did not fully participate in the disillusionment with the Third Republic that a growing number of elites and intellectuals experienced in that regime's final years.[34] And while his subsequent response to Vichy's National Revolution was ambivalent, his continued support for liberal values at the time helps to explain why he remained prominent after the Liberation.

In the early postwar years, Siegfried regularly engaged, most prominently in *Le Figaro*, in arguing against radical institutional or social reform, at a time when France's political mood had swung sharply to the left. For the remainder of his career, he commented extensively on national politics, continuing to tout a liberal-conservative approach as the best way forward for the crisis-prone Fourth Republic. While he acquiesced to an extent to the "neo-liberal" trend of the mid-twentieth century, accepting a degree of state intervention, he did so with a sense of resignation and often criticized the expansion of the French welfare state.[35] Tied to this hesitation was his ongoing concern about the role of the masses in politics; the appeal of the far right but above all the popularity of the French Communist Party, which he regarded as an alien presence on national soil, baffled him.

Siegfried's political views and engagement highlight the extent to which liberal ideas remained potent in French political culture during the early to mid-twentieth century. Since the 1980s, scholars have sought to recover the significance of the liberal tradition in France, in the process noting its diversity but also identifying some recurring features.[36] In contrast to the "negative liberty" upheld by many English liberals, their French homologues were more inclined to accept a role for the state, and were more historically and sociologically oriented in their thinking.[37] The revolutionary experience of 1789–99 also led French liberals, according to Aurelian Craiutu, to embrace moderation and tolerance, though scholars such as Michael Behrent note that this outlook also tended toward elitism.[38] Siegfried has been largely absent from this ongoing reassessment of French liberalism; this book argues that he warrants more prominent inclusion. Though not a theorist, his reflections on French politics were historically and sociologically informed, widely disseminated, and influential.

Siegfried's incorporation into the liberal tradition is, however, complicated by the controversy over his exclusionary views on French national identity. This book notes that he acknowledged his country's supposed commitment to universalist principles and expressed some reservations about negative eugenics, regarding the biological racism of contemporaries such as Alexis Carrel as crude. However, while Siegfried's analyses of different national and regional "temperaments," as he termed them, typically considered the influence of a variety of factors, including climate, geography, religion, and economics, he regarded race as a valid category of analysis and used it to define characteristics and establish hierarchies. Thus, while his notion of French identity was not completely static – he asserted that the French people were an evolving hybrid of ethnicities – it was essentialist. When it came to immigration, Siegfried strongly believed that certain populations, among whom he also established a hierarchy, were far more suitable for integration into French society than others. Jews, he felt, posed a particular challenge; while he asserted that they could

Introduction

make valuable contributions as individual citizens, he also believed that they were innately resistant to genuine assimilation. Hence, if their presence in France – or elsewhere, as he believed the case of the United States attested – grew too conspicuous, it would lead to an understandable backlash. Siegfried regarded himself as sympathetic to the Jewish people and there were contemporaries who agreed with him, but during and after the Second World War his views on this issue drew criticism.

Siegfried's rather defensive political outlook, taking pride in republican institutions but rejecting radical political and social change, had a parallel in his response to the evolution of modern capitalism and the emergence of a mass consumer society. Over the course of his life, Siegfried witnessed how the liberal capitalist order under which his family had prospered was utterly transformed by movements for social reform, frequent crises and wars, and the displacement of European economic hegemony by the United States. He was among the most prominent of a growing cluster of French and foreign commentators who believed that America was more than simply a new player on the international scene; it possessed a qualitatively different kind of economy, rooted in new principles and methods that were being emulated around the globe and producing a kind of society that was supposedly inimical to authentic European values. At first distinguished by a focus on mass production and consumption, this new industrial model, as Siegfried saw it, evolved to feature increasing bureaucratization of private business and government departments, the expansion of state involvement in many spheres of life, and an ongoing restructuring of the economy to cater to mass desires.

Siegfried was distressed by these changes and on various occasions criticized modern society as conformist, materialist, and even philistine. Yet he also marvelled at some of the benefits of technological improvement and organizational reform, advocating a partial incorporation of recent innovations while striving to preserve traditional humanist values. His career thus highlights the complexity of French elite responses to "modernity" in an era of upheaval. Marjorie Beale contends that in the decades leading up to the Second World War, France's dominant classes frequently evinced deep ambivalence about the results of technological innovation and the social and cultural shifts associated with it. Yet members of this same elite also devised modernizing responses that were often corporatist and technocratic, even as they hoped to preserve "traditional" values. Philip Nord has further explored these trends from the 1930s into the 1950s, highlighting how, despite intensifying left-wing demands for profound change at the time of the Liberation, institution-builders of a more conservative sort were able to direct postwar reformist impulses toward "a moderate statism [rather] than to dirigiste projects of left-wing cast."[39] Siegfried was prominent among those institution-builders, striving to ensure that Sciences Po and the Musée social responded to changing times while retaining many of their established goals.

As noted by Jackie Clarke, the concept of a mid-twentieth-century French elite that was traditionalist in outlook but pursued some modernizing projects rests on the assumption of an objective standard of what constitutes modernity.[40] I contend that Siegfried played a significant role in promoting the very notion of a binary opposition between "modernity," which he contended was being redefined by the United States as it apparently drifted away from the moorings of European culture, and a liberal, humanist tradition most fully articulated by France, though he also insisted that his country remained capable of meeting the challenge of innovation. Siegfried's role in the ongoing debate about what economic and social modernity should mean for France is another comparatively neglected facet of his career, further exploration of which illuminates his efforts to ensure the preservation of French status in the modern world.

Finally, crucial to any study of Siegfried's career is an assessment of his views on other cultures and global politics. His racist attitudes were evident during his global tour as a young man, but these were soon combined with a more specific concern about the future of French civilization in a world seemingly ever more dominated by the English-speaking nations. His early work on Canada is suggestive of these anxieties, while his subsequent studies of Britain and the United States highlighted contrasts between France and the leading English-speaking nations. This was especially the case with a United States transformed by technological and economic innovation, as well as new waves of immigrants, whom he regarded with suspicion. Increasingly, Siegfried evoked the need to defend "European" culture and values in the face of this American counter-model. His conception of Europe remained vague, however; in his writings, the continent often seemed to be France writ large.

During the 1930s, Siegfried broadened his purview, but the fate of French civilization remained a key concern. Travels to Latin America led to a portrait of a continent whose European heritage, which he stressed included a significant French intellectual and cultural influence was again threatened by the advance of American influence, as well as the growth of an Indigenous anti-colonial nationalism tinged by communism. These observations strongly influenced Siegfried's 1935 book *La crise de l'Europe*, which described a continent beset by intertwined American and anti-imperialist challlenges. His subsequent travel to the Mediterranean region during that decade, seeking further insight into the roots of and prospects for Western global leadership, intersected with his return to studying the geography of French politics, which now focused on the critical role of the Midi in shaping France's distinctive character.

With the onset of the Second World War in Europe, Siegfried was challenged to reconsider what the West stood for. His initial response was to promote Franco-British leadership in defending Western values, with an eye to encouraging American involvement. But after France's defeat and during the Occupation, he highlighted the West's Mediterranean roots in his 1943 book *Vue générale de la Méditerranée*. This book featured a sharpened focus on the salience of race, yet at the same time obscured the presence of Fascist Italy and Nazi Germany. Though Siegfried regarded the latter as a threatening distortion of Western values, he also continued to draw attention to the United States as a problematic counter-model.

As the war ended, he refined his conception of Western civilization yet again, now mindful of a potential Soviet threat but still fixated upon the United States; both were regarded as offshoots of Western civilization that, in their respective ways, could efface the latter's core values. Though Siegfried accepted the need for partnership with the US in the Cold War, he also hoped for close relations between France and the British Empire, and hesitantly began to see reconciliation with West Germany as a way forward. He also returned to travel, revisiting the Americas and South Asia, and touring Sub-Saharan Africa for the first time. He grew ever more anxious about the rising anti-colonial challenge to Western leadership, continuing to articulate his fears in racial terms. While professing some distaste for policies such as South African apartheid, Siegfried sympathized with what he regarded as the challenges whites faced in frontier zones. In cultural terms, he asserted that non-whites would be unable to carry on the work of civilization to the same standard as Europeans because they lacked technological and organizational originality. Events where European, and particularly French, status were visibly disrupted, notably the Suez Crisis of

1956, were deeply distressing to him, even more so because he believed they were facilitated by hypocritical American anticolonialism.

In his lifetime, André Siegfried was widely regarded as an urbane, cosmopolitan man, and an outstandingly perceptive and articulate commentator on French and international affairs, devoted to the cause of liberty and the life of the mind. There are good reasons for these observations; Siegfried was certainly among the most widely travelled intellectuals of his era, a clear thinker and writer who could engage audiences and present material in an accessible fashion, while conveying an image of being balanced and well informed. His commitment to liberal republicanism, though certainly elitist and increasingly conservative, was consistent and sincere. This helps to explain why Siegfried was regarded with considerable respect by the establishment of the Third and later Fourth Republics, and how his standing endured despite controversies, above all concerning his conduct during the Second World War.

However, to suggest that Siegfried's use of racial language and negative commentary about many cultures can be attributed primarily to historical context and should not be invested with too much significance, as Sanguin and other scholars have done, is debatable. Through his analyses and commentary, Siegfried invoked various explanatory factors for human behaviour, but the concept of race, in a cultural and in some cases biological sense, was integral to his entire interpretative approach. Whether he was expressing concern about the nature of America's challenge to European civilization, the quality of the French population, or the West's global standing, for Siegfried ascribing inherent characteristics to various populations was a driving force in his explanations. His career thus offers a powerful illustration of how racist thought permeated mainstream French republicanism in the early twentieth century.[41] His commitment to race as a category of analysis was firm; he held to it despite changes in thinking about this issue underway in France and elsewhere during this period.[42] Indeed, at times Siegfried would acknowledge the colour-blindness that was purportedly inherent in French republicanism, only to go on and question its feasibility. In the era of decolonization, he publicly contested the right and capacity of non-Western peoples to govern themselves.

The present work thus regards the assertions of scholars such as Birnbaum, Sternhell, and Tillmann about Siegfried's racism as compelling, but that in making their case, they have sidelined other elements of his broader intellectual project. While interpreting global developments through a racializing lens, Siegfried was also consistently devoted to advocating a liberal political vision for his country, as well as to preserve its international standing and cultural reach. In this regard, his primary focus was not on the French colonial empire; though fully committed to it, he wrote relatively little about it. Rather, to his mind, French values were integral to a Western civilization whose traditions were, ironically, imperilled by a dynamic offshoot. The influx of American-inspired social, economic, and cultural change challenged the legacy of French civilization in Quebec, Latin America, and Europe itself; it also furthered the intensification of anticolonial nationalism and potential decline of white supremacy. These dynamics preoccupied Siegfried as he witnessed the world order of his youth crumble.

With a focus on both the domestic and international dimensions of Siegfried's work, this book proceeds in a broadly chronological fashion. It seeks to ground his activities in their institutional context while reconstructing his views of French political life, global trends, and the transformations of the twentieth century, which he found both fascinating and unsettling. Chapters 1 and 2 focus on the period between his birth and the end of his work for the League of Nations; they outline how a privileged son of the French Protestant bourgeoisie had many advantages in his early life but also struggled to define his path. Chapters 3 and 4 concentrate on the interwar years, when Siegfried achieved renown both on the national and international stages and more fully articulated his vision of, and anxieties about, French society and a changing global order. Chapter 5 examines his activities during the Second World War, assessing the controversy that surrounds them. Chapters 6 and 7 explore the postwar years, showing how Siegfried's continued travel and international commentary combined with ongoing commentary on French politics.

# I

# An Extensive Education

André Siegfried understood very well that he came from the elite of the early Third Republic and was immensely proud of his family. This comes through quite clearly in his biography of his father Jules, and in a memoir of his childhood published late in life. The portrait that emerges from these books is that of an ambitious father, supported by a talented spouse, who enjoyed great success in business, developed an admirable political record, and was heavily engaged in civic and social initiatives. In some ways, the elder Siegfried was a very different man from his son, who seemed to share more fully his mother's intellectual and social orientation and came to feel that he never quite measured up to his father's expectations. Despite this, André paid relatively little attention to Julie Siegfried's many civic and social accomplishments in his recollections of his family and youth; in his early years, he evidently followed many of his father's directives, and later held him up as a shining example of national leadership.

Siegfried grew up immersed in his parents' commitment to establishing a moderate Third Republic, a regime that faced a great deal of opposition from the ultranationalist and Catholic right, as well as growing criticism from the emerging socialist left. As members of France's Protestant minority, it was essential for the Siegfrieds that the regime resist what they saw as reactionary encroachments. At the same time, as members of the bourgeoisie they wished to counter potential radicalism and class conflict through social reform. Their son, who was raised and educated to join the social and political elite, fully internalized these values, and in the years to come would advocate for them as a journalist and, later, a political candidate. At the same time, André Siegfried's commitment to a particular vision for his country was joined to curiosity about the wider world that was evident from an early age and nurtured by a global tour intended to round out his education. He began writing for newspapers and journals during this period, advocating the political and social values he held dear, while at the same time seeking to educate his readers about international developments. From the start, however, he did so in a way that emphasized difference and hierarchy; alongside his apparent talent for brisk analysis and clear expression was a propensity to disdain cultures that he regarded as inferior.

## THE SIEGFRIED FAMILY

A fiercely energetic man who left his mark in many fields, Jules Siegfried was born in Mulhouse in 1837, into a family that had done well in the cotton industry. Though he never went to university, his father apprenticed him in all aspects of the family business from the age of fourteen. After a decade, Jules struck out on his own, and, in 1861, equipped with what proved to be invaluable letters of introduction, made his way to the United States. Here he met with President Abraham Lincoln, developed connections in Washington, and travelled to Chicago and into the western states. Benefiting from information circulating in government circles and seeing an opportunity in the Union's need for cotton during the American Civil War, Siegfried established a firm in Bombay in 1862 and became very successful as a broker, buying from local producers and selling to British and French merchants. He soon accumulated a considerable fortune and relocated to Le Havre in 1866 while his brother Jacques, who went on to become a successful financier, remained in India. Jules's reasons for moving to Le Havre were initially commercial, but before long it became his home. In 1869, he married Julie Puaux, who was Norman-born but came from a southern family that included many Protestant pastors. Soon thereafter, the loss of Alsace-Lorraine in the Franco-Prussian War of 1870–71 removed any possibility of a return to Mulhouse. Jules deeply lamented the loss of his native province, where his mother still lived.[1]

He began a move into politics, starting at the municipal level by serving as a deputy mayor in the turbulent period following the proclamation of the Third Republic on 4 September 1870; he was heavily involved in the day-to-day governing of the city. After elected municipal officials were removed from their positions by the "Moral Order" government in 1874, he returned to private life. After an unsuccessful foray in the 1877 legislative elections, he returned to office the following year as deputy mayor on the republican ticket. After the death of the elderly Ulysse Guillemard, a veteran of the 1848 revolution, Siegfried became mayor in his own right, remaining in that post until he left for Paris to serve in the Chamber of Deputies following his election in 1885.[2] During the intervening years, he devoted himself to ensuring the city's economic expansion as well as to social reform. Though firmly opposed to socialism – he grew fond of Lord Randolph Churchill's adage, "If you wish to make democracy conservative, give it something to conserve" – he pursued various initiatives, such as social housing, improved hygiene, and public schools, including the city's first girls' school. According to his son, a deep and practical Reformed Protestant faith, which included daily reading of the Bible, was a crucial inspiration for Jules Siegfried. It also helps to explain a certain puritanism that informed his campaigns against vice, which made him unpopular in some quarters. In a city where religious distinctions remained important, his Protestantism, strong commitment to the Third Republic, suspicion of Catholic power, and support for laic education caused further controversy. While his son later stressed Jules's considerable popularity – which seems undeniable, considering his ongoing electoral success – some local papers were more critical, accusing him of being intolerant of dissent and inclined to be impetuous.[3] For André, however, the mutual hostility of the nationalist right and socialist left merely confirmed the correctness of his father's principles.

Though he went on to have a long and productive parliamentary career, at first Jules found the transition to national politics dispiriting. Perhaps lamenting the loss of the relative freedom of action that he had enjoyed as mayor and finding the combative and cynical atmosphere of the Chamber of Deputies depressing, he apparently considered resigning after his first year in office. However, travel with his family, as prescribed by his doctor, restored his usual optimism and he returned to the fray in the fall of 1886. He was in office until 1897, when he joined the Senate, remaining there until 1900. Out of parliament for two years, he returned to the Chamber in 1902 and served as a deputy until his death in 1922, by which time he had been the Chamber's *doyen* for several years. Given this lengthy career, it is perhaps surprising that he served in cabinet only briefly, as minister of commerce, industry, and colonies, under Alexandre Ribot between 1892 and 1893. His son concluded that his father's case illustrated that competence was not always the primary factor in constructing cabinets; prime ministers had to balance different interests and reward various loyalites. André's discussion also suggests that possibly his father's rigidity in wishing to be minister of commerce rather than holding any other portfolio, as well as his tendency to be outspoken, sometimes worked against him.[4] Nevertheless, this did not preclude a successful political career, as Jules was often a member of the governing coalition. Though remaining an economic liberal, the elder Siegfried promoted social reforms in the Chamber, including mutual aid; he even assented to state financing for the program, along with contributions from employees and employers. He was also a major patron of institutions that became crucial loci of elite education and social reform, the École libre des sciences politiques and the Musée social.[5] In addition, Jules Siegfried was a consistent and active supporter of French colonial expansion; his efforts in this realm included playing a key role in the formation of the *groupe colonial* in the French Senate.[6]

André consistently emphasized his father's commitment to the Third Republic and to the value of parliamentary institutions. He believed that Jules embodied a liberal-conservative outlook that was profoundly republican but admirably pragmatic, and displayed a willingness to work with politicians of other stripes. However, the reactionary views of many French nationalists at the time led him to align himself more frequently with the left, a stance that was particularly evident during the Dreyfus Affair, which fractured national politics beginning in the 1890s. Jules Siegfried, who was an acquaintance of Senator Auguste Scheurer Kestner, became a convert to the Dreyfusard cause. He suffered political consequences for this when he lost his Senate seat in 1900, though he was also criticized for not defining his position regarding an amnesty for those involved in the affair, a measure that would preclude further legal action by supporters of Dreyfus, though not Dreyfus himself.[7] Siegfried had to rely on left-leaning voters to return to the Chamber in 1902. For the next few years, he was obliged to count himself among the parliamentary supporters of the Radical-led government of Émile Combes, and voted for the controversial decision to separate church and state.[8] The fact that he had hesitantly, and temporarily, aligned with the left (though he would move to the right over the years) was symptomatic, in his son's eyes at least, of the tragic weakness of liberal conservatives in the Third Republic: "It was, I repeat, the misfortune of the Third Republic that men like Jules Siegfried could not be represented among the forces of conservation."[9]

André's mother, Julie Puaux (1848–1922), epitomized bourgeois Protestant women's activism in the early decades of the Third Republic. Via engagement in social causes, including campaigns against alcohol, tobacco, and pornography, she became one of France's most prominent feminists, counselling patient support for parliamentarians who supported the cause of women's suffrage. She established organizations for female workers and widows, became a longtime contributor to the newspaper *La Femme*, and was a co-founder of the Conseil national des femmes françaises, eventually becoming its president in 1913. This also led her into work with the International Council of Women, of which she became a vice-president; among the many international gatherings she attended was the Pan-African Conference of 1919, where she brought "words of encouragement" from white suffragists to the delegates. At the time of her death in 1922, she headed seven different charitable organizations.[10] Though recalling other leading feminists with whom she associated, such as Sarah Monod and Avril de Sainte-Croix, during the "heroic times" of their cause, and how as a youth he and his father had been the only males to attend gatherings of feminists "of all nations and ages" at the family home, André wrote very little about his mother's substantial activities. Instead, he stressed her intellectual and moral qualities, her talents as a writer, and – in contrast to her husband – her interest in religious doctrine. He praised her intelligence and deft handling of the family's many social gatherings, sometimes for small groups of family and friends, other times for politicians, speculating that "if charity or social and religious action had not absorbed her, she could have been the organizer of a Parisian salon of the first order."[11]

Siegfried depicted his parents' marriage as complementary in almost every way, a meeting of the best qualities of "the two Frances." His father, he suggested, embodied the drive, pragmatism, and self-discipline of the north, while his mother reflected the "spirit," intelligence, and cultivation of the south. "I do not think that the union of two French provinces has ever been happier."[12] Siegfried also regarded his mother as a source of immense strength for his father, noting how she provided him with invaluable advice and support, and deepened his religious commitment. Whereas some of the leading politicians of the Third Republic, notably Léon Gambetta and Georges Clemenceau, could not take solace in the joys of family, Jules Siegfried assuredly could: "[T]his was no doubt one of the secrets behind his confidence, and his invincible serenity."[13] After Julie's death in May 1922, her husband declined rapidly, passing away the following September.

The couple had four sons who reached adulthood, Jules, André, Robert, and Ernest. Their father had business ambitions for all of them, but ultimately only Jules pursued this route. Ernest was killed while serving with the Armée d'Orient during the First World War. Robert, who shared his brother's cultural and intellectual interests, also served in the war and survived, but committed suicide in 1923, apparently as a result of unrequited love.[14] The nature of André's relationship with his brothers is unclear, though late in life he did evoke some of the challenges of being a middle child, recalling how, as he matured, he tried to avoid "overwhelming" his younger siblings with "observations," recalling his experiences with his older brother Jules in particular.[15] That said, in the 1920s these two surviving brothers remained close enough to build adjoining villas in Vence, in the department of the Alpes-Maritimes.

Siegfried's extended family consisted of an interesting constellation of professions and personalities. His paternal uncle Jacques, a frequent guest at family gatherings, also facilitated Jules Siegfried's connections with banking and colonial milieux; unlike his brother and wife, who stressed the need for simplicity in their lives, Jacques embraced living well. André's maternal grandfather, François Puaux, described as possessing a "caustic wit" and "forthrightness" that made him popular with other guests, was another frequent presence, while his uncle, Frank Puaux, further encouraged an interest in colonial affairs, education, and, in particular, religious issues. So too did Auguste Decoppet, pastor of the Oratoire in Paris. Though not in a position to shape the family's everyday life, there were also relations in Italy and Switzerland with whom the Siegfrieds were in contact.[16]

Evidently, young André grew up in a comfortable, stimulating, and, it seems, happy environment, though he did not enjoy roughhousing with other boys and described himself as a rather melancholy child who cried easily and often liked to be alone. But his intellectual interests soon became apparent. From an early age, he travelled with his family, visiting relatives in southern France and Switzerland, and spending time in Britain and Spain. His early life in a port city, his awareness of his family's business and political interests, and his exposure to the adventure and travel stories that were widely read in the late nineteenth century, stimulated a lifelong fascination with

30 France in the World

the wider world. He subsequently recalled this growing awareness as follows:

> I thus learned geography by being attuned to the sea and international maritime relations. I did not need books to teach me that there were other continents. Family conversations at the table sufficed to learn that cotton was produced in the United States, logwood in Argentina, and coffee in Brazil, and I only had to look at the ships in port to know that there are black men who are Negroes and yellow men who are Chinese. In my reading, the novels of Jules Verne supported these discoveries, filling me with enthusiasm; Captain Hatteras in search of the North Pole, Cyrus Smith on his Mysterious Island, Mathias Sandorf and his Antekirta were familiar heroes to me.[17]

Siegfried was also quickly made aware of his family's social and political status. When he was five, they moved into a new home commissioned by his father, located on the coast. Known as the Bosphore, it helped to cement the Siegfrieds' prominence as republican notables. Visitors of various backgrounds called on weekday mornings and Saturdays. Some of them were officials, including "modest inspectors" who had been invited to give their views on a particular issue, such as public health or education; others were members of the popular classes looking for advice or support. There was also "a special room named, with a word that seems horrid to us today, the 'poor room.'" As Siegfried recalled, this was an era when sharp class distinctions existed and there was little embarrassment about it. His parents strongly believed in their obligation to the less fortunate but were comfortable with their elite status. When André accompanied his father on walks through the city, he met with ordinary people, but as the "son of a notable, for in our Normandy democracy, at least in its early stages, did not include, any more than it did in England, the practice of equality."[18]

Many prominent politicians were guests of the Siegfried family at the Bosphore. They included early leaders of the Third Republic, such as Adolphe Thiers, Charles Freycinet, Jules Ferry, and Léon Gambetta. Though André was too young to grasp the substance of many of the conversations that took place, he professed to recall, decades later, his father's impressions and reactions. Though Thiers's visit was apparently a pleasant one, afterwards Jules dismissed him as "a little man [with] a small mind"; by contrast, Gambetta's 1881 visit reportedly made a considerable impression upon both father and son, though André was only six years old at the time.[19] After Jules became a deputy, the family moved to Paris, settling in the eighth arrondissement. They continued to be very active hosts to smaller groups of family and friends, meetings of philanthropic organizations, and gatherings of politicians. His mother, often the only woman in attendance, oversaw these occasions with aplomb, and the quality of conversation was reportedly consistently high. With the passing of time, a newer generation of politicians came by; Jules Siegfried welcomed a spectrum of views into his home, though members of the nationalist right were not welcome; neither was Georges Clemenceau, whom Jules apparently disliked. Jean Jaurès, a moderate in the early stages of his political career, called once but after he became a socialist did not think it wise to visit the home of a prominent bourgeois politician; nor did the socialist leader Jules Guesde, though according to André, both would have been welcome.[20] He regretted, however, that his parents did not host more intellectuals and writers.

Reflecting on the influence of his parents, Siegfried grasped that his father's character and outlook differed considerably from his own, though he did not discuss in any detail how he might have identified more with his mother's intellectual, even spiritual predilections. He confessed that at times he found his father exhausting and his detachment from intellectual affairs dispiriting. Though deeply interested in the study of social problems and a patron of intellectual and educational institutions, Jules Siegfried did not identify with the associated milieu. "As for intellectual life, while he respected it (and my mother was there to defend it), in his eyes it was a secondary domain that remained largely foreign to him. His esteem for professors was mediocre." He primarily respected those in positions of command and did not really wish to see his son become an academic. As André recalled it, "he always hoped to see me become a deputy, and on top of that considered how I might go into business. 'A constituency in Pondicherry has opened up; quickly, you must leave for India. A mine is for sale in Africa, why not go there to see it?'" Thus, when André became a professor at the École libre, "he immediately wished that I would become its director, as he did not suppose that the activities of a professor could in themselves be truly interesting in a lasting way."[21] The sense of never really being able to keep up with his father evidently rankled Siegfried, even into his eighties; he also expressed some unease regarding his parents' views on social rank and austere values:

On the one hand they had an affectation of simplicity and lacking pretension, on the other hand the entire atmosphere of the house taught us that a Siegfried must maintain their standing. It was contradictory: "Noblesse oblige," they told us, yet at the same time they said, and repeated rather excessively, that we were nobody special. I have spent years, dozens of years, recovering from – if I have ever done so completely – this alternately hot and cold shower [*douche écossaise*]: in truth I have never "believed" that I was a Siegfried, but I am fond of comfort, luxury, and worldly pleasures, instead retaining a sort of repugnance for a certain pharisaism of simplicity. I admit frankly to not caring for "the simple life," which, moreover, my parents did not live.[22]

It would be misleading to focus too much on the negative, however. In their son's eyes, Jules Siegfried had made great contributions in the fields of business, social reform, and politics, while Julie Siegfried was a gifted organizer and philanthropist "constantly preoccupied with the intellectual and spiritual perspective." André conceded that his father, a pragmatic businessman rather than a great orator, was in some ways an outsider to the French elite, in particular the political system of the Third Republic. In his son's view, however, this simply highlighted some of the latter's faults, notably excessive insularity and too great a focus on speechmaking. In light of the many upheavals and changes Siegfried had witnessed, he prized his father as an exemplar of the progressive outlook, optimism, and confidence of the nineteenth century.[23]

### AN ELITE EDUCATION

André Siegfried came of age at a time when France was experiencing significant expansion and democratization in the field of education. But like many children of his background, he did not participate in the expanding field of primary education, which mingled different social classes. Instead, he was tutored at home, primarily by governesses of various nationalities. He did not recall being an especially gifted or engaged pupil, but did remember an early fascination with charts and maps that continued into adulthood. When the family left Le Havre for Paris, he began his formal schooling at the elite Petit-Lycée Condorcet, then moved on to the Lycée Condorcet itself, to

An Extensive Education

prepare for university. He characterized the education he received as rigorous, with a very full schedule. He was a disciplined student but also an anxious one, who was not captivated by study for its own sake. Interestingly, he was initially unsure about geography, at least as it was taught at the Lycée; philosophy was the first subject that interested him, and he credited his teacher, Jean Izoulet, with giving him "a taste for broad ideas."[24] His studies were complemented by the desire of his parents, especially his father, for him to be immersed in the world of politics: according to a 1938 profile of André prepared by the novelist and essayist Robert de Traz that appeared in the *Revue de Paris*, on occasion he missed classes because Jules had him attend proceedings of the Chamber of Deputies instead.[25]

Of course, school involved more than academics, and even institutions like the Lycée Condorcet could not fully insulate themselves from the tensions of the early Third Republic. Siegfried recalled that during the academic year 1887–88 there were a series of confrontations between Catholic and Jewish students that culminated in fighting before the school authorities intervened. In these confrontations, the Protestant students tended to side with their Jewish counterparts; Siegfried recalled another "Jewish" Siegfried named Georges who displayed notable gumption in these contests. At the same time, his own acute sense of social distinctions infused these memories of his youth. Not surprisingly, he tended to associate with his fellow Protestants, but social class also influenced who mixed with whom. As for the Jewish students, in his recollections Siegfried set them apart, with a touch of scorn: "[T]he Bloches and Levis were innumerable, to say nothing of those who had been able to leave a ghetto, and who perhaps had actually left it; in particular I think of a certain Oedlitz who would not write on Saturdays, sitting and doing nothing while we laboured, quills in hand, thinking that he was very lucky."[26]

Siegfried passed the *baccalauréat* in 1892. Continuing to live at the family home he went on to the Sorbonne, pursuing degrees in law and arts concurrently, obtaining both in 1895.[27] The path that he followed was not an unusual one for the male elite of the time, and in his 1938 profile Robert de Traz emphasized how the education that Siegfried received stressed an appreciation for the classics, rigorous training in analytical thought, and elegance of expression in speech and writing. De Traz lamented how this training had disappeared; rhetoric was no longer taught, and philosophy had been replaced by science. "Students no longer receive hardly any of these two years that were essential for

34 France in the World

inner formation, and which were determinative for M. André Siegfried, this sudden broadening of the intelligence, this illumination of the universe and of oneself."[28]

But while receiving in some ways a broadly generalist education, Siegfried was not indifferent to career plans. In his 1945 inaugural address to the Académie française, he recounted how in 1893 he and his father had met with some eminent teachers to seek advice. The influential historian Gabriel Monod encouraged him to pursue business but, at least in retrospect, it was a meeting with Émile Boutmy, the director of the École libre des sciences politiques, that proved to be decisive. Boutmy stressed how the students of the École libre were prepared for a variety of careers and might even become members of the Institut de France or the Académie française. André reportedly had little to say at the meeting but claimed that Boutmy's remark struck a chord, though at the time he never dreamed of achieving such a position.[29] In any event, the meeting marked the beginning of a lifelong association with the institution.

Established in 1872, the École libre des sciences politiques was, as Richard Kuisel puts it, "a private graduate school established by wealthy, public-spirited, Anglophile liberals" – including Jules and Jacques Siegfried – in the wake of the Franco-Prussian War, "with the aim of training talented members of the bourgeoisie in how to operate a modern state."[30] Its founders hoped that the new institution would imbue future French leaders with knowledge of international affairs, a commitment to economic liberalism, and a practical approach to social issues aimed at preserving class harmony while avoiding statist socialism. However, as noted by Philip Nord, the École libre also embodied a compromise between the nascent republican elite and conservative Catholic interests that enabled the latter to retain considerable influence.[31] The school soon became the primary route to the upper ranks of the civil service and was a prominent site for elite education and interaction; over time, it also attracted a considerable number of foreign students. The École granted diplomas, not degrees; students with political or higher civil service aspirations often attended classes there while simultaneously pursuing their degrees at the Sorbonne. Siegfried himself followed such a path; although he did not obtain a diploma, he was clearly marked by his time there.

Because of the relative paucity of documentation for this portion of Siegfried's life, it is difficult to draw precise conclusions about his intellectual influences. Still, some trends, based on his own assertions

# An Extensive Education

and some documentation from his later years, can be posited. While his university courses apparently stressed the classics and promoted eloquence, classes at the École libre concentrated on economics and public affairs. Siegfried's instructors no doubt broadened his understanding of global developments and likely encouraged his curiosity about other cultures, but they may also have promoted less cosmopolitan notions. Émile Boutmy, who remained director of the École libre until his death in 1906, published a study of the United States entitled *Élements d'une psychologie politique du peuple américain* (1890–92) that emphasized the "low quality" of new immigrants to America, a theme that later preoccupied Siegfried.[32] Siegfried himself stressed the influence of the historian Charles Seignobos in helping him to grasp the psychological underpinnings of politics, and the geographer Paul Vidal de la Blache for shaping his overall conceptual approach; the influence of Frédéric Le Play, the engineer and social reformer who stressed the importance of empirical analysis and elite leadership, is also discernable.[33] In addition, Siegfried admired the historians Jules Michelet and Hippolyte Taine, with the latter in particular stressing the role of race and geography in shaping national character.[34] Of course, the title of Siegfried's first book – *La démocratie en Nouvelle-Zélande* – and his subsequent explorations of the United States and French politics invite comparisons with Alexis de Tocqueville and suggest the latter was an influence, but interestingly Siegfried avoided referring to him explicitly in his writings or extant archives.

Siegfried frequently cited several writers over the years. They included Paul Morand and Paul Valéry, but, as noted by Birnbaum and Sternhell, the one Siegfried drew upon the most was Maurice Barrès (1862–1923), a crucial figure in shaping modern French nationalism. Barrès's novels reflected a complex intellectual and political evolution, beginning with anti-conformist literature, to political activism in support of General Georges Boulanger, to support for ultranationalist causes, and, finally, a shift toward more conservative attitudes and Catholicism. Siegfried's private papers contain extensive notes on Barrès's works, and especially in his later years he often acknowledged that Barrès had shaped his thinking since his youth, noting that when he studied philosophy in 1892–93, he and his classmates read Ernest Renan, Herbert Spencer, Paul Bourget, Anatole France, and, notably, Barrès. "For us the latter seemed full of novelty and imagination." Siegfried recalled being especially taken with Barrès's second trilogy,

*Le roman de l'énergie nationale* (1897–1902), above all its second volume *L'appel au soldat* (1900), a fictionalized account of its author's involvement in the Boulangist movement that threatened the Third Republic at the end of the 1880s; Siegfried claimed to have read the book five or six times. In his view, the Barrèsian triology "in its depth and as a splendid evocation of an era can be compared to Flaubert's *Sentimental Education.*"[35]

Given Barrès's history of ultranationalism, hostility to republican parliamentarism, anti-Semitism, and involvement with militant groups opposed to the regime before his conservative shift, Siegfried's lifelong enthusiasm for his writings may at first seem incongruous.[36] He was, after all, very strongly identified through his family and beliefs with a political system and values that Barrès often decried. On this point, it is worth underscoring the breadth of Barrès's literary appeal in his day – his admirers included the future socialist prime minister Léon Blum – and the variety of ways in which his writing and ideas were interpreted.[37] Siegfried seems to have admired Barrès's work above all for the insights offered by his political analysis of the Third Republic in its formative years. For instance, reflecting on Barrès's discussion of the Boulangists, he concluded, "In sum, I was less interested in Boulangism itself than the deep and careful analysis of the Republic's [political] forces in its opportunist, which is to say its most authentic, form." In his private papers, Siegfried also noted the tension between Barrés's political ambitions and literary efforts: "Barrès, this antiparliamentarian whom the parliamentary virus had struck in a manner so incurable that an electoral defeat [in 1893] left him breathless, who was only fully satisfied among the deputies that he despised, was not a major political actor but his genius was constantly fuelled by this milieu ... Through many re-readings of this trilogy, pencil in hand, I have noted phrases, expressions, metaphors, and adjectives likely to contain either a political lesson, or simply a reflection on the political behaviour of men."[38] Siegfried thus presented himself mainly as an admirer of Barrès's critical sense and eloquence.

However, it is certainly possible that Barrès's influence went further. As Christopher Churchill has shown in his work on Albert Camus, despite the latter's undeniable anti-fascist and democratic commitments, Barrès's conceptions of national rootedness, defined in opposition to an unsettling modernity and sharpened by foreign travel, left a lasting mark on Camus, even as he re-interpreted and reworked them to very different ends.[39] For Siegfried, Barrès might above all have been a keen political observer – as attested by his regular citations of the latter in the years to come – but it may also be that, in less direct ways, Barrès's definition of French identity in contrast to foreign influences may have shaped Siegfried's views on matters such as the foundations of French national identity, the character of Western civilization, and the effect of Americanization.[40]

Beyond explicit intellectual influences, Siegfried also credited more practical experiences, limited though they might have been, with shaping his outlook before the Great War. Writing in 1946, he candidly recalled, "I had ... three direct contacts, scarcely more, with reality: in the regiment, in touring the world, and finally in several electoral campaigns, which were not crowned with success, but which gave me a marvelous education in human behaviour."[41] The electoral campaigns will be discussed in chapter 2. Of the other two experiences, some basic information is available about Siegfried's military service. He joined the 119th Infantry Regiment and was promoted to corporal in 1896, later serving with the 24th Infantry Regiment at Lisieux in 1897 but subsequently returning to the 119th. After completing full-time service, he undertook regular brief periods of service and was made sergeant in 1900. He joined the territorial reserve in 1908, where he remained until he was called up in 1914.[42] Siegfried did not comment on how his military service, which would have led to him mixing with men from humbler backgrounds in a highly structured environment, might have affected his views on the character of French society. Since it was a rite of passage for adult males, perhaps he did not think it worth commenting upon, even in his old age. By contrast, the other experience he emphasized was one that few experienced: his round-the-world travel.

Even before he departed on this adventure, Siegfried had begun to write about international affairs as well as socio-economic issues. His earliest articles appeared in 1897 in *Le Signal*, a Protestant Dreyfusard newspaper. They treated a wide variety of topics, including the expansion of Russian influence in northern China, political developments in Austria-Hungary, economic competition between Germany and Britain, and labour and social legislation in Western Australia. This breadth of interests was combined with a consistent commitment to classical liberal economics and concern about France's international standing. Siegfried's hostility to what he regarded as overweening state intervention was evident in a critique of new regulations devised for the mining industry in Western Australia, which he predicted would stifle prosperity in that frontier territory. He concluded sharply that "the prosperity of an economy depends more upon the fruitful and free activity of merchants than to narrow and oppressive legislation!"[43] In articles on the Far East and Bohemia, he discerned opportunities for France to extend its international influence as it benefited from its diplomatic alignment with Russia and sought allies in its struggle against a Pan-Germanism "which threatens to become a danger to the security of Europe."[44] As for Britain, while it was an imperial rival Siegfried did not see it as a threat in the same way that Germany was. He did not underestimate British power – despite recent economic advances in Germany, it remained "great and strong." But while maintaining a critical stance, at a time when Anglophobia was a considerable force in France, he also expressed grudging respect for British imperialism. This was clear in an article devoted to the activities of Cecil Rhodes and the British South Africa Company, in which he concluded

> the cynicism and contempt for legality with which these men have invaded, without a declaration of war, the territory of another state with the obvious goal of purely and simply taking it over, cannot be condemned too strongly. But, on the other hand, how can the energy of these pioneers who, on their own without a subsidy from any government, have succeeded in founding a vast empire, not be admired! Here is a display of individual initiative and the spirit of enterprise that we scarcely recognize any more in Europe, especially in France.[45]

At this time, Siegfried also began promoting the Musée social, contributing an article on it to the *Journal des instituteurs* in 1897. The idea for such an institution, he explained, had begun to take shape following the Universal Exhibition of 1889, but the Musée itself had only been formally constituted in 1895. While some scholars have subsequently shown that the institute blended progressive and conservative agendas in its effort to stabilize the capitalist social order, Siegfried, unsurprisingly, stressed its enlightened outlook, describing it as reflecting a growing academic interest in poverty and social problems, and translating that theoretical knowledge by "men of action" into practical, effective policies. Studying hygiene, living conditions, and security, the Musée promoted a "social economy" in which, through a combination of insurance and savings, workers would be

An Extensive Education 39

able to navigate the crises they might confront in everyday life. Nor was the Musée solely focused upon France; it sponsored international missions to study social conditions, local legislation, and trade unions, garnering insights that would in turn shape policy. A result of private initiative and funding but serving broader public interests, the Musée, Siegfried noted, was already attracting notice in Europe and beyond.[46] Siegfried's connection to the Musée would only deepen in the years to come, culminating in his joining its executive committee in 1926, and becoming its president in 1941.[47]

### A GLOBAL FORAY

The provenance of the funding for and exact timing of Siegfried's world tour has been debated. It has been suggested that his twenty-three-month journey, which included visits to Canada, the United States, New Zealand, Australia, Japan, Korea, China, Indochina, the Philippines, and India was sponsored by the philanthropist Albert Kahn, who in 1898 initiated a bursary to send young Frenchmen and -women around the globe to promote a deeper understanding of non-European cultures, though Siegfried does not appear to have acknowledged Kahn's support and there is no reference to his participation in the records of the scholarship holders. In his 1945 response to the *discours de reception* for Siegfried's election to the Académie française, Duke Auguste-Armand de La Force indicated that Jules Siegfried financed his son's travel.[48] Indeed, Jules had also intervened with the ministries of foreign affairs and public instruction to secure a letter of introduction for André, to facilitate his dealings with French officials during his travels. The elder Siegfried suggested that the trip was a study tour that, at no expense to the government, could prove beneficial, particularly in the realm of educational policy.[49] More generally the journey clearly reflected the desire by members of the French elite, either privately or through support for universities, to ensure that their successors were imbued with a global vision that would help to sustain the country's international standing.[50] As to the timing, some sources have Siegfried travelling between 1898 and 1900, while others date it between 1900 and 1901.[51] It appears that Siegfried did not keep a journal, but he did write newspaper and journal articles about the places that he visited, and gave a talk on China and Japan in Fécamp in September 1900. The dates of the publications, the timing of his father's appeals, information from Siegfried's military service

40 France in the World

record placing him in Japan in 1899 and back in Le Havre in 1900, and the timing of his presentation in Fécamp, confirm that the earlier dates are the correct ones.[52] His precise itinerary has not been recorded, but it is known that he followed a westward route, first to North America, then to the Antipodes, then Asia, returning to Europe via the Suez Canal.

Siegfried's travel went beyond a tour of exotic places; he sought out people from different walks of life and delved into the workings of local politics, economics, and social life. His early writings from this period appeared in a variety of venues, ranging from the daily newspaper of his birthplace, *Le Petit Havre*, to more specialized periodicals and academic publications, such as the *Revue politique et parlementaire*; a few articles appeared in English-language publications. This corpus can be seen as an effort to establish himself as a commentator on international affairs; it also foreshadowed many of the themes that he would explore later in his career. His first articles detailed his time in Canada, in which he stressed the persistence of French culture in North America and the relative stability of Anglo-French relations. Visiting Saint-Hyacinthe, Quebec, he was struck by the vibrancy of the French language and customs there, describing the local accent as like that of Norman peasants and noting the considerable appeal of French books, though he acknowledged the presence of English words in the speech of the *Canadiens* and lamented how the Catholic Church stymied the circulation of works by authors such as Émile Zola, especially in rural areas. Relations between "English" and "French," he concluded, were generally satisfactory but hardly free of tensions or disruptions. The Fashoda Crisis, an imperial confrontation between France and England in 1898, had apparently given rise to concerns about what would become of French-Canadians if the two empires went to war. But Siegfried concluded that, despite occasional incidents, French Canadians were satisfied for the most part with their status, even though culturally they were very distinct from their English-speaking counterparts.[53] The *Canadiens*, he concluded, clung to traditional French mores in admiring fine oratory and gravitated toward the liberal professions, while their Anglophone counterparts were practical and mainly concerned with business. After decades of inferior status and despite some lasting hostility from English speakers, Francophones had secured equal rights and enjoyed a respectable presence in parliament and in government. This was due in no small part, Siegfried asserted, to the liberality and wisdom of Britain, which explained why the *Canadiens* were loyal subjects. He admired the current prime minister, Wilfrid Laurier, whom he saw as embodying the best qualities of both peoples.[54]

If Canada provided a model for the relatively stable co-existence of cultures, for Siegfried the United States was the vanguard of economic and social innovation. Newspaper articles derived from his time there stressed how the American melting pot was forging a new kind of society and that American ingenuity was transforming key fields. Visiting Philadelphia, he described how the University of Pennsylvania was adopting a fresh approach to teaching journalism, which incorporated courses in economics and political science to convey a practical understanding of how the newspaper business worked. The program also offered plenty of training in how to write articles that would appeal to a mass audience. Philadelphia was also the home of the Commercial Museum, which held all kinds of resources for businessmen, including samples of products from all over the globe and a vast array of business periodicals to promote informed decision-making; research services were also available. Though its mandate and goals differed from the Musée social's, Siegfried discerned parallels: both performed a public service but were the result of private initiative. "Such are the principal characteristics of this new and interesting undertaking, in whose organization is found again all of the typically American qualities of order, practicality, and speed."[55]

Siegfried was bemused by some American ways: as he visited Chicago, he noted his hosts' proclivity for telling him that everything he was shown was the biggest in the world. He also drew attention to the contrast between wide streets and impressive houses and the poverty of other districts, particularly those inhabited by recent immigrants. The sheer diversity of the latter – Italians, Germans, Poles, Jews, Czechs, French-Canadians, and many others – led him to liken his visit to a tour of an "ethnography museum." He expressed distaste about some immigrants, writing of an Italian bartender whom he met that "Southern dirtiness has followed him to these northern regions." But he also paid tribute to the rapidity with which many immigrants integrated into American society, concluding that, "[t]here is, in this city and throughout the American West, boundless life and energy."[56] In the years to come, Siegfried retained an admiration for American dynamism but grew ever more critical of its increasing ethnic diversity and the growing influence of its mass culture.

42 France in the World

Siegfried next visited Australia and New Zealand and soon wrote about the latter at length, developing insights about New Zealand politics and society that anticipated arguments he later advanced in his doctoral dissertation. Siegfried toured its major cities, met with various public figures – including the prime minister at the time, John Seddon – and attended political and civic meetings. His first reflections on what he saw appeared in the *Revue politique et parlementaire* in the winter of 1900. They portrayed an emerging nation in which "English" values and institutions had been strongly implanted in what he deemed a near-ideal environment. New Zealand was also the site of considerable political and social innovation, some of it intriguing, some of it troubling.[57]

Geographically, Siegfried concluded, the country was ideally suited to European settlement: "A temperate climate, similar to that of England, but more equable and softer, could lead the colonists settled in this faraway land to believe that they have not left Europe." Of the Māori, he had little to say beyond noting that at present they no longer "troubled" the settlers and benefited from representation in the form of four seats in the parliament. In his subsequent book on New Zealand, he would elaborate on these insights, to suggest that the local climate had destined the land for European settlement, while the Māori themselves were relative newcomers to the islands, unable to adapt to the modern world and fated to disappear. It was the British settlers who were rightly, Siegfried asserted, leaving an indelible mark on the landscape; the English were the dominant group, in part the result of planned colonization, but Irish and Scots had emigrated as well, giving the colony some diversity. The city of Dunedin had a Scottish character, while an Irish presence meant that Roman Catholics were a significant minority religion. Nevertheless, the overall effect was the establishment of a very "British" society, reflected in pragmatism, orderly cities, deep respect for religion among all social classes, and a strong bond with London. Analyzing the press, which he felt to be of generally high quality, Siegfried noted how it was oriented toward the imperial capital rather than the geographically closer United States or even Australia; the same could be said of the country as a whole. What concerned Siegfried was that despite its small population (approximately 700,000 at the time), New Zealand was adopting increasingly rigid immigration policies. The small Chinese community was among the first to be affected by this and was now shrinking. Siegfried added that while the Chinese constituted a "special case" because most did not intend to stay, were "dangerous" economic rivals, and aroused local opposition for unspecified "moral reasons," the general anti-immigration trend extended beyond them and threatened to stifle the growth and development of the country.[58]

This problem and some others were rooted in the growing "statism" of New Zealanders, according to Siegfried. In some ways, the country was a major source of political innovation, notably in the enactment of women's suffrage in 1893. Attending a feminist meeting in Auckland, Siegfried noted the moderation of the movement's leaders, the quality of their discourse, and the generally polite reaction of the wider public, though he added that they were taken less seriously when they tried to comment upon the workings of "high politics" or criticized male conduct. Nor could he refrain from commenting that "[e]legance had not completely banished itself from the setting, and through that several delegates tacitly consented to recognize that the right to vote, and eligibility, were not the only fineries that a women of the future could permit herself." Siegfried felt that women's suffrage was a significant change, but its effect ought not to be overestimated. In other key respects, he felt that New Zealand was going in the wrong direction. The growing power of the temperance movement represented a possible tyranny of the majority when it came to restricting alcohol consumption, though the "English" political culture of New Zealanders meant that the minority was willing to submit – something that, he was quick to add, would not be the case in France. More worrisome, however, was the labour legislation enacted by Seddon's coalition government. A system of compulsory arbitration and other measures excessively favoured unions and threatened to dissuade investors. New Zealand politics was about interests and not ideology, but too many looked to the state to meet their needs.[59]

Evidently, by his mid-twenties Siegfried was already fascinated by certain issues: the interaction between environment and population, the significance of ethnicity, the dynamics of politics and economics, and the role of religion and social movements. Over the course of his doctoral studies and in later years, he would pay even greater attention to conceptions of geography and race, but his commitment to liberal economics and representative systems was already abundantly clear. In retrospect, he also claimed that it was during this tour – in particular, the visits to Canada and New Zealand – that he developed an appreciation for the merits of the British imperial system and the stability that it provided, though this did not stop him from in criticizing it at times.[60]

The United States and the British Empire became subjects of lasting interest for Siegfried. During this period, however, he was also intrigued by Asia, melding personal observation and geopolitical analysis in his articles. Visiting Manila, he characterized the city as possessing a considerable Spanish charm, but added that as a result of war with the United States most of the Spaniards had fled; Siegfried was discomfited by those who remained. He described early morning activities in the port as follows:

It was a swarm of Chinese, Malays, and métis of all degrees. Some bathed in the river, which was dirtier and yellower than they were; others, sitting idly, watched with an entirely Oriental calm the Chinese who loaded or unloaded ships or maneuvered their junks. A little further away, women sitting on the ground sold tropical fruit, or rather waited lazily as buyers came forward, while nearly naked children rushed from group to group, without the slightest concern for mud or filth.[61]

Much of the city's character, he predicted, would in twenty years be swept away by the Americans. While their troops still had to contend with fierce resistance in the interior, their eventual domination seemed certain. "It is likely that within twenty years the American spirit will manifest itself in Manila with its succession of buildings, bars, and electric tramways. Travelers will certainly still show curiosity about the picturesque churches and monumental convents, but this will be no more than the melancholy memory of a rule that is extinct."[62]

Siegfried also believed that Korea was fated to be controlled by a great power, though at the time it was uncertain whether that power would be Russia or Japan. While Russian power seemed formidable, he refrained from making predictions, for the Japanese presence was deeply entrenched and would be fiercely defended in the event of war. As for the Koreans themselves, Siegfried emphasized their passivity in the face of these events. While finding some elements of the countryside attractive, when it came to the Korean people themselves, he was very harsh. Some Korean men, Siegfried observed, were physically impressive but others could be easily mistaken for women. Overall, he claimed, the male population seemed indolent. "As for the women, they are hideous, and I did not perceive a single one of them who was simply passable. Since the men do nothing, they have the toughest work and all of them appear to pass without any transition from youth to old age," despite the appeal of their traditional "costumes."[63]

If Siegfried's accounts of Korea and the Philippines were bluntly racist and dismissive, he was more ambivalent about what he saw in Japan and China, as both nations strove to respond to Western imperialism. The Japanese had embarked upon an aggressive program of modernization in a bid to revive their nation as a major power; in Siegfried's estimation, this strategy was rooted in a desire for greatness and real economic needs. But while incontestable progress had been made in adopting Western ways, the Japanese elite had also sown the seeds of future problems. The introduction of a constitutional regime brought with it the spectre of parliamentary instability, while the modernization of the armed forces led to the army and navy having considerable influence over the budget. As for the economy, "[e]ntirely absorbed by the economic program that Japan has implemented with so much vigour for the past ten years, the elites have hitherto left social questions not simply a secondary matter, they have forgotten them completely." Some workers in large-scale industries made a decent living, but in cities such as Tokyo and Osaka hundreds of thousands lived in squalor and there was practically no legislation aimed at addressing their problems. Following a conversation with the Japanese socialist Sen Katayama (later a co-founder of the Japanese Communist Party), Siegfried opined that the trade union movement was in its infancy and was at present largely restricted to better-off workers. Overall associational life was anemic, and Japanese workers generally lacked discipline and political awareness.[64]

China, by contrast, featured a vibrant associational life of considerable vintage, not just for workers but for beggars and thieves as well. But this capacity for social organization did not extend to politics, about which most Chinese, Siegfried contended, were indifferent. They were, however, very skilled at commerce; "[I]t is probably only a Norman who could get the better of a Chinese" in a business negotiation, he suggested. Despite this acumen, the cultural gap between China and the West was far wider than was the case with Japan. "This country is the complete opposite of Western peoples, and it is nearly impossible to make a comparison; what is white to us is black to them." Like its Japanese counterpart, the Chinese state took scant interest in social questions, but unlike Japan there had not been any substantial growth in industry.[65] Its future thus seemed even less certain than that of its island neighbour. Siegfried's interest in Chinese matters endured for a time. He published several articles on this subject in *Le Petit Havre*, one as late as 1903, and in 1908 he tried to arrange a meeting with Henri Cordier, an eminent sinologist and professor at the École libre, for advice about reading classical Chinese authors.[66] However, aside from some references to Japan and China in the courses that he taught, his interest in these two nations seems to have faded before the First World War.

— * —

By his mid-twenties, then, Siegfried had received an extensive education at leading French institutions, travelled the world, and begun to establish himself as a commentator on international affairs. Through his parents, extended family, and studies, he had developed a strong intellectual and cultural sensibility and an appreciation of politics, economics, and social affairs. He had also developed clear political views, rooted in his family's strong support for a liberal, laic republicanism, one that firmly advocated parliamentary democracy but also one where a competent elite directed a state that took an interest in social matters without threatening the dynamics of the free market. The masses, though entitled to decent conditions, should recognize their station, and behave appropriately. The nationalist right and the socialist left were regarded as extremes that disrupted the moderate, progressive path upon which liberal republicans believed that France should embark.

Regarding other states and cultures, Siegfried translated his impressions rapidly into readable opinion pieces that projected an image of authority while articulating often firmly held views in a lively manner. The language and stereotypes that he used must be seen in context, but it is nevertheless noteworthy that from the start his analyses were framed not only by his political and economic liberalism but also by an evident belief in the superiority of Europeans and the significance of race in defining culture. His opinions of Indigenous peoples in New Zealand, and the peoples of Korea and the Philippines, were disdainful. He displayed greater nuance in his discussions of Japan and China, but the latter was still held to be irremediably alien. Siegfried's outlook both reflected and contributed to an intensifying concern on the part of many intellectuals and politicians in Europe, the British Empire, and the Americas to establish the frontiers of "whiteness" at a time of emerging anxiety about Western global pre-eminence.[67] Within the family of Western nations, Siegfried expressed respect for the achievements of British imperialists and the dynamism of American society but found elements of both disquieting. His enthusiasm for the preservation of French culture in Canada, though tempered by concerns about excessive Catholic power, would give way to greater anxiety about the future of French civilization in the world in the years to come.

# 2

# Many Paths

In the years following his global tour, Siegfried extended his social and political engagement. Continuing his involvement with the Musée social, he also became involved in the *universités populaires* movement, which can be seen as an extension of his concerns about reducing class tensions. He also had persistent political ambitions, strongly encouraged by his father, but they remained unrealized. While his failure to win a seat in the Basses-Alpes was foreseeable, his rejection by the voters of Le Havre – twice – must have been a bitter experience. These disappointments, however, were mitigated by marriage and fatherhood; Siegfried was also successful in shifting his focus and securing an academic post at Sciences Po. He tried to profit from his electoral experiences by embarking on a study of regional electoral geography, *Tableau politique de la France de l'Ouest*, that in the long run would win him lasting renown. Though an extensively researched work, it also bore the imprint of his political experiences, reflecting on why elements of the French populace resisted the advance of republican values and remained attached to the political right, even as Siegfried also anticipated challenges from the left.

Throughout this period, he also continued to write about international developments, especially the "Anglo-Saxon" world. Through various lectures and articles and the publication of more detailed studies on New Zealand and Canada, he emerged as an authority on the English-speaking nations. His endorsement of British institutions and colonial practices continued; his scorn for those peoples who might stand in the way of European global leadership intensified, if anything. Yet he also expressed increasing concern about the emergence of the United States as a major power, but one that lacked the

Many Paths 49

culture and restraint of European nations. This was worrisome because American materialism could potentially displace a commitment to refinement and tradition, as the example of Canada – notably its French-speaking population – suggested.

The outbreak of the Great War set Siegfried on a different path, first in uniform as an interpreter, then into policy making and diplomacy, culminating in work for the Ministry of Foreign Affairs and the League of Nations. This chapter examines this period of his life in greater detail than in previous studies. It shows that although he published relatively little during these years, he retained his scholarly instincts, as indicated by his observations on Australia and his assessments of postwar diplomacy. Siegfried resigned his League of Nations position in 1922, a very difficult year for him because of the death of both of his parents, and compounded by the suicide of his brother Robert the following year. Given the available information, the profound effects of these losses can only be speculated upon. What is clear is that by 1923 he had recommitted himself to teaching, research, and writing; in the years that followed, he would move from being a respected commentator to becoming something of an intellectual celebrity.

## SOCIAL AND POLITICAL ENGAGEMENT

After completing his round-the-world voyage, Siegfried began working toward his doctorate at the Sorbonne; he also deepened his social activism, with meliorist goals in mind. In addition to his continuing involvement with the Musée social, at this time primarily in the form of contributing reports and presentations, he also joined an initiative aimed at reaching out to the French working classes. Launched in 1899, the universités populaires were intended to encourage social interaction and mutual enlightenment between working-class families and young, predominantly male elites. Initially, the movement enjoyed great success, with nearly two hundred institutes being established in Paris and the provinces, each offering a mixture of lectures, reading and discussion groups, and social activities. Momentum proved difficult to sustain in the longer term, however; attendance flagged, there was some friction between working-class audiences and bourgeois speakers, and political goals divided the movement. Some advocates were moderates whereas others had a more radical vision of what working-class education should entail. After 1904, many of the institutions fizzled, and by 1914 only a dozen remained.[1]

For a time, Siegfried was very active in one of the more prominent universités populaires, the Fondation Universitaire de Belleville, serving as its secretary-general between 1903 and 1905.[2] Rooted in an initiative of Jacques Bardoux, a historian, essayist, professor at the École libre, and later a senator, who sought to nurture a rapprochement between social classes, the Fondation's methods were at first influenced by the British example of social settlements. Established at Toynbee Hall, London, and elsewhere, the settlements involved students living in working-class districts with the aim of nurturing a true sense of community. But from Siegfried's perspective, this approach did not translate well into a French context. In England, he suggested, sharp class divisions paradoxically facilitated living in proximity, insofar as workers understood that the bourgeoisie lived near them but not like them. In France, where democratic sensibilities and distrust of authorities was stronger, elites would have to avoid "sermonizing" and adopt a lifestyle more akin to the workers of their district if they wanted their respect. In his words, "[t]he way of approaching people is to go with the simplest clothes that you have, and to mix with them exactly as comrades, forgetting even that you have or might have some intellectual or social superiority over them."[3]

The Fondation modified its activities over time, all the while seeking to encourage inter-class contact and harmony. As the idea of residential living lost its appeal among bourgeois students, the Fondation's executive abandoned this approach, instead taking on a worker and his family as residents to provide continuity. The executive also began to concentrate more on discussion groups and social events to encourage greater cohesion.[4] Siegfried was one of the organizers of the discussion group devoted to economics; in 1903, working with the geographer Henri Baulig, he also launched a new group that, somewhat controversially, explored France's history since 1870. Though initially concerned that the discussions might encourage political friction, Siegfried ultimately found that, thanks to the restraint of the presenters and the growing familiarity of the participants, the atmosphere did not become overheated. This was more generally true of the entire Fondation experience, he believed; writing in 1904, Siegfried concluded that it had succeeded in establishing a true sense of community and an even-tempered public spirit. Newcomers might be curt or pretentious, but many learned to adapt to the respectful atmosphere of the Fondation.[5]

Evidently, the institution absorbed a significant amount of Siegfried's time and energy, though it seems that after 1905 he became less active.

Given his comments about the need to downplay "social superiority" and his obvious concern about ensuring that class and political differences were, if not neutralized, then certainly tamed at the Fondation, it is not hard to see his activism as being partly rooted in a desire to defuse potential radicalism among workers. Such an outlook was in keeping with that of his parents and, arguably, reflected in his affiliation with the Musée social. It has also been suggested that Siegfried was uncomfortable mixing with the people of Belleville, though some of his contemporaries disputed this.[6] The writer Jean Schlumberger, who had been active in the Fondation, suggested that Siegfried's time in Belleville gave him a greater appreciation for a working-class perspective. "It was at the *université populaire* de Belleville where he first learned what books do not teach; a kind of companionship with men shaped by manual labour, from which sprang several friendships that he maintained until the end of his life."[7] Pierre Hamp, another writer who was involved in the Fondation and became a lifelong friend of Siegfried's, also stressed the latter's lack of pretension: "Repelled by the idea of intemperate debate, he encountered, with curiosity, individuals who differed from himself, and took the greatest interest in those who wished to check him, namely those fixed in the belief that the arrival of these bourgeois was an attempt to enslave the working class."[8]

Though his efforts were evidently sometimes construed as a subtle form of class domination, Siegfried thus participated in a broader trend of young elites reaching out to the working classes, doing so more intensively than some of his colleagues, however he may have felt about social distinctions. However, while he may have made some friends among the working people of Belleville, his work with the Fondation also nurtured contacts with fellow members of the educated bourgeoisie. Among those who participated in the work of the Fondation, aside from Schlumberger and Hamp, as well as Siegfried's brother Robert, were Marcel Rouffie, an editor for *Le Temps,* and the writer Daniel Halévy, with whom Siegfried remained in contact.[9]

At the time, Siegfried was also trying to launch a political career. That his first electoral run in 1902 was a failure is not entirely surprising. To be sure, he came from a prominent family whose father had become an established politician and enjoyed considerable resources. Jules Siegfried was also a supporter of the governing coalition presided over by René Waldeck-Rousseau, which had emerged victorious in the turbulent elections of 1898, shaped by divisions over the Dreyfus

Affair, and he now sought to consolidate its position. Siegfried *fils* also had some impressive credentials, despite his youth and inexperience; a first-rate education seasoned by extensive travel and immersion in political life. But the terrain upon which his first campaign was fought was hardly welcoming. The constituency of Castellane in the Basses-Alpes was a remote, poor, and thinly populated area, utterly outside Siegfried's own experience. The local incumbent, the right-wing deputy Count Boniface de Castellane (1867–1932), spent more of his time in Paris than in his own district and had only been elected in 1898. But his political grip was firm, strengthened by family ties – his father had also been a deputy for the district – and buttressed by the wealth afforded by his marriage to a wealthy American heiress, Anna Gould, which allowed him to develop an extensive system of patronage.[10]

Waldeck-Rousseau consulted with Jules Siegfried about the possibility of taking Castellane; in response, Siegfried recommended his own son as a candidate. The ensuing election was a bruising affair, ending with a clear victory for the incumbent, who received 2,485 votes against 1,622 for Siegfried, while a third candidate, a Radical-Socialist, got a mere 172 votes. Despite de Castellane's considerable lead, however, that was not the end of the matter. Siegfried and the other candidate appealed the result, citing a significant number of irregularities and calling for the election to be invalidated. In his submission to the parliamentary commission, Siegfried asserted that after four years of neglecting his electors, de Castellane had suddenly decided to provide them with charitable support and promised various public works projects. People were paid to appear at rallies and gatherings at which they were generously fed and entertained; most seriously, Siegfried claimed, de Castellane's agents had met one-on-one with electors in the week preceding the vote, and it seemed likely that their votes, or at least abstentions, had been bought.[11] Furthermore, Siegfried noted that de Castellane and his agents had taken advantage of Siegfried's Alsatian surname and lied to voters by describing him as a naturalized Prussian, a claim that Siegfried regarded, under the circumstances, as "defamation." He sued de Castellane and his secretary; among the most egregious pieces of evidence was a brochure of a song entitled "Siegfried the Dreyfusard," which included the following lines: "Siegfried the Dreyfusard/naturalized late in the day/loves Germans, Jews, and Protestants/abhors our soldiers/defends Judases."[12]

The victor responded energetically to the attempt to invalidate the election. Noting that his opponent had first appeared in the district only twenty-eight days before the vote, de Castellane argued that Siegfried hoped to overcome this disadvantage through extensive resources and official support. He also accused Siegfried of resorting to slander by accusing him of visiting prostitutes during the campaign.[13] While some of de Castellane's accusations may be exaggerated, Siegfried was undeniably a "parachute" candidate and had the support of the governing coalition as well as the local authorities, notably the prefect. On the other hand, Siegfried's argument that there had been electoral irregularities was buttressed by three convictions of electoral fraud by the local tribunal, which proved sufficiently convincing to invalidate the election. A new ballot was held in January 1903 but, as was often the case with deputies seeking re-election whose first win was invalidated, the outcome was not very different. After another nasty campaign – Siegfried's electoral advisor wound up duelling de Castellane's main agent – the incumbent scored another convincing victory over Siegfried with 2,348 to 1,840 votes. One of Siegfried's supporters, encouraged by Jules, challenged this result as well, but it was soon abandoned.[14]

Though the attacks on his origins and patriotism were personally galling, Siegfried's trial by fire was unsurprising in the rough-and-tumble politics of the early Third Republic. Though legislative elections were becoming increasingly competitive by this time, it was still common for some districts to be utterly dominated by incumbents, especially in rural departments such as the Basses-Alpes. Moreover, while the election of 1902 was not marked by the same level of unrest as that of 1898, partisan divisions remained fierce. Nor was Siegfried's defeat an isolated incident for Waldeck-Rousseau's coalition. Connecting electoral labels to political party membership or group affiliations in the Chamber of Deputies can be a tricky business when studying Third Republic politics but it seems clear that Siegfried, who ran on a platform of "republican defence," would have affiliated with the centre-right Alliance démocratique (AD) if he had won. His commitment to the republic and his economic liberalism mirrored the AD's platform, and his father was a leading member of the new party. In 1902, Waldeck-Rousseau's coalition was victorious but within that coalition the Alliance had not done as well as it had hoped, though it remained strong enough to play a major role in shaping government policy.[15]

Siegfried returned to the electoral fray in 1906, this time in seemingly more favourable conditions. With his father the deputy for the first district of Le Havre, André was chosen to represent the establishment republicans in the city's second district. Clearly, this environment was more promising than the Basses-Alpes, but there were still major obstacles. Siegfried's opponent was well-established; Louis Brindeau was a right-wing opponent of the government who had served as the city's mayor before being elected to the Chamber in 1895. While perhaps not descending to the level of the contest for the Basses-Alpes in 1902, the ensuing campaign was heated enough. Hecklers – including, on one occasion, members of a children's choir – disrupted some of Siegfried's speeches. Some attempts were also made to exchange bulletins with Jules Siegfried's name on them instead of André's to spoil ballots. Ultimately, Brindeau won the election on the first round with 9,194 out of a total of 18,183 ballots; Siegfried received 7,696 votes, with the two other candidates securing less than 500 votes each.[16]

Despite some underhandedness from Brindeau's campaign, this time Siegfried did not challenge the result. Local roots and considerable resources had made him a serious contender, but not enough to win. Though refraining from specific comment on the reasons for his defeat, in a 1908 article on the evolving French party system written for a Canadian publication, he observed, somewhat ruefully, that his country's upper middle class was moving to the right: "The liberal and Voltarian bourgeois sort, celebrated during the reign of Louis Philippe [1830–48], has had its day. Today the French bourgeoisie is conservative and Catholic."[17] Moreover, the moderate republicans who had steered the country through the Dreyfus crisis had now split into right- and left-leaning elements, leaving the regime without a political alternative in the centre. It is likely that Siegfried saw this religious, political, and social polarization as providing the context for the failure of his own campaign, whatever his personal shortcomings or the particularities of that contest.

Four years later, he tried again in Le Havre; this time, competition from the left proved to be a decisive factor in his defeat.[18] Brindeau and Siegfried were on the ballot again, along with a Radical Socialist, Valentino, and a Socialist, Le Chapelain. Siegfried ran as a supporter of the "Republican Federation," a rather confusing sobriquet as it was also the name of a major right-wing formation, to which he did not belong. Moreover, he was still clearly closer to the centre than

Brindeau, stressing the need for a moderate, laic republic though making clear his opposition to socialism. This platform did not prove to be especially effective; on the first round, Siegfried secured only 5,715 votes, nearly 2,000 fewer than in 1906; Brindeau also lost some, but not as many, 8,778 compared with his previous tally of 9,194. By contrast, the Radical candidate gained far more support than in the past – Valentino got 4,255 votes while the Socialist candidate scored 678. As no candidate secured a clear majority, there had to be a second ballot.

Under the Third Republic, in situations like this there was an established tradition of "republican discipline" whereby on the second round all pro-republican voters would rally to the candidate best positioned to defeat a right-wing opponent who ostensibly posed a threat to the regime. Siegfried invoked this precedent, stating that he wished to be "the candidate of all republicans." But his left-wing rivals were not convinced. Though his own party condemned him for it, Valentino refused to instruct his supporters on how to vote for the second round, instead criticizing Brindeau for his conservatism and Siegfried for his pro-capitalist views. Nor would the socialists support Siegfried, deeming him to be a "bourgeois" candidate just like Brindeau. Siegfried still picked up a significant number of votes on the second round, with a total of 7,687, but Brindeau secured 10,290 and was re-elected. Aside from a brief period of contemplating an attempt to replace his father in the Chamber following Jules Siegfried's death in 1922, Siegfried abandoned his quest for a seat.

In retrospect, some suggested that he was never really cut out to be a politician. The historian Édouard Bonnefous, who later worked closely with Siegfried in producing *L'année politique* after the Second World War, suggested that his personality was not suited to the political life of the time. "Unaffected and likeable at home, initially he often appeared distant. He detested the demagoguery and kind of familiarity that was required in political life." Though his intelligence and dedication would have made him an effective voice in parliamentary commissions, Bonnefous believed that the noisy left-right conflicts of the Chamber would have been distasteful to him. The Senate would have been a more congenial atmosphere, but typically it was only possible to become a senator after a long political career. Under proportional representation, with a list of party candidates, he might have fared better, but the system of the time worked against him.[19] In later years, Siegfried himself suggested that, at least in retrospect, things had turned out for the best. In a 1946 interview, he commented of his failed electoral bids that "[i]ntrigues and scheming of secondary interest were not to my taste, and I realized that I would not succeed on this path."[20]

Whatever Siegfried's personal qualities, there were also larger forces at work. His efforts to win Boniface de Castellane's seat represented an uphill struggle at best, with the outcome showing the power that well-entrenched incumbents could enjoy under the Third Republic, even if their views were not congenial to the government of the day. Similar forces were at work in Le Havre in 1906, while in 1910 the growing strength of the left and tensions between Radicals and the centre-right Alliance démocratique made Siegfried a less appealing candidate than he had been only a few years earlier. His status as a product of the establishment provided advantages but his origins and identification with the government could be and were used against him, at a time when official support and clientelism were gradually starting to lose some of their power in various districts. Writing in his 1913 book, *Tableau politique de la France de l'Ouest*, he noted sharply that in Normandy "official" candidates were defeated "nine times out of ten."[21] No doubt his personal experiences in Le Havre informed those words.

At the time, Siegfried's sense of disappointment must have been considerable, but amid these political defeats he also experienced personal fulfillment and other successes. In 1907, with none other than Minister of War General Georges Picquart, famed for his earlier role in the Dreyfus Affair, serving as a witness, Siegfried married Paule Laroche (1884–1964), the daughter of Hippolyte Laroche and Suzanne Marinier, in a Protestant ceremony at the Temple de l'Oratoire in Paris. In background and outlook, there were clear parallels between the two. In addition to a shared Protestantism, both were bourgeois, with their fathers enjoying successful and prominent careers. A former naval officer, Hippolyte Laroche moved into the civil service; it was his duties as a sub-prefect in Le Havre that led to André and Paule meeting. Hippolyte later served as the resident-general in Madagascar, and was elected as the deputy for La Flèche, in the Sarthe, in 1906. Paule Laroche, like her future husband, had been educated by governesses. In keeping with standard practices for a *bourgeoise*, she learned English, German, drawing, and painting, and spent a period as a *pensionnaire* in Heidelberg.[22]

Paule and André's subsequent domestic life differed from that of his parents in some ways. Both had multiple siblings, but the couple themselves had only one daughter, Claire, born in 1908. For the first six years of their marriage, they lived close to André's parents, but in 1913 they moved to an apartment on 8 rue du Courty, which was their Parisian residence for the rest of their lives. Their lifestyle was simpler than what André had known during his childhood, but it was certainly comfortable. And while they did not entertain on the scale that the elder Siegfrieds had – according to Sanguin "Paule detested society life" – the couple hosted teas for smaller groups, which often featured Britons, Americans, and family members. Paule was the hostess; André would often appear for an hour or so but then return to work in his study. The Siegfrieds also socialized in literary circles, with the poet Catherine Pozzi and writers that included Roger Martin du Gard, Julien Benda, Daniel Halévy, Louise Weiss, and Jean Guéhenno, as well as the publisher Bernard Groethuysen and Georges Boris, a journalist and economist who would later serve as an advisor to Léon Blum and Charles de Gaulle. Pozzi, who was well connected in Parisian literary circles and with whom André's brother Robert had been infatuated, kept a journal that offers some impressions of the gatherings, which featured theological and literary discussions, in the 1920s and early 1930s. André impressed Pozzi with his intelligence, though she also noted his anticlerical sentiments, informed by his Protestantism, and felt that his 1930 study of French politics, *Tableau des partis en France*, was mediocre.[23]

It seems that, like his parents, Siegfried had a happy marriage, with Paule providing constant encouragement and practical support over their many years together. Indeed, the limited amount of available evidence suggests that Paule was more self-effacing with André than Julie had been with Jules; she was also less visibly involved in civic activism, though in a 1945 interview with the Montreal newspaper *La Presse* she stressed her commitment to feminism and support for women's suffrage. Sharing her husband's interest in other cultures, notably when it came to art, she accompanied André on many of his travels and attended countless lectures. Xavier Leurquin, a former student at the École libre, recalled how "Madame Siegfried, his admirable companion, was always there. For years, no doubt, she knew that if the English ate porridge, this was a gesture of natural defense against the climate of their country, like horses being reheated with oats. Neverthess she always attended these annual rehearsals without wearying, always interested."[24] André seems to have been an appreciative husband, writing prose and poetry for Paule and commemorating special events in their lives. In a 1920 pamphlet on the seasons, which he wrote for her, the dedication, blending gratitude and restraint, reads: "à ma fidèle amie Paule."[25]

Relatively little is known about the life of the Siegfrieds' daughter Claire (1908–1984). She studied at the Lycée Victor Duruy, lived with her parents until 1935, and accompanied them on some of their travels, including their visit to North America that same year. She did not have a family of her own, and appears to have remained quite close to her parents. Having mastered both English and German, she worked at the American Library in Paris from 1946 until 1961. Though apparently not heavily involved in her father's research, she was reportedly very close to him, referring to him as "Adi," and was intensely proud of his achievements. A rare, surviving letter from her to André, written during the Second World War when Claire acted as the guardian of the family vacation home in Vence, suggests a tightly knit family in a time of crisis.[26]

Aside from the powerful consolation of an apparently happy family life, Siegfried's political setbacks were also mitigated by finding professional fulfillment through an appointment to the École libre des sciences politiques. In 1910, he recalled, he was one of three speakers invited to comment on British imperial developments, in particular the political role of Joseph Chamberlain, at a dinner. As it turned out, Siegfried was the only one who turned up; he improvised and spoke on the subject for forty-five minutes. Thereafter, the historian Anatole Leroy-Beaulieu, then director of the École libre (Émile Boutmy had passed away in 1906), offered him the position of chair in the political economy of Britain; Siegfried claimed that while he was hesitant at first, he soon accepted.[27] Of course, Siegfried was well known to the institution; he had been a student there and had connections to some of its faculty. Above all, as Sanguin notes, his father had played a key role in establishing the school and sat on its governing board. Leroy-Beaulieu may well have been influenced by these facts; indeed, his own nephew Pierre had also taught at Sciences Po before winning a seat in the Chamber of Deputies.[28] However, by this time Siegfried had earned a doctorate and was establishing a reputation as a commentator on international affairs, notably the British Empire. Family connections surely did him no harm in securing the appointment, but he had also positioned himself very well.

## AN EMERGING AUTHORITY

Even as he strove to become a deputy, Siegfried remained active as a journalist, writing for a variety of publications, especially *Le Petit Havre*. Some of his contributions derived from the trips he made to the United States in 1901, and again in 1904 to the World's Fair in St Louis. Others focused on Britain and its empire, commenting on developments in Australia, Canada, New Zealand, and Britain itself. He also assessed rising tensions in Europe, Asia, Latin America, and Africa, and traced the sometimes turbulent politics of his own country.[29] Moreover, he continued to be interested in social issues; for instance, following his 1901 visit to the United States, he published a comparative analysis of the American and French working classes, noting the higher wages, greater apparent contentment, and relative conservatism of the former.[30]

All the while, he also worked on his dissertation on New Zealand at the Faculty of Letters of the University of Paris, for which he had already gathered much material during his world tour. Though in later years, Siegfried stressed his intellectual debts as a geographer to Vidal de la Blache, his dissertation supervisor was Marcel Dubois, a former student of Vidal's, who had co-founded the *Annales de géographie* with his mentor in 1891. However, Dubois eventually broke with the Vidalian school of geography on intellectual, professional, and political grounds. Vidal's disciples often concentrated on regional studies and favoured a focus on physical geography, seeking to align their discipline with the social sciences. Politically, they tended toward the moderate left, inclining toward anticlericalism, and supporting Alfred Dreyfus. Dubois, by contrast, was a conservative Catholic and strong supporter of nationalist causes, co-founding the Ligue de la patrie française alongside figures such as Maurice Barrès. As for his intellectual outlook, Dubois favoured cultural geography, applying this approach to his work after he was named to the chair in colonial geography at the Sorbonne in 1892, when he was only thirty-six. He would go on to develop theories of colonization and promote the French empire, helping to prepare the colonial section of the 1900 Paris Exposition. Dubois also supervised theses devoted to various colonial topics, ranging from studies of New Caledonia and the Sahara to analyses of the colonization of British Columbia and a study of Newfoundland.[31] Politically, Siegfried's background and allegiances at the time were quite different from those of Dubois, but this does not appear to have unduly affected the preparation or defence of the thesis. Siegfried submitted the principal work on New Zealand in 1903 and his defence, chaired by the Protestant republican historian Charles Seignobos, was held on 4 May 1904, and judged a great success.[32] Both the dissertation and Siegfried's complementary thesis, devoted to the British colonial advocate Edward Gibbon Wakefield (1796–1862), were published by Armand Colin later that same year.

*La démocratie en Nouvelle-Zélande* bore aspects of Dubois's approach, which stressed the need to incorporate the study of history, politics, economics, and culture while framing an overall analysis in geographic terms. At the same time, there was also significant continuity with Siegfried's earlier writings on the territory. Tracing the early history of British colonization, including Anglo-French competition, and the development of political institutions, he reaffirmed how deeply the "English" character had made its mark on New Zealand, though in the process modifications had taken place. He held to his previously expressed view that New Zealanders were pragmatic, non-ideological, and in some ways progressive, but also overly inclined to become dependent upon the state. Siegfried praised some initiatives, such as the creation of old age pensions and the provision of credit for agricultural development, but retained his reservations about the potentially negative economic effect of compulsory arbitration even though it promoted social peace. Interestingly, he concluded that while the social structure of New Zealand was less hierarchical than that of Britain itself, "snobbery" remained prevalent, as he claimed it did in all "Anglo-Saxon" societies. Britons themselves rarely considered "colonials" to be social equals, yet "the British citizen, in fact, whether Australasian, Canadian, or English, is always ready to fall into line, and in every act of his political or social life feels the want of a leader."[33]

Compared with his earlier publications, what stands out in *La démocratie en Nouvelle-Zélande* is Siegfried's heightened focus on its status as a "white man's country." He had previously noted how the climate was very well suited to European settlement, but now went further by suggesting that the islands were destined for white settlement and that the Māori had become the previous inhabitants only because of circumstance. New Zealand's climate and geography, he asserted, "seems purposely designed to welcome the white race." The Māoris, "powerful, courageous, and warlike," had resisted European incursion fiercely and cruelly, but as a so-called tropical race brought by "chance migration" to a non-tropical climate, had never fully acclimatized; "thus it is that they, the conquered, find themselves, by a strange piece of irony, the race least qualified to prosper and survive there." While criticizing the Māori for their cruelty, Siegfried's analysis obscured the extensive violence involved in British colonial expansion, instead portraying the Indigenous population as doomed. Confronted with an increasingly vigorous settler presence, he predicted, "the time will come when [Māori] power and even their presence in New Zealand will be no more than a memory."[34] This assertion set Siegfried apart from one of his key sources, the New Zealand politician and writer William Pember Reeves. In works such as *The Long White Cloud* (1898) and *State Experiments in Australia and New Zealand* (1901), Reeves had also invoked New Zealand's climate and the status of the Māori as supposedly relative newcomers to legitimize colonial settlement, but he did not foresee their disappearance. Instead, he allowed the possibility of cooperation between the Māori and European settlers, albeit very much on the latter's terms.[35]

Siegfried reinforced his thesis that New Zealand was intended to be a country for whites by sharpening his opposition to non-white immigration. Whereas in 1900, he had expressed concern that New Zealand's restrictive immigration policies could stifle its development, he now opined that greater openness might cause trouble, stressing that the country's delicate social and racial balance needed to be preserved. He had previously written how restrictions had first affected New Zealand's small Chinese community, noting that they posed special economic and "moral" problems, but he was now more assertive about the need to exclude them. Chinese migrant workers, he noted, had spread throughout the Pacific region and were an often-underestimated threat to Western power. "In point of fact, the white man has no more powerful opponent." Hard-working and adaptable, Chinese migrants evoked intense racism from white populations, including that of New Zealand – an understandable reaction, in Siegfried's view. Economically, Chinese workers would undermine living standards; morally, they came without families and promoted vices. Siegfried thus condoned the implementation of sharp restrictions to ensure white supremacy: "[A]t the present time it can be said that the New Zealanders, by their brutal action and their inflexible prejudices, have succeeded in removing from themselves the yellow peril."[36]

In his complementary thesis on Edward Gibbon Wakefield, Siegfried offered a favourable assessment of the latter's theory of settler colonialism or "systematic colonization," as Wakefield himself referred to it. A controversial but influential figure in his day, Wakefield called for a degree of state intervention to ensure that overseas colonization was "balanced." Rather than allow a completely unregulated market in land, the state should ensure that prices were reasonable to ensure acquisition by settler families – gender balance was essential, in Wakefield's view. In this way, a stable social structure, featuring property owners and workers with good salaries, could take shape.[37] Siegfried concluded that while some of Wakefield's findings had not been accepted, his theories were valid and had produced positive results. He rejected criticisms that Wakefield simply wanted to reproduce "Old World" social hierarchies overseas, instead arguing that his goal was to ensure social stability. Siegfried also believed that Wakefield's advocacy for a degree of settler colonial autonomy was also well-founded, concluding that the legacy of his planned colonization scheme was a peaceful and prosperous country.[38] Overall, he found much to admire in Wakefield's efforts to favour market economics and class stability through an enlightened approach that stressed balance while accepting a degree of state involvement in establishing New Zealand as a "white man's country."

After completing his doctoral studies, Siegfried returned to North America in 1904. In the United States, his primary interest was the St Louis World's Fair, about which he wrote articles for *Le Petit Havre*. In them, he expressed admiration for American ambition but there were also plenty of deprecating remarks about St Louis itself. Visiting the different quarters of the city, Siegfried emphasized the squalor of Chinese and African-American enclaves, decrying the popularity of opium among whites and asserting the innate inferiority of black Americans: "The sad descendants of a race of slaves, mixed too suddenly with a superior race, these poor people hardly knew how to borrow only its vices and flaws. Why don't the whites of America want to admit their terrible responsibility?" He went on to explicitly juxtapose French civilization and American barbarism. "The 1900 [Paris] Exposition was the crowning achievement of the most civilized of all centuries, in the most civilized capital. The St. Louis World's Fair represents the immense and powerful effort of a young and strong race at the dawn of a new century, in an enormous, badly-finished city, still very near the crude Far West and its barbarism."[39]

It would be some time before Siegfried fully elaborated on this contrast, which would be a key theme of several of his subsequent works. Instead, he turned his attention to Canada, where he celebrated both the survival of French civilization but also worried about its prospects. In *Le Canada: Les deux races*, which appeared in 1906, he was more critical of Quebec's Catholic Church than in the past. The province was separated from France not simply by geography but also by the heritage of 1789. Though Siegfried credited the Church with helping to preserve French identity, it had done so only to promote its own values, resulting in an intolerant, somewhat backward society. There was really no place for a French Protestant like himself in Quebec, he lamented. Nevertheless, he still celebrated the French presence in the New World, insisting that a spiritual, even mystical, connection endured across the Atlantic.[40] In a public lecture given several years later, he depicted the *Canadiens* as living proof of French tenacity: "[I]t is a sign of the extraordinary vitality of our French soul which, defeated, trampled underfoot, and cursed by Destiny, always revives, and from the very milieu of its ruins cries out in confidence and hope in the future."[41]

The subtitle of his book on Canada, *Les deux races*, which had been suggested to Siegfried by his publisher, highlighted the challenge of preserving French identity in North America.[42] What did the future hold for French Canadians in a British dominion controlled by English speakers, many of whom, he pointed out, were hostile to them? On this point, he insisted that Quebec society needed to break free of clerical influence if it wished to modernize and prosper; ties with republican France could be helpful in this regard. Though French Canada was a "more refined, more distinguished, and more perfect" culture, it was "unable to conquer a [British] society that is more worldly and vulgar, but incontestably better adapted to the needs of a new country."[43] One factor that Siegfried saw as favouring long-term accommodation was the capacity of British institutions to accept French speakers, and the latter's ability to thrive within the British parliamentary system, as exemplified by individuals such as the current prime minister, Wilfrid Laurier. Even Henri Bourassa, a leading French-Canadian critic of British imperialism, embraced Westminster mores. Reflecting his emerging belief in regional and national "temperaments," Siegfried also suggested that the Norman origins and hence Atlantic orientation of many *Canadiens* facilitated their integration.[44]

Thus, while acknowledging tensions between English and French over matters such as participation in the Boer War, Siegfried believed that Quebec could prosper within the British Empire politically, while hoping for stronger ties with France. He was less optimistic when it came to the growth of American influence. The latter, he suggested, was already powerful in English Canada: parliamentary life in Ottawa, for example, consisted of "American actors on an English stage." In Western Canada, geography and immigration patterns ensured an even stronger orientation toward the United States. Siegfried did not fear annexation; rather, he argued that "[t]he danger does not take the form either of an attempt at conquest, a treaty of alliance or a plebiscite. It lies in the imperceptible daily transformation that by a slow steady progress is Americanizing the colony, its men, its investments and its manners." Though a common language facilitated the Americanization of English Canada, French-speaking civilization was also vulnerable, as the case of rapidly assimilating Francophone migrants to New England demonstrated. "You may resist British civilization, but American civilization submerges you every time!"[45]

Both *La démocratie en Nouvelle-Zélande* and *Le Canada* were generally well received, which helped to establish Siegfried's bona fides as an expert on the English-speaking world. To be sure, he was not alone in the field; in 1897, for example, Pierre Leroy-Beaulieu had published *Les nouvelles sociétés anglo-saxonnes,* and Siegfried's study of New Zealand was influenced by his friend, the academic and future deputy Albert Métin, who had published a study of social trends in Australia and New Zealand in 1901. However, Siegfried's works proved to have the most lasting influence. Writing on the fiftieth anniversary of the publication of *La démocratie en Nouvelle-Zélande,* the New Zealand historian Willis Airey observed that while the book was "not everywhere firm and coherent," it had succeeded in "putting its finger on many points that retrospect confirms and at least suggesting problems and doubts that are still with us."[46] As for *Le Canada: Les deux races,* it had met with some contemporary criticisms for its depiction of Catholicism in Quebec and its commentary on the long-term prospects for the unity of the country – and today, Siegfried's sidelining of regions such as the Maritimes, and total neglect of Canada's Indigenous peoples, might stand out more.[47] But the book had a long-term effect; it was held in high regard by influential Canadian intellectuals such as the historian Frank Underhill, who ensured that it was republished in 1966 as part of a series of classic studies of the country's history and politics.[48]

Siegfried's studies of New Zealand and Canada encapsulated many of the issues that had preoccupied him in the early stages of his career and would continue to interest him for years to come; the racially charged threat to a Eurocentric world order, the workings of the British Empire, the worrying rise of American influence, and the place of French civilization in a changing world. As we have seen, it was his expertise on the British Empire that helped secure his appointment to the École libre des sciences politiques in 1910. But with the completion of the book on Canada, Siegfried's focus shifted back to French politics, culminating in the publication of the *Tableau politique de la France de l'Ouest*.

## MAPPING FRENCH POLITICS

To conduct his research, Siegfried toured a total of fourteen departments in Western France. He consulted their archives for information about landholding and drew upon other official sources for population statistics, election returns, and data, such as the establishment of Catholic schools.[49] Some of these research materials are preserved in his archives, which also include drafts of the large number of maps that he used to support his findings. In addition to these sources, he also met with government officials and members of the local population, noting that some kinds of information, such as the nature of property ownership in a given area, could only be determined in this way.[50] Over the course of his research, he also presented some of his findings to the Musée social and consulted with Vidal de la Blache and Seignobos.[51]

Siegfried's broader goal in the *Tableau* was to explain why certain regions displayed enduring political "temperaments." Why was it, he wondered in the introduction to the book, that despite changes in political regime and shifting electoral alignments, specific areas persistently supported the same kinds of political formations over time? The answer lay with deeply rooted predilections: with a focus on explaining the past but an eye to predicting the future, Siegfried defined his terminology and goals: "Political opinions vary with circumstances, but the law by which they form is profound and stable. Behind external appearances, which scarcely recur twice, there are ways of being and feeling that persist. These ways of being, of conducting onself, of reacting to the action of circumstances, as an organism reacts to a given atmosphere or contagion, can be referred to as the political temperament. Each environment has its own, obeying its own laws. When the key is discovered, the evolution of the past becomes clearer, and at the same time tomorrow, to an extent, allows itself to appear."[52]

To discern a given region's temperament, the opinions of its elected politicians needed to be established by examining their professed goals during elections and analyzing their voting record on key issues. While often misleading, election rhetoric did reveal basic preferences and operated according to an intelligible code. As for the voting records, Siegfried chose to examine 100 key votes held in the Chamber of Deputies since 1871 to determine how the deputies of a given region leaned. Naturally, he also needed to explore what factors led the voters of a particular region to select a particular politician. Here, he would focus on legislative elections at the national level rather than local ones, where issues of personality were more likely to predominate, though they could certainly be a factor in the former as well. Siegfried conceded that individuals were not always able to translate their true preferences into votes; factors such as pressure and corruption came into play, and in small communities it was hard to preserve the integrity of the secret ballot. But such factors did not always win out, and in any case, he insisted, a detailed study of electoral behaviour over time would still reveal continuities: "In reality, in the end one becomes aware that between the electors and elected there is generally a profound harmony of temperament."[53]

Though declaring that he hoped eventually to study all of France during the era of the Third Republic in this way, that would be a life's work, so initially Siegfried had decided to focus upon the West. His own political activities encouraged him in this direction, and intellectually the region presented an interesting challenge insofar as it, in the aggregate, had been a bastion of resistance to the establishment of the Third Republic. Nevertheless, the West contained its own variations, with many districts displaying unique political dispositions. The task Siegfried set himself was to explain these variations down to the level of the canton, which allowed for a subtle analysis of political tendencies without going into excessive detail.[54]

Drawing on the work of Vidal de la Blache, Siegfried defined the West according to its topographical features, notably the relatively sparse and fragmented character of the population, the preference for husbandry over intensive agriculture, an ongoing transition from smaller- to larger-scale property, and, finally, the geological fault line of the Armorican Massif. These features displayed unevenly, and thus the region's frontiers were highly porous. Siegfried subdivided the West into three subsections. The "inner West" encompassed territory from the departments of the Vendée, Maine-et-Loire, Sarthe, and

Mayenne; he also included the northern section of Deux-Sèvres, which displayed similar features. Brittany comprised the next subsection; it included the Loire-Inférieure, Ille-et-Vilaine, Morbihan, Côtes-du-Nord, and Finistère. Finally, there was Normandy, which spanned the Seine-Inférieure, Eure, Calvados, Orne, Manche, and the electoral district of Dreux in the Eure-et-Loir. These sub-regional divisions were the result of different patterns of landholding, economic structures, noble and clerical influence, government activity, and "racial-historical" legacies, though other factors could come into play as well.

The inner West, in Siegfried's estimation, "constitutes, in France, the final stronghold of the counter-revolutionary spirit." A major reason for this was the prevalence of large-scale landowning in a region whose population was scattered. This social structure allowed big proprietors, many of noble background, to exert considerable influence over tenants even though their feudal rights had been abolished long ago. Alongside their economic clout, they retained their prestige and peasants still treated them with deference. The power of the clergy, Siegfried concluded, was also great, notably in the Vendée; here the peasant was "not only religious: moreover, they are afflicted by a kind of holy superstition toward the priest, to whom ancestral habit stipulates passive obedience. Here, then, is the true leader of the Vendean region!"[55]

Siegfried displayed a capacity for nuance as he noted variations within the region; for example, the Sarthe was a transitional zone with smaller proprietors and pro-democratic attitudes prevailing in its eastern cantons, while quasi-feudal conservatism dominated in western ones. He also acknowledged the significance of contingent circumstances in this department. In 1893, when the regime appeared to have moderated and conservatives had lost momentum, the republican vote increased; but in 1902 conservatives rallied against the regime's anticlerical laws and regained the initiative. Nevertheless, the Sarthe generally favoured the reactionary right, and while the latter's priorities shifted over time – from restoring the monarchy to the defence of Catholic interests – its underlying attitude had not changed, nor was it likely to. "To bring about a tranformation of this environment a total destruction of large-scale property, and a simultaneous popular rebellion against the electoral power of the priest, would be necessary."[56]

If feudal social relations and clericalism were the keys to understanding the interior West, for Siegfried race was the key to understanding Brittany. In his view, the Celtic Britons had had a formative effect upon the region since they invaded in the sixth century, defining its tripartite political geography in crucial ways. Continental Brittany, furthest inland, displayed only a residual Celtic presence; next came the *pays Gallo*, which evinced a stronger Breton presence but was still French-speaking; finally, there was westernmost, Breton-speaking Brittany. The inland regions, corresponding roughly to the Loire-Inférieure and Ille-et-Vilaine, intersected with the interior West. Siegfried regarded the neighbouring *pays Gallo* as one of the most subjugated societies in France; its people were fundamentally submissive to the clergy and nobility, prompting a transatlantic comparison: "I do not know of any land in the world, even in [French] Canada, where the authority of the clergy is so unrestricted." The social domination of the local nobility was also imposing, to the point that the common people of the region "subdued by conquests, surrounded by a powerful feudalism, [are] used to bowing their heads without saying anything," though they resented their situation.[57]

The atmosphere changed quite abruptly as one moved into Breton-speaking Brittany. This was due in the first instance to what Siegfried described as the innate qualities of the Celtic people. "They are independent, individualist to the point of indiscipline, sentimental and passionate in all things." Beyond that, economic and social trends were also significant. In some parts of the peninsula, the legacy of feudalism still determined social relations, but elsewhere it had broken down and republicans were gaining support. Other districts, such as Pontivy, evinced "a kind of Bonapartist spirit, anticlerical and democratic." Even socialism was beginning to make inroads, for instance among the workers of the city of Brest. This was a development that worried Siegfried, for, while he professed some admiration for the Breton spirit, he believed that its anarchic potential rendered it potentially unsuit-able for the modern world. He saw the socialist-leaning workers of Brest as unruly and naïve: "Do not believe, moreoever, that socialism will transform them; for them it will instead occasion a return to the classic primitivism of their race." He hoped that the socialist leaders in Brest would mature but remained dubious about their supporters and indeed about Brittany's prospects in general. The region was more integrated into France than often believed but lacked a strong middle class, increasing the appeal of political extremists to an inherently passionate people. The Bretons may have fervently embraced democ-racy, but the latter had not endowed them with "moral and social discipline."[58] They thus provided an especially acute example of a broader problem, for the question of how to reconcile authority and democracy had persisted in France since 1789 and had not yet, in Siegfried's view, been resolved.

The situation in Normandy was more reassuring. Here again the legacy of a medieval invasion for its "racial" characteristics was significant, but the overall temperament was calmer. Norman voters tended toward conservatism but were pragmatic and non-ideological. Indeed, in some ways their outlook was closer to that of the English than the French: "I sometimes ask myself if it would not be easier to adopt the English language when discussing the Normans." Geographically, Siegfried distinguished between Upper Normandy, with its cereal and dairy farms, and the *bocage* of Lower Normandy. In the rural districts of Upper Normandy such as the Pays de Caux, big landowners remained influential, while smaller farmers were business-minded and looked to the clergy as defenders of the existing order. Agricultural labourers had little chance to make headway and lived poorly, escaping their miseries through alcohol abuse. Politically, the region had only gradually adapted to the Republic as it stabilized, and its voters sought primarily to defend their material interests. The dominant city of the region – Rouen – displayed a similar general outlook. Siegfried noted that his native city of Le Havre looked to international trade and was thus something of an anomaly. Though socialism had garnered attention from some workers, the bulk of the population were practical but firm conservatives. Some districts were outliers: in the plains of the Eure, which Siegfried depicted as a frontier between Normandy and the Parisian basin, Bonapartism had some appeal. Overall, he concluded, the prevailing Norman tendency was to accept the Republic only after it had proven that it could offer stability and avoided radicalism.[59]

Lower Normandy was more egalitarian in its social structure but still conservative in outlook. Here a class of prosperous farmers remained deferential to local nobles, but the latter did not dominate them, nor did the clergy or the government. The region had prospered under the Second Empire, which had long-term implications. "Above all, the Bonarpartist spirit remains unchanged, in the persisting form of a materialist, laic and egalitarian conservatism, as distant from radicalism as it is from reaction." Though electors tended to vote for individuals rather than parties, their general stance made the region amenable to a conservative brand of republicanism. The population of Caen and its environs was more turbulent, the result of democratic tendencies among the lower classes, though in recent elections the situation had abated. Along the coast and further to the south, the Norman temperament commingled with influences from Maine and Brittany, but here Siegfried was less concerned about trends such as the rise of socialism than he had been elsewhere. For instance, in the city of Cherbourg – a creation of the French state – socialists had gained a foothold but the Norman environment, Siegfried opined, had a calming effect: "The political conditions thus scarcely differ from those in Brest. But the racial factor [*la race*] and the atmosphere are different: where Brittany creates anarchy, Normandy instinctively sets out its democratic demands in a framework of order and level-headedness."[60]

In the second, shorter part of the *Tableau politique*, Siegfried amassed his findings to determine which factors played the most important role in shaping political comportment in a region that still hesitated to fully accept the Republic. To be sure, the regime had tried to cultivate support, to some effect. One prominent example of relative success in this regard was provided by M. Hendlé, prefect of the Seine-Inférieure from 1882 to 1900, even though he was Jewish and an outsider. But Hendlé had succeeded only insofar as he had worked to highlight the moderation of the regime in response to the essential conservatism of the region. Moreover, his achievement was fragile and was largely undone by the upheavals of the Dreyfus Affair, a reminder that, unlike most of France, in the West the battle to implant republican values had yet to be won.[61]

Why was this so? In addressing this question, Siegfried revisited the salient if variable features of the region, noting that in many districts large-scale property-owners dominated, and that sparse populations hindered the inculcation of democratic values. Religion was a particularly crucial factor; though he noted that Catholic political activity was not inherently anti-republican or anti-democratic, in many areas of the West the values of 1789 were still contested by the clergy. The nobility also retained considerable influence and a broadly monarchist outlook, notwithstanding individual exceptions. The bourgeoisie, so crucial to the establishment of the Third Republic, was relatively small and weak in the West; moreover, it was uneasy with truly democratic mass politics. As for the masses, though there were pockets of independently minded workers, fishers, and farmers, most remained subordinate to the elites and the clergy. All of this meant that while Republican parties did have support – Siegfried identified a core of 26 to 27 per cent of the electorate over time – they did not dominate. The right was durable, and Bonapartism, while not straightforwardly conservative – it was also rooted in the revolutionary tradition and had a democratic element – also had lasting appeal. All of this meant that while in the rest of France the survival of the Third Republic seemed assured, in the West this fundamental struggle persisted: "The West in particular, if not on its periphery which has been affected by the spirit of the century, at least in its rural depths, still lives according to an old notion of authority ... In such an environment the new regime has not established itself in depth, and the resistance of the old persists, unyielding, vigorous, and effective."[62]

Favre and Sanguin rightly emphasize that the *Tableau*, though scholarly in its approach and argument, was also a very personal work, deeply rooted in Siegfried's efforts to secure election in Le Havre in 1906 and 1910, to the point that elements of his campaign speeches appear in the *Tableau* even as his research and writing also informed his campaigning. Alain Garrigou notes that, as a work by a supporter of the Third Republic seeking to ensure the regime's consolidation in recalcitrant districts, the *Tableau* was depicted by some contemporary reviewers, in newspapers such as *L'opinion* and *La dépeche du Midi*, as a guide for aspiring republican candidates.[63] On this matter, it is also worth pointing out that Siegfried was no less concerned to preserve the established moderate republican order against challenges from the left, notably the advance of socialism, as he was to promote the spread of republican values in the face of clerical conservatism. Indeed, at the end of the *Tableau politique* he suggested that, as class politics came to the fore, French governments might find the region's conservatism useful. "Who knows if governments of the future will not find there a kind of counterweight to growing pressure from the Fourth Estate?"[64]

Politically, the *Tableau* reflects Siegfried's liberal, moderate republican convictions. Intellectually, it indicates a more explicit debt to the Vidalian school of geography, with a greater focus upon the significance of the physical environment and a commitment to regional analysis, though Vidal's own approach was mutifaceted and did not neglect the human dimension of the discipline.[65] Siegfried also strongly emphasized continuity; though conceding that political formations changed names and programs, he approvingly quoted from Barrès's *L'appel au soldat* to support his belief in the persistence of distinctive political traditions over time: "There is the Jesuit tone, the Masonic tone, the Orleanist tone, the Opportunist tone, the Bonapartist tone, for each political party is the expression of a well-defined temperament."[66] This raises the question of essentialism in Siegfried's approach, which remains a matter of debate. It has been rightly pointed out that Siegfried's conclusions were far from simplistic – the expression sometimes associated with the *Tableau*, "granite produces the priest, limestone the schoolteacher," is a distortion of his approach. On the other hand, while attempting to provide a multifaceted analysis, Siegfried also clearly ascribed particular qualities to ethnic groups, an approach that would persist in his later work.[67]

Some commentators, including Vidal de la Blache and the reviewer for *Le Temps*, were enthusiastic at the prospect of Siegfried continuing his ambitious project on a national scale.[68] But it was not to be, certainly not to the extent that Siegfried originally intended. He may have been discouraged by the result of his extensive labours in writing the *Tableau*. Though it received some good reviews and would eventually be regarded as a pioneering work, this process took decades: after it first appeared, it took seven years to sell 450 copies of the weighty, detailed tome. Siegfried himself later blamed the Great War rather than a lack of commercial success for distracting him from further work on French politics – he had, he claimed, initially allotted twenty-five years to complete a country-wide study. Given the greater success of his earlier works on New Zealand and Canada, he may also have been tempted to pursue a more international direction in his writing even if the Great War had not intervened.[69] But he certainly never lost his interest in French politics, or French identity. In the *Tableau* he had sought to highlight the diversity of the latter, but when he turned his attention abroad it became a more unitary entity, defined in opposition to various challengers, notably America.

### NORTH AMERICA IN 1914

In 1914, Siegfried returned to visit and write about Canada and the United States, crossing vast expanses of the North American continent for two months and recording his impressions in a series of letters. Many of these appeared in *Le Petit Havre*, and eventually the collection was published as a book in 1916. He took account of the decade of change since his last visit; his earlier anxieties about the character and implications of Americanization were now sharper. Revisiting the issue of Canadian unity, Siegfried underscored its fragility. In its mores, the country was profoundly American; attending a parliamentary session in Ottawa, he commented that "[a]t first sight, the resemblances prevail over the contrast: all of these deputies simply appear to be Americans." This was the case even for French Canadians; it was only when they began speaking that their heritage came through, reflected in: "lively and frequent gestures, rapid delivery, [and] true oratory." Listening to an English-speaking member from Ontario, by contrast, Siegfried discerned "the nasal accent, pure Yankee, is dreadful, the tone is common and down to earth." However, his guide – a French-Canadian senator – pointed out that the man in question came from a United Empire Loyalist background; however American he sounded, he was fervently loyal to the British Empire. This led Siegfried to wonder, "Is it actually possible that, while American in manners the dominion remains politically British?" Tracing the evolution of its increasingly independent commercial and foreign policies, Siegfried concurred with Wilfrid Laurier's observation that "Canada is a nation." Sadly, Laurier had been defeated in the general election of 1911, undone by the mutual opposition of anglophone imperialists and francophone nationalists, both of whom decried his efforts to develop a separate Canadian navy. The former wanted greater integration into the empire, the latter more assurances that new ships would only be used for national defence. Laurier's downfall was a great loss, he concluded. "Canada has had no better pilot. Let us hope that he will be soon recalled to the bridge."[70]

American-style economic expansion, especially in Western Canada, was impressive but it intensified regional divisions. In cities such as Montreal and Toronto, there was a desire to protect domestic industry, but Western farmers wanted access to American goods and markets. When Laurier tried to negotiate an agreement with the US for free trade in agricultural products, he had met with fierce opposition from eastern industrial interests. But those interests could not prevent the rapid transformation of the West along what Siegfried regarded as American lines. Visiting the region, in Calgary Siegfried described how the discovery of oil had provoked a craze among all social classes for buying stocks and prospecting permits – even though the discoveries at that stage were very preliminary. "This entire, extraordinary boom is thus based upon simple hope." Canadian efforts to settle the country's Western provinces and thereby increase farming output for export were quite successful but had hit a snag. The rural population had grown rapidly but so had the urban one, too much so in Siegfried's estimation. This resulted in a large "floating" population that put

74 France in the World

pressure on local labour markets. In the expectation of great wealth, Canadians had also built too many railways and hotels, and now the result was economic stagnation. Siegfried concluded that while the Canadian Prairies had great economic potential, for the moment an excessively American-style approach had caused problems: "As is invariably the case in America during periods of great progress, the Canadians, who were justly aware of their magnificent possibilities, had counted upon the future somewhat excessively."[71]

Siegfried spent a greater proportion of his North American visit in the United States. Compared with previous trips, he ranged further afield, travelling extensively through the West and into the North. His belief that the country was starkly different from Europe in its racial and cultural character deepened; the fact that he spent more time in the West might help to explain this, though there was also a tradition of French visitors to the United States stressing its exotic nature.[72] Arriving in Denver after a long train ride from Chicago, he observed: "Here there is a kind of Spanish character: a languidness in the atmosphere, in the presence of the most beautiful panorama of mountains ... A Castilian or semi-Indian air among these bronzed men with the profile of eagles? ... I ask myself whether I am not, in Denver, at the outermost bounds of our Western civilization." Salt Lake City also struck him as exotic; he felt that French readers might find comparisons with Damascus helpful. The Mormon Tabernacle "is an intermediary between some kind of synagogue and immense Protestant temple ... [But in] crossing the Rocky Mountains, I did not really think that I had found a kind of new Holy Land there." As for San Francisco, Siegfried had seen it before the 1907 earthquake; it was now less "wild," but the city remained in its essence, without a doubt, "a frontier of races, worlds, and civilizations."[73]

Turning to the American people themselves, Siegfried observed that they were becoming more diverse than ever. Upon arriving in New York, he sensed that while there was no American "race" as such, immigrants were transformed by their surroundings to the point that they did possess "a common allure ... a people with its own personality."[74] But these comments pertained only to those of European ancestry. Siegfried had virtually nothing to say about the African American population aside from describing a porter on the train to Denver as, "in keeping with tradition," pleasant but lazy. In California, his attention focused on the growing opposition to immigration from Japan and China, which he evaluated in a way that echoed his interpretation of Asian immigration to New Zealand. The state needed more labourers, but Californians "do not want to make room for Asiatics." Overall, Siegfried's travels were leading him to become more skeptical about the future of the American people. In the nineteenth century, an American "race" had taken shape; predominantly Anglo-Saxon in heritage, physically impressive, and mentally energetic, it had been capable of absorbing some new elements. But now, especially in the West, immigrants came from Southern, Eastern, and even non-European states. "Racially" inferior, they banded together in isolated groups and concerned themselves with making money; they were also a source of labour unrest. Such trends undermined national cohesion and public spirit; "The national base of the American state – at least in the West, let us make that qualification – is thus less solid than is usually thought."[75]

Siegfried was also dubious about aspects of the American economy and the character of American politics, though he remained impressed by the country's vitality. Already gigantic, New York had grown tremendously over the ten years since his previous visit; further west, the relative pace of economic development was even greater in some areas. However, as he had observed in Western Canada, growth was sometimes too rapid, with businesses becoming overextended. This was the main reason, he concluded, why many railroads were currently failing. Though businessmen liked to point the finger at state regulation, and as a good classical liberal Siegfried conceded that this was likely a factor, ultimately he believed that the root problem was laying too much track and building too many stations. More generally, when it came to conducting business, "in spite of certain appearances North America is still far from constituting a settled, organized, and morally civilized society like that of Europe." As for politics, while from a historical point of view the United States was a venerable democracy, the electorate lacked sophistication compared with Europeans. Siegfried described a political rally held in Denver for Secretary of State William Jennings Bryan as carnival-like in its atmosphere. "American audiences do not have the refinement of ours. They more closely resemble gatherings of children and even (said without harmful intent, for it is perhaps a form of praise) audiences of savages." Commenting on politics in California, Siegfried noted how, until recently, private business had been able to dominate apparently democratic institutions. Now the population was rebelling against capitalist excesses and political corruption. The result was an increasing use of referenda and recall votes. But as turbulent as American politics were, he conceded some admiration, albeit of a patronizing kind: "The day when Americans become completely reasonable, peaceful and timid, our old planet will to me seem less lively, colourful, and lacking an indefinable but necessary youthfulness."[76]

Siegfried's tour ended abruptly when he learned that war was breaking out in Europe. He made his way back to New York, where the steamer *La Lorraine* took him and other mobilized passengers back to France. During his return journey through the West, he was struck by how unaware the population was of European developments. Upon arrival in New York, he saw, to his mind, further evidence of the deep ethnic divisions in the United States as groups of Germans, Austro-Hungarian subjects, and others paraded in the streets. But he was pleased to note that whereas in earlier years he had detected a strong anti-French sentiment among Americans, rooted in suspicion of Catholicism and disdain for "Latins," there was now more sympathy. To be sure, in some parts of the US – particularly the West, where German immigrants were plentiful – feelings were bound to be different, but in New York Siegfried judged public opinion as pro-French, perhaps even more than it was pro-British. Years of propaganda, university exchanges, and other diplomatic efforts had paid off, and it was widely accepted among Americans that the Germans were the aggressors.

Still, as he left the United States for France, Siegfried could not help but to underscore differences. Despite expressions of support, it was evident to him that many Americans wanted nothing to do with European quarrels, and that others wished only to profit from them. Siegfried professed to understand why many Americans did not envy Europeans at this time, but he also referenced willful ignorance and crass materialism: "[T]heir blissful sense of security, their concern to remain apart and above all to not lose a dollar in adventure seems exceedingly dull to me. There is more grandeur in those for whom battle is a necessity and who simply accept it."[77]

### THE GREAT WAR AND AFTER

Thirty-nine years old when the war broke out, Siegfried was one of many French soldiers approaching or of middle age. He was probably fortunate that his linguistic skills allowed him to serve an interpreter, though he still came face-to-face with some of the harsh realities of the conflict. At the time of his mobilization, he was a member of the 24th Territorial Infantry Regiment, holding the rank of sergeant. He was soon assigned to the heavy artillery unit of the First Canadian Division in Flanders, which operated around Armentières in 1915. Promoted to the rank of adjutant and transferring into the 19th Escadron du train later that same year, he was then transferred to the 25th Royal Garrison Artillery, or "Phipps," Brigade of the British Expeditionary Force, serving in the Nord.[78] He remained with this unit until 1917, when he was transferred to work with the financial service of the French blockade effort against Germany. The key figure in effecting this change was probably Siegfried's friend Albert Métin, who had become a deputy cabinet minister before being named undersecretary for the blockade. Siegfried now returned to Paris to join Métin's staff, where he could wear civilian clothes, and alternated between working at the blockade section in the morning and processing telegraphs in the afternoon.[79]

In the latter stages of the war, Siegfried was thus no longer at the front lines, but he had spent a significant amount of time there. Writing on the first anniversary of his death in 1960, his friend Pierre Hamp depicted him as adapting calmly to the rigours of the forward areas while retaining his keen powers of analysis. Though he apparently regretted that any chance of Franco-German reconciliation had been dashed – there was little left between the two nations but hatred, he observed to Hamp at the time – Siegfried tried to make the most of his surroundings. He recounted how serving with the Canadians in this area had given him an opportunity to appreciate the qualities of French Flanders, "where the war smashed houses but not the people's character." Despite the devastation, the population had bravely adapted to the shelling and destruction; even children who had lost limbs continued to play, using wooden substitutes. The Flemish also got along well with the Commonwealth troops, who found the region's *estaminets* reminiscent of their own pubs. As for Siegfried himself, Hamp suggested that "he managed as best as possible, as if he was accustomed to privation."[80] Of course, Hamp's article was part of a memorial tribute and thus unlikely to be critical, but it does appear that Siegfried executed his duties without controversy and made the best of a trying situation, while trying to remain engaged in intellectual activity. He corresponded with Max Leclerc about the publication of his letters from his 1914 North American visit, and translated a book authored by a correspondent for the London *Times* that described a visit to the front in the early stages of the war.[81]

Further indication of Siegfried's wartime experiences and impressions can be gleaned from an address that he gave to the Empire Club of Canada in Toronto after the fighting ended. He recalled that the war was initially expected to be brief, but of course had turned into a gruelling contest, one in which early German advances had deprived France of many natural resources. As a result, the entire nation had to mobilize; its people heroically answered the call. Siegfried acknowledged the decisive contribution made by French women, recalling his time in Armentières where, despite the proximity of German fire, the cotton mills continued to operate. "The labor was done by girls of 17, 18, and 19. They were shelled, and at the time of the shelling the workers went to the cellars, and sometimes they were wounded, but I was told by the inspectors of labor that the next day not a girl was missing." Perhaps inspired by Barrèsian conceptions of national rootedness, he also invoked memories of an elderly peasant farming his land as close as 1,000 yards from the trenches because his country needed food. "There is," he added, "in the mind of the French peasant something which I think has struck your soldiers. It is the very peculiar kind of love he has for his country. For you the country, the Empire, does many fine things – I don't know exactly what – but I know it is something fine. For us, and especially for the French citizen at the war ... it is the soil of France; it is the land of France."[82] Privately, he made a similar observation in the preface to a book of poetry he completed for Paule in 1920, commenting that his wartime service had reawakened a childhood appreciation of nature, particularly the glories of the French countryside. "For nearly three years during the war I again had the opportunity to live with nature, but this time amidst the fields themselves, close to the earth and in the intimate company of those who cultivated it."[83]

In his comments to the Empire Club, Siegfried had also placed the French war effort in a broader international perspective. He expressed profound gratitude to France's allies for their sacrifices on the battlefield, predicting that the deep bonds established between French citizens and Allied soldiers constituted an "everlasting" friendship. But while readily acknowledging that France could not have triumphed on its own, he also suggested that its unprecedented wartime effort and triumph might lead other nations to reconsider their previous impressions of the country; "[W]e have shown qualities of organization which people did not expect from us; for we were always spoken of as being charming people, of course, but light. Gentlemen ...

we remain all that, but we claim that we are able to organize, and I think that during those four years we have been organizing victory." In so doing, he continued, France had shown that it was not, as had often been suggested since 1870, in decline. "We knew what France was, though people did not know it, we expected the time would come when we would be allowed to show it; and now, after forty years of ordeal, and after four years of the horrors of war, the Day has come, and the light is shining in France after so many days of darkness."[84] Though presented within the context of his commitment to Allied solidarity, there is more than a hint here that Siegfried believed his country had not always received its due respect.

Siegfried's Toronto speech had come near the end of a lengthy official visit to the British dominions of Australia, New Zealand, and Canada, as a member of a mission assembled in the spring of 1918 by Clemenceau's government. Initially, the plan was to visit Australia in the hope of bolstering France's image there and promoting stronger postwar economic and cultural relations; New Zealand and Canada were soon added to the itinerary. The French government chose Albert Métin to head the mission, and he requested that Siefgried serve as its general secretary.[85] The mission set out in August 1918, but tragedy struck when Métin died of a stroke en route, in San Francisco. Though wishing to accompany his friend's body home, Siegfried was instructed to continue the journey. Apparently, the French government hoped to send the philosopher Henri Bergson in Métin's place, but he was unable to travel in time. General Paul Pau, its senior military member, now assumed leadership but Siegfried was also required to assume a more prominent role, both in analyzing political and economic data as well as participating in public engagements.[86]

The mission visited Australia during the fall of 1918, travelling widely and meeting with national and local politicians, chambers of commerce, and trade union leaders. Siegfried was particularly interested in promoting French culture at Australian universities. He met with professors in Sydney, Melbourne, Adelaide, and Perth with an eye to establishing connections through funding travel to France by Australian teachers of French, and "took advantage of every opportunity," Pau reported, "to promote French culture and intellectual leadership."[87]

The delegation encountered some political challenges. In Queensland, it received a cool reception as elements of the population – notably Irish workers – suspected the French of wanting to promote conscription. The mission denied having any such motive; its members also stressed, in response to questioning, that France had played no role in causing the outbreak of war, though they did not convince all their interlocutors. For the most part, however, the mission's members were struck by the level of official cordiality and public enthusiasm. Their visit to Melbourne went especially well; they met with acting prime minister William Watt, and Siegfried also had discussions with Labor party leaders. The French consul in Sydney reported that Pau cut a fine military figure, and noted that "M. Siegfried's great cultivation, modesty, and affability," along with the qualities of other members, "charmed everyone." Though no binding agreements were reached, there were extensive discussions about lowering Australian tariffs for French goods, and at the time the mission departed at the end of 1918, the situation seemed promising. However, the official report that followed warned that if the French government did not follow up this promising start with innovative American-style public diplomacy, the considerable fund of goodwill that had been built up would dissipate.[88]

The delegation also spent a month in New Zealand – where Siegfried's reputation as an authority on the country facilitated access to various notables – but upon returning to France he concentrated on writing about Australia.[89] He was almost certainly the primary author of the extensive official report of the mission, which bears all the hallmarks of his approach and style. Assessing Australia's potential as a future trading partner, the report stressed that its economic expansion was being held back by its low population and barriers to trade and immigration, but added that most Australians did not seem to be troubled by this. "In fact, [Australia] gives the impression of being a happy country, where there are no poor, and salaries are sufficient to ensure everyone a decent, even pleasant life, where social equality prevails and where the white race gives obvious signs of health and prosperity." Whether this situation could endure was another matter. Australians were all too aware that they were surrounded by "immense reservoirs of men of the yellow race," and were already looking to the USA as a second protector, given the waning of British power. The report fully endorsed these fears: "If the yellow man was able to force entry into the Commowealth's territory, Australian civilization in its current form could not continue to exist."[90] Renewed contact with the Pacific had apparently intensified Siegfried's earlier fears regarding the supposed "Yellow Peril."

Siegfried's military service ended in September 1919. He continued to write occasional articles for *Le Petit Havre* and to give lectures – some of them deriving from his visit to Australia – but now embarked upon a diplomatic career, joining the new Service français de la Société des Nations (SFSDN) established in December of that year. Part of a broader effort by the French Foreign Ministry to build upon its wartime efforts in economic diplomacy, the SFSDN was headed by Jean Gout, who had previously been the director of the blockade services. Siegfried was among the latter's staff – many of whom did not have careers rooted in the diplomatic corps – who accompanied Gout into the new service. He began as the deputy head of its economic and financial section and was promoted to section head in 1920.[91]

The SFSDN's personnel were soon heavily involved in the various international gatherings that sought to stabilize postwar Europe. Siegfried served on the delegations to three conferences. The first, held in Brussels in the fall of 1920, was a financial conference organized by the League aimed at coordinating postwar economic recovery. It established some agreements on general principles but achieved little in the way of concrete policies, partly because the major powers had excluded discussion of inter-Allied debts or German reparations. The second conference, held at Barcelona in the spring of 1921, was devoted to communications and achieved some practical results in the form of conventions on the freedom of transit and the regime of international waterways.[92] The third and best-known was the Genoa Conference of April-May 1922, where British prime minister David Lloyd George sought to achieve a breakthrough in European recovery and reconstruction by integrating the Soviet Union into international affairs; promoting the peaceful revision of the peace treaties with Germany, Austria, and Hungary; and securing American involvement in European recovery. Ambitious in scope, the conference fell short, undermined by the signing of the Treaty of Rapallo between Germany and the Soviet Union as well as French-led opposition to treaty revision and a general lack of preparation; moreover, the United States had refused to participate.[93]

Intensely involved in the work of the delegations, Siegfried sent reports to Gout in which he detailed various proceedings but also offered general observations. At Brussels in 1920, he judged that the conference was unlikely to achieve much in the way of concrete results but felt that it still provided an opportunity to show that France was getting its house in order and was prepared to play a leading role in world affairs, notwithstanding foreign criticisms that it was in financial and social turmoil. Near the end of the conference, he reported to Gout that: "As I indicated to you in one of my preceding letters, France's position remains excellent. Our financial overview made a strong impression: France is cited as one of the rare stable countries, set upon reestablishing its economic and financial equilibrium, and capable of doing so. This position, in tandem with the fact that we are victors, gives us an undoubted prestige, which the conference has indisputably highlighted." By contrast, the delegation noted in its final report, the British left an impression of being excessively self-interested.[94] In Barcelona the following spring, Siegfried counselled a policy of restraint, suggesting that France's image would suffer if it opposed any of the transportation conventions. After the conference ended, he felt that the delegation's performance had been less effective than in Brussels.[95]

This focus upon sustaining France's image remained important for Siegfried at the Genoa conference, but he also sensed that the tasks assigned to him were of secondary importance, and he grew increasingly preoccupied by family concerns. As the conference opened, he emphasized the importance of its success for the British prime minister, whose performance impressed him: "Lloyd George pilots the conference, of which he is the true and only leader, with perfect ease. The way in which his smiles and frowns are reported makes one think of the court of Louis XIV. It is clear that he is above all concerned that the conference does not fail, and for that he is ready to make plenty of concessions." As for the French delegation, it had to be mindful of public opinion at home – where a general desire to hold firm in dealing with both Germany and the Soviet Union prevailed – while at the same time appearing open to dialogue. As the conference continued, Siegfried continued to analyze the proceedings but stressed that "I continue to believe that these economic and financial discussions are only a smokescreen and pretext, allowing the Russian question to come to a head." He was frustrated by a softening of France's position regarding Soviet compensation for nationalized foreign assets, though it was soon reversed. However, he was also increasingly distressed by news from home that his mother's health was failing. He planned to return to France once the commissions, save for the one dealing with the USSR, had finished their work.[96]

Julie Siegfried passed away on 28 May 1922; her husband died only months later, on 26 September. Within a matter of weeks, their son had resigned from his position with the French service of the League of Nations; were the deaths of his parents the main reason why he did so? His motives can only be guessed at, for he does not appear to have committed an explanation to paper. Years later, François Goguel suggested that Siegfried simply did not have the bureaucratic temperament required to stay in such a job. The records of the French service also suggest that its workload was increasing and that its personnel were frustrated because they were not entitled to the same benefits, particularly housing, that colleagues in the Ministry of Foreign Affairs received.[97] Possibly a combination of these factors led Siegfried to quit. At the time, he also expressed interest in running for his father's vacated parliamentary seat, but in Le Havre the local supporters of the Alliance démocratique decided that René Coty, the future final president of the Fourth Republic, whose electoral and war records were more impressive, and who presented himself as "the faithful disciple" of Jules Siegfried, would be their candidate instead.[98] For André the matter was settled; the academy it would be. Though he later joined the French delegation to the Geneva financial conference of 1927, this was only temporary; for the rest of his life his focus remained on teaching and writing.[99]

— * —

The significance of Siegfried's experiences as a candidate, soldier, and diplomat are evident. His unsuccessful electoral bids shaped his insights into the dynamics of French politics, setting the stage not only for the publication of the *Tableau* but also subsequent analyses of national politics that would reach much wider audiences than his in-depth study of regional electoral geography had. Though aspects of his wartime experiences remain obscure, they clearly reinforced his interest in the English-speaking world, even as he juxtaposed the values and merits of the "Anglo-Saxons" with those of an exhausted but triumphant France. His involvement in diplomacy afforded him fresh insights into the international trends that he had often written about, while at the same time shaping his awareness of how deeply circumstances had changed after the Great War. In the years to come, Siegfried devoted the bulk of his time to making sense of the interwar era, both in terms of French politics and global trends. Though he would write about a great many developments, preoccupations that were already evident by 1914 – the challenge that the United States posed to French and, more broadly, European civilization, and the existence of potential threats to white global hegemony – remained paramount.

# 3

# France and the Anglo-Saxons

Siegfried resumed his duties full-time at Sciences Po in 1923. He was soon recognized as the school's most prominent teacher, winning the admiration of many students, and going on to defend the institution when it came under increasing criticism for elitism and conservatism. He also returned to researching and writing about the English-speaking nations, travelling first to Britain, then to the United States, with the support of the Musée social. These travels produced two books that attracted considerable attention, securing his status as a leading French interpreter of the Anglo-Saxon world. He was increasingly in demand as an interlocutor between France, Britain, and the United States, continuing to publish in France but also contributing to English-language journals to decipher his country to a foreign audience and offer what he described as a European perspective on international trends. A second study of Britain appeared in 1931; devoted to assessing the country's response to the Great Depression, it sparked greater controversy than the first. Siegfried also wrote about the Great Depression's effect on the United States and published an in-depth second study of Canada, in which the themes of Americanization and the survival of French culture figured prominently.

This chapter contends that Siegfried's teaching and writing ultimately served to highlight the differences between France and the English-speaking nations. It was not that he intended to promote animosity; indeed, he saw himself as encouraging mutual understanding, and was often, though not always, perceived in such terms across both the Channel and the Atlantic. Yet, in his writings, there were consistent themes – the profound contrast between British and French economic assumptions and behaviour and the ever-widening gap between American and European mores, which he, arguably, conflated with French ones – that underscored the distinctive character of the English-speaking nations. He considered Britain as European and the United States as being part of Western civilization, but both were outliers that posed challenges for intra-European and trans-Atlantic cooperation. And while he discerned a deep kinship between Britain and the USA, he saw them as being on different trajectories. Britain was in a relative though avoidable decline, while, conversely, the Great Depression had only partly halted America's growing economic and cultural reach. The latter was very evident in Canada, where French traditions faced formidable challenges. As the Second World War loomed, Siegfried promoted cooperation between the Western democracies, but his efforts in this regard still bore traces of his previous emphases on their differing values and institutions.

## THE EDUCATOR

The Sciences Po to which Siegfried returned remained an elite institution whose staff was immensely proud of its work. A 1927 brochure, for example, highlighted how the school, created to provide new leadership for the country after the devastating defeat of 1870–71, had lived up to the intentions of its founders during the Great War. Many of its students, graduates, and staff had sacrificed themselves for the nation; as France sought to rebuild, it had greater need than ever of the leadership that Sciences Po provided.[1] The school's graduates utterly dominated the upper reaches of the state bureaucracy, but this formidable placement record rested on a narrow social base. Sizeable enrollment fees limited the student pool, meaning that the 2,000 to 2,500 people who attended Sciences Po annually during this period came primarily from the Parisian upper middle classes. There were also some foreigners and a smattering of students from the provinces, but the latter often regarded themselves as outsiders.[2]

Sciences Po offered a two-year diploma that promised both a wide-ranging liberal education and more specific skills applicable to a variety of prestigious careers. An additional complementary year, available to authorized students, provided further training for the admission exams to the *grand corps* of the French state – the Inspection des finances, the Conseil d'État, the Cour des comptes, and the Corps diplomatique. In terms of curriculum, the laissez-faire liberal views that had predominated when Siegfried was a student remained strong, and overall Sciences Po evinced a broadly conservative though hardly uniform outlook. During this period, its faculty included figures such as the conservative republican Joseph Barthelémy, who taught legislative history; the laissez-faire professor of political economy Jacques Rueff; and the monarchist sympathizer Raphaël Alibert, a professor of public administration. The liberal historian Élie Halévy, whose work Siegfried admired, was also a prominent faculty member.[3] In the 1930s, new administrators such as Roger Seydoux – a former student of Siegfried's – sought to adapt Sciences Po to a changing political climate.[4] Siegfried himself played a significant role in these efforts, which were undertaken with the goal of preserving the private character and liberal outlook of Sciences Po as much as possible, in an era where greater state intervention loomed.

Though he had taken up his post in 1910, given the interruptions of the war and his forays into diplomacy it was only during the second half of the 1920s and the 1930s that Siegfried truly attained renown as a professor. Among his regular courses were "The politics of the great commercial powers, except France," later renamed "The commercial policies of the British Empire, the United States, and the Far East," which he often co-taught with the historian Georges Blondel; another was "economic geography," which also had an international and comparative focus. In addition to these offerings, until 1932 Siegfried also oversaw preparatory courses for students planning to write the *concours d'entrée* for the Ministry of Foreign Affairs.[5]

Lecture notes from this period in Siegfried's papers highlight his organization, precision, and desire to inform and engage his audience, employing an approach that encouraged students to identify the essences of economies, nations, and cultures, and to classify them hierarchically. For example, England was typified as an "old" nation in economic terms; it was rich in skilled personnel and capital but in need of primary materials, while "new" nations, such as the Latin American states, had plenty of the latter but gaps in the former. The United States, he suggested, was a transitional case, still rich in resources but increasingly an exporter of manufactured goods. Stressing the implications of economic orientation for trade deficits and balances of payments, he concluded that the two categories were, ideally, complementary. Mature economies should partner with emerging ones or transform them into colonies, though current trends indicated that the colonies would eventually seek emancipation. Another serious challenge for industrial nations was that if demand for their products fell, they faced mass unemployment, lower salaries, and potentially lower birthrates.[6] With the advent of the Great Depression, the travails of Britain and especially Germany illustrated these problems acutely: Siegfried seemed to imply that France's less industrialized but more "balanced" economy was better positioned to weather the storm.

Siegfried also differentiated between "saving" and "spending" nations. Saving nations, he proposed, tended to have predominantly rural economies and were more pessimistic about the future, stressing the need for preservation in the interest of the family: the French, Chinese, and northern Italians fit this characterization. By contrast, the Germans and Anglo-Saxons, and some "primitive peoples," as Siegfried put it, in warmer climes, were more optimistic about the future, less inclined to regard wealth in static terms, and more willing to consume. Frugal nations such as France were less economically dynamic but because they preserved their resources were more independent, though such an orientation could also encourage inaction.[7] Race, too, was a significant factor in Siegfried's analysis of economic relations, as a set of notes devoted to the issue of the "yellow peril" suggest. Facing population pressures and possessing formidable business talents, Asians presented an economic, ethnic, and political challenge to whites. Economically, their labour was cheaper, and they were extremely ambitious; ethnically, they threatened to overwhelm certain territories unless they were excluded. Politically, the situation was less worrisome, at least for the time being. While Japan was increasingly assertive in defence of its interests, China lacked the unity to do so, and in the short to medium term Siegfried did not see them as a direct threat to Europe. But he concluded that "the yellow race is a great race, likely our equal"; challenges lay ahead.[8]

The records of Siegfried's preparatory classes for the foreign ministry entrance exam shed further light on his teaching methods and motivations. He required students to make succinct oral presentations and prepare expositions on assigned topics, warning them that "[n]owadays we write very badly (at your age, people have always written badly)," and entreating them to strive for clarity, precision, and vigour. For oral presentations, he stressed the need to organize one's thoughts and observe time limits. The subjects assigned were often highly topical and reflected some of his long-standing interests. For instance, among the options he gave his 1924–25 class were explaining why Great Britain was so determined to restore the value of the pound following the Great War, and why Italy had been able to industrialize despite lacking natural resources. Among the choices for written expositions was a question asking students how they would arrive at a trade agreement with the new Soviet regime, and another instructing them to explain how they would prepare for a journey to California to study the "problem" of Chinese and Japanese immigration.[9]

What kind of an impression did Siegfried make upon his students? Roger Seydoux recalled him as a precise and meticulous but also highly engaging lecturer, who drew upon an amazing breadth of knowledge as well as vast personal experience. He described Siegfried's introductory lecture for a course given in 1930 as follows:

> As he enters, rich and lengthy applause breaks out. Students cry "bravo" as if they were at the theatre. At the Sorbonne or the rue Soufflot such a demonstration would perhaps appear inappropriate. Here the perspective is different: the School is a sort of club, and we are cheering not only the professor but the star of the house. Sitting slightly in profile, he begins his course, sometimes throwing a quick glance over his notes. He used a bizarre device, derived from old-fashioned glasses, with notorial pince-nez and a dowager's lorgnette. [His] very animated head dominates a neck of disproportionate height; the features are strongly pronounced, the brows bushy. The brush-cut mustache accentuates the ruggedness of a face that is British in appearance, but which, through a liveliness of expression, remains Latin. The dominant impression is one of youth. To assign him an age would be risky: he is one of those men who reaches their forties very quickly and seems to remain there indefinitely. He speaks with a steady and clear voice, in a tone more like that of a [popular] lecturer than a professor, with a slight affectation and a deliberately French pronunciation of English terms that has earned him many excellent imitators.[10]

Claude des Portes, another former student who went on to become a high-level civil servant in a career that spanned from the late 1930s to the early 1980s, provided a similar portrait in a book about Sciences Po published in 1935:

> His economic geography course, celebrated all over the world, is a series of picturesque scenes and shrewdly drawn characters, in which he knows how to embed indispensable figures ...

For thirty years he has travelled the globe, keen to see everything with his own eyes, and not fearing to expose himself to need. This has yielded him a profound understanding of places and peoples. Every day, not only the students of the School benefit from this, but also an entire Parisian public who listen to him with respect and pleasure ... he remains faithful to the École des sciences politiques, of which he is ... the most outstanding personality, because he incarnates at once the spirit of liberalism, the spirit of observation, the spirit of the salon, and indeed spirit itself.[11]

Siegfried also made an impression on foreign students, such as the American Laurence Wylie, who went on to become a leading scholar of contemporary France. Speaking at the symposium held in Siegfried's honour in 1975, Wylie recalled with amusement how during an exam in June 1930 his renowned teacher had been perplexed to discover that "Madamoiselle Laurence Wylie" was in fact a young man. More seriously, he continued,

André Siegfried opened my eyes: with him the details of everyday life possessed a significance that escaped other observers. I remember my sensation of discovery when he analyzed the publicity for a brand of cigarettes, whose posters were then covering the walls of America. I must have seen "Reach for a Lucky instead of a sweet!" thousands of times without grasping the complexity of this slogan. André Siegfried explained to us that it reflected one of the characteristics of an advanced capitalist country, where entire sectors of the economy compete with one another: in this case the tobacco industry was seeking gain at the expense of the sugar industry.[12]

What did Siegfried, in turn, think of his students? The evidence suggests that he was demanding. Regarding female students – who during the interwar years constituted between 10 and 13 per cent of the student body, a dismissive adage has been attributed to him: "A young girl who is not too ugly is five boys who do not work."[13] In a report to the director of Sciences Po on his preparatory course for foreign affairs, Siegfried characterized his group as generally able, but also felt that there was plenty of room for improvement. The students' oral presentations were well-informed, but they tended to read from

## 90    France in the World

their notes instead of addressing the audience and struggled to keep within the time limit. In their written work, they displayed knowledge of the issues but an inability to appreciate another point of view or convey an idea vigorously. There were also problems with their writing. "As for the style, it always leaves something to be desired, through lack of precision in the use of terms and above all disregard for nuances. Taking into account their (excusable) ignorance of our language, these flaws are particularly noticeable among foreigners, notably the Americans, who often have ideas but express them in disorder."[14]

Siegfried may have bemoaned his students' shortcomings, but he also seems to have genuinely enjoyed working with them. In a preface he contributed to des Portes's 1935 book, he noted some of the challenges of teaching, such as the difficulty in sustaining the attention of young minds and trying to anticipate often unpredictable student opinions. He was quick to add, though, that the reinvigoration that contact with young people provided more than compensated for this.

> We age markedly in study, in the muffled calm of libraries and the security of offices. But when, after having conscientiously prepared a class, the familiar call of the usher introduces you in the amphitheatre – "Professor, it's ringing" – it seems that, in an atmosphere humming with life, one will fly over an ocean of youth ... I flatter myself as being curious, but did curiosity alone lead me to travel through so many countries if I had not been sustained, through so many journeys, by the sentiment that I would share my observations with these battalions of young people keen to learn about them?

Naturally, he was also proud of his students' later accomplishments, especially since so many rose to prominence. "As parents do with their children, I now measure the swift passage of time with the classes [*promotions*] of youth whom I knew and prepared as candidates. It is rare for me to go to one of our embassies or legations without finding former students ... I even find that they are beginning to become dangerously important in the hierarchy!"[15]

The depth of Siegfried's commitment to Sciences Po became particularly apparent after the elections of 1936. The French left had long criticized the school as elitist, suggesting that its faculty evinced a strong conservatism, even muted hostility to republican democracy.

Following the victory of the Popular Front and the formation of a new government by the Socialist leader Léon Blum, there was talk of replacing Sciences Po with a publicly funded, more accessible institution that truly reflected the democratic character of French society. Minister of Education Jean Zay, a left-leaning member of the Radical Party, spearheaded the effort, setting out a proposal for the creation of an École d'administration. The administrators of Sciences Po responded with a public relations campaign, intensive lobbying in parliament, and attempts to work out a deal with Zay that conceded a new public institution but sought to preserve the Sciences Po as well.[16] The political struggle continued until the outbreak of war; Siegfried participated in the lobbying and in discussions with Zay, but his primary role was to enhance the school's public image. For instance, in an interview with the mass daily *Le Petit Parisien* in February 1938, he recounted the many services the École libre had performed for France. Created in response to the defeat of 1870–71, he explained, it had always been a national institution. Though it was privately funded, its monies were devoted solely to its work, including financial support for students. On this point, he added, new scholarships were being established, showing that the school was not as exclusive as critics suggested. As for politics, its faculty were of diverse backgrounds and views rather than a group of anti-republican reactionaries. Noting that his extensive travel and dealings with foreign students allowed him to appreciate the international significance of the institution, Siegfried did not oppose the creation of a publicly funded École d'administration but argued that it was essential that Sciences Po be able to continue its fine work.[17]

By the time the Second World War broke out, Science Po's lobbying, along with a rightward shift in the political climate that reduced Zay's freedom to manoeuvre, meant that the challenge to it had been parried, at least for the time being. By 1939, the government of the day was prepared to have the École libre become the feeder institution for an upper-level Centre des hautes études administratives; the proposed École d'administration had faded from the agenda. In the meantime, Sciences Po was reducing some of its emphasis on laissez-faire liberalism, hiring new faculty devoted to topics such as industrial organization and labour relations, and engaging more fully with various, often non-conformist, intellectual currents ranging from pacifism to technocracy.[18] The debate over Sciences Po would continue under Vichy and after the Liberation, but during the 1930s it had

92             France in the World

displayed the capacity to adapt, and as one of its most prominent faculty members Siegfried embodied the determination of French elites to maintain their core values while responding to change.

### ANALYZING BRITAIN

Beyond his duties at Sciences Po, Siegfried devoted considerable time to travel, research, and writing. In the early 1920s, he focused on events across the Channel at a time when Franco-British relations were under great strain, the result of diverging policies toward Germany and suspicion of each other's motives. In the eyes of many French politicians and ordinary citizens, the British, by encouraging more lenient treatment of the former enemy as a potential economic partner, were reverting to a self-interested policy that abandoned their wartime ally. Conversely, many Britons felt that the French were adopting an excessively hard line and scuppering chances for a stable peace; elements of an increasingly angry press and political elite contended that the Third Republic sought hegemony on the Continent.[19] However, there were voices on both sides that sought to preserve cooperation, among them the Association France–Grande Bretagne and the Musée social, which had long regarded the English-speaking nations as worthy of close attention. To that end, the two co-sponsored a series of monographs aimed at improving French understanding of Britain, and the Musée funded a 1923 visit to Britain by Siegfried, who, after meeting with political and industrial leaders, recorded his initial impressions in a detailed letter to industrialist and social reformer Georges Risler, its president at the time. Outlining many of the trends that he would examine in the book, he noted the salience of anti-French sentiment:

> From the viewpoint of Franco-English relations I have nothing good to tell you. I have met many friends of France, but not one who currently approves of us. They accuse us of destabilizing Europe, keeping it in a state of crisis without hope, not so much in the goal of ensuring that we are paid [reparations], but to dominate it. They speak of Napoleon and Louis XIV all the time. Disturbingly, it appears that in the schools ten to twelve-year old boys have begun to talk about France as a rival and enemy again. The "advanced" elements of Liberalism and Labour are against us, as is non-conformist opinion.[20]

More generally, he argued, the mood in Britain was bleak, the result of continued economic troubles and enduring mass unemployment. Though historically an exporting nation where support for free trade was strong, circumstances were now leading some politicians to reconsider their priorities. However, Siegfried doubted that this would result in a profound policy shift, suggesting that that the British economy could only thrive if it retained an open approach. "England gives the impression of self-destruction by shutting itself behind a wall, within overly narrow frontiers. It needs a world base: if it cuts itself off from this base, it will wither."

Returning to France, Siegfried was keen to write but somewhat apprehensive about how his work would be received. "I have the elements of a study which, while I would be the first to admit is superficial, could be worthwhile. The difficulty will be to produce a book that is not outmoded the very moment that it appears."[21] He thus worked quickly and the book appeared in the spring of 1924. Despite his concerns about superficiality, the final product offered a detailed discussion of economic and political developments in Britain since the Great War. Concentrating first on economics, Siegfried assessed the clash between pro-imperial and pro-free-trade impulses. The war years, he noted, had encouraged a trend toward pro-imperial cooperation, while the postwar downturn had created pressures to defend homegrown industry. But free-trade views remained strong in certain sectors, and after the war British negotiators had sought to encourage access to foreign markets, notably European ones. British governments also pursued deflationary policies after 1918 in a quest to restore the pound to its former rate of exchange. Their efforts had restored some standing to the currency and reassured financial interests, but also had a negative effect upon various industries, possibly exacerbating the crisis. Indeed, significant quarters of opinion were asking whether Britain was trying to play an economic role that it could no longer really afford.[22] The volume of its exports had fallen, and unemployment remained high, leading Siegfried to wonder whether the British Isles were overpopulated.

British opinion was divided about how to tackle the economic and social problems. While Siegfried noted the complexity of the country's economy, in general those industries that catered to domestic and imperial markets called for re-orientating trade away from Europe, a shift supported by publications such as *The Round Table* and Lord Beaverbrook's *Daily Express*. By contrast, the free traders, consisting of export industries and the commercial and financial sectors, were more inclined to see the current crisis as a temporary one and urged the continuation of traditional policies in the long term. In examining the political consequences of this debate, Siegfried explained the workings and evolution of the British system in some detail. The years since 1914, he stressed, had witnessed major changes – the growing concentration of power in the hands of the prime minister, the rise of coalition politics and the transition from a two- to a three-party system, and votes for women. About the latter, he had surprisingly little to say; he was more interested in the fragmentation of Lloyd George's wartime coalition and how the vagaries of the British electoral system had led to rapid changes of political fortune. The Unionists were the premier party of social defence, their support stretching from much of the elite to elements of the working class. In 1922, they had decided to reassert their separate identity by sundering their coalition with Lloyd George's Liberals. The Liberal party itself had been in disarray since 1916, split between a faction under Lloyd George that aligned with the Unionists and a group under former prime minister H.H. Asquith that retained an independent stance. The Labour party was on the rise as it attracted workers away from the Liberals, but it faced significant internal divisions. Its factions ranged from moderate trade unionists to the reformist intellectuals of the Fabian Society to what Siegfried deemed "certain violent tendencies, especially in Scotland."[23]

Siegfried closed his political analysis by assessing the national elections of December 1923. These had been triggered by Baldwin, who wanted to shift toward protectionism, but because of a pledge by his predecessor Andrew Bonar Law not to change the customs tariff, decided that a new mandate was needed. This decision, Siegfried contended, "was to all intents and purposes a form of political suicide," as pro-free trade sentiment remained powerful.[24] Thanks to Britain's first-past-the-post system, the Unionists had been able to win a majority of the seats in the Commons in 1922 with only 38 per cent of the vote, but they now faced a growing Labour party and a Liberal party reunited on the principle of defending free trade. Though the shift in voting percentages was limited, the seat totals shifted markedly, with the Unionists losing eighty-six MPs. "The respective positions of the parties were thus completely upset, without any corresponding change in the country."[25] Since no party had a majority, the option was for either a coalition or a minority government. The Liberals would no longer align with the Conservatives and instead decided to allow

Labour, which had won second place in terms of the seat count, to form a minority government with their support. The book ended with a brief account of Ramsay MacDonald assuming office as Britain's first Labour prime minister in January 1924.

In a work that was intended to promote mutual understanding, the pessimism that Siegfried had privately expressed to Risler regarding Anglo-French relations was toned down in *L'Angleterre d'aujourd'hui*. Nevertheless, his analysis still emphasized contrasts between the two nations. Britain was an industrial, commercial nation that viewed other states – Germany included – primarily in terms of potential trade, while France remained substantially agricultural and focused on its domestic market. "Whereas for the French foreign markets are only a supplement, for the British they constitute the essential factor not only of their prosperity but of their very existence."[26] Politically, whereas in Britain there was a tendency to concentrate executive power, in Third Republic France the individual deputy retained greater clout. The relationship between religion and politics was also profoundly different. In France, the Catholic Church was deeply contested by the left, but in Britain religious influences from various denominations were evident throughout the party system. The Protestant ethos of the British people also powerfully shaped their dealings with France and other European nations. "In their attitude towards Europe the British people have been impregnated with the spirit of Protestantism, with its official idealism, its way of treating all questions from a moral point of view, its conviction that Protestant Britain is the salt of the earth, and finally its unconscious phariseeism which persuades the British that they are doing their duty when they are really serving their own interests."[27]

That said, Siegfried tried to conclude *L'Angleterre d'aujourd'hui* on a more positive note, with some general recommendations about Franco-British relations. France had to bear in mind the essential features of the "English" – for, despite paying some attention to the diversity of the British Isles in his electoral and economic analyses, Scotland, Wales, and Northern Ireland were on the margins of his discussion. Siegfried accepted the supposedly popular French perception that "they" were egoists who tended to react instinctively. But despite their insularity and conservatism, the English, he discerned, were direct and without malice. "The French, who are so-called light and frivolous, feel themselves old and wise alongside this ingenuous people who never lose the mentality of grown-up boys with their understanding and love of nature, children and animals. Added to

96 France in the World

these traits is a mixture of roughness and simplicity, of honesty and of ignorant disregard for others, caused by a capacity for forgetting which is almost akin to unfaithfulness. We must make up our minds to take the British as we find them, and after giving up all ideas of altering them, simply try to understand them." France still had plenty of friends across the Channel, though currently their point of view was in the minority. At present, other elements, including pacifists and business interests who wanted to renew trade with Germany, dominated the public sphere. Nevertheless, Siegfried closed by insisting that there were reserves of British goodwill toward France: "Let us remain convinced that every British government, no matter of what party, will always listen with a sympathetic ear to our proposals provided that they are practical and straightforward, and also that every British government will invariably respect as legitimate and just France's desire for peace and life."[28]

These conciliatory comments appear to have worked, for *L'Angleterre d'aujourd'hui* was generally well received on both sides of the Channel. The financial attaché at the French embassy in London praised it for clarifying "to our compatriots why they generally understand their insular neighbours so poorly." For the author Joseph Aynard, writing in the *Journal des débats* (at the request of one of the book's sponsors, the Association France–Grande Bretagne), the book was a useful tool for mutual understanding.[29] Influential British readers were also generally receptive. Lionel Curtis, the director of the Royal Institute of International Affairs, claimed that it was "the most penetrating analysis of the position of the whole country which I have ever read." The pro-imperial Conservative politician Leo Amery praised Siegfried's "account of the psychology of our attitude on currency questions," though he did suggest that the Frenchman overestimated the strength of "free trade prejudice" in Britain.[30] R.H. Tawney, writing for the American *New Republic*, suggested that Siegfried was too indulgent in his assessment of the British psyche but concluded that "he has written a brilliant book, which will be instructive to all, and not least to English, readers."[31]

The following year, Siegfried travelled to the United States to research what became *Les États-Unis d'aujourd'hui*, but he was far from being done with Britain. He spent the fall of 1927 as an associated member of All Souls College in Oxford, where he updated his views on Britain's political economy. In a letter to Jacques Chapsal, then a junior colleague at (and later the administrator of) Sciences Po, he related how he was enjoying Oxford but found it to be lacking in intellectual vitality, which he felt was indicative of a growing national malaise. "England's problem, and especially Oxford's problem, can be summarized in this verse from the New Testament: Can one put new wine into old vessels?" Though retaining his admiration for the British – "They are in all cases magnificent in their energy and, even in their pessimism, their confidence" – he emphasized that they still faced formidable challenges.[32]

Siegfried made clear how serious he believed these challenges were in articles for the London *Times* and the American journal *Foreign Affairs* that appeared in 1928.[33] He noted that some of the advantages that Britain enjoyed at the height of its power had begun to fade as early as the 1880s; in general terms, he suggested, the country was failing to transition from the nineteenth to the twentieth century. As new forms of energy like oil became available, Britain's early advantage in coal reserves grew less meaningful. The country's exports were falling, and a good deal of its industrial base was outdated. The fact that Britain had been spared massive wartime destruction, did not, ironically, give it the opportunity to rebuild. This made it more difficult to compete, as did high production costs. One of the main reasons for the latter was that British governments had struggled mightily to restore the value of the pound after the war to preserve London's status as a financial centre, making British goods quite expensive. But Siegfried also contended that British workers enjoyed an excessivly high standard of living, with their unions tenaciously resisting any changes that might threaten this. High consumption then drained national savings and reduced potential investment capital. "In this sense, England is less an exporter today than formerly. Perhaps she is relatively more a nation living on an income."[34]

Siegfried returned to London in 1930, as the effect of the Great Depression on Britain was becoming evident. He discerned a critical shift in the national mood: "[I]t is in their *morale* that they are suffering even more than in material ways. At least, such is my impression. And as a result, they are in danger of giving way to a pessimism unjustified by the circumstances."[35] He insisted that the British retained the capacity to adapt, but the tone of his 1931 book *La crise britannique au XXe siècle* – portions of which were excerpted in the *Times* – seemed at odds with this claim.[36] In that book, Siegfried examined the psychological and cultural aspects of Britain's dilemma, offering a comparison with France in the process. He continued to insist that British workers were overpaid and that they overconsumed. As for the hundreds of thousands who were out of work, the benefits they received were so high that they were disinclined to find a job. Citing his Sciences Po colleague Jacques Rueff, Siegfried contended that lower wages would make British goods more competitive and eventually alleviate unemployment. Ultimately, he claimed, the problem was rooted in the national psyche, as the organization of British households showed:

> The English workman spends freely, chiefly because he is not clever at organising his life. His wife is also somewhat lacking in *savoir-faire*. She does not take a keen delight in shopping economically, nor does she pride herself on her cooking, and the way in which she brings up her children is open to criticism. As a housekeeper she has no sense of, nor delight in, economy as we have in France, and therefore she requires higher wages to maintain a very ordinary standard. Do not imagine that the French workman, though he receives less than half as much money, lives only half as well. This English standard of living means, to a certain extent, the right to live shiftlessly without exertion, and at the same time to be well paid for doing so.[37]

Siegfried thus saw the root of Britain's problems in an overly indulged working class, a perspective that suggests a hardening of his views on class compared to his days with the Fondation universitaire de Belleville. More generally, he observed, in a mass democratic society where the working class was ascendant, it was hard to resist pressures to redistribute national wealth downwards. Britain's upper classes possessed a sense of social obligation and tended to give way, while the civil service was increasingly colonized by the middle and lower classes. In France, by contrast, the peasantry remained strong and so did the commitment to individual property, a state of affairs that Siegfried thoroughly approved of.[38]

What options, then, did Britain have? Siegfried favoured a laissez-faire approach but noted that the political obstacles were considerable, and that the current intellectual climate favoured state intervention. Moreover, protectionism was gaining appeal. Siegfried conceded that it might deserve a chance but felt that such a policy "overlooks the flaws in the international economic equilibrium, which a self-contained unit like the United States, or even a partially self-supporting country like France, may possibly ignore, but which England, dependent upon foreign trade, cannot neglect for long without mortal danger to her very existence." There was the option of greater trade with the empire, though the reality was that most British trade was with foreign states while elements of the empire – the Dominions in particular – had their own economic interests and policies. It might be possible for Britain to focus more upon its crown colonies, but ultimately the country was "condemned to a world-wide policy." In terms of international alliances, here too there was a choice to be made, either to focus upon the English-speaking nations, including the United States, or to opt for Europe. Siegfried hoped that Britain would make the latter choice but believed that the salience of "racial feeling" and other factors favoured the Anglo-Saxons. In the end, he predicted, England's leaders would try to avoid choosing at all: "Faithful to her tradition and her genius, she will hover between the two groups, without giving herself completely to one or to the other."[39]

Though the closing sentence of *La crise britannique* stressed the country's "unlimited powers of adaptation and life," the overall portrait was of a nation in decline. France had experienced a similar reversal of fortune in 1870, and while the country "has now recovered from that mood of discouragement ... her dreams of world power have gone for ever." Would Britain suffer the same fate? Siegfried indicated that he hoped not, but he detected an air of decadence among the elite and population at large. "Do not go to post-War England if you are in need of a tonic. It is not sufficiently invigorating. On the other hand, at the very moment when wealth, power, and culture are becoming dissociated, one finds there a refinement that is unequalled elsewhere." The British needed to modernize their industry, and their engineers and managers required a more rounded education in comparison to their continental counterparts. Siegfried acknowledged some positive trends, such as newer industries developing in the south of the country and talented engineering graduates from Cambridge. But the way ahead was not entirely clear; if the country exhausted "the capital accumulated by earlier generations ... England risks finding herself on the brink of a precipice."[40]

These observations aroused consternation among British officials. When Siegfried published some of his findings in the *Revue de Paris* in February 1931, the British ambassador in Paris feared that it would reinforce European fears about the United Kingdom's economic weakness and recommended that a response be published. The Foreign Office agreed, commenting that "The Lords Commissioners [of the

Treasury] will realise that an article of this sort from the pen of so eminent a writer as Monsieur Siegfried will be widely read and that the gloomy picture which he draws of the economic future of this country is in no way likely to increase the confidence of public opinion on the Continent in the future of British industry."[41] How exactly British officials proceeded is uncertain but it is noteworthy that Sir Walter Layton, editor of the *Economist*, published a study of Britain's economy in the following issue of the *Revue*, in which he stressed its capacity for growth and innovation.[42]

The British press greeted Siegfried's book with some respect but also a good deal of criticism. *The New Statesman and Nation* was cautiously positive, concluding that "though no Englishman will agree with it all, this is a tonic and stimulating, because able and honest, critique of our national situation."[43] Alfred Zimmern, an international relations specialist, expressed admiration for Siegfried's abilities but suggested that some of his attitudes were outmoded. "M. Siegfried, in spite of his pin-pricks, has written an extraordinarily charming book. But is it he, or his subject, which still lives in the atmosphere of the past?" The left-wing political theorist Harold Laski criticized Siegfried for his narrow class perspective, which ignored the perspective of the trade unions: "I doubt whether he talked to anyone who did not possess, if not the Curzon manner, at least the Oxford temper."[44]

Siegfried felt compelled to respond to a review of *La crise britannique* by the editor of *The Observer*, the prominent journalist J.L. Garvin. Garvin's lengthy review praised the book as "a model of compression and clear skill," but also took Siegfried to task for underestimating the British people's resilience. He suggested that Siegfried had neglected to acknowledge the great cost of the First World War to Britain as it stood shoulder to shoulder with its French ally. In his response to Garvin, Siegfried said that he had only sought to provide an objective account, and that he and many other Frenchmen wanted to see England strong again. Indeed, it was his respect for the country that had led him to be so frank. Garvin's reply was polite but still objected to Siegfried's language. "Upon the one hand I thought your conspectus of the facts invaluable. On the other hand, the tone seemed to me in a good many pages unnecessarily grating, and you know how utterly true is the German phrase 'the tone makes the music.' ... I heartily wish that you had seen more of the best we can show. A second edition of your book is certain to be called for and if you add something in the tone of a friend, believe me, it will be appreciated."[45]

As it turned out, a new edition of the book was published in 1933, to which Siegfried added a preface in which he conceded that Britain had weathered the global economic crisis after abandoning the gold standard, "having proved once more to the world her capacity for defence and resistance." He also stressed that many of Britain's problems were shared by other European nations. But he held to his overall conclusions, reiterating that formidable challenges lay ahead.[46]

Siegfried remained a respected commentator on Britain but his analysis of the state of its economy was not soon forgotten. A Foreign Office report on leading French personalities completed in January 1938 characterized him in the following terms: "His approach to his subject is dispassionate, intellectual, and economic, and he takes insufficient account of moral forces – hence Great Britain's rapid recovery after being forced off the gold standard took him by surprise. He has generously admitted his mistake in this connexion, but still sees a fundamental weakness in Great Britain's economic position."[47] Siegfried continued to underscore the multifaceted gap between the two countries. He conceded that Britain was linked to France by geography, history, and culture, and noted that the two countries had experienced parallel postwar crises. Though he affirmed his desire that Britain emerge strengthened from its ordeals as a major partner in European civilization, he discerned a fundamental contrast between a France whose economy was largely self-sufficient and characterized by frugality, and the consumption-oriented, collectivist society that Britain was becoming. Britain's transatlantic cousins had also embarked upon this undesirable path, with profound international implications.

## THE AMERICAN CHALLENGE

While Siegfried had already visited the United States several times and formed opinions on its qualities and deficiencies, his return to the country in the 1920s strengthened his conviction that it was headed on a very different path from France, and Europe more generally; its values and society now offered a starkly alternative way of life. He advanced his interpretation in depth in *Les États-Unis d'aujourd'hui*, which appeared in 1927 and became his most successful book, enjoying impressive sales and winning him accolades from both sides of the Atlantic. Given its significance, it is important to appreciate the degree to which its author depicted the United States as almost the antithesis of French values.

As with *L'Angleterre d'aujourd'hui*, the new book was the product of research supported by the Musée social. In keeping with the think tank's mandate, Siegfried assessed American production methods and their implications, but he also wished to conduct a broader social analysis.[48] To that end, he travelled widely throughout the US for six months. His correspondence shows that he met with individuals in a variety of fields ranging from industrialists, journalists, and social reformers to the actor Douglas Fairbanks.[49] His views were further informed by official statistics and the works of writers such as Walter Lippmann and Sinclair Lewis.[50] However, these sources were melded with personal impressions that insisted upon the derivative and sometimes alien character of American culture. Commenting on his visit to Los Angeles, Siegfried concluded that "[i]f it is a matter of remaking Chicago or St. Louis here, very good – they have succeeded! But they have not created a capital of beauty." Returning to El Paso, Texas, for the first time since the turn of the century, he found the city depressingly standardized. One of the few consolations was the Mexican community, which he deemed to be racially alien but, fortunately, leavened by European culture. "Without a doubt these Mexicans are above all Indians: their skin is brown, verging on red; their eyes have the languor of exotic races. But Spain has left all of them, including the poorest, a little of its incomparable elegance. Some of these men with large hats, underneath which a fine profile becomes apparent, a melancholic distinction that very few of the neighbouring [American] businessmen could claim. And some of these women have a purity of features that recall madonnas, an elegant walk, even a nobility, which sets back, dare it be said, the triumphant vulgarity of American typists."[51] For Siegfried, even a slight trace of Old World culture gave Mexicans a refinement that their white American counterparts lacked.

In correspondence with Jacques Chapsal, Siegfried elaborated upon his reactions, at first in the context of a discussion of American universities. He was impressed by some programs, notably Harvard's business school, commenting that its students "are not taught the techniques of business, but the general culture necessary for business ... we certainly have a lot to learn from what they are doing." But he also expressed major reservations. American universities, he opined, had too many mediocre students, which degraded the quality of education – though he conceded that this was also a problem in France. He also despaired at the priorities of US institutions: "They have formed, to excess, football, baseball, and hockey teams.

They have been won over by the megalomania of numbers. The universities which originally resembled ours, such as Johns Hopkins in Baltimore, have also been overcome by a kind of building craze [*la maladie de la pierre*]. Their presidents have essentially become architects." Above all, he was struck by what he characterized as a combination of material prosperity, racial decline, and cultural impoverishment in the United States:

> In material terms we have far to go, in truth we are terribly
> behind. But in terms of individual value and general culture,
> the difference in value with Europe is considerable. By
> establishing foreign races in the American melting pot and
> standardizing individuals in order to enhance their material
> productivity, some kind of flame has been extinguished. When
> you see a brilliant individual, a quick eye, an intelligence with
> rapid reactions, it is nearly always a foreigner (French, Italian,
> Russian). When you make [a person] American-style he is
> superior in efficiency, but the flame is not there. If the goal
> of civilization is to produce things, they have succeeded.
> If it is to produce men, they have failed.[52]

These criticisms were only somewhat muted in *Les États-Unis d'aujourd'hui*. Siegfried began the book with an exploration of "the ethnic situation," giving considerable attention to mass immigration and the xenophobic reaction it had triggered, which found expression in forms ranging from Prohibition to the revival of the Ku Klux Klan. He was uneasy about elements of this backlash, noting how the encouragement of biological racism by writers such as Madison Grant and Lothrop Stoddard was leading to intolerable state intervention in the form of sterilization: "[E]ugenics may eventually relegate the 'sacred rights of man' to the limbo of half-forgotten achievements."[53] But while Siegfried distanced himself from the "Anglo-Saxon" emphasis on negative eugenics, many of his anxieties echoed those of racists in the US.[54] Though he conceded that they made contributions to their new country, he believed that the newcomers from Southern and Eastern Europe were inferior. They resisted assimilation; at best, their "Americanism" would be "morally shrunk in comparison to the vigor of the pioneers." He saw Jews as especially problematic in this regard, giving a nod to the "great value of Jewish collaboration" but going on to condemn the Jewish presence as excessive, observing that in New York "one is crammed into the subway along with countless stenographers with swarthy complexions, hook noses, and a flavor of the ghetto."[55]

Proceeding to a discussion of "the colour problem," Siegfried expressed some unease about racism in the United States but endorsed the view that African Americans were both inferior and threatening. Having "inherited from the English a horror of intermarriage between white and coloured people that is little less than fanatic," white Americans now faced "an insoluble problem." In the southern states, the Jim Crow laws had established a comprehensive system of discrimination, buttressed by popular sentiment: "[T]he lower we descend in the social scale, the more violent is the hatred of the negro." At the heart of the system was sexual fear – which Siegfried legitimated, noting "those instincts of barbarity and bestiality that the blacks have inherited, and which may suddenly break forth in an attempt at rape." He continued stereotyping in his depiction of African American women, who possessed an "indescribable attraction," even though white men typically denied it: "It is a mystery which alarms and humiliates thoughtful Americans on account of the biological and moral perils to which it leads."[56] A growing number of African Americans were migrating to the North, again prompting a racist response despite notional civic and legal equality. In the South, Siegfried explained, African Americans remained deferential, but in the North there was potentially troubling militancy: "W.E. Burghardt Du Bois, that penetrating coloured writer who maintains that the blacks can equal the whites in everything, demands uncompromised social equality ... this American *élite* is strengthening the unity of the black race all over the world." This worried Siegfried, who concluded that "the colour problem is an abyss into which we can look only with terror"; in his view, "[t]he only answer is that the whites must learn to live side by side with a race that they cannot possibly assimilate. However, they can comfort themselves with the knowledge that the percentage of blacks is diminishing."[57] A gradual erasure of the African American presence seemed the best way forward, in Siegfried's view.

Central though race was to his analysis, Siegfried also stressed the importance of religion to grasping the American national character. While noting distinctions between the various Christian denominations as well as the split between modernists and fundamentalists, he discerned a fundamental spiritual unity in what he labelled an essentially Calvinist nation. The typical American, he argued, displayed "incontestable" good faith but also an "insufferable" sense of "self-satisfaction as a member of God's elect," an attitude that bolstered many Americans' conviction of Anglo-Saxon superiority. The Puritan ethos also encouraged an intolerance of dissent, as evidenced by the trial of John Scopes for teaching evolution. Siegfried saw little affinity between such an outlook and his own French Protestantism, a minority tradition that cherished individual freedom. Instead, he felt that the American variant encouraged conformist materialism, especially in the case of the modernists, who emphasized "the confusion of spirituality and worldliness."[58]

Indeed, worldliness was the order of the day in the US. Astounded at the growth of the nation's economy, Siegfried confessed his enthusiasm for American dynamism. The freewheeling era of the trusts, he argued, had given way to an era of greater state involvement and regulation, aimed at maximizing efficiency and output. While fewer skills were now required for the production process itself, executives and managers were becoming better educated and more broadly cultured. Businessmen such as Henry Ford were instrumental in these changes, but Siegfried also praised the American government for displaying "rare intelligence and moral authority" in encouraging the reform of industrial methods. While stressing that America had advantages over Europe in the form of a huge standardized internal market, he also gave the country its due. "Never before in history have social forces converged on so vast and intensive a scale, but even the extent of the created wealth is less remarkable than the dynamic forces of the human impulse that has brought this wealth into being."[59] Impressed as he was, however, Siegfried doubted that such expansion could last. He was also dismayed at the regimentation that resulted from the unceasing emphasis upon production: "In its pursuit of wealth and power, America has abandoned the ideal of liberty to follow that of prosperity."[60]

In his analysis of American politics, Siegfried discussed the Republicans and the Democrats in some detail but felt that to truly understand what was going on in the United States one had to turn to civic associations, lobby groups, and the press. He was impressed with their vibrancy yet feared their use as instruments of manipulation. The apparatus for shaping public opinion meant that "given the malleability of the people, there appears to be no limit beyond which they cannot be led." His conclusions about politics thus reinforced those concerning economics; materialism was creating a nation of conformists. Nor did he take comfort in the sometimes hesitant yet inexorable expansion of America's international role. Not only was it distancing itself from Europe diplomatically, as civilizations the two were steadily diverging. "[In] her enthusiasm to perfect her material success," he mused, "has not America risked quenching the flames of individual liberty which Europe has always regarded as one of the chief treasures of civilization?"[61]

*Les États-Unis d'aujourd'hui* was one of a cluster of French books on America that appeared during the late 1920s; both André Tardieu and Lucien Romier published studies of America the same year that Siegfried did. All three found a receptive audience in France but it was Siegfried's book that received the most accolades. Remaining in print until 1947, it won the Prix Montyon of the Académie française and established Siegfried as a pre-eminent interpreter of the United States.[62] French reviews were generally quite positive, though they reflected clashing visions of national identity. Thus, the monarchist historian Jacques Bainville felt that Siegfried had captured how nationalist reactions to foreign threats were inevitable – and well-founded: "Nationalism is an attitude of defense in a country where the essential national element believes itself to be threatened. That is precisely the case in the United States." Alfred Berl, reviewing for *Paix et droit*, the journal of the Alliance Israélite Universelle, took a very different view. Though referring to Siegfried as a "remarkable talent," he felt that the book was too pessimistic about the prospects for Jewish integration into societies such as the United States, observing that "moral union can be established without complete fusion."[63]

Across the Atlantic, Siegfried's book provoked considerable self-examination. The English translation, *America Comes of Age*, sold over 20,000 copies within its first year of publication and was the subject of lectures, reading groups, and the occasional sermon.[64] At a time when Americans themselves were debating the social consequences of rapid growth, and their government had sharply curtailed immigration amid a climate of xenophobia, Siegfried's analysis was often judged to be unusually perceptive.[65] The Chicago *News* found him occasionally prone to "exaggeration and distortion," but concluded that his arguments were "worthy of being carefully weighed."[66] The *Los Angeles Record* suggested that while "many people" found Siegfried's book objectionable, this was only because "it is too penetrating, tells too much of the truth and exposes our faults with painful candor."[67]

But some American commentators disputed Siegfried's core conclusions. The historian Charles Beard, writing in *The New Republic*, dismissed the contention that the United States was particularly obsessed with wealth, asserting that "no larger proportion of the total human energy in this country is devoted to acquiring material goods than in any European country."[68] The reviewer for *Outlook* chided Siegfried for his elevation of an abstract conception of liberty over the benefits of greater comfort. "I have heard grandmother's tales of pioneer days, and I am willing to trade a little freedom of action for central heating, electric lights, and a shower-bath."[69]

While Siegfried's emphasis on American materialism provoked some dissent, widespread American hostility toward Slavic, Latin, and Jewish immigrants perhaps explains why his racist analysis apparently elicited few objections.[70] The San Francisco author Rebecca Godchaux disputed Siegfried's characterization of Jews, but her comments remained private.[71] Ernest Boyd, writing in Boston's *Independent*, suggested that the book underestimated the cohesion of American society, but still felt that it "may well take its place beside Alexis de Tocqueville's *Democracy in America*."[72] H.L. Mencken, writing in *The Nation*, believed that Siegfried's national identity made him more inclined to sympathize with newcomers: "Dr. Siegfried, as a Frenchman, is unable to grasp the 'equity' of having recent immigrants endure the continuing domination of Protestant Nordics."[73] The associate editor of *The American Hebrew* apparently did not take exception to the book's anti-Semitic passages; indeed, he initially thought that Siegfried might be Jewish. He invited him to contribute to his publication, which Siegfried eventually did, though he wrote about French rather than American Jews.[74]

For the remainder of the interwar era, Siegfried was widely regarded on both sides of the Atlantic as a perceptive if sometimes sharply critical observer who could promote mutual understanding. He published on Franco- and European-American relations in periodicals such as *The Harvard Business Review*, *The Atlantic Monthly*, *Foreign Affairs*, and *The Yale Review*.[75] In these writings, he reiterated his belief in the growing cultural distance between America and France, and Europe as a whole. This was the result, he explained, of various changes in American society. While referring to the effect of "Slavo-Latin" immigration as one factor, in *The Atlantic Monthly* he revisited an earlier observation concerning the shift of the country's centre of gravity toward the West and the rise of new productive techniques. "Lincoln, with his Bible and his classical tradition, was easier for Europe to understand than Ford, with his total absence of tradition and his proud creation of new methods and new standards, especially conceived for a world entirely different from our own."[76]

Europeans, Siegfried contended, could not afford to ignore America's growing power, but nor should they unthinkingly adopt the American model of production. Instead, the continent should follow the path that Siegfried had previously recommended for France, which was to respect artisanal traditions and individuality. "Experience has taught us that American industry succeeds when the machine can be substituted for the man, and automatism for individuality ... On the contrary, Europe, and especially France, is likely to win when the reverse is true."[77] Such comments did not preclude Siegfried from receiving further recognition in the United States. His article for the *Yale Review* entitled "Will Europe Be Americanized?" won the journal's best article prize for 1930, with the citation also describing *Les États-Unis d'aujourd'hui* as "one of the most important books of the post-war period."[78]

By this time, the American economy had to contend with the onset of the Great Depression. While Siegfried soon acknowledged the profundity of the latter's effect, his subsequent commentary on US affairs during the 1930s stressed continuities as well. He was visiting the country at the time of the stock market crash of 1929, which he attributed to over-consumption and imprudent speculation. Having long stressed the centrality of economic prosperity to American identity, Siegfried argued that a downturn of this scale posed a fundamental challenge to the national psyche: "The United States' weakness is that it was conceived and constructed only for expansion ... When the tide ceases to rise, when there is a retreat or even simply a halt, all America is unhinged."[79] When he returned to the United States in 1935, President Franklin Roosevelt's efforts to address mass unemployment and poverty through the New Deal were well underway. As an economic liberal, Siegfried predictably disliked Roosevelt's interventionist approach. Though he conceded that economic activity had revived to some degree, he was troubled by the fact that it depended upon "artificial," government-funded consumption. "The crisis," he lamented, "has reached a stage where the cure is evidently worse than the sickness."[80]

In a 1937 pamphlet, Siegfried reflected on the evolution of the United States in a more integrated fashion. The Depression and New Deal were having profound effects upon the nation's political culture, he concluded. America had "aged" to the point where, as in Europe, politics were increasingly focused on encouraging redistribution rather than production. But he generally avoided stressing European-American commonalities; in fact, he favourably contrasted the American response to growing hardship with that of French citizens. "[Americans] admit that they are ruined and see that, from the moment when they have to live more simply, it is best to resign oneself to it with good humor ... We cannot liken ourselves to them in this respect." He also believed that traditional American optimism would soon revive, even if the circumstances did not warrant it: "Americans will believe themselves to be economically youthful longer than they will actually remain so."[81]

For all that, lasting changes were underway. In a lengthy review of the influential study *Middletown in Transition* (1937) by Robert S. Lynd and Helen Lynd, which assessed the evolving social structures and attitudes of Muncie, Indiana, Siegfried reiterated that recent trends were leading the people of the American heartland to embrace a hitherto-rejected dependence on the state, abandoning the "traditional philosophy of the pioneers, based upon individual initiative and responsibility."[82] He also continued to stress the alien character of the US. Its massive size – akin to that of Africa or Asia – meant that it lacked Europe's "human" dimensions and was still at a different stage of historical evolution. He also held to his belief in the deleterious effect of mass immigration; notwithstanding some standardization in dress and deportment, "mediocre" arrivals from Southern and Eastern Europe had unbalanced the blending of British, Irish, Germanic, and Jewish mentalities that had been underway by the late nineteenth century. "In France I can see perhaps only Marseille, with its composite population of Italians, Africans, Armenians, Spaniards, etc, which can provide a scene able to evoke the extraordinary crowds of San Francisco, Chicago, and New-York."[83] The result, he stressed in a lecture to Sciences Po students in the spring of 1938, was that "European problems do not resemble American ones *at all*."[84]

### THE FUTURE OF FRENCH CIVILIZATION

As the foregoing pages have argued, in his analyses of Britain and the United States Siegfried often developed comparisons with France and, more generally, Europe that highlighted contrasts in economic and social structures, and, above all, in mentalities. He advanced similar ideas in various studies of French politics during this period, and they are evident in a new book on Canada that appeared in 1937. Compared with the pre-1914 period, when his writings on France centred on the conflict between liberal progress and conservative reaction – with socialism an increasingly worrisome presence – Siegfried now further accentuated the conservatism and individualism of French society, contrasting it with Anglo-Saxon perspectives and policies. His study of Canada, though intended and presented as a general survey, also highlighted what he characterized as ongoing tensions between British, American, and French values. With the approach of the Second World War, he shifted ground somewhat, trying to make the case for the essential unity of interests between the democratic powers as they confronted the growing threat of Nazi Germany. Yet even then he continued to highlight the significant differences between France and the "Anglo-Saxons."

Some of Siegfried's earliest and most wide-ranging reflections on these matters appeared in a 1926 paper delivered to the Royal Institute of International Affairs. Here he sought to dispel any illusions about an overly close relationship between France and the United States, instead pointing to the deep affinities between America and Britain. He asserted a contrast between contemporary French and American values to the point where they were practically opposites: "While the French still think politically in terms of 'liberté, égalité, fraternité, the Americans practically live and act on the basis of a doctrine of discipline, authority, and race-hierarchy. Unconsciously, but obviously, they despise the French for their democratic individualism and for their failure in organising production and society on a collective basis." In contrast, he claimed, American hostility toward Britain was largely rooted in the past and was now giving way to feelings of solidarity, based in part upon the desire to form "a common Protestant and Anglo-Saxon front against the 'foreigners.'" Siegfried concluded that "[t]he character of Anglo-American relations thus appears clearly defined; you may at times be enemies, but you are at any rate brother-enemies ... It is a family affair." For the British, the question was whether to align themselves with the United States or to seek deeper cooperation with Europe. If Britain rejected the latter option, then France would have to explore options with Germany. Such a policy might displease London, but Britain had left its neighbour with few options. Siegfried suggested that British policy on this score was hypocritical: "We French have well understood that to please you we must not quarrel too much with the Germans, but that, at the same time, we should not be too friendly with them."[85]

France itself undeniably faced many challenges in the postwar world; Siegfried reiterated that it was an "old" country whose values and strengths were frequently at odds with the emergent order of mass production and consumption. With its utilitarian techniques and huge domestic market, the United States was perfectly suited for such a system but, given its prevailing tradition of high quality and artisanal goods, France was not. In the *Harvard Business Review*, Siegfried mused whether "[i]n order to comply with circumstances and to survive as a great industrial power, must [France] give up the very essence of her ancient economic activity, or does there remain, even now, some room for the traditional ways and means of the old French civilization?" French individualism, the product of a heavily rural base and a high degree of economic self-sufficiency, could discourage technical innovation and social cooperation but there were also benefits. Individualism nurtured pride in one's work, and Siegfried concluded that French industry would fare best by concentrating on the production of high-quality goods for international markets. To be sure, there were also more modern elements in the French economy, such as the automobile industry, that were drawn to American-style methods, but even in this case going too far in the direction of emulation would likely be wrong-headed. "For many years, and especially in the beginning of motor cars, France has enjoyed an international reputation for the sale of fine cars. If it would now try to do what Ford has done for many years, it would probably fail, owing to the absence of mass production. It can win only if it gives as much attention to invention and care as to cheapness in production." Put otherwise, the possibilities for adaptation were limited, if the French wanted to preserve the qualities that made them distinct.[86]

Siegfried's interpretation of contemporary French politics also stressed the powerful hold of established traditions. Developing his ideas at the Royal Institute of International Affairs and a lecture series delivered at the Williamstown Institute of Politics in Massachussetts, in 1930 he published the *Tableau des partis en France*, which appeared that same year in English under the title *France: A Study in Nationality*.[87] After sketching an image of a France whose "personality ... was a finished product by the end of the eighteenth century," Siegfried stressed the extent to which the legacy of the Revolution still dominated its politics. "At the very moment when the France of 1789 is already superseded by new social structures, she is still obliged to devote a great deal of her energy to struggle against the tradition of the *ancien régime*." This, he claimed, distorted the country's political culture. On the left, "the French democrat feels obliged to support any policy which may be supposed to lead to progress. He must be *advanced*."[88] On the right, conservatives shrank from identifying themselves clearly as such, while in the centre the Radical Party was less militant than its name suggested. The gap between this "logomacy" and the quotidian realities of French politics was often considerable, for in their daily lives, Siegfried asserted, the French people tended to be conservative, prizing frugality and routine. Citing with approval the writings of Paul Morand, he posited that "in a way, France resembles China, where life does not follow any political plan but is attracted to a center of gravity lying far deeper and thus more stable."[89]

Siegfried did not deny that industrialization was affecting the structure of French society and politics, but still stressed the importance of long-term continuities in a fractious political system. Economic change had given rise to the Socialist and, more recently, Communist parties, but their political effect was ambiguous. The Socialists, he suggested, clung to Marxism but were now essentially advanced Republicans, with little to distinguish between their right fringe and the Radical Socialists. As for the Communists, many of their members were basically "Red" Republicans, but the party itself followed Moscow's dictates, making it hard to situate properly on the political spectrum. Another result of industrialization was to encourage the bourgeoisie toward conservatism, in response to working-class militancy. But even here, the weight of old conflicts, notably the struggle against the Church, had a complicating effect. It was primarily the job of the political centre to preserve order while continuing to respect the republican tradition, but it was fragmented, notably along religious lines, and lacked disciplined parties. The right was also divided, though its supporters' identification with Catholicism provided a potential unifying thread. They had some real power but were also controversial because of the influence of "1789" on French political culture. Siegfried concluded that "[t]he right never seems to realize that its influence is compromising, and that it would do much better to give its help in silence."[90]

Though depicting French democracy as rather messy in comparison with its Anglo-Saxon counterparts, Siegfried still admired its ideals. Discussing the pattern of politics since the First World War, he traced the alternation between rightist and leftist coalitions in power as they formed in reaction to one another. The left, he felt, was good at rallying in times of a perceived threat to the Republic but less steady when it came to everyday government. The right was more reliable on that score, but any administration that went too far in a conservative direction risked alienating the public and incurring a left-wing revival. For Siegfried, the outstanding politician of the era was Raymond Poincaré, who had managed to restore the country's finances after the "muddle" of the left-leaning Cartel des gauches. But even Poincaré's skills had their limits, meaning that a leftist coalition would likely soon revive. Such was the essence of French politics: "Our democracy is Latin in origins, and therefore unlike the Anglo-Saxon democracies where practical social accomplishments are the first consideration." This was not necessarily a failing, in Siegfried's eyes; he made clear his abiding commitment to the principles of individualism that the French democratic system was intended to preserve. Currently, he suggested, the world favoured the Anglo-Saxon focus on efficiency, but if a shift back toward a more idealist brand of politics took place, he predicted that French individualism would attract renewed interest.[91]

A letter from Siegfried to Marshal Hubert Lyautey, France's famed exponent and practitioner of colonial expansion, sheds further light on Siegfried's views on these matters, specifically in developing a contrast between France and Britain. Thanking Lyautey for attending a lecture he gave on "spiritual forces in England," Siegfried concurred with the marshal's observation about the need to understand the hierarchial and aristocratic character of British society, going so far as to conclude that "*an egalitarian democracy in England is inconceivable.*" For France, however, the situation was totally different: "To me France seems to be above all a democracy of individuals." In asserting this view, Siegfried dissented from Lyautey, a conservative critic of the Third Republic who stressed the critical role of elites in the functioning of French society. However, Siegfried may have mollified his interlocutor by suggesting that the French were more suited to individualist democracy because "to me the average level of the population appears superior to that in England; people are more educated, more quickwitted, more equipped with possibilties." This was the case both at home but also abroad, which meant that overseas "he [the Frenchman] becomes a ruling elite."[92] Expressing himself with greater candour than in most of his publications, Siegfried justified French suitability for democratic individualism partly on the basis of having a superior population, which, he had implied to Lyautey, was destined to lead.

Siegfried's juxtaposition of French individualism and Anglo-Saxon efficiency won praise, though some of the findings posited in *Tableau des partis en France* were questioned. His Sciences Po colleague Joseph Barthélemy admired "the wisdom and precision of your observations," and the social Catholic activist Robert Garric admired Siegfried's "great lucidity." The Socialist politician Albert Thomas, then head of the International Labour Office in Geneva, was more tentative. He wondered if French workers really shared in the petit-bourgeois mentality that Siegfried discerned at the core of the national psyche, though he agreed fully that "it is our old political mystique which, alone, could provide resistance to productivism, Americanism, whatever name one gives it."[93] Other criticisms emanated from the United States. Louis Gottschalk of the University of Chicago commented that the book downplayed the level of French industrialization. Columbia University scholar Carlton Hayes disputed the significance of supposed French individualism: "[O]f course the French are individualists – about some things – as are the other Latin peoples and most nations of the continent, but they display relatively great conformity in their school system, in their obedience to army demands, and in their patriotism."[94]

Siegfried also highlighted the contrasts between Anglo-Saxon and French values in works with an ostensibly more international focus, notably his second book on Canada, which was based in part on observations during his visit to North America in 1935.[95] The title of the work, *Le Canada: Puissance internationale*, reflected an intention to shift the focus away from English-French relations at the heart of Siegfried's 1906 study to the country's growing international presence. To an extent, Siegfried moved in this direction. He revisited the role of geography in shaping Canadian identity, suggesting that the country's "narrow" zone of settlement led it "to seek a centre of gravity outside her own borders." He also concluded that because of its British heritage and American geography, Canada would become an important mediator.[96] The evolution of the Canadian economy, the significance of regional differences, and the country's likely importance to the aviation sector all received attention, though the total exclusion of Indigenous peoples and the Martimes as a region persisted.

The precarity of Canadian national identity and uncertain future of its French component were very much at the core of the book, however. Though noting variations in attitudes, Siegfried reaffirmed that, in general, English Canadians still "resent the French Canadians with a hostility which is instinctive and congenital. Nothing can be done about it."[97] English Canadians, he predicted, would continue to pursue imperial ties and loyalty to the Crown. As for French Canadians, while Siegfried did not deny the fact of ongoing industrialization in Quebec, he asserted that French Canadians remained for the most part rural, Catholic, and traditional. They thus provided a contrast with – arguably, a bulwark against – an influx of American methods and values that was ever more prevalent. Siegfried underscored this point by contrasting the methods of French-Canadian farmers with the American-style approach increasingly adopted in Western Canada. "The French-Canadian peasant has conserved the qualities of our French peasantry: he works hard and is thrifty, above all preoccupied with living on the land and raising his family there, without giving himself over to the desire for speculation ... Americans, perhaps, ask too much of the land when they call upon it to enrich them, and to do so quickly."[98]

But Siegfried feared that the traditional virtues of the French-Canadian peasantry would not ensure its cultural survival; nor could Canada's future be taken for granted in the face of Americanization. There was still considerable loyalty to British institutions, yet American influence grew stronger every day. Immigration from Britain continued to reinforce some ties with the "mother country," but the increasing proportion of arrivals from continental Europe would likely assimilate as they had in the United States. "Former" Germans, Slavs, and others would become "North American, but not inevitably British or Anglo-Saxon." Even French Canadians might find American influences sapping "those reserves of spiritual nourishment which formerly provided their defence."[99] Siegfried admitted that Canada had managed, "contrary to the dictates of geography itself," to assert its independence, but economically and socially Canadians were "riveted" upon the United States.[100] The country was thus, in his eyes, a site for the contestation of enduring French and Anglo-Saxon, particularly American, values.

In Canada itself, these arguments provoked some disquiet; though the book received considerable praise, various aspects of Siegfried's analysis, ranging from economic trends to his commentary on the role of the Catholic Church, aroused criticism.[101] In particular, his views on Canadian identity sparked contrasting responses. Canada's Governor General, the Scottish-born writer John Buchan (Lord Tweedsmuir), endorsed Siegfried's characterization of French Canadians, concurring that they were "a force of social persistence and stability, and also a barrier of good breeding and tradition against modern vulgarization." The Archbishop of Quebec also praised his "concern to serve French civilization."[102] But others felt that Siegfried overstated American influence and underestimated the resilience of

Canadian identity. Henri de Lageneste, France's chargé d'affaires in Ottawa, reported that French Canadians there felt that he had "insisted too strongly upon Americanization." W.M. Conacher, reviewing the book for *Queen's Quarterly*, found that that Siegfried exaggerated the strength of French-Canadian traditionalism. "He aims at canalizing the whole race, keeping it apart in a vine and fig-tree existence – the simple child of nature."[103] Such commentaries suggested that Siegfried had sacrificed nuance in his portrait of Canada to his larger vision of French traditionalism juxtaposed with an Anglo-Saxon, and above all American, fixation upon modernization.

As war loomed at the end of the 1930s, Siegfried felt compelled to make a case for democratic solidarity between France and the English-speaking powers, but even when he tried to do so he posited contrasts. In a 1939 article for *Foreign Affairs*, he praised Britain and its empire as a bastion of liberalism but also concluded that as a model it had an inherently limited appeal. "One might wonder, therefore, whether the English people, which has supplied the most perfect example of liberty, of parliamentary government, or rule by public opinion, has not succeeded in doing so by virtue of its very success in preserving a tradition of social superiorities and inferiorities – in a word, of aristocracy." This was a contradiction that the French democratic tradition, and indeed French logic, could not bear. "This, probably, is why the British constitution, though it figures as a beacon in French schools of law and political science, fails to cast its beams upon French political practice."[104]

Siegfried's attitudes toward the United States were even more conflicted. During the Czechoslovakian Crisis of 1938, for example, he privately expressed resentment over American pressure on France and Britain to stand up to Germany, observing that "it is fine for the Americans, who were nearly not in the [First World War], to hint that we will have to make war ... I find this attitude simply shocking."[105] His public comments were more restrained, but even when speaking in favour of Franco-American cooperation he drew attention to the barriers that persisted. In a 1939 talk delivered at the French Information Center in New York, he cautioned that the mentalities of the two democracies were very different and that relations had to be cultivated with care. In his contribution to *Foreign Affairs* published that same year, he praised American values for having a broader appeal than those of the British but added that those of the French Revolution went even further, transcending the bounds of race – though he felt that doing so was potentially unwise. "America's message of freedom, of emancipation, is addressed to all men who are white; but only to whites. The yellow races, the black races, are not invited to take advantage of it. I do not say that this is not a more reasonable message than the French one, from the standpoint of sound social and political organization. But it cannot have the universal appeal that the French Revolution has had."[106] He thus asserted the uniquely progressive nature of the French democratic tradition, only to suggest that in advancing notions of racial equality it overlooked the unfitness of nonwhites for democracy; in this sense, the practices of a partially segregated United States made more sense to him.

— * —

Siegfried presented himself as a sympathetic but objective observer of the Anglo-Saxon nations; his publications asserted that France should cultivate good relations with them, though it must do so with a realistic appreciation of sharply contrasting national traditions. But in much of his interwar writing, there is a deep pessimism regarding affinities between France, Britain, and America. He hoped that Britain would align with France in reshaping an increasingly troubled Europe but underscored how different social structures were across the Channel, and expressed doubts whether Britain could really depart from a commitment to Anglo-Saxon solidarity. The United States posed an even greater challenge; it shared a revolutionary tradition with France, but geography, race, religion, and economics made for nigh-unbridgable differences in outlook. America had to be courted as a potential ally, but its influence – so evident in Canada, where it confronted a long-standing but potentially fragile French presence – was problematic. Siegfried's interepretations were nuanced by in-depth analysis and favourable commentary on aspects of British politics and American economics, winning him respect in the English-speaking nations as well as at home. But the portrait of France that emerges from the writings discussed in this chapter is one of a nation and its principles that, though inherently impressive, were nevertheless on the defensive. Siegfried was critical of aspects of the Third Republic's political culture, though he regarded his nation's more balanced economy and undying commitment to the principles of individual liberty as qualities to be treasured. Over the course of the 1930s, he would range well beyond the English-speaking nations, while also seeking to deepen his understanding of French political dynamics. But he still located his country at the heart of an emerging clash of civilizations and races.

# 4

# Horizons Old and New

On 28 April 1933, Siegfried, having just been appointed to the Chair of Economic and Political Geography at the Collège de France, gave his inaugural lecture. After acknowledging the great honour he had received, he outlined his conception of geography as a discipline, quoting Vidal de la Blache: "[T]he human element fundamentally forms part of all geography."[1] He then described his research and teaching plans, which would focus on two themes. One would be economic geography; his goal was to examine Europe's place in a rapidly changing world. The continent's economy and mentality, he explained, were still showing the effects of the Great War, even as the globe faced an unprecedented qualitative change in everyday life spearheaded by the United States. Siegfried's courses in economic geography would examine Europe's status in relation to other continents, with reference to a variety of case studies.

The other main theme would be the political geography of France in the modern era. The country's personality, he asserted, had been well-formed since the eighteenth century and had proven highly durable, but could not avoid the revolutionary social changes now underway. Siegfried hoped to shed light on the continuities and changes in French politics by returning to the study of electoral geography. There was no way that he could survey the entire country, as had been his goal before 1914, but he hoped that by carrying out a detailed analysis of the Midi – a region critical to the country's political development, but one that was not well understood – he would elucidate the laws driving French politics, moving beyond the expressions of mystification often made by foreigners and French citizens alike.

Siegfried conceded that the two themes might seem disparate but asserted that there were points of connection. Both grew out of his formative experiences, notably his world tour and his repeated electoral campaigns. Furthermore, he would tackle both projects in the spirit of taking a journey. This entailed more than physical displacement; it required embracing a state of mind: "[A] kind of release of the intelligence takes place; it functions as if freed from the constraints of the goal and realization." This approach, he surmised, reflected the high ideals of disinterested research that the Collège stood for.[2]

In the years that followed, Siegfried adhered to much of the path traced out in this lecture. It was an individual path – while he added involvement with the Collège de France to his ongoing activities with Sciences Po and the Musée social and displayed some interest in the complex intellectual ferment of the era, he tended to avoid overly deep attachments to other iniatives. As we have seen, he continued to visit the English-speaking nations, but in the 1930s he also researched the Midi while travelling through Europe and Latin America and spending time in Palestine and Egypt. His work on the Midi led him to highlight the contribution of Protestantism to the French republican tradition, as well as the centrality of the Mediterranean to French identity. As for his travels beyond the Hexagon, Siegfried's European ventures suggested a more differentiated sense of the continent, though such nuances tended to fade when he returned to discussing Europe as a whole. Latin America, to his mind, demonstrated how the intertwining of American influence and Indigenous nationalism threatened the imprint of Latin civilization and French culture. These findings supported his broader claims that the key challenges to European values, as notably embodied by his own country, and European international leadership, emanated from Americanization and anti-imperial nationalists who were, paradoxically, influenced by Western values.

### VARIETIES OF ENGAGEMENT

Siegfried's growing prominence was reflected in his election in January 1932 to the Académie des sciences morales et politiques, one of the five *académies* of the Institut de France; he was chosen as the successor to the diplomat and journalist Auguste Gauvain. The election dossier suggests that the *Tableau politique*, which had won the Milne-Edwards Prize from the Société géographique, had helped to establish his reputation despite its rather tepid sales. So too had his earlier studies of New Zealand and Canada and his recent work on Britain, but it was his 1927 book on the United States that was regarded as having the greatest effect, helping him to be elected over the historian and geographer Albert Petit.[3] Thereafter, Siegfried participated regularly in the activities of the Académie, presenting papers on the economic situation in the United States and the geography of French politics.[4]

Securing election to the Collège de France proved to be more controversial. Elected by their peers, chairs at the Collège were expected to be leading intellectuals who would continue researching on the frontiers of knowledge while delivering free public lectures. As Marguerite Bistis puts it, faculty at the Collège were typically "arbiters of the *goût public* shaping the intellectual outlook and sensibility of their times."[5] A chair was thus a real prize; complicating Siegfried's quest for one was a determined rival, the historian Bernard Faÿ. A right-wing Catholic, the relatively youthful Faÿ – born in 1893 – had quickly earned a reputation as an expert in American history and literature on both sides of the Atlantic, having completed an MA at Columbia, and had won the Jusserand Medal from the American Historical Association and runner-up status for the Pulitzer Prize in History (foreigners were not eligible for the prize itself).[6]

Siegfried first proposed his candidature for a Chair in American Civilization at the Collège in November 1931. He had, however, missed the formal deadline, because he had been travelling in Latin America. Though he initially requested special consideration for these circumstances, he subsequently withdrew his application to avoid controversy.[7] It appears that there had also been considerable politicking behind the scenes. Faÿ fought hard to secure his own election by enlisting the support of the prominent centre-right politician and three-time prime minister, André Tardieu. Like Faÿ an admirer of American dynamism who also judged its political system superior to that of the late Third Republic, Tardieu reportedly detested Siegfried despite some similarities in their background. What precise bearing any of these factors had on the actual deliberations is unknown, but Faÿ was elected in February 1932, at the age of thirty-eight the youngest holder of a chair in the Collège's history.[8]

Undeterred, Siegfried applied again the following year, this time for a chair in political and economic geography. Supported by Collège de France faculty members such as Charles Andler, Marcel Mauss, Sylvain Lévi, and Isidore Lévy, Siegfried stood for election to the position at an assembly of the professors on 8 January 1933; the other candidates were Édouard Dolléans of the Paris Faculty of Law and C. Brouilhet of the Université de Strasbourg. Unanimously elected by the forty-three faculty members in attendance, on 19 February Siegfried was officially named to the chair, on the same day that the historian Lucien Febvre, the co-founder (with Marc Bloch) of *Annales*, was elected to the Collège.[9] Siegfried remained at the institution until 1946. Retirement was mandatory at age seventy, so he had in fact been due to end his term there in 1945, but given early post-Second World War circumstances he and several other faculty members were extended for one additional year.[10]

From 1933 to 1940, Siegfried offered two courses every year at the Collège. One of these, on aspects of the geography of political opinion in the Midi, was held on Tuesday mornings. Later described as the more "intimate" and specialized of his two classes, its specific content varied each year, reflecting the evolution of Siegfried's research as he travelled to different departments. His lectures also gave him the opportunity to offer more personal observations on political life. The other course, held on Friday afternoons, related to his broader interests in international economic geography. Here again the specific focus varied from year to year, and often reflected his previous or current research projects, ranging from Britain and Canada's places in the international economy, to methods of production in the United States, to the Suez and Panama Canals. It also allowed Siegfried to develop and refine his ideas about Europe's changing international status. The course attracted a large and diverse audience; it was among the first classes offered by the Collège to be broadcast on the radio.[11]

Siegfried also showed interest in shaping the evolution of the Collège. He was an active member of its Assembly of Professors, which determined both the chairs to be established and which applicants would fill them. Siegfried's lobbying efforts had mixed results; his attempt to create a chair in comparative European civilizations in 1935 was to no avail, and in 1936 his choice for a chair in the history of labour, Robert Jarry, did not advance past the candidate stage.[12] The following year, by contrast, Siegfried was pleased to report to Mario Roques, a scholar of linguistics and comparative literature, that his efforts to support the creation of a chair in lexicology and in favour of Roque's candidacy for it were successful. But later that year, his lobbying for Henri Labouret, a former administrator in French West Africa, as the candidate for a chair in colonial history did not bear fruit. Unable to attend the Assembly of Professors, Siegfried had written a letter of support for Labouret in which he stressed the latter's practical knowledge – based, like his own, on extensive travel and personal contact – as well as his connections to other French and foreign colonial administrators. The letter is interesting insofar as it hints at Siegfried's views on colonialism, about which he published little – he stressed, for instance, the need for cooperation between the European powers in the colonial sphere – but it did not have the desired effect, as Labouret came in third in the balloting.[13]

Notwithstanding such reversals, Siegfried cherished his post to the Collège, prizing the institution above all as a site for the preservation of intellectual liberty. In a 1938 article for the *Revue de Paris*, which reviewed the institution's history, structure, and function, he noted how, since its creation by François I, the leading goal of its faculty was to "maintain the Collège in the spirit desired for it by its great founder, namely, to preserve the practice of free research there." Though the faculty was diverse, they shared this broader goal. With minimal oversight, they chose the chairs to be established – the Collège was not obliged to cover every subject, nor did it have to preserve a chair in a particular discipline once it was vacated. When elections were held, different factions sometimes took shape to support particular candidates, but with "the electors being extraordinarily different from each other, they do not succeed in forming truly dangerous coalitions." Once a chair was selected, the holder had considerable autonomy in organizing their work as long as they offered courses – never teaching the same lesson twice – and carried out original research. In this way, the Collège's long history of autonomy was preserved. While Siegfried did not deny that some French regimes had failed to respect fully the institution's independence, he asserted that the Third Republic had been scrupulous in this regard. It was crucial that it continue doing so, for "in our time liberty has become a delicate plant, shaken by storms; even if it is not menaced here, it needs to be attentively cared for and defended. There are those regimes, whose winds from the east peristently bring foul smells, where the application of the Collège's program would become impossible."[14] After the defeat in 1940 and the creation of the Vichy regime, Siegfried would see this commitment to liberal values tested first-hand.

In addition to his activities at the Institut and the Collège de France, Siegfried continued to teach at Sciences Po and remained active with the Musée social. His writings also raise questions about connections to other intellectual networks. For instance, his research aligned with the growth of scholarly and public interest in the study of the "psychology of peoples" during the interwar years. As shown by Egbert Klautke and Carole Reynaud Paligot, proponents of the study of the psychology of peoples, a field whose roots dated to mid-nineteenth-century Germany but also gained adherents in France, eschewed notions of biologically "pure" races but did promote a historical, cultural, and inegalitarian conception of race that included a belief in the heritability of psychological traits. Earlier enthusiasts for this approach included Émile Boutmy and Gustave Le Bon, and during the interwar years several books on national psychologies appeared, including Louis Cazamian's *Ce qu'il faut connaître de l'âme anglaise* (1927), Régis Michaud's *L'âme américain* (1929), Louis Reynaud's *L'âme allemande* (1933), Jules Legras's *L'âme russe* (1934), and Count de Sforza's *L'âme italienne* (1934). Adherents outside of France included the Spanish-born writer and historian Salvador de Madariaga, who taught at Oxford. While there were variations in emphasis and approach, collectively these authors accentuated enduring national "mentalities" and "essences."[15]

Siegfried was certainly a participant in this trend. He was of course mentored by Boutmy and knew Le Bon, attending some of the luncheon discussions that the latter had hosted since the turn of the century. Le Bon greatly admired Siegfried's *Les États-Unis d'aujourd'hui*, which, to his mind, revealed the lack of awareness about "the psychology of foreign peoples" in France.[16] It is also noteworthy that during the 1930s, Siegfried began to refer explicitly to the nineteenth-century historian Hippolyte Taine, who had influenced the emergence of the psychology of peoples as a scholarly approach. For instance, in a 1936 lecture contrasting European and American civilization, Siegfried invoked Taine's formula of "milieu, heredity, and moment" as a framework for comparison.[17] However, he does not appear to have had much personal contact with the wider interwar cohort of writers focused on national psychologies. Though his papers show that he did follow the work of Madariaga, making notes on the latter's writings about Jews and Anglo-German relations, they do not contain correspondence between the two writers.[18]

Siegfried did lend his support to the establishment, in his home city, of L'Institut Havrais de Sociologie économique et de Psychologie des Peuples in December 1937. The Institut was the brainchild of Abel Miroglio (1895–1978), who studied at the École normale supérieure and the École nationale des langues orientales vivantes. Miroglio taught philosophy at a variety of secondary schools, moving to Le Havre in 1936. A devoted advocate of Siegfried's work, he sought to promote the psychology of peoples as a bona fide discipline. The development of the Institut was disrupted by the Second World War, however, and it only got fully underway after the conflict.[19] Even then, while Siegfried remained supportive, he did not pour his energy into consolidating a new discipline; Miroglio was its champion.

Siegfried's involvement in promoting the psychology of peoples as a discipline thus had its limits. This was arguably even more the case with another emerging scholarly approach – the Annales school. In some respects, it seemed natural that a connection would develop, given Siegfried's interest in persistent political temperaments, which complemented the goal of the Annales's founders, Lucien Febvre and Marc Bloch, to shift scholarly focus away from studying events toward assessing deeper structural trends and mentalities. Indeed, Febvre and Bloch courted Siegfried; he joined the editorial board of *Annales*, and they hoped he would become a regular contributor. Febvre appears to have genuinely admired Siegfried's work, giving several of his books favourable reviews, but there were also professional interests at work. As Febvre put it, "his name would do much good"; Bloch sought Siegfried's support for a chair at the Collège de France. Siegfried accepted the invitation, lectured to the Annales group about his research and supported Bloch's candidacy, but his level of involvement was not what the co-founders had hoped.[20]

Siegfried did engage – though again in a limited way – in ongoing debates about how France should respond to the economic and political crises of the 1930s. Scholars such as Nord and Clarke have enriched understanding of these debates by tracing interactions between seemingly incongruent political trends and actors. Various intellectual currents – including elements of the trade union movement, dissident socialists, reformist social Catholics, and "non-conformist" intellectuals who sought to liberate France from what they referred to as the "established disorder" of the Third Republic – converged, at least to a degree, in calling for a break with laissez-faire economics and moving toward an "organized" economy and society. Among the key proponents of this shift were the members of X-Crise, officially known as the Centre polytechnicien d'études économiques, a think tank founded by graduates of the elite École Polytechnique. Its members, mostly engineers and businessmen, envisioned a dynamic French economy in which *techniciens* provided oversight, guiding enterprises toward maximum productivity, and ensuring social peace. One of the most influential leaders of X-Crise was Jean Coutrot, a Great War veteran who, though trained an engineer, also had broader philosophical interests. Corresponding with figures ranging from the Jesuit theologian and paleontologist Pierre Teilhard de Chardin to the British writer Aldous Huxley, Coutrot concluded that a new era in civilization was dawning. While technological changes were profoundly disorienting, he believed that through "scientific humanism," society's material and spiritual needs could be reconciled with a productive, managed economic order.[21]

To that end, in 1936 Coutrot established the Centre d'études des problèmes humaines (CEPH), another think tank. It sought to bring together people from various disciplines and political tendencies to explore the best way of restoring human equilibrium within an ever-changing material environment. The result would be, as Nord puts it, "a total renovation of the human species." The group first met at the Cistercian monastery of Pontigny in July 1936. Those in attendance included members of X-Crise, some moderate trade union leaders, Teilhard de Chardin, the educator Maria Montessori, and Siegfried.[22]

In some ways, the latter's involvement is not surprising, as some of his writings drew attention to the social and psychological challenges posed by accelerating economic growth and technological change. In a 1934 presentation at Sciences Po, for example, Siegfried noted that the world economic crisis had resulted in some profound policy shifts, none more shocking than in the United States where the Roosevelt administration had intervened significantly in the economy. While unenthusiastic about this new course, Siegfried hesitated to suggest that his own country necessarily knew better. "We have lost the spirit of invention in political matters: at this time the driving forces of the world are not here. Too often our attitude toward renovators is one of skepticism, if not irony."[23] Yet while he shared some admiration for the spirit of innovation promoted by the CEPH, he did not become a prominent member, though a 1938 talk given at the Académie des sciences morales et politiques engaged with some of its ideas. In that lecture, Siegfried echoed Coutrot's diagnosis that humanity was entering an era of unprecedented technological change, but his commitment to individual liberty strongly tempered his willingness to accept technocratic reform. "If humanity allows itself to be dominated by technical preoccupations, it is to be feared that the machine, with all of the social necessities that it entails, will lead the individual into a kind of enslavement."[24]

Such concerns, along with a dose of intellectual snobbery, also led Siegfried to avoid establishing relations with the medical researcher and eugenics promoter Dr Alexis Carrel, whom the CEPH had also initially hoped to recruit. A Nobel Prize winner who had spent much of his career in New York at the Rockefeller Institute, in his later years Carrel became a scientific popularizer, promoting the idea of human renewal in his book *L'homme, cet inconnu*, which first appeared in 1935 and became an international bestseller. There were some points of contact between Carrel's vision and that of Jean Coutrot, which helps to explain why the physician had been invited to join the CEPH's executive committee. But there were differences as well. Carrel's vision was more explicitly authoritarian, stressing the importance of cultivating new elites; he condemned egalitarianism and supposed societal degeneration, and had flirted with far-right politics before the war. He was also an advocate of eugenics; though he focused on "positive" measures to promote racial health, he did not rule out the adoption of negative ones, such as sterilization.[25]

As it turned out, Carrel never attended any meetings of the CEPH; he was more interested in founding his own think tank, a "Centre for the Study of Human Civilization." Siegfried was among those whose support he sought; Dr André Missenard, a colleague of Carrel's, approached Siegfried in early 1939. After a meeting over lunch, things initially seemed promising, but it seems nothing came of the overture. In fact, well before the meeting Siegfried had privately expressed disdain for Carrel, writing in a 1936 letter that his work "is interesting, but is banal vulgarization; I have often met with him in New York; when he talks he is a fanatic and I would not be surprised if he was in all a simpleton [*qu'il fut en somme un primaire*] ... these scientists do not have the spirit of finesse; I suppose that in order to do experiments well one must have patience, and a little housekeeping ability; but there is no need for general culture."[26]

More amenable to Siegfried's outlook was the attempt, spearheaded by Louis Rougier, a philosopher and professor at the Université de Besançon, to re-energize French liberalism at the end of the 1930s. In 1938, an international gathering of economic and political liberals, including Friedrich Hayek, Ludwig von Mises, Wilhelm Röpke, André Maurois, Jacques Rueff, Raymond Aron, Ernest Mercier, and Siegfried was held in Paris to celebrate the appearance of the American journalist Walter Lippmann's book *The Good Society* in French translation. This "Colloque Lippmann," as it became known, set the stage for the formation of the Centre international d'études pour le renouveau du libéralisme (CIRL) the following year. Given his prominence, Siegfried's affiliation was considered highly desirable, yet he does not appear to have played a prominent role in this short-lived, albeit influential group, which helped to shape the economic policies of the Daladier government in 1938–40.[27]

Siegfried, thus, took an interest in contemporary intellectual trends and political engagement, but within limits. He also expressed interest in expanding the scope of geography as a discipline, noting how the spatial characteristics of some phenomena, notably wind, colour, and smell, had long been commented upon by travellers and writers, and had been identified by scholars as potential subjects of study, but remained neglected. He believed that all three could be useful in their own way for demarcating frontiers. The study of Mediterranean and Atlantic winds, for instance, could be crucial to grasping regional differences within France. Individual continents and spaces also had their own distinct colours, though there were also intermediate zones. As for the geography of smells, Siegfried insisted that countries, continents, and civilizations had distinct odours. "Blacks say that whites smell like cadavers, and foreigners that the French smell of fried potatoes ... One of the essential points of the program would be to determine, for example, the domain of odours for this or that civilization. If I went, for example, to the East and India by way of Marseille and the Rhône Valley, where would I encounter the first whiffs of Asiatic or African scents?" Such questions were not trivial, he insisted. "[I]t is precisely in these quasi-imponderables where the most fecund and suggestive observations reside."[28] But he does not seem to have been very interested in establishing institutions to nurture such an approach.

## REVISITING FRENCH POLITICS

As he researched the political geography of the Midi during the 1930s, Siegfried adopted an approach similar to the one that he had employed for the *Tableau politique*. He travelled throughout the region over the course of the decade, typically during the summer or autumn, meeting with local experts and notables to gain further insight. Drawing on these sources, he gathered geographic, demographic, and electoral data for various departments.[29] Letters from the summer of 1936 about his research on the department of the Aveyron are suggestive. After reviewing documents procured by a research assistant, he spent ten days in the department, focusing on the southern electoral districts of Saint-Affrique and Millau. At Saint-Affrique, he met with Émile Borel, mathematician and, until recently, the deputy for the district, who had served since 1924 (and had been Minister of the Navy in 1925) before losing his seat in the 1936 elections. In Millau, Siegfried met with Morine Comby, a professor at Nîmes with whom he had previously worked and who he anticipated could shed light on local politics; "[H]e had the advantage, for me, beyond being very intelligent and cultivated, of being a popular democrat [member of the Parti Démocrate Populaire], which from my point of view was a novelty."[30]

Siegfried's impressions of the Aveyron focused upon distinctive topographical features, the underlying mentality of the population, and the dynamics of local politics. "Geographically it has large proportions that are not even French; these immense expanses and quasi-deserts of limestone plateaus, with their bright colours (yellow and dark green from several rare trees), are, rather, African or Spanish." The local peasantry reminded him of French Canadians; "[T]hey have the same incuriosity, the same sense of effort, the same taste for hard work, [and] the same love of money." But the Aveyronnais were more ambitious, willing to leave for Paris or elsewhere in the Midi to make their fortune. Politically, "the Aveyron is simple: it is a clerical region, but one that needs the government and rallies to the Republic during periods of calm in order to have government manna; but it reverts to clericalism in times of struggle and when the Republic is perceived not to be gaining ground." This environment had rendered Émile Borel's position delicate. Siegfried believed that it would be difficult for him to regain the seat he had lost, for "his majority is made of personal votes."

In 1938, Siegfried spent two weeks in the Aude, which was the political base of the Sarraut brothers, Albert and Maurice, both of whom were leading figures in the centrist Radical Party. Albert Sarraut was a former governor general of Indochina, two-time prime minister, and frequent cabinet minister; Maurice Sarraut was the editor of *La dépêche de Toulouse*, an influential regional newspaper. Siegfried arranged to meet with Maurice at the beginning of his visit, but even before that his research had led him to form some clear views about political developments in the department. As had been the case with the *Tableau politique*, he was attentive to ongoing shifts in local politics, but also located these trends within a broader context of enduring temperaments. He discerned that the Aude tended toward

Radicalism but noted that the Radical Party was itself in transition; it had been on the left, but under pressure from the Socialists was now becoming "a party of resistance." This realignment brought the threat of being compromised by a growing association with the right, meaning that the more "advanced" elements of the party might defect to the Socialists. However, Siegfried saw continuities as well: "[W]hat is permanent is the percentage of temperaments of the right, left, and extreme left; these temperaments change name but are still the same, and it is this which truly determines the political personality of the department." Even the fact that the district of Narbonne had elected the Socialist Léon Blum instead of a Radical candidate was the result of long-term trends since it had always been "violent," in Siegfried's estimation. In 1871, he noted, it had a pro-revolutionary commune, while Ernest Ferroul, who had served as Narbonne's deputy and mayor, "was the leader of a quasi-insurrectional movement," specifically the 1907 winegrowers' protests that had been violently repressed.[31]

Siegfried elaborated upon these impressions in a paper delivered to the Société d'histoire de la Troisième République, of which he was vice-president, in the winter of 1939. The Aude, he explained, consisted of two regions, one with a predominantly Mediterranean climate, the other dominated by the Atlantic. The former was a wine-growing region where residents inclined toward an artisanal or working-class mentality, while the latter featured fields of wheat and maize, with a corresponding peasant outlook. Local attitudes were also conditioned by distant history: Greeks and Romans had brought "subtlety," and during the Middle Ages the Albigensians had endowed part of the region with a "sense of resistance, notably opposition by the Midi to the conquering north." These features inclined the eastern part of the department toward extremism, while in the West "the fundamental political complexion will be moderation."[32]

Siegfried contended that electoral data confirmed these lasting trends, notwithstanding some anomalies. For instance, he suggested that the far left in Narbonne sometimes displayed "Boulangist" tendencies; the wine growers' insurrection of 1907, he argued, did not fit the traditional mold of party politics, instead displaying "a plebiscitary spirit, bringing together men of the left and right, rich and poor, proletarians and property owners, in a common action." But in most of the department, the Radicals had managed to reassert themselves and now the overall picture was one of stability. "The right appears to have 25% of the registered voters, the left around 55%, among whom the governmental left has 30% and the extremist (or opposition) left 25%, very approximately of course. Moreover, the geographic distribution is rather distinct: Narbonne is on the far left, Carcassonne the left, and Castelnaudary if not on the right at least inclined towards moderation."[33] These trends were due to geography and social structure but also particular circumstances, notably the role of the Sarraut family in consolidating local Radicalism. Despite this nod to contingency, in the question-and-answer period that ensued – participants included the writer Daniel Halévy and the historian Adrien Dansette – Siegfried reaffirmed his insistence on the durability of political temperaments. For example, in response to a query from Dansette he explained that the Bonapartist tradition continued through the late nineteenth century in the form of support for Boulangism and then Ernest Ferroul.[34]

Similar kinds of observations found their way into Siegfried's lectures on the geography of political opinion in the Midi at the Collège de France and echoed in his reflections on the unique contribution that the region made to French national identity. Siegfried held that France was both a "Western" country, linked to the Atlantic and Anglo-American civilization, and a "European" one, with its eastern frontier reaching into the central part of the continent. But its Mediterranean coast set the country further apart: it put France "in quasi-direct contact with the East"; Siegfried even suggested parenthetically that "those who understand the French peasant understand the Japanese peasant." Though quick to point out that the Midi contained different frontiers and climates, he discerned an underlying regional unity in relation, even opposition, to Paris and the North. Politically its people were not a race but were rather defined by "a certain way of life, of producing ... a particular conception of power, of the individual in [relation to] the state."[35] Yet, although the Midi was a distinctive region, its ethos also powerfully defined France as a whole, giving it a unique geographic reach and promoting a way of life that underscored the individual autonomy to which Siegfried was deeply committed.

Siegfried's work on the Midi also reflected a growing interest in religious matters. He had long recognized the role of the Catholic clergy in shaping political comportment but, given the history of the Midi, the effect of Protestantism also had to be considered. In departments such as the Ardèche, it was a key factor in explaining political differences.

Indeed, it was "exclusively" Protestantism, he asserted in a 1935 lecture, that accounted for left-wing support in some mountainous districts of the Ardèche while Catholicism encouraged right-wing voting in others. Protestantism was also a key factor in ensuring left-wing support elsewhere in the department, though here it was reinforced by other factors, such as a more egalitarian social structure. Siegfried's view of the Ardèche was not entirely static; he noted that it might be possible for the right to gain support among more conservative Protestants.[36] Overall, though, he stressed a correlation between Protestantism and support for the moderate republican left.

Siegfried's increased attention to the political significance of Protestantism was also informed by personal interests. He acknowledged that one of the reasons he had decided to focus upon the Midi in his return to electoral geography were his own Protestant *ardèchois* roots on his mother's side.[37] He also began taking a more public interest in moral and spiritual issues during this period. In 1933, he presided over a meeting of the Assemblée du désert, an annual gathering in Mialet (Gard) that commemorated the persecution of French Protestants; the title of the meeting recalled the name of their clandestine gatherings. In his address, Siegfried recalled this long history of repression, quoting – without irony, it seems – the Catholic nationalist Maurice Barrès as he celebrated the gathering at "a place of significance for the soul." Stressing the Protestant commitment to freedom of conscience, he closed by emphasizing how "1789" reflected perfectly this "demand for the sacred domain of the individual."[38] His correspondence from this period confirms his views about the distinctive character of French Protestantism. In a 1936 letter, he posited major contrasts between it and other traditions that featured a greater focus on worldly deeds and success. "France, with its rational and classical tradition, is rarely tempted by these seductions. But Nordics – Germans, English, Americans – slip more easily into a state of mind where they end up, without remorse, serving Nature rather than God. The English and Americans, who are more hypocritical, pretend to have made a mistake: the Germans, more cynical, serve Nature as such, without even believing that it is good."[39] The rationalist, liberal character of French Protestantism was, in his view, evidently a boon to the nation.

Siegfried also reflected on the Jewish contribution to French civilization. He had paid considerable – and largely negative – attention to Jews in *Les États-Unis d'aujourd'hui*. Correspondence about that book with the editor of the journal *The American Hebrew* had led him to contribute an article, in 1929, on the status of Jews in France. Perhaps not surprisingly, the tone of this piece was less harsh, but Siegfried continued to regard Jews as an unsettling presence, and as being in the final analysis responsible for outbursts of anti-Semitism. Though numerically small, he explained, the French Jewish community had made a major contribution to the country. "It is a fact that the Jew is ranked among the best citizens. He has a sense of social and civic duty which is hardly surpassed anywhere ... France being, as everyone knows, an utterly individualistic country, such a sense of social duty among Jewish people (which also exists to a high degree among the French Protestants) is an interesting factor for the welfare of the community at large." When it came to intellectual matters the situation was more complex, however. Notwithstanding old beliefs, he suggested, Jews were not especially focused on money; rather, they sought cultural prominence. In this sense, they had a distinctive contribution to make, which could be valuable – provided, Siegfried added, that it remained proportionate:

> In philosophy, in literature, in art, the Jewish intellectual often
> appears ... as the most cruel and sophisticated critic of present
> affairs ... Such Jewish contributors are utterly French, and yet
> they bring a touch of something which does not quite belong
> to our traditional atmosphere ... Anti-Semites will complain
> of such a contribution, which, spiritually speaking, may not be
> 100% French. I am ready to accept it and even to welcome it.
> I think, and many think with me, that it plays in the social body
> the role of a ferment of extra-ordinary vitalizing power. It is
> only a question of percentage, and, provided the dose is not
> overdone, the effect can be deemed incomparably beneficent ...
> If harmonized to the needs of the community which they
> have adopted, [Jewish] collaboration is of the greatest
> possible value.[40]

Though seeking to distance himself from anti-Semites, Siegfried made it clear that France's Jewish minority should remain small and respectful of national traditions, to which they were not always inherently suited. In this respect they were different from French Protestants – both shared the experience of being minorities, as well as certain social attitudes, but, he concluded, the Protestant emphasis on individual liberty was at the heart of the republican French ethos in a way that Jewish values were not. Though Jews – provided there were not too many of them – could integrate and contribute, they would always remain, in critical ways, a people apart.

Siegfried elaborated on this theme in a lecture delivered to the Cercle d'études juives in 1930. Here he insisted that "the assimilation of the Jew has never been complete; something within him remains irremediably outside the community [*l'association*]." Describing the Jewish people as a "palimpsest with traces from nation to nation," he quoted Maurice Barrès to the effect that Jews were never entirely integrated by their host country. He then proceeded to compare the status of Jews in France to that in the United States. In France, he asserted, there was no "Jewish question" per se. Anti-Semitism did exist, but rather than being rooted in economics or ethnicity, it was the result of a supposedly singular Jewish mentality. "Perhaps [Henri] Bergson would have never conceived of his philosophy of time if he had not been a Jew ... Léon Blum as a social apostle is certainly from another spiritual race than Jaurès." In contrast, the "Jewish question" in the United States was fuelled not only by spiritual distinctiveness but also by "heavy doses" of migration over the past century, with many arrivals from "the Orient," in contrast to the situation in Western Europe. Commenting on the Anglo-Jewish author Israel Zangwill's exploration of Jewish assimilation into American society, as presented in his 1908 play *The Melting Pot*, Siegfried conceded that in business, language, and civic responsibility, "the American Jew" integrated rapidly. But, he insisted, "his intellect remains distinct, as well as his mystique." Siegfried concluded by reiterating the value of Jewish culture as a "ferment," but added, "let us have the courage to admit that an excessive dose of this ferment can risk becoming noxious."[41] The highly conditional nature of his proclaimed toleration for Jews remained evident in the years to come, with troubling consequences.

Siegfried generally avoided explicitly partisan comments during this period, but his political views were clear enough. He continued to support the liberal, moderate republican tradition that had done so much to forge the current regime, and still admired politicians within this tradition, such as Poincaré. In his view, France's reactionary right remained unable to play a constructive role, while on the left the Socialists and Communists posed a collectivist danger. He despaired at the election of the Popular Front, commenting privately in August 1936 that "I confess to being disheartened, and it is very uncomfortable to feel that one is governed by firebrands." Two years later, he was very fearful that if France was plunged into war at the behest of left-wing politicians it would be radicalized, as it had been during the Franco-Prussian War. This concern about a "war-revolution nexus" explains his support for the Munich Accords in 1938, an attitude shared, admittedly, by a broad spectrum of French opinion. Siegfried disdained politicians, especially those on the left, who advocated a tougher line in dealing with Germany: "What frightens me is that there is, in France as in England, a war party: these men, concerned above all with fighting Fascism and Hitlerism, without fearing that it might lead us to ruin ... The men of 1871 were madmen (as Thiers put it): I have the impression that Pierre Cot [a Radical deputy] and others are also madmen."[42]

A 1937 lecture about his father, delivered to the Société d'histoire de la Troisième République, also reflected Siegfried's dissatisfaction with the state of French politics at the time, and his convictions about how the situation could be improved. Jules Siegfried, he suggested, was too cosmopolitan, too businesslike, too puritanical, in a way too "Anglo-Saxon" to truly thrive in the current French system, given as it was to excessive verbiage and the influence of "southern" values, a comment at odds with the more positive things he had to say about the Midi in other contexts. It was a shame, Siegfried concluded, that his father's practical achievements in business, social affairs, and politics were not more widely emulated.[43] The workings of the late Third Republic, he implied, were too populist, demagogic, and socially radical; a France governed by a moderate elite, faithful to the liberal values of 1789 while mindful of the supposed realities of national identity, offered the proper way forward.

### ASSESSING LATIN AMERICA

Siegfried travelled extensively in Latin America during the 1930s; having spent much time in North America, he evidently wished to understand its southern counterpart better. In 1931, after accepting an invitation from the Institute of the University of Paris in Chile and Argentina, he toured the continent for three months, stopping in the French Antilles before visiting Panama and Venezuela, then spending two weeks in Peru, over a month in Chile, and finishing with visits to Argentina, Uruguay, and Brazil. In the process, he delivered lectures about French politics and society in a variety of settings.[44] Then, in

1935, as part of his visit to North America he spent a busy few weeks in Mexico, during which he delivered a total of seven public lectures on topics that included economic geography and the crisis of Europe's international status, but focused primarily on exposés of French politics and promoting his country's contributions to civilization.[45] In 1937, he spent four weeks in Brazil, again delivering various public lectures in several cities to promote Franco-Brazilian intellectual and cultural ties. Finally, in 1938 he returned to Colombia and Panama, studying the Canal region, which fascinated him.[46]

While the Latin American visits provided occasions for praising the virtues of French democracy, they also offered new opportunities for observation and reflection. Siegfried's first journey was recounted in a series of letters to *Le Petit Havre*, subsequently published in book form as *En Amérique du Sud*, then brought out by his British publisher Jonathan Cape as *Impressions of South America* in 1933.[47] The following year he published the more analytical study *Amérique latine* with Armand Colin. His travels to Mexico and Brazil were also described in subsequent letters to *Le Petit Havre*, while the Panama Canal featured in a comparative study with the Suez Canal, which appeared in 1940.[48] Aside from specific analyses of particular states, Siegfried depicted Latin America as a site for considering the implications of growing American power, a rising assertiveness on the part of non-white peoples, and the prospects for the Latin, and more specifically the French, perspective in the modern world.

As usual, Siegfried framed his analyses of economic and political trends with an overview of geographic features and ethnic composition. His brief stop in the French Antilles in 1931 gives an indication of the general approach. Here he found the geography and built environment of "our old colonies" reminiscent of that of the metropole, but the population was radically different. It seemed "to consist of black athletes, the women wearing brilliantly coloured dresses, with romantic Madras handkerchiefs about their heads." Unfortunately, he commented without elaboration, "politics have not allowed these 'good savages' to live in the native innocence pictured by Jean Jacques Rousseau."[49] As one moved to the South American continent, he observed, the similarities to French landscapes faded. Whether it was the vast mountain ranges of the Andes, the deep jungles of the Canal Zone and Brazil, or the endless horizons of the Pampas, the scale of the continent, he concluded, was utterly unlike that of Europe, instead paralleling that of North America.

But if geography brought the two continents together, history and race pulled them in different directions. "The Anglo-Saxon Protestants of the North and the Latin Catholics of the South evolved within the frameworks of distinct civilizations, each marked by their origins." In North America, whites had established themselves as the dominant group almost everywhere, while South America was far more complex. In the continent's southeastern cone, recent waves of European immigration ensured white dominance in Uruguay, and much of Chile, Argentina, and southern Brazil. Europeans had also settled along the Pacific coast, but as one moved away from the shoreline into the Andes, Indigenous peoples – whom he described as "mongoloids" with obscure roots in Asia – or people of mixed blood who should "in no way be considered as belonging to our race" dominated. Here the elites, themselves generally of purer European background, were anxious. "Theoretically the master of these regions, will our race be able to maintain itself there in the long term, other than as an occupying body in the capitals, ports, trading posts or mines? Having to ask the question shows how serious [the matter] already is." Siegfried seemed less concerned about the third ethnic zone, which spanned northwards from Rio de Janeiro through the Caribbean and featured a significant African presence and extensive intermixing. Here he did not regard the inhabitants as threatening; "With the Negro gaiety, sensuality, carelessness, and easy-going good humour reign, which makes for an atmosphere very different from one impregnated by Spanish sadness and incurable Indian reserve." [50] Still, white supremacy in South America clearly had its limits, and this concerned him.

Siegfried's 1931 visit coincided with a period of economic and political upheaval throughout much of South America, problems that he often attributed to its peoples' innate characteristics. Though acknowledging that conditions differed from state to state, in broad strokes he concluded that the continent's people had access to tremendous resources but did not make the best use of them. A lack of coal and limited population size hindered efforts to industrialize, meaning that most states still had essentially colonial economies dependent on foreign investment and the export of primary products. Another major underlying problem was a propensity to borrow and spend heavily. Like their counterparts to the North, South Americans partook of a powerful and sometimes misguided economic optimism. This was enhanced by what he characterized as a Spanish and Portuguese inclination to be ostentatious, despite the financial prudence of some groups like the Castilians, whom he judged akin to the French in this regard. Latin American elites also spent a great deal of time and money abroad, weakening the balance of trade. Nor did they spend borrowed money wisely: "From my hotel window in Santiago I look out on unfinished buildings fifteen storeys high, for which there was no need, and which bring in no income."[51]

As for South American politics, it was a combustible mix. Siegfried noted that there were significant class tensions in some countries and that these sometimes overlapped with racial divides. In Chile during the country's 1931 presidential elections, he met with the Labor candidate, Senator Manuel Hidalgo Plaza, who seemed to embody the salience of such divisions. "He was a workman, evidently of Indian descent, and Marxian by creed. The arguments that he put forward in our conversation against the small property owner, and in favour of large-scale exploitation as in Russia, using American methods, were pure Orthodox Communism." This was not the case everywhere, Siegfried conceded; in Argentina, notwithstanding socialist activity in Buenos Aires, "there are no rivalries of either race or caste, [so] the situation is comparatively simple." Regarding Brazil, the population was incredibly diverse and the gap between rich and poor was great, but he maintained that there was a good deal of passivity in the face of upheavals and authoritarian rule. This did not bother Siegfried overly, for he believed that "democracy requires a certain homogeneity of race and culture ... In North America, the Southern states are to a certain extent in an analogous situation, and so cannot be considered a real democracy either ... in spite of its very sincere democratic sentiment, for the present at any rate democracy in Brazil cannot be anything more than a façade."[52]

Beneath the rhetoric and ideological posturing, he concluded, South American politics was often reducible to a competition for power and resources. "Napoleon once said that a revolution was simply an idea that had found bayonets to express it. In South America this definition would have to be adapted, for there it would be a group of interests, not an idea, [which] has found the bayonets. Imbued with our European ideas, we are tempted to look for the causes in political ideals, but in these factional quarrels it is simply greed in most cases." Extending his political analysis in *Amérique latine*, Siegfried discerned key structural weaknesses. Despite sometimes elaborate and high-minded constitutions, elected assemblies were too weak and presidents wielded excessive power, a trend he attributed largely to the legacy of Spanish

Catholic rule. The church lacked liberal traditions and the state had little respect for autonomy; the result was that the population, while possessing some impressive qualities as individuals, lacked civic-mindedness and a general respect for legality. They were vulnerable to demagogic populism that could potentially take on a more racial and revolutionary form, for instance with Indigenous-based movements in the Andean countries. More generally, political office held out the promise of resources and power, tempting the unscrupulous, while the weakness of civic and social organization encouraged military coups. Siegfried cautioned against seeing this in terms of officers simply desiring control; some sincerely believed that they could serve the nation. Interestingly, he commented that while at present such coups were dominated by officers, if subordinate military elements ever wielded power the result could be radical social reforms, "following the too-well known formula of workers and soldiers' committees."[53]

Internationally, South America stood at a crossroads; it could either remain primarily Latin in its ethos or drift further into the orbit of the United States. Geography and the current economic situation favoured the latter, but Spanish and Portuguese heritage bolstered the former; fortunately, it also facilitated French influence in the intellectual and cultural spheres. Siegfried took heart at the extent to which French values continued to influence the South American elite: "I know of no country where the cultured people are more thoroughly conversant with the French language down to its most intimate details, and appreciate better our literature and trend of thought, or interest themselves more spontaneously and seriously in our intellectual and artistic activities." But there was no cause for complacency, he added, for current developments tended to work against these patterns. Politically, France was a cradle of democratic values but socially it remained aristocratic in spirit; it was to the elites rather than the masses that French values appealed. "It is our traditional liberalism that can be found in the doctrines of Latin American jurists and political philosophers." The rise of democratic and revolutionary currents, and the spread of modern technology and values, thus posed a threat. "When democracy triumphs, it is then that the masses abandon the French inspiration. They turn to Russia if they wish to destroy, and towards the United States should they desire to organize, buy motor cars, or be amused. Here is a contradiction which we must accept because the French democracy is aristocratic at heart. We would gain little by standardizing ourselves, for in so doing we should only remain common." In the end, Siegfried predicted, despite the growing appeal of the American model, even among South American intellectuals, the Latin spirit would endure. "The Spanish tongue, the Catholic influence, and above all the family tradition of the Iberian peninsula, are ramparts which the American invasion cannot scale."[54]

To a considerable extent, then, Siegfried regarded Latin America as beset by a struggle between civilization and primitivism, but also between alternate variants of civilization. The values of Latin Europe had profoundly shaped the region, but in many instances they were being checked by the presence of Africans and or threatened by an Indigenous political revival; Latin America was thus not fully part of Western civilization.[55] Siegfried's reflections on the region also exposed his fundamental convictions about the limitations of democracy, the benefits of an elitist liberal approach, and the fundamental clash between Latin and Anglo-Saxon values.

Siegfried's visits were partly intended to promote French thought and culture in a part of the world where the Third Republic feared its influence was waning. His prestige, officials hoped, would win over elements of the Latin American populace, especially its elites. British diplomats in the region, concerned about competition, feared that would be the case: reporting on the 1931 sojourn in Peru, the British ambassador in Lima observed that "From our point of view, Prof Siegfried's tour will be bad business."[56] In fact, his views met with some criticism. The French ambassador in Lima felt that his lecture on French adaptation to the global economy at the University of San Marcos had not been fully appreciated, partly because of the university rector's "communist tendencies" and partly because members of the audience, some of them with Indigenous ancestry, could not understand Siegfried, who had delivered his remarks in French.[57] In Colombia, Siegfried's early writings on his travels to Latin America aroused offence, to the point that the liberal newspaper *El tiempo* suggested that he "perhaps believes that we are part of the Sandwich Isles." Even the French ambassador to Bogota felt that it was unfortunate for someone of Siegfried's reputation to venture generalizations, for instance about military dominance of Colombian politics, that were outdated, unfair, and likely to offend.[58] The Peruvian writer and politician Luis Alberto Sánchez, who translated Siegfried's 1934 book *Amérique latine* into Spanish, saw merit in the Frenchman's economic analyses but felt that some of his observations were superficial – the result of rapid travel – and dated. Sánchez also observed that Siegfried relied too heavily upon the perspective of local established elites and questioned his proclivity to see Indigenous activism as Communist-influenced.[59]

Despite such criticisms, Siegfried's writings on Latin America, translated into English and Spanish, reached a variety of audiences, and the French Ministry of Foreign Affairs continued to see him as an asset. During his 1935 visit to Mexico, the French chargé d'affaires was delighted with the local reception that his eminent visitor received. Some effort had been made to publicize Siegfried's lectures in advance, to good effect. The stock of his books that had been ordered in advance and made available at a discounted price sold out more quickly than anticipated, and the lectures were well attended, with never fewer than 600 people – from the local French colony but also many members of the Mexican elite and intelligentsia – turning up. Siegfried also had the opportunity to meet with officials such as the ministers of education, finance, and foreign affairs, and he and Paule – who took a much-appreciated interest in Mexican art – had opportunities to tour. Despite ongoing political turmoil, he reportedly managed to avoid being "captured" by a particular faction, instead promoting the values of French democracy. For instance, one lecture devoted to various French statesmen noted the different perspectives of figures such as Gambetta, Jaurès, Clemenceau, and Poincaré, but ended by stressing their shared patriotism. "A country is great through its institutions and its men ... France has at least had its men." In all, the French legation stressed "the very pleasing results obtained by our compatriot, who knew, even though he denied doing so, how to make the most noble propaganda, and to enlighten in an admirable way France's position in the contemporary world."[60]

While admitting of variations in different states, Siegfried continued to hold to his vision of Latin America as a continent where European values were dangerously contested. His visit to Mexico reinforced his anxieties about the radical potential of an Indigenous presence; he exclaimed in one of his letters for *Le Petit Havre* that "[f]or a long time I believed that the Indian was dying a slow death in America. What a mistake! He has reconquered all of Mexico, where the Aztec kings are national heros and the conqueror Cortez does not have a statue." He was even more blunt in a letter to Jacques Chapsal at the Sciences Po, describing his stay as "fascinating but very worrisome from the point of view of the future of the white race: the Indians have control and are in the process of undoing Cortez's work. It's a kind of

Bolshevism, above all a rudimentary Indian nationalism. The result is the same thing."[61] Though in public he suggested that compared with their counterparts in Peru, Mexico's Indigenous peoples were not as politically aware, and that Mexican national identity was of a civic rather than ethnic character, he nevertheless depicted the ongoing revolution as a throwing off of the Spanish colonial heritage. In a country where social inequality was severe and where the Catholic Church possessed great wealth and power, revolutionary measures aimed at redistributing property and curbing clerical power were understandable, if excessive. However, it was not clear that a better future lay ahead; the current Mexican regime did not respect individual liberties and the Indigenous population was incapable of managing landholdings effectively. Barriers to industrialization, among them overly powerful unions that demanded excessive wages, were considerable. As he took his leave of Mexico, Siegfried tried to sound reassuring by underscoring the resilience of "Latinity": "[I]n Latin countries life always has a charm, an easy-going quality and a certain kind of humanity, even in disorder, which makes one love living there."[62] But he clearly regarded the ongoing Mexican revolution as another example of the damaging non-white rejection of European inspiration and leadership.

Neither Brazil nor Colombia, which Siegfried visited in 1937 and 1938 respectively, were as perturbing in this regard, but nor did they invalidate his earlier impressions of Latin America. In Brazil, Siegfried's generally warm welcome was disrupted by some critical comments from the country's foreign minister, Pimentel Brandão, who suggested at a luncheon that European affairs were more troubled than the French academic's presentation of events suggested. But Siegfried was unconvinced, replying that there were still European states where liberalism thrived.[63] In subsequent writings about Brazil, he depicted the country as still having much to learn from Europe. Unable to pay its debts, Brazil exemplified both the vast resources of the Americas and the obstacles that existed to developing them properly. Reflecting "American" attitudes, Brazilian farmers quickly exhausted the land that they cultivated and then moved on; there was little of the typically French inclination toward restraint. The country was industrializing and had goods to export but depended on foreign capital and had trouble conquering markets. The labour force was another obstacle, for Brazil was still underpopulated, and its ethnic composition, in Siegfried's view, was problematic.

Elaborating on the latter point, he observed that given the persistence of a large Indigenous community, the importation of slaves from Africa, and waves of migration from Europe, "there is no Brazilian race, any more than there is a French race or a British race." But while Siegfried concluded that Brazilian racial attitudes were relatively tolerant in comparison to those in the United States, this did not lead to social equality – a fact that he explained by invoking stereotypes to justify the hierarchies that existed. "Coloured people enjoy full social and political rights. Yet cases where a man of Negro blood has risen high on the ladder are rare, for the black man contents himself naturally with more modest situations." In general, the "laziness" of the African-Brazilian and the "unsuitability" of the Indigenous peoples accounted for the low quality of the labour force. Siegfried did take some comfort though, in the continuing appeal of France to Brazilian elites, observing in a letter to Georges Risler, "There is great sympathy for French culture. The lectures that I gave drew a large audience, who understood French admirably. There are several French professors here, who are all doing very well. I hope to have contributed through my lectures to maintaining Franco-Brazilian intellectual friendship."[64]

He also expressed some optimism about the situation in Colombia, perhaps seeking to avoid the controversy that had accompanied his previous visit. In July 1938, along with René Huyghe, director of paintings at the Louvre, and the anthropologist Paul Rivet, from the Musée de l'Homme, he served as a member of the French delegation to an exposition in Bogota marking the 400th anniversary of the city's founding. In a wide-ranging discussion of Colombia's heritage and prospects, he observed that despite serious travails at the turn of the century in the form of war and the separation of Panama, since then the country had enjoyed an impressive degree of stability. Though its population was diverse, encompassing a Spanish elite, Black labourers, and a large Indigenous population, the latter did not pose the same problems as existed in Mexico or Peru because it was more assimilated; "[T]he mixing of the conquerors with the natives has produced a new people, less strongly Indian than elsewhere ... the predominance of the white race has also made itself felt more clearly." Blessed with coasts on both oceans and access to oil, the country evinced great economic potential, though it was still heavily dependent on foreign investment. Internationally, Colombians sought to preserve their independence from European interference, but relations with the United States were more complex. While mindful of past US

Horizons Old and New    143

interventions, they respected its wealth and technological prowess, and Roosevelt's Good Neighbor policy had helped to allay old tensions. For all that, there was good reason for France to take a continuing interest in Colombia on cultural and economic grounds. Invoking "the natural sympathy that brings together all the nations that have agreed to call themselves Latin," Siegfried noted that "Colombia places itself in this group and, in this respect, a Frenchman cannot feel himself to be a foreigner there." The Colombian elite took great interest in French art and literature; these cultural ties, he suggested, could be complemented by further initiatives on the part of French industry. While the United States was clearly the dominant economic power in the region, there was no reason why it should simply be given a monopoly. Given its location and resources, Colombia could be a valuable ally in the event of war.[65]

Such observations were in keeping with Siegfried's other affirmations of Franco-Latin American affinity. This notion of "pan-Latinity" was not new. Since the nineteenth century, and especially after the defeat of 1870–71, various French intellectuals, often though not always on the political right, had promoted their country as the natural leader of the Latin nations of Europe and the Americas. It was a way of compensating for France's decline in international status and of competing with German, British, and eventually American international ambitions. In the early twentieth century, the nurturing of Franco-Latin American ties took on a more institutional form, as embodied for example in the creation of the Comité France-Amérique in 1909. Attempts to bolster connections intensified during the First World War and, after 1918, the Quai d'Orsay remained active in this regard, committing more resources to cultural propaganda. Pan-Latinity remained a crucial theme but there was now less overt emphasis on French leadership and more on reciprocity, though still with the goal of competing with foreign influence – now above all emanating from the United States.[66]

In his emphasis on strengthening cultural affinities and economic involvement rather than asserting explicit French leadership, Siegfried's writings reinforced this evolution. So did his frequent comments about the threat of Americanization; here he tended to focus not so much on direct US political intervention as on the influence of American technology and values. On the other hand, his proclivity for assessing ethnic composition distanced France from Latin American nations, especially when they contained a large Indigenous population. To the extent that "Latin" values were solidly established through European dominance, and that liberal values were rooted in local elites, French connections were assured. But the revival of Indigenous identities, the rise of democratic – even revolutionary – politics, and the spread of American values all posed threats in this regard. Siegfried's worries about the growing effect of Indigenous radicalism and Americanization, as expressed in the Latin American context, echoed in his writings on global challenges to European hegemony.

## THE CRISIS OF EUROPEAN HEGEMONY

During the late 1920s and early 1930s, Siegfried travelled to Germany, several Eastern European states, and Scandinavia. These visits, it seems, enhanced his sense of the continent's diversity. He found Germany to be in some respects a very modern country, reminiscent of the United States to a degree but also appreciative of intellectual life and French culture. Yet Germany was also closer to Russia, a land of radical social and political experimentation; the Germans did not emulate the Russian approach completely, but Siegfried believed that they were affected by unsettling currents that had largely bypassed a still-bourgeois France. As for Eastern Europe, he remarked following a 1932 visit to Romania, only its ruling classes had been touched by "European civilization proper"; the peasant and artisan population remained deeply traditional, even alien in the case of those peoples who had formerly been under Turkish rule. "When one speaks of Europe in the singular," he observed, "one is unaware of these nuances; however, they are essential for anyone wanting to discuss the future of our old continent."[67] But when Siegfried turned to considering the continent's status and prospects as a whole, these distinctions were soon obscured. His focus was very much on the economies and cultures of northwestern Europe, in particular those of Britain and especially France.

Siegfried's angst about the challenges to Europe presented by the American "model" had already been articulated in the 1920s; he now broadened his discussion to consider other, related trends on a global scale. His evolving thoughts on these issues were advanced in a 1932 lecture given to a group of Protestant businessmen. They were fully developed in a 1935 book entitled *La crise de l'Europe.*[68] Taking a longer-term perspective, Siegfried contended that although the roots of Europe's global dominance could be dated to the Renaissance, it had only truly reached its height during the industrial era. He focused

Horizons Old and New

heavily on the economics of European pre-eminence, noting how capital investment, technological innovation, migration flows, consumer demand, and the activities of experts and administrators had all been mutually reinforcing. An equilibrium had emerged, whereby the "old" countries of Europe provided industrial goods while the rest of the globe provided markets and raw materials. It was the depth and sophistication of European economies that ensured a favourable position, Siegfried concluded, noting that it was above all British maritime and imperial power that allowed for the creation of, as Élie Halévy had put it, "an international mercantile republic." Recalling his world tour in 1898–1900, Siegfried conceded that he had fully partaken of the opinion that such dominance was only natural. "By divine right – I know I remember this perfectly, so I am not exaggerating – Europe considered herself a privileged continent, the king of continents in fact."[69]

But over the past thirty years, he continued, the situation had changed dramatically; Europe now faced a two-pronged assault. The first came from regions that had been conquered and settled by Europeans, but were now asserting their autonomy and increasingly looked to the United States for leadership. They were countries of "the white race" – more fervently so than many Europeans were, Siegfried found, as "the excessively rigid policy of White Australia and the colour bar in South Africa" indicated; such similarities in settlement and development helped to explain why American influence over these nations was growing. As for the United States itself, while it had been dealt a serious blow by the Depression Siegfried believed that American influence would continue to expand. "From now on we must recognize that there exist two directing centres for the white race and Western civilization, and Europe, though traditionally accustomed to reign supreme, is now only one of them."[70]

The second trend, in Siegfried's view, was "the emancipation of the coloured races," as described by the American author Lothrop Stoddard in his 1921 book *The Rising Tide of Color*. Nonwhites were now appropriating European technology for their own ends. Recalling his time in South America, Siegfried suggested that "primitive people and members of outworn ancient civilizations" might actually employ new tools more effectively than their white counterparts: "On the narrow giddy roads of the Andes the Indian drives a Buick or a Ford with a coolness which compels our admiration."[71] Europeans, he explained, sought to bring spiritual values and material progress to non-whites, but the latter had focused on the undeniable misdeeds that had been committed by some colonizers, overlooking the nobler aspects of the European imperial project. Like the whites of the Americas and Australasia, the peoples of Africa, Asia, and Latin America now sought to modernize, free of European tutelage; the war had contributed to this assertiveness and created opportunities to develop their economies. Siegfried was taken by the extent to which even non-white Christians were determined to go their own way, citing the example of a meeting of the International Council of Protestant Missions held in Jerusalem in 1928, where one-quarter of the delegates came from Africa and Asia and exerted an influence that was "even greater than their numbers justified." Distressed at what he deemed European passivity in response to these trends, he also worried that just as the "new" white nations were susceptible to American influence, so too were the non-white masses of the globe. "They look to the Americans, too, for advice in women's fashions, for cinemas, for the so-called scientific ideas, and even for amusements."[72] In sum, notwithstanding the severe effect of the Great Depression and the intensification of political extremism in Europe at the time, for Siegfried the continent's most imposing challenges were apparently the international appeal of the American economic and social model, coupled with growing non-white assertiveness.

Yet as worrisome as he believed the situation was, he refused to despair at Europe's prospects. At least some European investors would benefit from overseas industrialization, and European experts would likely be hired as consultants. As local consumers became wealthier and more discerning, the appeal of at least some high-quality European goods over local ones was bound to grow, thus ensuring that businesses from "the old continent" could still tap into overseas markets, as long as they continued to innovate and improve. "Thus we are forced to take refuge in the superiority of our goods, and are drawn into a cycle of progress which it is fatal to stop." Even here, Siegfried could not avoid invoking stereotypes: "There is something infernal in this rhythm, which recalls the haunted striving of the Wandering Jew." Still, the challenges of remaining competitive were very real. Non-white workers were far cheaper, largely because their employers were not compelled to pay for expensive social provisions; conversely, the United States possessed the advantages of a huge, relatively uniform internal market, permitting mass production and consumption with high wages. But there was still a way ahead for Europe, Siegfried insisted. Asians, for example, might be able to copy European innovations but still lacked creative genius; so, for that matter, did the United States. "The Americans, as we know, are interested only in solving simple problems. They only mine the easiest minerals, and they avoid industries which avoid too close application, too great patience, and too careful calculation." Economically, Europe had lost the Americas and was losing the Far East but could still hope to hold sway in Africa and "Western Asia." Moreover, "Europe still retains two vital factors: her genius for creative invention, and her appreciation of spirituality, both of which are bound up with her traditional culture. We are thus forced to rely upon our own superiority, the unique stronghold into which the overseas countries can penetrate only with difficulty: quality, 'services,' international finance – this is where Europe undoubtedly excels." The United States was catching up, but its economy was still not as evolved in this regard.[73]

Having argued that the continent could still compete economically, Siegfried nevertheless predicted that difficult choices lay ahead. Even if Europeans could still provide high-quality goods and services, these could not sustain the continent's current population and what he deemed its unreasonable expectations of high living standards and social welfare. One option was to embrace a controlled economy, as Nazi Germany was currently attempting and of which he clearly disapproved; "Life there is virtually on a war-time basis, which has meant loss of liberty, a reduced standard of living, a strong police, [and] concentration camps – everything served up with a coating of mysticism to make the pill easier to swallow." Another option was some variant of Americanization, as increasingly adopted in Britain and France, where "the common people are enjoying an increasing amount of cheap semi-luxury which seems to satisfy them."[74] But that option would ultimately be soul-destroying, Siegfried contended. In a closing passage that blended a commitment to intellectual liberty with an evocation of the continent's racial identity, he warned:

If Europe conforms to the present trend and sells her soul to mass production, she will undermine the foundations of the civilization on which she lives. The hero who best symbolizes our old continent is Prometheus. When he stole the fire from Jupiter to give it to man, he may have offended the gods, but he called into being that hidden soul of our Western civilization, the revolt against fatality and supine passivity. From this revolt has gushed forth our technical invention and our undisciplined creative genius. Let us not be crushed by the American masses or the Asiatic masses. Let us remain true to the spirit of the Caucasian host, for even the most punctilious racialists cannot pretend that it was not Aryan.[75]

Siegfried thus emphasized how the racial and cultural bases of European superiority were intertwined; the foundations of European greatness could be traced to the continent's whiteness, as well as a commitment to freedom, creativity, and innovation. Though he did not make explicit assertions on this occasion, the latter qualities coincided significantly with characteristics that Siegfried had often ascribed to France in particular – devotion to liberty, a focus on quality and service, and attention to detail, though in the case of financial services British pre-eminence was undeniable. Moreover, his admonition for Europe to remain true to its values as it looked to an uncertain future echoed his earlier writings about challenges to French identity in a rapidly changing, American-influenced world. He continued to advance similar views during these years, for instance in a preface to a book entitled *Le destin des races blanches*, by the legal scholar and essayist Henri Decugis.[76]

In the winter of 1937–38, Siegfried visited Palestine and Egypt, a journey that suggested a growing interest in the Mediterranean region's significance for Western culture. The focal point of his travels was the Suez Canal, which he compared to the Panama Canal as an illustration of the realignments underway in global politics, but he also commented on other developments in the Middle East for *Le Petit Havre*. To his mind, the region was another instance of Western-led progress that faced fierce local resistance. The establishment of petroleum pipelines required the British and French militaries to establish a "freedom of the desert" akin to the freedom of the seas. The British had major strategic interests in Palestine, bolstered by a commitment to support Jewish settlement, but this had placed them in an untenable situation. The Palestinian Arabs, unable to cope with such rapid changes, were in revolt; "The current crisis here has taken on the character of a terrorist movement, above all anti-Jewish but tending to become anti-European."[77]

Travelling from Palestine to Egypt, he marvelled at the Suez Canal but grasped that the turbulent political environment made its future uncertain. Despite an enormous "Asiatic" peasant population that cared little about modern comforts, a long history of foreign control and a powerful Islamic sentiment that hindered the incorporation of minority groups into nationalist movements, an Egyptian patriotism rooted in the middle classes had been sparked by Wilsonian rhetoric. It was given a voice by the Wafd movement, which sought to reduce foreign control over the economy and increase opportunities for Egyptians. Control over the Canal, which had been built and was still run by foreign interests, was prominent in the broader dispute. Siegfried doubted that turning it over to non-Westerners, even if they had "diplomas," would be advisable, as they lacked the "spirit of initiative" and "genius for administration" that were the hallmarks of European civilization.[78] "Orientals," he asserted, did not apply laws without taking individual interests into account, though he conceded that such an attitude existed to some extent in France as well, in contrast to the "Anglo-Saxon" countries. Who managed the shipment of goods had broader implications, he noted, for intercontinental contact could also promote the spread of disease. Recalling the writings of the nineteenth-century racial theorist Count Arthur de Gobineau, Siegfried commented that Asia was "the continent of prestige but ... also that of contamination"; Suez was on the front line in this regard, having become part of the West's advanced defence system against contagion. Perhaps Egyptian doctors might take over these duties, but true Western methods would still be lacking. Events in Egypt encapsulated a broader trend whereby nonwhites, having benefited from European technology and culture, believed that they should be masters of their own destiny in all respects. With the possible exception of the Japanese, Siegfried doubted whether they were up to this task. "The nationalism of these *nouveaux riches* of civilization, whose ambitions we have unleashed, does not seem to ensure that the world progresses."[79]

A similar message emerged from his subsequent book, *Suez, Panama et les routes maritimes mondiales*, which appeared in the winter of 1940. The book's first section, dealing with Suez, was often celebratory in tone, especially with respect to France's Ferdinand de Lesseps, who was depicted as a heroic figure, overcoming political, financial, and practical obstacles – including loss of the right to use forced labour from Egypt and being compelled to hire "free" workmen. The Canal, Siegfried concluded, was a singular humanitarian achievement, promoting commerce for all, a private initiative that reflected "ideals which were among the finest things produced by nineteenth-century Liberalism during this period."[80] Even the subsequent British occupation of Egypt did not undermine this achievement, for the Canal remained an international venture – though also a quintessentially French accomplishment. It was essential that the company and operations remain under the control of Westerners for as long as possible, though "Greeks, Italians, Syrians, and sometimes the Jews" could play a useful practical role. But the day of reckoning could not be avoided. In 1968, the Canal Company's concession would expire and new arrangements would have to be finalized: "[T]he only workable solution will be one which is satisfactory at once to Egypt and to Europe – again supposing that thirty years from now Europe is still able to impose her will."[81]

If Suez reflected the glories of nineteenth-century Eurocentric civilization, Panama symbolized the changing international order of the twentieth. Here too, de Lesseps had made heroic efforts to build a transoceanic crossing, but financially overreached and underestimated the challenges involved, not the least of which were the tropical diseases that decimated the French-led undertaking. As the venture unravelled and was utterly discredited in an ensuing political-financial scandal, the United States was well positioned to intervene. It supported Panamanian secession from Colombia, and then proceeded to complete the canal. Whereas in *La crise de l'Europe* Siegfried had emphasized the limits of American ingenuity, here he was more respectful. The Americans had medical advances at their disposal that the French had lacked, and the fact that their project was a state-led enterprise gave it resources that its predecessor could never hope to attain. Siegfried concluded that the final product "does honour to the American race, and classes them with the Romans among the great creative geniuses of the universe." For the labourers themselves – many of them Jamaican – he had far less respect, characterizing them as "lazy and vain," but able to work in the difficult climate and motivated by "American customs" and "the atmosphere of materialistic civilization in which they were now living."[82]

Comparing the two canals, Siegfried noted that they reflected predominant patterns of world trade. In terms of the proportion of trade Britain still led the way, dominating the Suez route to a proportionately greater extent than the United States did in the case of the Panama Canal. Nevertheless, the building and operation of the latter reflected America's growing clout; "[T]he Old Continent remains the principal centre of world trade, but it is no longer the only centre. New currents have now been set in motion beyond its confines, for North America has already become an independent centre. All this is rather like the twilight of the Roman Empire, when a vast structure, which yesterday had been universal, began to break up. However, the present structure still exists." The endurance of this structure, he concluded, illustrated the possibility for continuing international trade and linkages despite the recent outbreak of war in Europe. Moreover, both canals were products of Western civilization, administered to ensure "the rights of international commerce." The capacity to do so, the "creative genius" that entailed a "sense of large-scale administration" remained "the sole prerogative of the white race, and even of a limited section of that race." Other peoples were misguided in thinking that they could simply emulate whites. "Doubtless that is true enough so far as daily routine and current business is concerned, but when it comes to maintaining material civilization at the high level to which we have brought it, then it is a horse of another colour, as the saying goes."[83]

— * —

On the eve of the Second World War, Siegfried had in many ways fulfilled the agenda that he had set for himself when he addressed the Collège de France in 1933. He had carried out extensive research into the political geography of the Midi; doing so confirmed his belief in enduring political temperaments but also the significance of French Protestantism in shaping the nation's commitment to liberty. He acknowledged dysfunction in French political life but saw his country as a precious repository of individualism at a time when the latter was imperilled.

As we have seen, during these years he also travelled widely, beyond the Anglo-Saxon nations that had been his primary focus in the 1920s. He gained brief exposure to Central and Eastern Europe, and a more in-depth view of developments in Latin America, whose New World geography and ethnically mixed population placed it, to his mind, on the frontiers of Western civilization. While Siegfried hoped that the Latin character – which included a significant French cultural influence – of the continent would be preserved, these qualities had become more precarious given the growth of American influence and Indigenous nationalism.

These observations fed into his broader conceptualization of global politics in this period, in which a largely unitary and French-inflected conception of European values was threatened by Americanization and anti-imperial nationalism in various parts of the world. These challenges were intertwined; American goods, values, and mental habits seemed to be gaining ground everywhere, winning over local populations while threatening established elites and ties to European culture. The Suez and Panama canals were particularly revealing case studies for Siegfried, highlighting how the magnificent achievements of Europeans such as de Lesseps now faced increasingly formidable American competition.

Siegfried was not alone in his fixation on challenges to European supremacy; various commentators perceived a continent in crisis. In response, some, such as Lothrop Stoddard and Oswald Spengler, sought to articulate a sense of transnational, albeit threatened, white identity. Others, such as Arnold Toynbee, instead emphasized a conception of Western civilization as defined by liberal, democratic, and Christian values, though still associated with whiteness.[84] For his part, Siegfried invoked a transnational white identity associated with unmatched technological and organizational prowess, but also stressed growing Western fragmentation due primarily to the appeal of a United States that increasingly diverged from traditional European values. This challenge continued to loom large in his thinking even when the outbreak of the Second World War compelled him to reflect on intra-European conflict.

# 5

# War and Occupation

In the opening months of the war, Siegfried did his patriotic duty, using his influence to promote the Anglo-French alliance while encouraging greater American involvement in the conflict. He called for a renewal of the partnership of 1917–18, with France providing intellectual and spiritual leadership, supported by the political genius of Britain and the material power of America. To his mind, the struggle against Nazism meant quashing a deadly threat to individualist values, which were properly the preserve of whites. Anxious about the radically egalitarian implications of invoking the French Revolutionary tradition, Siegfried envisioned a war effort that would preserve Western global supremacy and established liberal institutions. Though mindful of the threat posed by the Third Reich, he tended to discuss it in abstract terms, while at the same time reminding his audiences of the dangers of Communism and more generally an excessively materialist conception of progress.

Following France's crushing defeat and the advent of the Vichy regime, Siegfried decided to remain in Paris and maintain his established activities as best he could. As a result, he participated in various accommodations made by Sciences Po, the Collège de France, and the Musée social to the conditions of the occupation and the prerogatives of the National Revolution, though his refusal to serve on Vichy's Conseil national signalled a desire to maintain some distance. In his writing, he made some adjustments to the new ideological environment, paying more attention to issues such as leadership and incorporating a more biological dimension into his conceptualization of race; some of his publications from these years clearly contributed to a xenophobic, exclusionary climate. This was the case even when

Siegfried's conclusions derived from preoccupations that dated to the pre-war years, notably his negative attitudes about recent immigration to the United States.

It would, however, be unfair to suggest that he entirely abandoned his liberal convictions during this period. A distaste for authoritarianism is evident in some of his wartime writings, as is an attachment to the principles and achievements of the officially reviled Third Republic. Siegfried continued to pursue projects that he commenced in the 1930s, such as the roots of Western supremacy and the character of Mediterranean civilization; doing so reinforced his belief that modern materialism, as embodied by the United States, was undermining ideals at the core of European civilization, but did not lead to support for a Nazi-dominated New Order. Instead, Siegfried appears to have remained sympathetic to the Western allies, and to have had some contact with elements of the Resistance. This helps to explain why, despite controversy about his wartime conduct and writings, he remained highly respected into the postwar years.

## FRANCE AT WAR, 1939–40

As noted in chapter 3, by 1939 Siegfried had begun arguing for a renewal of democratic solidarity, making one of his most detailed cases for it in *Foreign Affairs*, whose editor, Hamilton Fish, was a strong supporter of US ties with Britain and France.[1] Yet his analysis, though invoking a rich ideological heritage, was carefully circumscribed. He declared that the values of the French Revolution were under attack and must be defended, but that their potentially radical complications were to be avoided. The underlying principle of the Revolution, he asserted, was "that respect is due to every individual human being – considered as a thinking being, capable of reflection, judgment, decision." This principle, he continued, was intended to apply to people of all backgrounds; for that reason, it was "magnificent and perhaps also dangerous." It challenged the prerogatives of ruling elites by asserting the claims of a quasi-mystical conception of "the People." Its conception of equality transcended the bounds of nation or race. It was "obliged" to be anticlerical in opposition to the claims of the Catholic Church, even though its commitment to the values of human liberty and dignity accorded with the message of the Gospels.[2]

There was thus a serious risk of going too far. "In her resolve to destroy absolutism [France] has always been ready to smite her

War and Occupation

government, somewhat as though in hitting the apple William Tell had also killed his son." Siegfried reiterated that he saw the acceptance of racial equality as impractical. "In the first burst of their enthusiasm, the French had not given a thought to limitations of race." He also remained preoccupied by a broader global tendency toward materialism and conformity that threatened to swamp individual freedoms, though he conceded that such trends were especially dangerous when coupled with totalitarian political ambitions. "Aspiring to the dominion of Europe, the aggressor governments are actually putting material progress at the service of passions that emanate from sheer brutality." Soviet tyranny had to be resisted despite the current alignment between some French radicals and Marxism. "The battle that must be offered to National Socialist or Fascist tyranny is not very different, though the case is clearer." Finally, despite the fierce conflicts of the past, the defenders of 1789 now had a powerful ally in the Church and its message of "respect for human individuality."[3]

Siegfried's invocation of revolutionary principles was, then, quite selective. He disputed racial equality and called for the preservation of individualism in the context of aligning with traditional religious values. He also equated the Soviet, Nazi, and Fascist threats. And while calling for cooperation between the Western democracies, he still highlighted important contrasts between British, American, and French political cultures. Britain's institutions bore the influence of its aristocracy, and its democratic tradition tended toward insularity, though "in everything that pertains to governmental practice the lessons that England has given to other countries are much more valuable than anything that could be learned from revolutionary France." Turning to the United States, Siegfried commented that "[a]s a Frenchman shaped by the Revolution of '89 I feel closer to the American democracy, which sprang as ours sprang from the philosophy of the eighteenth century." But even though America's social structure was more egalitarian than France's, its appeal as a democracy was limited by the fact that it applied only to whites, even though Siegfried judged this situation more "reasonable" than the French approach.[4] In his eyes, the looming confrontation between liberal democracies and totalitarian states was framed by a general crisis of social change and potentially destabilizing challenges to racial hierarchies.

Siegfried continued to travel, teach, and write during the ensuing "Phoney War" of 1939–40. Less than three weeks after the declaration of war he was in the Azores; in 1940, he visited Portugal and Algeria, and returned to the Eastern Mediterranean, stopping in Tunis, Alexandria, Jerusalem, Beirut – where he spent time with High Commissioner Gabriel Puaux, a relative from his mother's family – Damascus, and Aleppo. He finished the journey in Turkey, meeting with President Ismet Inönü in Ankara, and delivering a lecture at Istanbul University.[5] During his stay in Jerusalem, Siegfried held a wide-ranging discussion with faculty at the Hebrew University; he came away convinced that, despite varying national origins and the trappings of Western culture, Palestine's Jewish community was irremediably foreign. "I understood, in a flash of inspiration, that they could certainly hate the Muslims, even kill each other, but ultimately their conception of society, based on a totalitarian mystique, was the same: an Oriental conception." In his Istanbul lecture, he considered the key role of the Mediterranean in shaping Western civilization, a subject to which he devoted growing attention in the years to come. Not surprisingly, he offered his own country as a leading exemplar of this deep historical connection: "A Frenchman for example, especially on the Mediterranean coast, has two thousand years behind him and knows it. When he looks around, or beneath him, everywhere he grasps the trace of successive and superposed civilizations, of which he constitutes the upper layer."[6]

But further analysis of the Mediterranean would have to wait, for during the months of the *drôle de guerre* Siegfried was intensely busy, performing tasks on behalf of his government while continuing to teach. Doing so, he explained to his economic geography course at the Collège de France in the winter of 1940, served "to affirm – in the age of propaganda – the search for the truth for its own sake." But while stressing his objectivity, Siegfried's course notes highlighted the weaknesses of France's enemies. In a comparative ranking of countries, which he presented in February 1940, based upon natural resources, the quality of the population, strategic location, and politico-economic stability, both Germany and the USSR scored lower than France, Britain, or the United States. Germany had a good strategic position and a talented populace but was lacking in natural resources and its people lacked a sense of balance. As for the Soviet Union – which Siegfried always referred to as "Russia" – while its vast size and resources could not be denied, it was strategically vulnerable, and its people possessed only limited capacities.[7]

Though Siegfried evidently disliked the term "propaganda," in various lectures and writings he continued to promote Anglo-French solidarity, while still underscoring differences between the two countries. For example, in late 1939 he delivered a series of broadcasts on British democracy for Radio Paris, in which he stressed that, while full of contradictions and arguably unsuitable for export outside the Dominions, the system had the great merit of stability. Britain's monarchy enjoyed wide support as long as it preserved its nonpartisan role. Its parliamentary system was profoundly different from its French counterpart, characterized by a higher degree of ministerial stability and a greater concentration of executive power, as well as a less politicized civil service. In contrast to French deputies, British MPS were more tightly disciplined and governed less, which helped to explain, in Siegfried's opinion, the solidity of British finances. The unelected House of Lords had lost some of its powers over time but remained important and still provided some cabinet ministers. Overall, he praised the British system as a vigorous mixture of liberty, democracy, and self-restraint.[8]

Siegfried also commended these virtues to English-speaking audiences, contributing an appreciation of the British Empire to the *Oxford Pamphlets on World Affairs* series in 1940. Here he urged the defence of the empire for the sake of Western, indeed global, civilization, which he predicted "would not survive the decline of the white race." Because Britain had given its Dominions considerable autonomy, he explained, the empire – now more properly a commonwealth – was stronger than ever, "the political expression of an Anglo-Saxon civilization founded on liberalism." This system benefited Europe, America, and the wider world, by guaranteeing freedom of the seas and encouraging connections between different continents, but also through the diffusion of liberal ideals. Were Britain's presence in the Far East to crumble, Siegfried predicted, the primacy of the "white race" outside Europe would be endangered, which would be catastrophic. In the West, were Britain to be supplanted by Nazi Germany, pernicious beliefs would come to the fore; "[M]aterial efficiency might not be less, but a certain dignity of political life, linked with respect for the rights of the individual and with his freedom as a citizen, would be gravely endangered."[9] Siegfried thus urged the defence of liberal values, but these would remain restricted to whites, whose global hegemony must also be upheld.

Beyond his writings, Siegfried engaged in practical efforts to deepen Anglo-French cooperation. As early as the spring of 1938, the Royal Institute of International Affairs (Chatham House) and the French

Centre d'études de politique étrangère (CEPE) had established a joint study group to that end. With the outbreak of war, the British Foreign Office was drawn in; within weeks, the historian Arnold Toynbee – a scholar interested in promoting connections between Britain and Europe, and an acquaintance of Siegfried – began promoting closer Anglo-French cooperation, out of which ideas of a union or federation were soon bruited. Study groups were established by Chatham House (much of whose staff was now based in Oxford) and CEPE to examine the possibilities; Siegfried was a participant in the latter.[10] He visited Oxford in November 1939 to discuss the development of common war aims and presented a report he co-authored to the CEPE in February 1940. This document assessed the prospects of a Franco-British union within the context of a broader revitalization of international organizations envisioned for the poswar era. Noting that the question of what to do with Germany would greatly complicate the creation of a postwar European federation, the report concluded that it was advisable to concentrate first upon a smaller-scale project, in this case a federation between Britain and France. Even here, there were plenty of obstacles and the authors recommended moving gradually, implementing limited agreements first while avoiding getting bogged down in finer points of detail.[11] Nevertheless, by April discussions had advanced to the point where Toynbee drafted an "Act of Perpetual Association" between the two countries.

Following the German offensive against Western Europe that began on 10 May 1940, these discussions took on greater urgency. There had already been arguments that Toynbee's proposal was too timid; as catastrophe loomed the following month, there was a dramatic call for an "indissoluble union," aimed at bolstering French resistance. It was of course unsuccessful in its goal, as Marshal Pétain's administration took office and instead sought terms with the Third Reich.[12] By this time Siegfried had left Paris, and it seems that he was not heavily involved in these last-ditch efforts. Though he had expressed admiration for the British, given his focus on the distinctiveness of their traditions he would likely have continued to advocate a gradual approach. In any case, it was now a moot point.

Siegfried had also promoted Franco-American ties during this period. Writing in the *Revue de Paris*, he made the case that despite old traditions and current disputes, there were powerful reasons for the United States to take an interest in supporting the democratic powers. To be sure, America had a long tradition of regarding itself as self-sufficient, and isolationist sentiment was potent; indeed, Siegfried was dismayed at the apparent indifference of many Americans to recent threats to Western power, and white prestige. "I remain struck by the fact that, during the blockade of Tientsin [Tianjin] by the Japanese, public opinion in the United States was not more disturbed by an ordeal whose repercussions affected, in sum, all people of the white race." But America could not avoid entanglement in the wider world. Moreover, there was an idealistic quality to US foreign policy, shaped by Protestant ethics and a belief in the superiority of democracy. The United States was also a critic of totalitarian regimes, which Siegfried attributed partly to Jewish influence but primarily to deeper American values, contending that: "Jewish propaganda has played an important role in this arousal of an entire people against a system of government that contradicts some of the most evident principles of Western civilization, to be sure, but one can argue, without fear of making a mistake, that Puritan protest alone has sufficed." US leaders were also aware of threats such as growing German influence in Latin America. Above all, the United States had long benefited from the liberal international order sustained by the British Empire. Though acknowledging currents of anti-British opinion, Siegfried predicted that Anglo-Saxon solidarity, based upon national interests and a shared heritage, meant that America would likely intervene if the British Empire faced ruin. He asserted that it would not seek to supplant Britain, however: "The United States does not have the ambition to do, in the world, what England has done; perhaps it does not have the genius for it."[13] Future events, of course, confounded this prediction.

Siegfried made more idealistic and urgent appeals to French and American audiences in the spring of 1940, again in the pages of the *Revue de Paris* and *Foreign Affairs*. In both cases, he depicted the three leading democracies as making their own invaluable contributions to Western civilization. Bemoaning the current division of Europe "into two hostile zones," he concluded that "the Western civilization to which we bind ourselves could only then survive by seeking, beyond the oceans, necessary compensations," which meant ensuring US involvement. France, Britain, and the United States were now the leading advocates of liberalism, to the point that two of them had taken up arms to defend it. For the moment, France was the leading military force, but Siegfried asserted that its most important contribution was ultimately intellectual; "I would place, at the centre, the magnificent confidence of the French in human intelligence, which is to say humanity itself ... Any thought filtered by the French mind, is imbued with order and clarity. Moreover it becomes transmissible, like a currency having value everywhere, which everyone can use."[14] Britain's role was more practical, though equally significant; "[I]t is especially in business and politics that the English contribution is inseparable from the development of our civilization." Sadly, the liberal principles at the heart of Britain's achievements were currently on the defensive, because the country had embraced protectionism.[15]

Turning to the United States, Siegfried concentrated not just on its material prowess but also its national ideals. America had perfected the techniques of mass production, but the motivation for this splendid material achievement was ultimately a principle "to enhance the dignity of the human being by continually raising the plane on which he lives. America has sought to make men better by making them happier. America is the country of social progress."[16] In combination, Franco-Anglo-American values prized human dignity and liberty. By contrast, a world dominated by Germany would be unrecognizable. "The concept of a free humanity in which all men are equal, at least in the respect owing to them as human beings, is replaced by the iron doctrine that a few supermen have been created to exploit the masses that are born congenitally inferior." The United States could not ignore these developments, but at present the situation remained agonizingly unclear: "One may guess sooner or later the United States will decide to accept world responsibilities transcending the limits of the American continent. Its physical power, its prestige, its wealth, its unparalleled industrial equipment, the fact that it is part and parcel of Western civilization – all drive it in that direction. But until it makes its decision Europe alone must uphold the world order on which our civilization depends."[17]

Though displaying tinges of resentment toward American non-intervention, Siegfried had, in his way, sought to make a compelling case for US solidarity with Britain and France. By the spring of 1940, he was preparing to do more. With money from James Hazen Hyde, a Paris-based American financier who was a leading supporter of the Alliance française in the United States, arrangements had been made by the Collège de France and the Ministry of Education for him to give lectures at several provincial universities in support of Franco-American solidarity.[18] Plans were also underway for him to spend the 1940–41 academic year at Harvard. Even after the German invasion, the French defeat, and the installation of the Vichy regime, the new minister of education initially recommended that Siegfried still go to the United States.[19] For reasons that are not entirely clear – it may have been that Siegfried simply decided it was more appropriate for him to stay, as former associates later suggested – the exchange did not proceed.

Siegfried's activities in support of French cultural diplomacy during the phony war of 1939–40 reflected some general features of the Third Republic's propaganda efforts at the time. Headed by the playwright Jean Giraudoux, the Commissariat général à l'information and the governments that supervised it have been criticized for chaotic organization, meagre funding, and crafting messages that were too elevated and lacking in conviction.[20] To be sure, Siegfried's own proclamations of French virtues, invocations of solidarity with Britain, and analyses of American attitudes were aimed at an educated audience, and his tone could certainly be guarded. Nevertheless, as Robert Young has pointed out, as far as the United States was concerned French efforts to gain support for their cause in a relatively restrained manner appear to have had some effect, as indicated by increasingly sympathetic press coverage and the shock wave that resonated throughout America following the French collapse.[21]

### RESPONDING TO OCCUPATION

As of 27 May 1940, Siegfried and his family were still in Paris, but he had arranged to stay with Madame Métin in the Breton commune of Ploubazlanec. Correspondence from July indicates that the family had relocated there, though there is no record, it seems, of their experiences during that terrible summer. While the Siegfrieds had the resources and connections that eased some of the difficulties of that period, the psychological shock was no doubt severe; the fact that Siegfried himself apparently chose not to write about it in any detail is suggestive.[22] By 21 July, however, he was already planning a return to Paris, writing to the administrator of the Collège de France to confirm that its administration was still in Paris and that new arrangements for pay were being made.[23]

Writing shortly after Siegfried's death, his friend Pierre Hamp praised this decision to remain and resume his normal activities. It would have been relatively easy, Hamp asserted, for Siegfried to emigrate to Britain or America, but instead he chose solidarity in shared adversity:

Sharing in the misfortune of his country was a position of conscience for him ... He ate only what his ration card entitled him to. He behaved in [a spirit of] national solidarity and continued his work as a professor in Paris when he could have easily taken refuge at Vence, in Mas Saint-Dont, among the perfumes of the same kinds that enchanted Virgil ...
He continued in his roles of professor at the Institut d'études politiques and president of the Musée social, as if the German army had never occupied Paris. Every day he was there to sustain methods and to form men. In the minds of his students he remade France.[24]

Hamp's emphasis on continuity in Siegfried's routine was at least partially borne out in the case of the Académie des sciences morales et politiques. He attended sessions regularly, presenting on topics such as Paul Cambon's role in French diplomacy, and international maritime routes during the war; articles on these subjects also appeared in *Le Temps* and *Le Figaro*. Siegfried also commented on colleagues' presentations, including one by the Marquis de Canisy of the Paris Chamber of Commerce that discussed professional training, and another by former cabinet minister Louis Germain-Martin recounting a journey through the North Pacific in 1920. And while Siegfried did not participate in the commissions of the Institut, he did serve on prize juries, notably the Prix Santour for 1941.[25]

The situation at the Collège de France proved more complicated. Its chief administrator, Edmond Faral, made it clear that faculty members had to make their own decisions but was personally keen to resume the work of the Collège as soon as possible, even though three faculty members were soon arrested and four more, classified as Jewish, were removed from their positions. Faral did request two exemptions from the anti-Jewish laws but otherwise applied the regulations; he also acted to forestall potential protests following the arrest of the left-leaning physicist Paul Langevin. In contrast to suggestions from Marshal Pétain that replacements for the chairs vacated by arrests and purges be deferred for the time being, Faral countered that it was important to maintain the institution at full strength, though its faculty apparently balked at accepting excessively pro-Vichy candidates.[26]

Like the other faculty at the Collège who avoided repressive measures or racial legislation, Siegfried did not raise any objections, at least not in public. He also participated in some meetings of the Assembly of Professors, supporting Étienne Gilson, a scholar of medieval philosophy, in an unsuccessful attempt in 1943 to have the Chair in sociology previously held by Maurice Halbwachs – vacated because of the anti-Semitic laws – replaced with one in the history of the moral sciences.[27] As for teaching, Siegfried continued to give courses on the geography of regional opinion and the international economy, in the latter case now focusing on the Mediterranean as the progenitor of Western civilization and a crossroads between civilizations.[28]

In contrast to the Collège, at both Sciences Po and the Musée social, Siegfried played a leadership role. Given its reputation for having an "Anglo-Saxon" orientation, Sciences Po was suspect in the eyes of the German occupiers, who shut it down on 26 July 1940, following up with searches and the seizure of some materials. The school's chief administrator, Roger Seydoux, responded by meeting with Karl Epting of the German embassy, whom he had known before the war through the German Institute in Paris, to determine how it might be reopened. Subsequently, some of the school's courses deemed objectionable by the occupation authorities were dropped. In addition, several faculty members – notably the economist Jacques Rueff, who was Jewish – left for the unoccupied zone. New courses and staff were also brought in to appeal to the occupier's sensibilities, including a course on "German unity." All of this facilitated the reopening of the École libre that fall; it also established a satellite campus in Lyon, beyond direct German control for the time being, which catered to displaced students.[29]

The institution also made various accommodations to the Vichy regime. Sciences Po was not a monolithic bastion of Pétainism – some former students found their way into the Resistance – but there were links to the new order through various alumni as well as faculty members, including two of Vichy's justice ministers, Raphaël Alibert and Joseph Barthélemy. The École libre also welcomed prominent members of the administration as lecturers. They included Jean Bichelonne, who became minister of industrial production, and the famed former tennis player Jean Borotra, now a high-ranking official in the education ministry. Moreover, Sciences Po introduced a physical education requirement and new, very difficult, entrance exams for women, aimed at reducing female enrollments. Such changes were very much in keeping with Vichy's mania for fitness and its animus toward women's employment outside the home.[30]

Regarding Siegfried's individual role, he continued to give courses on economic geography, international exchanges, and the United States at the Rue St Guillaume in Paris. He also taught, it seems, at the Centre d'études politiques in Lyon. Here classes were given in highly concentrated time periods, but it seems that whether they were delivered in Paris or Lyon, the content of Siegfried's courses remained much as they had before the war.[31] For instance, in a lecture on Anglo-American relations delivered in Lyon in May 1941, he emphasized that despite some friction it would be wrong to see the British and the Americans as rivals. Both were invested in preserving an Anglo-Saxon world order based on commercial and political liberalism and the presence of the "white race" outside Europe. It was vital to understand this relationship in the contemporary era, where the focus was shifting from nations to continents and civilizations. Similarly, in a course given at Sciences Po in 1941–42 on American civilization, Siegfried restated many of his earlier criticisms of the United States' economic and ethnic structures, as well as the view that "[t]he European is ... no doubt superior as an individual (but in a more difficult environment)." He closed by surmising that it was increasingly unlikely that America would remain aloof from the growing international crisis.[32]

There were some changes in Siegfried's outlook as well, though, notably his conceptualization of race. Beyond the cultural and historical dimensions that he had long assigned to the term, in his wartime lectures he adopted categories derived from racial anthropology as well. For instance, in his 1942–43 course on the geography of politics in Languedoc, he retained his usual geological, sociological, and cultural-historical foci but also drew distinctions within the population based on cephalic indexes – measuring the ratio of breadth to length in human skulls – an approach that harkened back to the nineteenth century.[33] Tillmann notes that Siegfried contacted Paul Lester, assistant director of anthropology at the Musée de l'homme, with a request to develop a map of the races of Europe; under Lester's direction, Musée staff produced a "very simplified" map, derived mainly from the work of the German racial anthropologist Egon von Eickstedt, which demarcated the chief racial groups of Europe while suppressing "small circles" that denoted "enclaves of foreign races in the principal domain of a given race." Moreover, Birnbaum has shown that Siegfried took interest in the work of the racist thinker Georges Montandon, making extensive notes on his writings and developing an increasing interest in the characteristics of the "Mediterranean race," though in his wartime publications he avoided identifying openly with Montandon's ideas.[34]

Aside from teaching his classes, Siegfried played a key role in a reorganization of the École libre aimed at adapting it to a more technocratic and interventionist era and at blunting criticisms that it was elitist, even dilettantish. Beginning in 1941, he headed the school's Comité des études, which was charged with updating its programs. In their early sessions, members of the Comité lamented that youth tended to focus too much on grades and short-term career preparation rather than acquiring general culture and good habits. But they accepted that the École had to adapt to the times by providing the foundations for training in more technical subjects.[35] Among the key changes recommended by the Comité, which was implemented in 1943, was the creation of a new one-year preparatory program for entering students who had not completed a postsecondary diploma. Simply put, the members of the committee found that since the Great War, entering students who only had a baccalaureate were insufficiently prepared. They would now be required to complete a series of courses, including one on economic geography taught by Siegfried, to an acceptable standard before they could proceed to more specialized studies during the second and third year.[36]

These plans resonated broadly with the priorities of the Vichy regime as it sought to reverse the supposed laxity of the late Third Republic. But the reforms were also the product of impulses at work within the École libre before the war broke out, and they also looked ahead to the postwar era. Indeed, by the time the school implemented its new first-year program, many of its administrators and staff had distanced themselves from Vichy, with some of them developing Resistance contacts. In part, this was in response to the growing prospects of an Allied victory, as well as the increasingly repressive tactics of the Germans and the Vichy authorities. Abel Bonnard, minister of education after Pierre Laval's return to office in 1942, was therefore suspicious of Sciences Po and some of its faculty, including Siegfried. An undated note on Siegfried from Bonnard's files characterizes the former's outlook in the following terms: "clearly Anglophile last year, speaking of 'my friend Roosevelt,' calmer and more circumspect this year – yet looks down upon racism."[37] This brief but telling comment suggests that Siegfried paid attention to the ever-shifting political context but was also regarded with some suspicion by a radicalizing regime.

166 France in the World

For Siegfried had kept his distance from Vichy in some ways; in January 1941, he was nominated to its Conseil national, an unelected consultative body whose members included former parliamentarians and other representative elites. He refused the nomination, however, and was removed from the nominal roll in November.[38] He did not attend the first meeting of the Conseil's commission on national administrative reform, though when approached by the government for advice he complied. His input influenced the commission to include Normandy as one of the provinces envisaged within a regionalist-inspired administrative overhaul. It is worth noting, however, that in his memo to Admiral Jean Fernet, the secretary general of the Conseil national, Siegfried defended the virtues of the department as an administrative unit and expressed reservations about the lack of consultation that characterized the current process, in comparison to the initial wave of administrative reform during the French Revolution.[39]

The ambiguity of Siegfried's relationship with Vichy is also suggested by his association with the Comité d'études pour la France. The Comité was a think tank that explored a wide range of political, economic, and social issues and counted among its members several other Sciences Po staff and faculty, including Seydoux, as well as the engineer-social reformer Auguste Detoeuf and the demographer Alfred Sauvy. However, Vichy officials also attended, and the Comité – which eventually had hundreds of members – kept the regime informed about its deliberations. Indeed, some of its proposals echoed classic Vichy concerns – a fixation on France's decadence; the need for practical, moral, and civic education; and the desire to nurture strong leaders, for example. Exactly how prominent a role Siegfried played in the Comité is unclear, though it is worth noting that around this time he also led one or two discussions for a forum based in Lyon hosted by Paul Bastid, a former Radical deputy and a critic of Vichy, which in 1942 evolved into the Comité général d'études, a think tank for the Resistance. He was also reportedly involved in an anti-Vichy group hosted by the engineer Jean de Traz, which had been meeting since the armistice, and by 1942 was forwarding information to the Gaullists.[40]

By spring 1942, Siegfried was growing more confident of an eventual Allied victory. In May of that year, he breakfasted with Pastor Marc Boegner, head of the French Protestant Federation, during which he suggested that the Allied occupations of Diego Suarez and New Caledonia were "inevitable," and that Dakar might be their next target. Boegner observed of Siegfried, "He pursues very effective teaching at the Collège de France and the [École libre des] sciences politiques. His authority over [our] youth is greater than ever due to the firmness of his attitude." The following month, in a meeting with an unnamed American diplomat, Siegfried asserted that the war would eventually turn in favour of the Allies and claimed that a landing in France would receive considerable support from its army and populace.[41] This does not necessarily mean that Siegfried's attitudes toward the Western allies were uniformly positive, of course. In January 1946, the journal *Les Lettres françaises*, which had its roots in the intellectual resistance, claimed that following a lecture he gave in New York in 1945, in response to audience questions Siegfried expressed anger about wartime Allied conduct. He strongly criticized the Allied bombing of France, and admitted that during the war he had wondered who among "his friends in London and Washington" would have collaborated under German occupation.[42] If this account can be fully credited – and here the postwar political context, in which Siegfried's conservatism clashed with *Les Lettres françaises*'s left-wing stance, should be borne in mind – it still seems clear that Siegfried desired an Allied victory.

As the war went on, Sciences Po's dealings with Vichy and the occupation authorities became increasingly fraught. When Joseph Barthélemy, having left his post as Vichy's minister of justice, sought to return to the classroom in 1943, the administration refused. Barthélemy later accused his former colleagues of hypocrisy, singling out Siegfried by claiming that he "had initially given the regime his invaluable support; he was not long in withdrawing it and has just been rewarded by his accession to the most illustrious state body," the latter a reference to Siegfried's election to the Académie française in 1944.[43] Sciences Po also aroused the ire of the Vichy authorities because it helped to obstruct the recruitment of its students for the hated Service du travail obligatoire, which would have sent them to work in Germany. Despite a grilling from Abel Bonnard in 1943 on the institution's stance, Roger Seydoux was undeterred, and in fact began to nurture various contacts with prominent resisters, notably Michel Debré, a former colleague who had eventually left France and rallied to de Gaulle. In 1944, Seydoux hid Debré and a group of men he was meeting from the Gestapo. At the Liberation, despite earlier accommodations to the Germans and Vichy, the Sciences Po administration could point to these pro-resistance activities and other good works, such as the aid sent to POWs who had graduated from the school. Shortly after the war, Siegfried wrote the preface to the *livre d'or* of the École libre, which commemorated those affiliated with the school who gave their lives for France.[44]

At the Musée social, too, there was also a complicated mixture of cooperation and dissent. Georges Risler died in March 1941 and Siegfried, though he had long sought to avoid administrative leadership, began presiding over the governing board (he was vice-president at the time) and then formally assumed the position of president in February 1942. Between the wars, the composition of the Musée social's supporters had evolved; industrialists became less prominent whereas professionals and academics were increasingly visible. The institution's primary focus remained the promotion of social peace, and it remained heavily concerned with matters such as housing. But it also displayed greater interest in preserving and enhancing rural life and promoting large families, the latter having been of great interest to Risler. Scholarship on the Musée during the war years is limited, but the minutes of its governing board indicate that in the early phases of the occupation its administrators intended to curtail its operations quite severely.[45] There would be no meetings of its various sections and its *Cahiers* would not be published. However, the library would remain open to researchers and the institution would make its headquarters available to various groups that wished to hold meetings. These groups soon included the Comité d'études pour la France as well as the clearly pro-Vichy Institut d'études corporatives et sociales, though in the latter case the Musée's executive clarified that, while they were willing to allow the Institut's meetings to be held on the premises, it could not establish its secretariat there.[46]

By the time Siegfried formally assumed the presidency – following "the insistent entreaties of his colleagues" – in early 1942, things were changing. As the war dragged on and Vichy continued to initiate social legislation, the Musée's executive committee decided that some activities should resume. The Section agricole thus renewed its activities, as did the Section d'hygiène urbaine et rurale. Moreover, under Siegfried's leadership a new Section d'études sociales was launched. It intended to assess new legislation, such as the Vichy regime's Charte du travail, to encourage cooperation between different agencies and ministries, and to study major social problems. The executive also agreed that it would seek permission to publish the *Bulletin du Musée social* again.[47] Doing so proved difficult at a time of increasing censorship, and eventually the executive decided simply to print occasional issues, presenting "the most interesting studies." Several such issues subsequently appeared in 1943–44.[48]

Thus, after an early period of passivity, the Musée social became increasingly active during the Occupation. It also depended on financial support from the Secours national, the Vichy regime's quasi-official aid organization, to keep going. In 1943, the executive cancelled an intended exposition because the Secours national also planned to hold one on its premises, and they believed that this would reduce the number of their possible attendees. Instead, they planned to co-host an exposition with the Secours national in the future, though this never materialized. The Musée also sent a representative to the inaugural Salon des urbanistes in 1943; this gesture was noted approvingly by Minister of National Education Bonnard and by many of the officials of the Société français des urbanistes, who credited the Musée as an inspiration for many of their initiatives. Finally, the various sections of the Musée studied problems that were certainly relevant from Vichy's standpoint, even if growing German control and wartime disruptions made implementing measures increasingly difficult. For instance, the Musée's Section d'études sociales assessed the effect of the regime's Charte du travail on social institutions and the Section agricole considered the "scientific organization of work" in rural areas.[49]

Although as its president, Siegfried wanted the Musée to focus on concrete matters, his own research unavoidably shaped his thinking on social issues. The promotion of hygiene had long been one of the Musée's principal concerns; in July 1942, Siegfried addressed the issue by returning to his comparative study of Suez and Panama, reaffirming that "Salubrity is a work in progress, which must be constantly maintained against the disintegrative forces that menace it. Its preservation is essential to our Western civilization."[50] In a discussion of housing published in 1944, Siegfried relied on his view of the French national character when explaining the challenges that the country faced in this realm. Unlike Scandinavians, Anglo-Saxons, and Central Europeans, who had to contend with harsher conditions, France's more temperate climate translated into fewer concerns about the quality of housing. The French people's individualism meant that they were preoccupied with ensuring that they would always have a home free from the control of others, but good food and sociability took priority over tidiness. Catholic values also encouraged an indifference to material well-being, though Siegfried noted that Protestantism could go too far in the other direction. He also conceded regional distinctions – "There is moreover a noticeable difference in this regard between our northern departments and those of the Midi, which have been clearly seen during the sad days of the exodus, when the inhabitants of the Nord, Alsace, and Lorraine came into contact with their southern compatriots; they were surprised and somewhat offended." He did not seek to denigrate the many positive qualities of the French character, but "there is no doubt that the French must receive better civic, hygienic, and social education, instilling in them concern for their health, having a healthy life in a healthy dwelling, for bodily dignity and respect for the law, for others' property and common property, showing them the advantages of comfort and the life of the mind, which is inconceivable without a certain form of housing."[51]

However, though the Musée responded to Vichy's social policy interests, in his address to the inaugural meeting of its Section d'études sociales in 1942, Siegfried asserted that there was no need for a complete break with the organization's liberal heritage or the initiatives of the preceding regime: "The social achievement of the Third Republic is very considerable; I am not one of those who refuses it the praise that it deserves."[52] In June 1943, he returned to these issues in a talk entitled "Social Engineers" given at the Musée. In it, he traced the history of the institution, explaining that it had been founded by men who were firmly liberal in their views but also possessed a social conscience. Four decades on, Siegfried continued, state intervention and the expansion of social policy were the order of the day, practised by governments of the right and left – Fascists, Nazis, Soviets, and even Roosevelt through the New Deal. Liberals now had to respond. "The human person must now be defended against a state whose administrative rigour excludes human sentiment more and more." As the title of his lecture suggested, Siegfried believed that concessions had to be made. New personnel, "representing the social [dimension] within the economy – social engineers, social workers, superintendants, etc" – had to be trained. But liberal principles must be preserved as Europe sought to remain economically competitive, for challenges from other continents lay ahead.[53] He made similar points in remarks delivered to the Musée's Grand Council in December 1943 and again in liberated Paris in January 1945, when he confirmed the institution's devotion to liberalism and private initiative.[54] Though the Musée had cooperated with the authorities in significant ways under his leadership, Siegfried still presented it as reflecting liberal principles.

## WARTIME WRITINGS

Siegfried's wartime journalism evinces a blend of long-held views, adaptations to the new political context, and occasional hints of dissent. In 1941 and 1942, he contributed articles to *Le Temps*, *Le Figaro*, and *La Dépêche*; the focus here is on the first two. Both were permitted to appear during the occupation, and were of a broadly conservative bent, but whereas *Le Temps* generally toed the Vichy line, *Le Figaro* occasionally got into trouble with the censors. It was eventually suspended on 1 November 1942; this prohibition and its more independent stance ensured that it was able to reappear after Liberation, which was not the case for *Le Temps*.[55] Many of the articles that Siegfried contributed to these papers reflected his ongoing interests. Some were reflections on his previous travels or on the state of geography as a discipline, while others were essentially book reviews; still others, such as one entitled "Sociologie téléphonique" were intended to be lighter pieces.[56] But he also commented on international developments, the problems that France faced, and the bureaucratic and managerial character of modern society. Writing for *Le Temps* in June 1941, for example, Siegfried lamented how serving the state was increasingly indistinguishable from working for a large company; indeed, many civil servants no longer possessed a sense of the public interest. Such "arrivisme" had become increasingly acute in France over the past half-century; the country required "a serious correction."[57] With its critique of decline and calls for renewal, the article reflected the mood of the time, though Siegfried refrained from advocating repressive measures and did not specifically invoke the ideals of the National Revolution; moreover, such calls for reform emanated from across the political spectrum, including the Resistance. Siegfried retained a tone of cautious ambiguity in later articles as well. In the summer of 1942, he lamented the many trials that France had experienced, suggesting that the divisions of the interwar years revealed how the country had placed too much importance on reflection, analysis, and "mental operations" and not enough on decisive action and a sense of unity – "France first" was a popular slogan during his childhood, he noted. But in a later article he seemed to equivocate, defending the importance of intelligence and independent inquiry: "The danger would be that in the name of action, we do not want to enslave thought."[58]

172    France in the World

This call to preserve the domain of the intellect resurfaced in other contexts, including in articles that, at first glance, suggested an accommodation to Vichy's priorities. For example, in a discussion of sport and politics – a topic Siegfried had rarely broached before the war but one of interest to the regime – he noted that sport had been neglected by the educational system under the Third Republic and was generally dissociated from politics before the war, but the situation was now changing. He deemed this a generally positive development but also saw pitfalls: "The [political] party is tending to give way to a disciplined group, under a leader accepting of risk. In this system the muscle regains, in relation to the brain, an importance that it had lost. We admit that, in our hierarchy of values, there is a need for revaluing, but let us add that tomorrow the brain must be defended." Beyond this possible allusion to Vichy's anti-intellectual stance, Siegfried also distanced himself to a degree from the regime's traditionalist leanings despite his own reservations about rapid social change. He observed that while he was an admirer of the French peasantry, alterations to the country's social structure were irrevocable. "It would be dangerous to ignore this, by speaking and reasoning as if the France that we love has always existed in full, as if France hasn't changed."[59]

Cultivating leaders and imbuing them with the proper values was a major concern of the Vichy regime, and Siegfried explored this subject at several junctures. He contributed a piece on Marshal Lyautey – a Vichy favourite – to *Le Figaro* in 1941, praising him as "a free spirit." Another essay explored the career of the magnate Andrew Carnegie, in which Siegfried affirmed the need for effective leaders, though he added that Carnegie himself recognized the need to learn from subordinates as well.[60] Interestingly, Siegfried also offered his father Jules – even though he had been a prominent politician of the now-discredited Third Republic – as an example of leadership in several fields, later developing this argument in a full-length biography. Following the death of one of his mentors, the historian Charles Seignobos, in 1942, Siegfried eulogized him as a rigorous scholar who was "Germanic" in his precision but above all praised him as a non-conformist, a Protestant from the Ardèche who adopted the "viewpoint of the left" and was not afraid to challenge conformity. "In an era when unbridled propaganda systematically obscures issues, the memory of this implacable intellectual probity is refreshing. Seignobos expressed one of the most authentic traits of the French mind."[61] Such words might be interpreted as a comment on the conditions of the occupation and the National Revolution.

Regarding international developments, Siegfried sought to educate his readers about the widening geographic scope of the war. In the summer and autumn of 1941, he discussed the growing significance of the North Atlantic in the conflict and evaluated American foreign policy. Emphasizing the strength of the bond between America and Britain, he questioned whether, in an age where technology was shrinking vast distances, the US could truly remain isolationist. After all, its leaders were already taking a growing interest in securing the North Atlantic and Arctic; to the south they kept a careful watch on potential threats to the Panama Canal.[62] Siegfried also looked eastward, commenting on the potential role of land routes through Asia and the strategic centrality of Turkey. He was particularly fearful about the implications of a Japanese advance into the Pacific. Here his long-standing worries about the future of white hegemony resurfaced; writing in *Le Figaro* on 10 September 1941, he depicted Australia's armed forces as a bulwark of white civilization against an Asian peril.[63] After Pearl Harbor, he stressed the grave threat that Japan's entry into the conflict posed for Britain's imperial presence in the Far East.[64]

Indeed, the state of Western civilization was much on Siegfried's mind during these months. In a substantial essay published in the conservative *Revue des deux mondes* in September 1941, he discussed the roots of the West's global leadership and assessed the challenges that it now faced. Developing themes that he had begun exploring before the French defeat, Siegfried began with the Greeks, who he believed had imbued the West with "the critical spirit, the habit of observing phenomena and contemplating problems freely." It was this conception of the individual shaping their own destiny that distinguished Occident from Orient; it drew frontiers between religion and reason, and between religion and the state, that were absent in Asia or among adherents of Islam. Siegfried then turned to the Jewish contribution to Western values, contending that Judaism was the principal source of the Western notion "of a personal god and man's relationship with him ... the conception of the individual, considered as a moral unity, comes from the Jewish tradition. The law as a moral, imperative command, distinct from the scientific law discerned by Greece, became a new basis for conduct." While the West had incorporated these values in a distinct way, their Jewish roots meant that there were also links to the East. "These ancient Jewish notions are Eastern but the West, in adopting them, adapts and transposes them, to the point of nearly contradicting the original inspiration, and nevertheless the relation is evident."[65] Siegfried went on to explain how, from the intellectual and spiritual base provided by the Greeks and Jews, the Romans provided order and juridical expression of these values by regulating property and the civic independence of the individual. Subsequently, technology became the source of Western supremacy; it was rooted in a conception of science emanating from northwestern Europe, whose harsher climate necessitated practical responses to nature.

For 150 years, technological prowess had been the root of Western dominance, Siegfried observed, but it was only the concrete manifestation of a more complex system of power rooted in spiritual values, notably a belief in individual freedom, and even a propensity for rebellion. "Europe, which continues the tradition of Prometheus each day, essentially expresses this non-conformism, in which an authentic form of the true spirit of initiative must be contrasted with the tranquility within inertia that characterizes the Orient." Various factors – the human-scale geography of the Mediterranean, which encouraged a balanced interaction between humans and nature; the innate superiority of whites; the values imparted by a shared Christian faith – all reinforced Western leadership. Even Europe's long history of conflict, though destabilizing, also encouraged vitality and innovation. For the time being, Siegfried asserted, "the West remains young and hitherto has given no serious sign of aging." Neither "blacks" nor "reds" could hope to match the "white race"; "the yellows" had more capacity but were ultimately imitative.[66]

But Siegfried was not sanguine about longer-term trends. The materialism that was part of the West's heritage could lead to a shallow mass society. Alternately, "liberalism could be lost amidst the abuses of an irresistible statism that favours, even imposes, conformity, that is to say a state of mind directly contrary to the true Western tradition." Perhaps the greatest threat was rooted within "the extra-European division of the white race." Where the latter dominated – America, Australia, South Africa, Russia as well – geography and climate did not encourage a sense of balance, as in the Mediterranean. In this "Far-West," he suggested, "the white race loses some of its traditional characteristics." In particular, the Greek sense of curiosity and individualism was absent in the United States; while the American system of production grew ever more efficient, the tendency toward conformity gained concomitant strength. Europe would also move in this direction if a hegemon – which Siegfried did not name, though his meaning seemed clear enough – dominated the continent and militarization stifled the energies which fuelled "its fecund but dangerous diversity ... Whatever the future holds, it will be difficult for Western civilization, swept along by a rapid, nearly disorienting, transformation, to maintain the characteristics that enable us to describe its personality."[67]

The article advances some arguments introduced in Siegfried's earlier works, notably *La crise de l'Europe* of 1935, but there are noteworthy modifications. For one, he characterized the Jewish contribution to Western values in relatively positive terms, though he continued to identify Judaism with the "East" and, thus, alien. Moreover, his concerns about the future of liberalism and domination by a militaristic hegemon are expressed more urgently. Indeed, Bernard Bruneteau has argued that the article offered a significant alternative to the visions of a German-dominated "New Order" promoted by various collaborationist intellectuals at the time, with Siegfried positing a more pluralist vision of European identity.[68] This interpretation has merit, but it must be borne in mind that Siegfried continued to decry Americanization and the cultural decline of whites who no longer fully identified with "authentic" European values.

Later that same year, in a discussion of French immigration policy, Siegfried cited a specific instance of how the example of the United States should not be emulated. In an article that was to become infamous, appearing in *Le Temps* in December 1941, he argued that Slavic and Latin immigration to the US, and the backlash that resulted, clearly demonstrated the problems that uncontrolled mass immigration caused. Popular opinion held that after three generations assimilation was complete, but Siegfried questioned whether that was truly the case; unsuitable immigration, he claimed, could "inject not only a physical but also a moral, at its root refractory, element, and as a result the people who receive it find themselves internally modified, even if external appearances no longer reveal anything." Immigration could not be taken lightly, for some groups integrated far more readily than others. "Did France know these things when a wave of foreigners penetrated after the war, twenty years ago? It is to be regretted that she [acted] as if she did not know."[69] In a wartime context where xenophobia was intense and officially promoted, Siegfried drew upon his widely affirmed expertise on the United States to criticize recent immigration to France, further legitimizing fear and hostility.

It is also worth noting that Siegfried expressed gratitude when an excerpt from *La crise de l'Europe* appeared in a 1942 collection titled *Anthologie de la nouvelle Europe*, edited by the far-right journalist Alfred Fabre-Luce, who at the time had advocated collaboration with the Third Reich. The anthology, which featured a wide range of contributions, including excerpts from Charles Maurras and Adolf Hitler, was intended, Fabre-Luce explained, to trace the intellectual underpinnings of the new European order. To his mind, the key features of this revolutionary thinking included an acceptance of the primacy of power, the embrace of charismatic leadership and hierarchy, the rejection of liberal democracy and Marxist socialism, and the necessity of European imperialism. The excerpt from Siegfried suggested that, despite fierce economic competition from Asia and the United States, Europe remained superior in terms of its creative genius and spirit.[70] Siegfried's excerpt did not explicitly reinforce an authoritarian vision of the new European order, and in his note to Fabre-Luce he indicated that different conclusions could be drawn from the assembled texts. But Siegfried also noted that he did not think current developments invalidated the broader conclusions he had drawn in the excerpt. "For myself I continue to believe that Europe is the first among continents."[71]

The troubling ambivalence of Siegfried's views in the context of the Occupation is also evident in his comments on the evolution of the American economy, which appeared six months after Pearl Harbor. In June 1942 – the same month in which he suggested to US diplomats that the French would welcome an Allied liberation – he wrote in *Le Figaro* about the revival of statist tendencies in connection with America's wartime mobilization, which he characterized as a renewed effort on the part of the "brain trust" of New Dealers. He identified the key figures influencing Roosevelt as "Baruch, Frankfurter, Brandeis, Henry Morgenthau, Douglas." If the country persisted in this direction, he concluded, the result would be "a directed economy, neither fascist nor communist but democratic, possibly demagogic, respecting the principles of the American constitution but nevertheless turning its back on the spirit of initiative and individualism which in the past made the United States great."[72] Siegfried had expressed reservations about the New Deal since its inception, but now explicitly identified the decline of economic liberalism and, thus, American values, with the Roosevelt administration, key members of whom were Jewish.

In at least one case, Siegfried's wartime journalism elicited an intense private reaction. Birnbaum cites a letter sent in response to Siegfried's December 1941 comments on immigration by Paul Grunebaum-Ballin, formerly a state councillor of the Third Republic until he was removed from office because he was Jewish. He had attended school with Siegfried's brother and knew his father. In the letter, Grunebaum-Ballin made it clear how much Siegfried's article in *Le Temps* had upset him. "I know well that these horrible times constrain those who make a profession of writing for the newspapers – all monitored – to [make] many ... concessions. But you, sir! Was it also necessary for you to prostrate yourself before the altar of racism?" Michael Marrus and Robert Paxton suggest that Siegfried's article exemplifies the pervasiveness of xenophobia in France at the time, which extended to those who kept their distance from or even opposed Vichy.[73] Their point is compelling; it seems unlikely that Siegfried was ignorant of the inferences that many readers would make. Perhaps he decided that it was acceptable for him to express previously held views in much the same way as he had before the war. If that is the case, at best it represents a deeply distressing lapse in judgment.

With both *Le Figaro* and *Le Temps* shut down following the German occupation of all of France in response to the Allied landings in North Africa in November 1942, Siegfried lost his principal journalistic venues but remained active in other ways, publishing a biography of his father that had its roots in a 1937 lecture.[74] Though obviously a very personal work, the book also placed its subject in a historical context and noted some of his limitations while celebrating his many accomplishments. Presented as a study in in leadership, *Jules Siegfried* detailed his achievements as a businessman, "a social leader," and a politician. Siegfried depicted his father as a man of action who sometimes grew impatient with a society that prized contemplation and stability, whose people were too content to settle into comfortable employment. "Jules Siegfried, who had the mentality of a leader, was basically disdainful of civil servants and more generally employees with fixed remuneration: he only held in high regard people capable of beginning, of creating something, and then being in charge of collaborators chosen by them."[75] His father was something of an outsider, whose familial connections to central Europe and affinity for Anglo-Saxon and Protestant cultures set him apart from France's Latin mores; he wanted his country to be more dynamic and export-oriented, its citizens less reliant upon the state.

In praising his father's virtues, Siegfried critiqued the failings of the Third Republic and, indeed, his country's political culture more generally. He lamented, for instance, that more politicians of the early Third Republic had not shared his father's passion for social reform, focusing on practical improvements for working people. Jules Siegfried, he admitted, was less cultured than many of his parliamentary contemporaries, but such qualities counted for too much in a system that was "too verbal, which assigned too much importance to pure eloquence and clever manoeuvring, to the detriment of achievements." The biography also detailed the elder Siegfried's disdain for corruption, noting that when he first became a deputy "he had the impression of having entered into a den of thieves." Unsurprisingly, his son believed that some of the problem was geographic: "Let us add that, in a France whose centre of gravity is too Meridional, this Alsatian cut a figure, not as an eccentric but as a citizen who was slightly different, whose temperament surprised his fellow citizens a bit."[76]

Yet, while presenting his father as a moral man who struggled with the games of parliamentary politics and noting that he was in many ways a conservative who abhorred disorder, Siegfried also highlighted Jules's devotion to liberalism and the laic Republic, noting his early support for Dreyfus and his general opposition to the Catholic and reactionary right. Overall, he recalled the early years of the Third Republic as a hopeful time: "In the environment that I lived, it was said that the Republic would be the most effective instrument of French revival, since the people, in their entirety, were its first collaborator: in fact, as in the time of the great Revolution, this people had never dreamed of separating the Republic from the country."[77] It is difficult to see such an analysis as a solid endorsement of the National Revolution.

Siegfried published a much shorter volume the following year. Entitled *Quelques maximes*, it was, like the biography of Jules Siegfried, a personal work, but one that explicitly reflected his desire to be a moralist and to give comfort to his fellow citizens. As he explained in the preface, periods of crisis could nurture contemplation and insight into the human condition; La Rochefoucauld had produced a series of maxims during the Fronde of the mid-seventeenth century, Rivarol had done so during the Revolution, and Doudon produced comparable reflections in 1848. The time had arguably come for a new set of maxims: "We have 'great catastrophes,' and nothing prevents us from hoping that tomorrow they will be 'great catastrophes in the past,' with 'a long rest ahead.' The time has come, therefore, to reflect upon what we have seen and perhaps express, in the form of aphorisms, what we can learn about human behaviour, at a time when their destinies are subjected to some rough twists and turns. I believe that maxims arise from a contrast, and that they are often a sort of protest." This literary form, he added, had a particularly Latin quality. Noting how in the United States the Gideon Society directed travellers toward Bible passages for inspiration, Siegfried described how his own mischievous suggestion that a "Société Rochefoucauld" should be established to promote the latter's maxims had elicited cries of "cynical Frenchman!" from some American inter-locutors. "But cynicism, for many people, is simply the truth that displeases them … We Latins have, in this regard, an intellectual sincerity that the Anglo-Saxons do not possess." Siegfried hoped that by offering some of his own maxims he could help to revive a rich tradition, which presented an alternative to modern sloganeering, and provide insight in troubled times.[78]

Grouped according to four themes – "man, the workings of the soul, conduct, and politics" – some of the adages are generic but others reflect Siegfried's personal convictions, echoing some of the criticisms that he had made of French society during the war years: "Intelligence only works well when detached in relation to action; all direct contact distorts it. Many people see properly, conclude well, and do nothing." Others did seem essentially cynical: "I believe that a committed and authentic Christian would not survive past noon. An anchorite, perhaps."[79] The potentially most controversial maxims, dealing with politics, combined Siegfried's ethnic stereotypes – "Orientals know how to bow before a fait accompli. Westerners never do" – with a few adages that possibly implied an unease with the current situation; "Politicians all say that they are sacrificing themselves for the country when taking power: they must never be believed." There was also a defence of classical liberalism, at least in economic terms. "State-guided economics have the same drawbacks as lying: it erects an artificial structure whose logic cannot be maintained, and collapses."[80]

Though some of their contents might be interpreted as muted criti-cisms of the Vichy regime, neither *Jules Siegfried* nor *Quelques maximes* occasioned hostility from the authorities. Indeed, neither seems to have evoked much public comment – apparently, only 250 copies of *Jules Siegfried* were printed at the time, though the biography did receive a positive review in the *Revue d'histoire diplomatique.*[81] Siegfried's third wartime book, *Vue générale de la Méditeranée*, published by Gallimard in 1943, was more prominent. The culmination of his growing interest in the region as a formative influence upon European identity, as indicated by his travel before the defeat and then teaching at the Collège de France, it continued his practice of wide-ranging geographic and cultural analyses.[82] After providing an overview of its geological characteristics, Siegfried examined the economy of the region while also highlighting its timelessness; "[T]oday, a given scene of the Greek or Lebanese countryside evokes Homeric agriculture." Nevertheless, industrialization and larger-scale capitalist agriculture were becoming more established, with some wine-growing regions resembling "a new California" under the influence of American-style technocracy, which decried the "anarchic individual" and promoted the "mass man." Much was being lost in this way, Siegfried lamented. "The personal and familial character of the social contacts of yesterday were characterized by great simplicity, dignity, and even equality, independently of differences in fortune ... By contrast, the new economic system increases differences, for the boss or management of big business are far removed from the quasi-anonymous groups of employees who, all too often, have lost even the hope of becoming proprietors."[83]

What, then, did this mean for the future of a region that had played such a decisive role in shaping Western values? Siegfried suggested that given the tendency toward increasing bureaucracy, technology, and mass production, the Mediterranean was in some ways ill-suited to the contemporary world. Yet if its traditional values were submerged, Western society would lose an important part of itself. "The notions of paterfamilias, clan, patrimony, familial solidarity, [and] the Mediterranean conception of the role of women, are all matters of the past rather than the future. It is an archaism that is not without advantages, as it maintains the prestige of certain values that Western humanity needs and whose loss would place it in prolonged jeopardy."[84]

Some of the arguments advanced in the book – including Siegfried's concern about maintaining the region as a barrier against the spread of disease from Asia – were familiar. But there were also innovations, notably in the sixth chapter, where he discussed the composition of the Mediterranean "race" in explicitly anthropological terms, noting that he was drawing on work in this field; such an approach contrasted with the historical-cultural conception of the term that he had previously favoured. As discussed by Birnbaum, Siegfried had been introduced to the work of the racist thinker Georges Montandon on the different sub-groups of "the white race." These sub-groups, classified according to the cephalic index, were discussed in detail in *Vue générale*, to the point where Siegfried distinguished between sub-groups within individual departments of Mediterranean France. However, he did not cite Montandon. Instead, he relied on the writer Émile Littré for his definitions, briefly referring to the American economist and racial theorist William Ripley and the British anthropologist A.C. Haddon, who emphasized that racial classification systems were ultimately subjective. Siegfried had prefaced his discussion by conceding that there were no pure races, though in contrast to those who denied the utility of the concept he asserted that the study of races was a legitimate endeavour. He also posited a degree of mutability within races that demonstrated the role of cultural influence; "[D]iverse races have been the vehicles for civilizations, but the latter, in their turn, have transformed races."[85]

However, while distancing his approach from a rigidly biological conception of race to an extent, Siegfried did not hesitate to establish hierarchies in discussing the ethnic composition of the Mediterranean. He readily conceded that the background of the population was diverse; the key was whether the mixture was of good quality or not. "Not all human mixtures are good, but there are excellent ones, and we can, in some cases, discern the crossbreeds who are generators of progress and civilization." In the case of the Mediterranean, Nordic and Slavic elements had brought a "sense of command" as well as a capacity for hard work and frugality to a people who "are more brilliant, but less solid." There was a lesser "Mongol" contribution in the form of the Turks, who were ethnically and culturally "marginal" to Mediterranean civilization but possessed "an uprightness of character that distinguishes them from such neighbouring races." There was even a slight "negro penetration" evident in border regions of Egypt and Morocco, though as a whole, he claimed, "the Mediterranean remains an incontestable domain of the white race."[86]

It seems reasonable to posit that censorship, or self-censorship, explains why Siegfried did not discuss the potential effect of German hegemony on the Mediterranean, or mention its Jewish communities, in the book – though such matters do not appear to have been a major focus for him in his earlier travels to, or writings about, the region. On the other hand, *Vue générale* did afford him the opportunity to link values – such as artisanal tradition and intellectual independence – that he had long identified with France to the Mediterranean in general, which he then presented as the desirable alternative to the mass society embodied by the United States. His resulting emphasis on the unique contribution of Mediterranean values resonated with readers, though sometimes in unexpected ways. Claude Bied-Charreton, writing in *La cité nouvelle*, observed that Siegfried "leaves the door open to any future development or adventure. But he insists upon the loss for Western civilization that a decline in the Mediterranean contribution would represent." The collaborationist Georges Albertini, writing for *L'atelier*, took things further, suggesting that Siegfried's portrait of the region implied the necessity of German hegemony. "It is clear, in fact, that Mediterranean civilization is threatened in particular by America and Russia. Only Germany can save some of the irreplaceable values that were born on its shores. Mr. Siegfried does not say it, and I do not know if he thinks it. But it is a conclusion that one cannot prevent oneself from drawing, from the pages, admirable in depth, which he has devoted to the most humanised and most bathed in sea in history on the surface of the globe."[87] It is indeed unlikely that Siegfried approved of German hegemony in Europe, but his goal of articulating a racialized and traditional Mediterranean identity in opposition to excessive materialism had left his work, at this stage of the war, vulnerable to appropriation by a proponent of the Third Reich's hegemony.

### THE LIBERATION

As the war entered its final stages, Siegfried hoped for the revival of a moderate republic. Hints of this are discernable in his May 1944 preface to Roger Thabault's book *Mon village: Ses hommes, ses routes, son école*, which became an influential portrait of rural life in the postwar era. Siegfried praised the author's analysis of the transformation of French rural life as seen through the experience of the village of Mazières-en-Gâtine and appreciated the reference to his 1913 work *Tableau politique de la France de l'Ouest*. He also noted approvingly how Mazières provided an example of "how and why the Republic implanted itself in communes which, in the beginning, did not belong to it."[88] But while Siegfried missed the Third Republic, at least in its pre-1914 incarnation, he feared that a new one, restored in the wake of Vichy, would be too radical because of growing Communist influence within the Resistance.

His comments to the seventy-ninth annual meeting of the Société de l'Histoire du Protestantisme Français, in which he explored the career of the Protestant pastor and moderate revolutionary Jean-Paul Rabaut Saint-Étienne, reflected this preoccupation. Siegfried reaffirmed the profound connection between the French Protestant tradition and the values of 1789 that he had explored during his work on the Midi. Recalling that he had attended the meeting of the Société fifty years before when it had marked the 100th anniversary of Rabaut's execution during the Terror, he contrasted the circumstances: "[U]nder the Republic, which respected liberty, praise for it was academic; today this liberty, three-quarters lost, is a threatened inheritance that must be defended." For much of his political career, Rabaut had fought such a battle, notably for Protestant rights, against the forces of reaction. But as the political atmosphere of France shifted during the Revolution, his unswerving commitment to the moderate values of 1789 was deemed intolerable by the far left. The twin threat of reaction and radicalism was something that the defenders of the liberal revolutionary tradition would always have to bear in mind, Siegfried warned. This did not mean that the situation was hopeless: "What is encouraging is the immense hope of the late 18th century. That window, then so magnificently opened to the great sky of free life, could it be shut again? We tell ourselves that would be impossible. When one breathes that air of summits, one can no longer live among the lowest depths of politics: sooner or later, humanity must regain altitude." It was vital that French Protestants remain true to liberal principles, just as Rabaut had, despite the costs. Rather oddly, though, Siegfried ended his address by citing Maurice Barrès about the value of holding to one's convictions; "I love these writers, these orators who, like stars in space, occupy fixed positions in our political sky, in relation to which we can draw bearings."[89]

In early August 1944, following the advice of Roger Seydoux, André, Paule, and some acquaintances left central Paris for the relative safety of Vaucresson, a commune at the city's western limits; they feared that the Germans would engage in roundups and hostage-taking as Allied forces approached. They returned to Paris on 18 August, just before the Resistance began its uprising. In the chaotic days that followed, before General Leclerc's forces arrived on 25 August, Siegfried witnessed some fighting and experienced a close call, briefly hiding in a stranger's apartment on 19 August to avoid a German patrol. But he survived unscathed, and on 26 August he went to the offices of *Le Figaro* to witness the victory procession down the Champs-Elysées. His description of what he saw was both emotional and analytical: "The impression is complex: there are elements of a Popular Front procession, something of America (like a Hollywood parade), a revolutionary element that evokes 1830 or 1848, and finally, dominating the ensemble an air of Valmy. In an hour I gained a better understanding of our entire Parisian revolutionary tradition than I had in years of reading history."[90] Siegfried later recounted his witnessing of the battle for, and celebration of, the city's liberation to the British historian Arnold Toynbee, at the International Paris Peace Conference of 1946. Noting that Siegfried "was looking old, frail, and starved, but he was animated by a glow of intellectual exhilaration," Toynbee also recalled that Claire Siegfried, who was joining them for lunch at the British delegation's hotel, reacted quite differently to her father's reporting of his experiences. "While Siegfried was speaking, I had been looking at his daughter's face ... Mlle Siegfried did not see, with the same eyes, the experience that the speaker had been recounting with such gusto. Mlle Siegfried's job had been a tougher one than her father's. She had had to keep the octogenarian [*sic*] observer alive." Toynbee's recollections are suggestive of the toll that the occupation had taken on the comparatively fortunate Siegfried family.[91]

Siegfried had not remained in reflective mode for too long in the summer of 1944, though; he moved quickly to shape public opinion as best he could. Within days of the liberation of Paris, his first article for a revived *Le Figaro* appeared, in which he argued that France had to work enthusiastically with Britain and the United States to reassert Western values: "liberty, respect for rights, for the individual, the sincere desire to improve the conditions of human life."[92] In meetings with American and British officials, he expressed confidence in de Gaulle's ability to restore authority; evidently, his impression of the Free French leader had improved. When Siegfried had discussed the political situation in France with American officials in June 1942, he identified Generals Giraud or Weygand, rather than de Gaulle, as the men best positioned to lead a French movement in support of the Allied cause. But when he met with US diplomats again in September 1944, he indicated that while still very worried about the Communists and the domination of political life by certain resistance groups, he and other moderates were pleasantly surprised by de Gaulle's emphasis on restoring order. Similarly, in meetings with British officials that same month, he stressed the importance of securing de Gaulle's legal authority, though he doubted whether many resistance leaders would prove to be effective parliamentarians. British officials debated what to make of his views; Ambassador Duff Cooper dismissed Siegfried as "one of those ineffective political theorists who spend their lives talking to people more important than themselves and writing books which are slightly out of date before they are published." However, other observers, notably Arnold Toynbee, defended Siegfried as "one of the few French men who have an inside knowledge and understanding of English-speaking countries."[93]

It is noteworthy that General de Gaulle himself sought out Siegfried's assessment of the national mood. He met with Siegfried on 5 September, during which the latter explained his thinking in some detail. Asked what he thought of the internal situation in France, Siegfried replied that while a segment of the population, perhaps especially in the provinces, might be satisfied with a return to the old system, the Resistance was a strongly republican but also left-leaning movement. Many people wanted "something new," and this climate of opinion could not be ignored. Siegfried conceded that the Communists currently enjoyed considerable esteem because of their contribution to the Resistance, though he added that there was an element of popular mistrust because they were tied to Russian interests; nor could the threat of a takeover be entirely ruled out. Nevertheless, he believed that in the current situation it was in de Gaulle's interest to govern with the Parti communiste français, as he was currently doing. As for the other political forces in France, Siegfried asserted that the Socialists had been greatly weakened by the conduct of "many" of their members during the Occupation. Commenting on the right – which for Siegfried meant the reactionary right – he declared that it needed institutional expression but advised that the government should position itself against it, for it was a republican tradition to oppose reaction. Turning to the economy, he stressed the need to embrace liberal principles, even if the general populace did not understand all aspects of such an approach; "[T]here is, in the mass of the population, a clear desire to free themselves from the oppressive regulations of the state-guided economy ... That said, we cannot delude ourselves: liberalism is an aristocratic sentiment extraordinarily restricted in its appeal." De Gaulle acknowledged this point but countered that "now and for a long time to come, we cannot hope for anything other than a state-directed economy."[94]

Despite this difference of opinion, the two men agreed on most other issues. Siegfried approved of de Gaulle's overall political strategy, entreating the general with a phrase very similar to one he had written in the *Tableau politique* in 1913. The main challenge of the moment, he asserted, was to "restore authority in democracy," which certainly reflected de Gaulle's own priorities. The general closed the meeting by encouraging Siegfried to renew his contacts with the English-speaking nations. "It would be very useful, [de Gaulle] said, to make known to the Anglo-Saxon the state of mind in France. I hope that you can do it. The Americans, President Roosevelt first of all, do not know France and are concerned about it. They believe that France is communist or fascist, but do not take into account the state of mind that you have analyzed. If America and England are persuaded that France is sincerely democratic and republican, its international position will be greatly strengthened."[95]

Appreciated though the general's support surely was, Siegfried probably did not need his encouragement to embark on such a task. In articles for *Le Figaro*, he was unstinting in his praise for the British and American role in withstanding the Nazi onslaught and restoring freedom to the French people. While echoing the Gaullist argument that Paris had liberated itself and praising the Free French leader, he stressed that "these efforts would have remained in vain without the powerful and massive presence of the Allied armies." After four years of censorship, Siegfried also revisited ideas that he had advanced in 1940, stating that the war was ultimately about the survival of liberal Western civilization. Having avoided explicit comment on the National Revolution during the war, he now condemned the regime as the antithesis of what France truly stood for. "The Marshal's government took responsibility for anti-Semitic persecution, renounced with a sort of enraged joy all of the principles of 1789, and violated the most sacred rules of justice with its special courts." With its freedom and dignity restored, he concluded, France could now rebuild on the foundation of its true values.[96]

When it came to what kind of path the country should take toward reconstruction, Siegfried cautioned against social radicalism and unnecessary state intervention. Writing at the end of October 1944, for example, he expressed concern about the future of the bourgeoisie. While he conceded that this class could be excessively materialistic and that some of its members had compromised themselves during the Occupation, as long as it retained the values of competence and service it was worth preserving. On the matter of state intervention, Siegfried asserted, "left to himself the Frenchman, in most cases, would no doubt instinctively give himself over to such a [liberal] program ... based upon saving, private ownership and the passionate quest for personal independence ... It is paradoxical that the quasi-totality of current political programs appear to neglect or even contradict these principles." The following month, Siegfried published two articles devoted to reconstruction in which he made the case against a focus on reviving consumption, notwithstanding popular desires, instead recommending a faster pace of reconstruction with the goal of restor- ing a favourable trade balance.[97] These arguments were welcomed by Minister of National Economy Pierre Mendès France, who favoured a similar approach. Mendès France, a former student of Siegfried's at the École libre, thanked him for his support; "I am happy that a pen as qualified as yours has undertaken to show the public the gravity of the reconstruction problem."[98]

— \* —

As his treatment by de Gaulle and Mendès France suggests, Siegfried's insights were often welcomed by the Liberation-era authorities, and it seems that his wartime conduct was generally regarded as honour- able. Interestingly, the attitudes of British officials at the time were more complex. R.H. Speaight of the Foreign Office, commenting on Siegfried's praise for Britain in the immediate aftermath of the Liberation, questioned its sincerity: "Although [Siegfried] is generous enough in his tributes to us now, he seems to have played a very nega- tive role during the German occupation, and although he did not openly collaborate I have not heard that he risked his skin in any way for the sake of the cause which he professes to have so much at heart." But another Foreign Office official, William Stewart, provided a more favourable estimation. "I heard six months ago from one of the under- ground leaders – Mathieu-[Fréville] – of [Siegfried's] support for the Resistance; and his first article in the liberated Paris press was a very generous tribute to Great Britain and the United States – but particu- larly Great Britain."[99] Which, then, is the more accurate portrait – that of a consistent supporter of the democracies, or of a man who adjusted his views according to circumstances?

Siegfried avoided collaborationism but had accommodated himself to Vichy and the Occupation in significant ways. He carried on with his teaching and involvement with the Institut and took over running the Musée social; such commitments necessitated engaging with the regime and adjusting to its plans, though Siegfried also evinced a degree of skepticism about aspects of the National Revolution and cooperation with Germany. He had fully supported the Anglo-French alliance in 1939–40, hoped that the United States would soon join the war against Nazism, and privately expressed confidence in a democratic victory in 1942. In that sense, his support for the English-speaking democracies in 1944 shows a degree of continuity. The same can be said about his commitment to the idea of France as a liberal republic, which remained discernible in some of his wartime writings and speeches.

But during these years, there were both interventions and silences that attracted criticism, both at the time and since. While not abandoning his core political beliefs, Siegfried addressed issues – such as the need for strong leadership – that chimed with Vichyite rhetoric. His critique of France's interwar immigration policy served to endorse official xenophobia and antisemitism. Furthermore, his unabashed commitment to Western supremacy and willingness to engage in criticisms of the American civilizational "model" in his book on the Mediterranean and other publications had problematic implications. Many of his views predated the war, and they were broadly in line with the outlook of more conservative elements of the resistance, but there were also points of contact with the discourse of the National Revolution. None of this prevented Siegfried from retaining a position of prominence and respect after the Liberation, but it does explain why his actions between 1940 and 1944 have become a source of controversy.

# 6

# Facing the Postwar World

In early September 1945, during her journey to North America with André, who was a member of the French delegation at the San Francisco Conference, Paule Siegfried gave an interview to Montreal's *La Presse* – a rare record of her public views – in which she reflected on the current situation in France. Though overjoyed to travel again, she emphasized the devastating effect of the German occupation and the harsh conditions her fellow citizens still faced. Her elderly mother, living in Morvan, had experienced three German invasions, and Paule herself stressed how painful the memories of occupation were: "Finally the nightmare has ended, but the vision of the enemy plundering Europe, as they have pillaged France, is often present in my mind."[1] Looking ahead, she was immensely proud that French women could now vote; though, sadly, she had not been present to cast a ballot, her daughter Claire had. Women could now participate fully in public affairs, which would greatly benefit families, and fields such as hygiene. Paule warned, however, that the challenge of rebuilding would be immense, and stressed that the power of the Communists had to be reduced as much as possible.

André fully shared Paule's concerns about the situation in France, and in the years to come devoted considerable energy to promoting his vision of how to implement economic revival and political reinvention. His election to the Académie française, though not free of dissension, signified his legitimacy in the emerging new order, amid continuing divisions emanating from the war years. In his public prescriptions for the French economy, though he realized that a degree of state intervention was unavoidable, in keeping with his liberal beliefs he argued that it should be limited. He also strove to ensure that Sciences Po and the Musée social preserved as much autonomy as possible. As for the configuration of France's new political system, while critical of the reactionary right Siegfried frequently advocated moderate conservative solutions that would blunt the more radical plans coming from the left, favouring a regime with structures reminiscent of the Third Republic.

The restoration of France's international standing was also a key concern as André took stock of the postwar world. Taking full advantage of his renewed ability to travel, beyond visits to Britain and continental Europe, and to North America in 1945, he and Paule spent several months in Latin America. In 1948, they toured sub-Saharan Africa for the first time, and in 1950 ventured to South Asia. In his accounts of these journeys, Siegfried retained his capacity for synthesis and concise observations, but conveyed to his readers the implications of the emerging Cold War order and the intensification of anti-colonial nationalism. In his writings, France emerges as a country facing formidable challenges, but one that has retained vibrancy and potential; through selective partnerships with other European states, it might yet preserve a prominent role.

### POSTWAR PROMINENCE

Siegfried arguably reached the height of his prestige in the early postwar years. As France was still being liberated, he received the greatest recognition of his career to date; election to the Académie française on 12 October 1944, along with the physicist Louis de Broglie and the physician Louis Pasteur Vallery-Radot. These elections were part of a broader attempt to reform an institution that had been compromised by the conduct of some its members during the Occupation. Before the war, the Académie had become a bastion of right-wing views, as the election of Charles Maurras to its ranks in 1938 suggested. After 1940, some of its members, most notably Abel Bonnard, Abel Hermant, and Cardinal Alfred Baudrillart supported the policy of collaboration, while an even larger number endorsed the spirit of the National Revolution while evincing some reluctance about Germany. But there was also a dissident minority more critical of Vichy, which included the writers François Mauriac and Georges Duhamel, as well as the poet Paul Valéry, whose work Siegfried admired and sometimes quoted. Other figures, such as the historian Paul Hazard and the writer Jérôme Tharaud, also moved in this direction despite the latter's anti-Communist and anti-Semitic views. In January 1942, Duhamel was elected provisional secretary of the Academy following the death of André Bellessort. This gave the dissidents greater influence, and thereafter the Académie distanced itself from the regime and began to support some of its opponents; at the Liberation, there was a general sense that, as Gisèle Sapiro puts it, its honour had been saved. Having suspended elections during the war, it now proceeded to choose three new members with views judged suitable to the new political climate. In fact, Siegfried's name had been on a "wish list," drafted by Gaston Palewski, of individuals that de Gaulle wished to see join the Académie.[2]

As it turned out, Siegfried's election proved to be somewhat controversial. Only seventeen voting members were present for the vote, below the regular quorum of twenty. But the fact that the Académie had not chosen new members during the Occupation and that in the interim some members had either passed away, gone into exile, or, like Bonnard, been suspended, meant that it currently only had twenty-eight sitting members rather than a full complement of forty, so the elections proceeded. De Broglie was elected unanimously, while Pasteur Vallory-Radot, who had played an active role in the Resistance, received fifteen votes with two blank ballots. Siegfried was elected with thirteen votes, but the four remaining ballots were marked with a cross, rather than just left blank – an expression of hostility to the candidate, though the precise reasons for this are unknown.[3]

Assessing the backgrounds of those chosen to join the Académie between 1944 and 1947, Gisèle Sapiro includes Siegfried among the growing number of academics being elected, compared with the literary elites and various professionals who had hitherto tended to dominate. Siegfried regarded himself as part of the "left-wing" faction of the Académie, though, as he explained, this simply meant endorsing liberal humanism rather than "the most authentic principle of authority, emanating from the most orthodox Old Regime." Arguably, his defence of French traditions and Western values were in keeping with the conservative outlook of many *académiciens*, but he identified with a pro-resistance, anti-Vichy outlook as the adherents of the traditional right sought to reassert themselves after the war.[4]

The politics of collaboration and resistance also shaped the closing stages of Siegfried's association with the Collège de France. His rival for the chair in American civilization in 1931, Bernard Faÿ, who had enthusiastically supported Vichy, was removed from his professorship on 24 June 1945 and subsequently tried and imprisoned for collaboration, though he later escaped and lived out the remainder of his life in exile.[5] Siegfried was actively involved in the election of his replacement, Marcel Giraud, a professor at the Lycée Carnot who was building a reputation with his scholarship on Canada's Métis peoples. By the time of Giraud's election, Siegfried had known him for a decade; Giraud had contacted him for guidance concerning his research in 1934, and Siegfried later served as a member of the jury for Giraud's *thèse*. After Faÿ's removal, the Collège's Assembly of Professors, at Siegfried's suggestion and with support from the *Annaliste* historian Lucien Febvre, retitled the position as the Chair in the History of North American Civilization. In a clear shot at Faÿ, Siegfried explained the reason for the decision as follows: "[T]he Chair of American Civilization had been conceived of by its previous holder in a much more general form. In changing the title, the Collège seeks to give a properly scientific character to this [field of] teaching." The Assembly duly proposed Giraud as the candidate for the position to the Ministry of Education, which in turn sought the opinion of the Académie des sciences morales et politiques. Siegfried then made the case for Giraud's appointment to his colleagues in this body, stressing the quality of his work and its potential to deepen cultural relations between Europe and North America.[6] These arguments proved compelling, as Giraud joined the Collège in 1947. Having been made an honorary professor, Siegfried continued to remain active in Collège matters after his formal retirement, for example supporting the creation of a Chair in the Psychology of Graphic Arts in November 1949.[7]

Siegfried may have identified with the opponents of Vichy when it came to academic politics, but when it came to his cherished École libre he found himself engaged in a rearguard action against Liberation-era reformist impulses. By the fall of 1944, it was already apparent that various left-wing politicians were seeking to create a state-run school of national administration, more socially democratic in its recruitment, to displace the École libre; the Communists wanted to see it disappear altogether. On 20 February 1945, the PCF group in the Consultative Assembly called on the provisional government to confiscate the property of Sciences Po and turn it over to a new "École des sciences politiques nationale et démocratique." This was necessary, they argued, because Sciences Po was an elitist institution, which had harboured pro-Vichy and collaborationist sentiments during the Occupation.[8] The proposal was not simply a rhetorical gesture; it was

Facing the Postwar World

to be examined by the Assembly's Commission on State Reform, some of whose members – notably the Radical Pierre Cot and the Socialist André Philip – found elements of the PCF's critique compelling.[9]

However, the leadership of Sciences Po was already preparing a response, which did not reject state intervention outright but sought to preserve as much autonomy as possible. Having refused to play a major administrative role in the 1930s, in January 1945 Siegfried now agreed to replace the ailing Paul Tirard as president of the institution's governing board. Moreover, the latter's entire membership resigned, creating an opportunity to alter its composition; some previous members subsequently returned, but individuals who were regarded as tainted by association with Vichy did not. There were also some new faces, among them Siegfried's fellow academician Georges Duhamel, who was highly respected for his pro-resistance stance under the Occupation. Such modifications bolstered Sciences Po's efforts to counter left-wing charges of past support for Vichy. To that end, Siegfried and Seydoux also conducted press interviews; on 30 March, for example, Siegfried assured the mass-circulation *France-soir* that Sciences Po had aligned with the Resistance and had purged pro-Vichy faculty, while Seydoux made the case that the school no longer adhered solely to the tenets of classical liberalism. Then in April, they circulated a detailed, 33-page refutation of the PCF's allegations to over a hundred individuals, mostly members of the Consultative Assembly. They continued lobbying along these lines into the summer, sending letters to ministers in the Provisional Government.[10]

Their efforts bore fruit. Political figures such as the Christian Democrat trade union leader Gaston Tessier and the conservative politician (and later prime minister) Joseph Laniel, wrote letters of support. Siegfried and Seydoux also secured a meeting with de Gaulle himself on 20 June, at which Siegfried indicated that the institution was willing to modify its charter but expressed fear about its expropriation, as demanded by figures like Pierre Cot. Siegfried argued that the school must preserve its "individuality," contending that it played an important international role that was worth sustaining. De Gaulle was reassuring, stressing that "Mr. Pierre Cot's positions are always extreme and do not correspond to those of the government."[11] The general's administration was in fact developing a counter proposal that addressed Siegfried's and Seydoux's concerns. The key figure here was Michel Debré; charged by de Gaulle with devising an alternative plan, Debré negotiated a scheme in which a state-run École nationale d'administration (ENA) would be established, but its students would primarily come from new political science institutes that would be affiliated with local universities. There would be several of these but the most important one would be in Paris. Between June and September, Siegfried, supported by Seydoux, was involved in negotiations about the proposal, which was presented to the Consultative Assembly on 9 October. Some vigorous debate ensued, but the proposal was endorsed, and in a decree of 22 March 1946 the École libre was dissolved and replaced by two bodies, the Institut d'études politiques (IEP), a teaching institution, and the Fondation nationale des sciences politiques (FNSP), which would focus upon research.[12]

Despite the formal disappearance of the École libre, Siegfried was evidently pleased with this outcome. In a 1952 lecture delivered in Nice, he told his audience that, given long-term trends and the postwar political context, some extension of state control was inevitable. Unlike some of his colleagues, he had accepted this as a necessity but took comfort in the fact that the negotiations had managed to preserve much of the character of Sciences Po.[13] Subsequent scholarship has borne out his claim. As Nord argues, while the classic École libre disappeared, there are solid grounds for characterizing the developments of 1945–46 as a successful effort in conservative adaptation. To be sure, along with the new institutional configuration came a shift in outlook more amenable to the interventionist, technocratic ethos of postwar reconstruction. But key figures such as Siegfried retained their core views and enjoyed considerable clout in running the new institutions. Siegfried became the first director of the FNSP, while Seydoux took charge at the IEP; he was to be supported by a seventeen-member board, five of whom would come from the FNSP. In addition, two members of the FNSP – its president (i.e., Siegfried) and senior administrator – joined the administrative council for the new ENA. Finally, it was quickly apparent that the IEP would be the main "feeder school" for the ENA; their approaches were harmonized, there was some overlap in teaching staff, and though not the result of deliberate planning, their two principal buildings were just a courtyard apart.[14]

As it turned out, Seydoux did not remain at the IEP for very long, departing in 1947 to embark upon a diplomatic career. But before doing so, he was effusive in his praise for Siegfried's efforts. "For the past ten years the old ship of the Rue Saint-Guillaume has endured harsh storms and has had to avoid many reefs. If it has been able to maintain its course, and today can navigate calmer waters, it is because those who were at the helm had an experienced and courageous pilot with them." After Siegfried's death, Seydoux reiterated in *Le Figaro littéraire* that "Thanks to him, the old house of the Rue Saint-Guillaume, allied with the university but in no way subjugated to the state, sees its work confirmed and enlarged."[15]

In his teaching at Sciences Po, Siegfried kept abreast of current events and updated his lectures, but some of his views proved jarring in the postwar era. At least one former student, future Canadian prime minister Pierre Trudeau, found elements of Siegfried's views outmoded. When he studied at Sciences Po in 1946–47 – having previously attended Harvard – Trudeau's political and religious convictions were undergoing a complex shift from conservative, Catholic Quebec nationalism to more liberal and pro-federal views, though he remained an observant Catholic and was drawn to the doctrine of personalism. Trudeau was acquainted with Siegfried's work, some of which had been part of the curriculum at the Collège Brébeuf in Montreal, where he was educated; indeed, he later cited Siegfried in support of the view that Quebec universities were too conservative and required reform. But it appears that Trudeau was unimpressed by Siegfried's postwar lectures. He noted how Siegfried asserted the continuation, even enhancement, of global white supremacy in 1946 compared with what it had been in 1918; he also witnessed Siegfried repeat his long-standing view that Jewish immigration to the United States was a potential threat to the American population, and that anti-Semitism could be seen as an understandable reaction to it. He also disdained Siegfried's opinion that the massive geography of North America was "beyond the human scale"; in an April 1947 talk, Trudeau ridiculed this idea, noting how "a whole generation of people in France [had been] taught at Sciences Po to believe in the imminent collapse of the American continent, where rivers, boundaries, buildings and institutions defy the 'law' of grandeur."[16]

It cannot be said that Trudeau's negative view of Siegfried was necessarily typical, however. Other foreign students, such as Jacqueline Bouvier, who attended classes at the FNSP in 1949–50 as part of Smith College's junior year in Paris program, do not appear to have taken such a view.[17] And there is evidence of Siegfried's lasting ability to captivate audiences. One Sciences Po graduate who completed his diploma in 1951 and went on to become a journalist was admiring to the point of seeming intimidated: "Siegfried was the institution, he was god-like ... he had an exceptional elegance in his bearing, conduct and speech. It was a truly aristocratic style, the best. In listening to him you had the impression that things were luminous and clear. But he could not be thought of as being approachable."[18]

Siegfried also led the Musée social through the postwar years, and here too a case can be made for continuity within adaptation. That was the goal that Siegfried outlined in his address at the celebration of the institution's fiftieth anniversary held on 21 March 1945. Before an audience of various notables and government representatives, he traced the establishment of the Musée as a response to the short-comings of the liberal capitalist order of the late nineteenth century, noting that the founders sought a synthesis of liberalism with modest state intervention.[19] For decades, the institution had deepened understanding of social issues through its rich library, support for studies of other nations – including his own journeys to Britain and America in the 1920s – and the research carried out by its various sections. Siegfried hoped that the Musée would continue these activities in the spirit of open-minded investigation but added that it would have to contend with the emerging "administrative age," with its ever-increasing mechanization and bureaucratization. He feared that the focus on the collective was reaching the point at which industry was becoming "totalitarian" and the individual was being swamped by "administrative tyranny." Despite these sweeping changes, he insisted, the Musée would seek to provide constructive advice while respecting its long-held traditions. "No doubt it represents most particularly independent work and institutions. It is very attached to institutions derived from private initiative."[20]

However, the Musée's good work would be imperilled if it did not receive a significant injection of funding. The Comte de Chambrun had launched the institution with a generous endowment and provided it with a legacy in his will but the purchasing power of these funds, like many private fortunes, had been greatly diminished. At an executive committee meeting held in the fall of 1944, Siegfried stressed the need to adapt to the current political environment by developing contacts with various ministries and the trade unions. At the commemorative ceremony itself, he called upon the state, and all those who wanted to see the institution continue its mission, to provide support.[21] Eventually, in 1946, the Ministry of Labour offered funds, but on the condition that the Musée cooperate with its research initiatives. Siegfried and the executive committee agreed to these terms. The following year, they also secured aid from the Centre de la recherche scientifique by signing a convention between the Musée and the Fondation nationale des sciences politiques. The agreement stipulated that representatives from the FNSP and the Centre would join the Musée's governing board – given the overlap that existed, notably in the person of Siegfried himself, this was easily done.[22]

Despite these changes, the Musée preserved a good deal of autonomy. During negotiations for a convention between it and the FNSP, Siegfried had been reassured by Jacques Chapsal – with whom, of course, he had worked for years at Sciences Po and then the FNSP itself – that the Musée's independence would be respected: it was only a matter of coordinating research activities and including some representatives on the executive. The Musée's board regarded the outcome of the negotiations as a success, and in a 1949 letter to the Musée's director, Henri Aubrun, Siegfried expressed satisfaction with the current situation: "Our topics for discussion were well chosen and interesting; they seem to have engaged our audience, which remains faithful. I know that this result is due largely to you, and I value the depth of competence, intelligence, and devotion that you bring to the running of the Musée."[23]

An examination of the articles published in the Musée's *Cahiers* during this period suggests that while having to trim the scope of its activities, in important respects the organization continued to operate as it had done before the war. Retaining a general commitment to liberal principles and private initiatives, its members traced developments in other countries as well as the effect of technological innovation and social change. Various articles explored the evolution of welfare and public health initiatives, and other social developments, in various European states, the Americas, and even the Soviet Union. For his part, Siegfried discussed topics that reflected his broader interests at the time but were also relevant to the Musée.[24] The topics he addressed included the decline of a sense of culture among the labouring classes and the troubling status of skilled workers, who were now in short supply.[25] He also lamented the fact that few people were saving – in the nineteenth century, savings had facilitated capital accumulation but the effect of two world wars, the growing fiscal demands of the state, and the desire of the popular classes to consume had undermined this useful propensity.[26]

Siegfried also reaffirmed that social policy could not be developed in isolation from considerations of economic competitiveness – or ethnicity. Adopting a stance reminiscent of his controversial *Le Temps* article of December 1941, in 1946 he contributed a piece to the *Cahiers* outlining the lessons that France could learn from the US experience of immigration. Insisting that proper integration required favourable conditions and at least three generations, Siegfried contended that France's predicament was especially challenging. As an "old" country, it was harder for it to absorb outsiders, even though there was a need for foreign labour. Worse, there were also "quality" elements of the French population, especially among the young, who believed that they would have to emigrate to realize their dreams. For these people, Siegfried believed that the best approach was "give to those who are disillusioned an internal climate that could retain them." As for immigrants, some nationalities – Italians, Spaniards, and to a lesser extent, Poles – could eventually integrate. "But the Chinese will always remain foreigners." Selectivity about who was admitted was vital, even if it ran against the country's tradition of toleration: "We have an instinctive horror of racial barriers, of the divisions that nationalism or exclusivity stubbornly attempts to establish between human beings." But it was precisely because of these sentiments that France had to be cautious; "[P]rudence dictates that we must never forget that assimilation has its laws, which cannot be bypassed."[27]

## SEEKING A MODERATE REPUBLIC

In the wake of Vichy's authoritarianism, but also in the face of a sharp turn to the left in French politics after the war, Siegfried made the case for a liberal, moderate republic that respected the legacy of 1789 while avoiding extremes. This preference is discernable even in his more academic works on French politics during this period. In 1945, he and Pastor Marc Boegner co-edited a volume in which he reaffirmed, through a study of Protestants in the Cévennes Mountains, which spanned several French departments, the powerful connection between their religious tradition, commitment to freedom, and support for republicanism. A distinctive community whose religious practice was open to Anglo-Saxon influences such as revivalism, the *cévenols* were socially diverse but characterized by an abiding tradition of civic-mindedness and opposition to state tyranny. This translated into widespread support for the values of 1789, republicanism, and more specifically for Radicalism under the Third Republic, even though the notion of supporting a "religion of government" went against the community's traditions.[28]

Protestant political behaviour was also at the heart of Siegfried's *Géographie électorale de l'Ardèche*, which appeared in 1949. In its consideration of multiple causal factors in explaining voting patterns, the work still reflected the approach adopted for the 1913 *Tableau politique*. Siegfried assessed a range of variables, including altitude – he found that higher elevations favoured the right and lower ones the left – as well as ethnic composition; he analyzed the population in racial terms, continuing to employ the cephalic index that he had adopted during the war. Ultimately, however, he arrived at a nearly monocausal explanation, asserting that the key force in shaping political views in the Ardèche was a sharp Protestant-Catholic division; "[W]hen in play this factor dominates, even cancels all others."[29] Centuries of persecution meant that the Protestant community, though harbouring different theological beliefs and some class divisions, had gravitated toward political liberalism under the Third Republic. Observant Catholics typically responded by opposing the heritage of 1789, Radicalism, and Freemasonry, nurturing powerful and lasting divisions in the region. Indeed, the political and religious right was so hostile, Siegfried argued, that its supporters sometimes voted for the far left against more moderate elements to prevent a consolidation of the republican system. This trend, he concluded, was symptomatic of a larger problem, which had contributed significantly to undermining the Third Republic; the Catholic right had never truly reconciled itself to the regime, preferring to engage in a *politique du pire* which prevented the consolidation of a moderate, "liberal" conservative party that would stabilize the system.[30] As we shall see, Siegfried hoped that postwar politics would take on a different form.

*Géographie électorale de l'Ardèche* proved to be Siegfried's last major contribution to the field. In the book's preface, he noted that it was originally intended to be part of a broader study of the Midi under the Third Republic that he had begun working on in the 1930s, but his progress had been disrupted by the Occupation and he now feared – rightly, as it turned out – that it would never be finished.[31] Ironically, it was around this time that *Tableau politique de la France de l'Ouest* became increasingly regarded as a foundational work in French political science. It had attracted some renewed attention during the late 1930s and early 1940s, but it was in the context of the early postwar years, and the evolution of political science as a discipline in France, that the book's reputation was truly cemented. The key figure in bringing this about was François Goguel; though he apparently had reservations about Siegfried's more "popular" works based upon his travels, he believed that the latter's approach to electoral geography could be "perfected" by the application of even more rigorous methods. In Goguel's estimation, the scholarly depth of the *Tableau* warranted its recognition as a pioneering work, and Siegfried as a "founding father" of an emerging field. Goguel, his students, and other scholars thus cited the *Tableau* as a foundational study.[32]

Interestingly though, few scholars have made much of the fact that while Siegfried was being consecrated as a founder of French political science, he was also commenting on national politics more extensively than ever, and, more explicitly, from a conservative standpoint, for which his column in *Le Figaro* gave him an influential platform. Under the editorship of Pierre Brisson, the paper emerged as the leading voice of moderate conservatism in postwar France. Brisson was a formidable presence but was certainly not alone in shaping its political line. He regarded Siegfried as a key advisor, while also consulting with figures such as François Mauriac and Raymond Aron. In his memoirs, Aron expressed some reservations about this arrangement, suggesting that Brisson's outlook was insular, and that Siegfried's knowledge of economics was dated; he "would not willingly discuss current economic problems" and "had probably not read Keynes." Nevertheless, Siegfried's influence on Brisson appears to have been considerable.[33] Furthermore, he had another venue for his ideas in *L'année politique*, a revival of a compendium published between 1874 and 1906. The new publication was initially edited by Roger Seydoux and Édouard Bonnefous, another former student of Siegfried's. From the appearance of the first volume in 1946 until his death, Siegfried wrote every preface, which served as an overview and analysis of annual political developments. This gave him further opportunity to present his well-informed but hardly disinterested take on the unfolding drama of the French Fourth Republic.[34]

Siegfried consistently opposed what he deemed was excessive state intervention in Liberation-era France. He did not minimize the challenges that lay ahead but implied that pragmatic, innovative rebuilding – without too much government spending – was possible. In late December 1944, he had joined Minister of Reconstruction Raoul Dautry on a visit to his home city of Le Havre, which had been decimated by Allied bombing and German sabotage. Siegfried was impressed by Dautry's exchanges with the local population, in which the minister insisted upon the need to focus reconstruction efforts on the city's port, its chief source of prosperity. When a local engineer pointed to the lack of resources, Dautry replied "An engineer is someone who keeps striving! [*Un ingénieur, c'est quelqu'un qui s'ingénie!*]." Siegfried approvingly commented that "[f]rom this point of view, no country has as many engineers as France does."[35] In subsequent articles, he reiterated that the French people had the capacity to rebuild, but he also grew increasingly critical of what he saw as inappropriate government involvement. He reminded readers, for example, that France needed large firms that could make money; even the Soviets did not think that nationalized industries could consistently operate at a loss. By the summer of 1945, Siegfried feared that the French people were gripped by pessimism, evidenced by strikes and social divisions. They needed to commit to reconstruction so that the country could regain international respect. "For France has preserved a unique position among nations, not just that of any power, but of a country whose civilization has enlightened the world. *Noblesse oblige.* Much is asked of us; we would disappoint if we did not give much."[36]

These strictures were accompanied by frequent comments on the effort to establish new republican institutions. In the run-up to the elections for the new Constituent Assembly held on 21 October 1945, Siegfried criticized Communist and Socialist demands for a unicameral system, which he suggested would encourage unchecked radicalism. He advocated retaining elements of the Third Republic's constitution, including a senate. After the left performed very strongly on the ballot, he expressed dismay, speculating that a desire to "liberate the people" from "aristocratic" leadership might lead to a new kind of tyranny, under the control of a bureaucracy or party. His frustration grew during the fall and winter of 1945; then, on 18 January 1946, two days before de Gaulle resigned as head of government in response to deteriorating relations with the Assembly, Siegfried wrote his most frantic column yet, depicting individual initiative and private property as being under siege, putting the nation's very identity at risk; "[W]hat would France be if it was no longer individualist, betraying the profound spirit and tradition of political liberty?"[37] Fearing the potential effect of his words, the Ministry of Finance responded directly to him, arguing that the government was in fact encouraging savings and protecting the interests of property owners.[38]

The left-leaning Constituent Assembly subsequently produced a draft constitution that called for a unicameral system; it was put to a referendum on 5 May 1946. Siegfried and other contributors to

*Le Figaro* energetically supported the "no" campaign. He wrote several editorials on the subject, which subsequently appeared as a pamphlet entitled *Que penser la constitution?* He contended that a unicameral assembly would further the destructive tradition of the revolutionary far left, harkening back to the repression of the Jacobins.[39] Invoking the more positive heritage of a "liberal" 1789 and the constructive aspects of the Third Republic, he called upon voters to reject the draft and uphold France's parliamentary traditions. As it turned out, the draft constitution, despite the endorsement of the Communists and Socialists, was narrowly rejected. Thereafter, a revised document, which incorporated a relatively weak second chamber, known as the Council of the Republic, was approved in October of that same year, though only by a minority of the electorate – the margin of "yes" votes was thin, and eight million voters abstained. The passing of this revised document gave Siegfried some satisfaction, but he still perceived serious flaws in the new system. Surveying the events of 1946 in *L'année politique*, he argued that while the new Fourth Republic bore a superficial resemblance to the Third, mass parties with excessive influence still threatened to stifle true pluralist democracy and encouraged paralysis in day-to-day government. The Constitution of 1946 was still "Jacobin" insofar as it privileged the National Assembly; though "counterweights, in the form of a President of the Republic and a Council of the Republic, have been introduced, one senses that a persistent mistrust [emanating from the left] seeks to limit, even diminish their role." Siegfried continued to insist upon the long-term significance of these flaws in the years to come.[40]

Siegfried was particularly concerned about the Communists. The rhetoric he deployed against the PCF was less virulent than that of some right-wing commentators, but he was adamant in stressing its fundamentally alien character. Citing his long-held view that, while many French voters tended to favour militant parties they were also firm believers in private property, he asserted that "it is very clear that not all, not even a majority, of the people who vote communist are communist; furthermore France is not Marxist."[41] Naturally he was relieved at the expulsion of the PCF from the governing coalition in 1947, which he argued reflected a desire within the country at large for greater order and a desire for a revival of liberalism against *dirigisme*.[42]

The other mass parties were less threatening but, in Siegfried's eyes, posed problems of their own. The SFIO (Section française de l'international ouvrière) still notionally adhered to Marxist doctrine but its voters and many of its members held more moderate views, and as a result the party often struggled to remain true to its principles. The MRP also lacked coherence, torn between its commitment to democracy and its belief in the efficacy of state intervention; these conflicts were further complicated by Catholic influences. Initially, Siegfried was unsure what to make of de Gaulle's Rassemblement du peuple français (RPF), which appeared on the scene in the spring of 1947. He did not see it as a manifestation of the far-right anti-parliamentary tradition, as some left-wing commentators of the time did, though he came to regard the RPF as a political spoiler. But he avoided criticizing de Gaulle too harshly, instead hoping that some of his supporters would integrate into the system – which after several years turned out to be the case, albeit without the general's approval.[43]

Overall, Siegfried was a prominent voice calling for what Richard Vinen suggests many French conservatives wanted at the time – a looser party system, with individual deputies playing a greater role, united in the defence of an ostensibly moderate republic against extremism.[44] Over the course of 1948, Siegfried discerned signs of growing stability, suggesting that as the mass parties lost some of their strength, the pattern of politics began to resemble that of the Third Republic – which in Siegfried's view was a good thing. Surveying the situation at the end of the year, he observed that "the country carries on"; despite "the instability of postwar adjustment, a potential stability is asserting itself"; there was strong public support for a centrist regime, he believed. This amounted to a tacit endorsement of the "Third Force" – the coalition of the SFIO, MRP, and smaller parties that dominated French politics by this time, and opposed by the Communists and the RPF. He likened this situation to that of the early Third Republic, when the moderate republicans had worked to stabilize the country in the face of opposition from the extreme left and extreme right.[45]

Siegfried's views on the state of French politics can also be discerned, more obliquely, in his 1948 book *La Suisse, démocratie témoin*. Though it was framed as a monographic study in the tradition of his earlier works on English-speaking nations, it is not difficult to identify some prescriptions for France in the book. For Siegfried, Switzerland offered a welcome respite from the penury of postwar Europe. Though aware that the country had endured shortages during the conflict, in comparison to its neighbours it seemed prosperous: "Our first impression is that of a cornucopia, of an abounding mass of riches."[46] The task

Siegfried set for himself was to determine how the Swiss, despite many internal divisions, had managed to construct a stable democracy and a dynamic economy – things that he wanted for his own country.

Dissecting Switzerland's challenging geography and considerable linguistic and religious diversity, he explained that while the German-speaking Swiss accounted for nearly three-quarters of the population, the earlier presence of Christianization and the effect of Zwinglian rather than authoritarian Lutheran Protestantism happily distinguished them from Germans. To be sure, there was friction, but the overall impression was one of harmony.[47] The country's sturdy, localized democratic traditions – rooted originally in ancient barbarian practices – helped to explain this. Describing a cantonal gathering held in the town of Glarus, Siegfried noted the role of tradition but also the practical and constructive character of the meeting: "I am particularly struck by the fact that all the speakers discuss the objective merits and demerits of the proposals, and are not guided, as in other countries, by considerations of party politics." Centralization was a potential problem, but for the time being Siegfried believed that the virtues of the system were intact. That was also the case with the Swiss economy, for, despite its limited natural resources, the country had developed an advanced industrial sector while preserving a tradition of artisanal quality. The system was not perfect – it lacked some of "that creative imagination proper to the French genius" and there was a threat of decline "from an excess of cerebral concentration" – but as a whole Siegfried was most impressed by Swiss practices.[48] He was also taken with the country's ongoing ability to navigate the shifting currents of international trade, developing an impressive reputation in the tourism, banking, and finance sectors. Swiss prosperity was susceptible to fluctuating economic conditions, but the country undeniably demonstrated the results that could be achieved through continuous striving to produce high-quality goods and deliver crucial services within an open economic environment.

Siegfried did not think that the Swiss model could simply be exported to France, for the "temperaments" of the two countries were quite different. His comparison of their political systems shows the extent of his dismay with the state of French politics at the time: "The debates in the French Chamber are the lists in which opposing doctrines confront each other. The sessions of the National Council in Bern are more like meetings of an administrative body affecting only indirectly those who are not immediately concerned – but what an efficient administration!" Given this contrast, he expressed some surprise – though also a hint of pride – that "[t]hese astounding people, who have everything, good sense, technique, a civic sense, education, a fine culture and the highest civilization," still admired France and desired the "human spirit" that it possessed, even though "[n]ature has given it to France in the form of folly; Switzerland has it in the form of wisdom."[49]

Other, more popular books, further reflected Siegfried's concerns about the state of his country. One of them, *Savoir parler en public*, was intended to provide advice using references to classical and modern examples of great orators. Siegfried devoted a large proportion of the book to portraits of Léon Gambetta, Georges Clemenceau, Aristide Briand, Jean Jaurès, René Waldeck-Rousseau, Raymond Poincaré, and the philosopher Henri Bergson. He was blunt in explaining why none of his examples were contemporary politicians: "Please forgive me for the choices that I have made, to remember the orators of the Third Republic. I admit to playing the role of *laudator temporis acti* [praiser of times past], but who are the great orators of the Fourth Republic whom I could have added to this record of achievement?"[50]

A similar attitude informed *La Fontaine: Machiavel français*, an edited collection of the seventeenth-century poet's influential fables, some of which were widely studied in French schools. Siegfried lauded the fables for containing practical insights into human nature that modern politicians had clearly forgotten. His lukewarm estimation of contemporary ministers was clear, though he extended his criticisms to politicians of the Third Republic and foreign leaders as well. He wondered, for instance, if France's leaders would have evacuated the Rhineland early and allowed German troops to occupy it in 1936 had they truly absorbed the lesson of "The Lion in Love," which clearly showed that, just as "Samson must not let his hair be cut, the lion must not let its claws be clipped: a disarmed state no longer counts."[51] In *Géographie humoristique de Paris*, which appeared in 1951, Siegfried again adopted a light-hearted tone, but also sought to make the point that an exploration of apparently minor curiosities could highlight important trends. The book mapped the evolving social elite of Paris from the mid-nineteenth to the mid-twentieth century, with case studies ranging from members of various academic bodies to those still holding ducal titles to financial elites. Along the way, Siegfried offered observations on how status differentiated according to telephone exchanges, metro stops, and banking.[52] In the process, he made the point that while society evolved, the durability of class structures was evident in the city's spatial configuration. Siegfried noted that eastern Paris, with its more "popular" class composition, was socially marginalized despite its political significance. With respect to political change, he conceded that Popular Front and post-Liberation reforms meant that as a group the regents of the Banque de France had become more state-oriented. Ultimately, though, elites were persistently concentrated in the western half of the city, with academics preferring the Left Bank and financial elites the Right. Social planning could only have limited effect: "Through careful study of the evidence, the addresses of such important personalities across an entire century, I have formed the impression that, in the choice of a residence, their freedom only seems apparent; by virtue of laws deeper than their own will, they end up establishing themselves where they must. In this case sociology resembles natural history."[53]

The reservations and critiques that Siegfried advanced in these works also reflected his ongoing concern over the evolution of the Fourth Republic. Though it provided a degree of stability, the centrist Third Force also contained many internal fissures – between clericals and anticlericals, *dirigistes* and economic liberals, and moderates and militants – that made constructing durable ministries very difficult. The upper chamber was too weak to compensate for such problems. Collectively, these flaws – notwithstanding the efforts of the Socialist president Vincent Auriol, whom Siegfried respected – nurtured a troubling instability that damaged France's international reputation, especially among the Anglo-Saxon powers.[54] National elections were scheduled for June 1951: given the appeal of the Communists and de Gaulle's anti-system RPF, the stakes were very high. Siegfried emphasized in *Le Figaro* that France's reputation for political instability needed to be rectified.[55]

As it turned out, a coalition of moderate formations went on to narrowly defeat both the PCF and RPF, thanks to a complex electoral system of alliances that favoured the centre against the two mass parties. Evidently relieved, after the election Siegfried published a series of editorials that advocated for a government of the moderate centre-right. However, he also reiterated his bewilderment at the fact that one-quarter of the French electorate voted for the PCF, a fact that he attributed to a long national tradition of voting for the "loudest" protest party. On the other hand, he was also concerned that if any French government were too right wing, it would spur the formation

Facing the Postwar World

of an opposing left-wing coalition, causing further polarization and instability. In an editorial entitled "For an Intelligent Right," he deplored the destabilizing effect of the "anti-regime" right and argued that conservatives should now focus on defending individual and property rights, while respecting France's constitutional traditions.[56] From his perspective, France's 1951 shift to the right and the waning of Resistance-informed politics were promising signs. Before too long, however, his commentary on Fourth Republic politics would resume a more negative tone.

## FRANCE FACES THE POSTWAR WORLD

Siegfried was as concerned about the international situation as he was distressed about the state of French politics. In the closing stages of the war, he outlined the challenges faced by the West in general, and France in particular. At the Collège de France, he devoted one of his courses for the winter of 1944–45 to exploring the "Characteristics and Limits of Western Civilization"; that summer he presented his findings at Oxford, where he delivered the annual Romanes Lecture. His contention was that Western identity – rooted in a Greek conception of knowledge, a Judeo-Christian conception of the individual, and technological proficiency – was now threatened by a loss of equilibrium. Confidence in technology and human mastery of nature were advancing to the point of hubris and had collectivist social implications; "[O]ur civilization is becoming mechanical and materialistic: individual ambition is becoming a social claim for material equality ultimately ending in socialist distribution." Of the leading "mass mechanical civilizations" – German national socialism, Russian communism, and American capitalism – the most destructive had thankfully been vanquished, but even the more peaceful American variant promoted an excessively materialist notion of progress. It threatened to "standardize" private life, and to corrupt other civilizations that criticized the West's supposed lack of spirituality but nevertheless sought to appropriate its advanced technology. The West was also playing the role of "sorcerer's apprentice" by developing weaponry that allowed nations to destroy themselves.[57]

Above all, Siegfried feared that the West's unique quality of non-conformity would be lost. "The West has not renounced this idea, but an entire segment of the West is tempted to abandon or pervert it." Both the United States and Russia, by virtue of their geography and cultural development, lacked classic features of the Western heritage and thus posed problems in this regard; "The maxim according to which man is the measure of things no longer has meaning on the Russian steppe or American prairie." He tried to avoid sounding overly pessimistic, pointing out that the United States was a powerful repository of Christianity and eighteenth-century humanism, and suggesting that the Russian people were still marked by "the evangelizing tradition" and a natural "humanism." Nevertheless, Western leadership was passing to two indisputably non-European powers.

How were France, and, more broadly, Europe, to respond? Siegfried had few illusions about the difficulties involved. In a January 1945 address to reporters, he detailed the moral and material devastation of his country. In addition to the prodigious destruction of resources and huge loss of life, the country's psychology had become distorted. The need to conduct sabotage and to disrupt production for Germany meant that "[i]dleness, selective striking became commendable … Ambush, plunder, attack by force of arms thus became acts worthy of praise." This made an orderly transition to recovery difficult. In a talk given at the Royal Institute of International Affairs (Chatham House) a few weeks later, Siegfried conveyed a similar message. "That we have suffered under the occupation in France you may know physically but you cannot know morally, so when speaking of Franco-British relations in the future Europe I think it is necessary to start by saying that the plight of the continent is much worse than you can imagine."[58]

To reclaim its international standing, France needed allies. Even before the war ended, Siegfried was involved in early dialogues about closer economic cooperation within Europe, chairing a discussion group that explored the possibility of a future West European customs union. In his 1945 lecture at Chatham House, he signalled that an effective partnership between France and Britain would also be vital. While noting significant friction between the two nations in the past and acknowledging that a degree of mistrust persisted, Siegfried contended that Britain and France were nevertheless united in the goal of building "a common civilization." While Britons might be inclined to regard Europe with disdain, he commented, "[t]his mad-house is so near to you that you cannot ignore it." Notwithstanding its Atlantic orientation, Britain also possessed ties to Europe, and, like France, Belgium, and Holland, retained major colonial interests. European solidarity was thus critical, for the continent "is the real source of culture in the world, and if she were to disappear the culture which exists outside Europe would hardly be sufficient to keep the level of human civilization high enough."[59]

Germany was excluded from Siegfried's definition of Europe, at least for the foreseeable future. "I have admired the Germans as everybody has, for their technical skill, their philosophy and their great works of art, perhaps above all for their great aptitude for going to the very bottom of a question; but really in the long run you cannot work with them because they are not working for Western civilisation." When asked whether he could foresee an improvement in Franco-German relations, he reportedly responded that "[i]t would be a great danger if the German menace were again forgotten or underestimated after the present war. Perhaps in forty or fifty years it would have disappeared, but in 1918 he had heard the same language spoken ... It would be better this time to be more severe in the beginning and finally to find some means by which they could serve as peaceful members of the European community. Whether the Germans would ever be educated to adopt the British form of government he very much doubted." Both Russia and the United States, despite their divergence from aspects of Western civilization, were more suitable as allies, the former because of "geographical equilibrium" and the latter because of shared values, even if Franco-American relations could never be on the same level as Anglo-American ties.[60] The rapidly changing postwar environment soon led Siegfried to revisit some of these views, but at the time he clearly hoped that wartime alliances would endure and new intra-European associations would take hold.

Despite the challenges ahead, the French could take comfort in the fact that they had at least retained their unique culture and language, which could be major sources of renovation. "France will shine if its science, literature, higher education, and high culture remain at its level, and if it shows through its bearing the world that it remains attached, not in word but at heart, to the ideal that made it a leader in the world." Siegfried was enthusiastic about efforts to realize this potential: speaking in 1945 to Rayonnement Français, an association that encouraged contacts between elites from the Allied nations, particularly military officers, and their French counterparts, he underscored the particular value of the French language in this respect: "For a thought, filtered by the French mind, having been imbued with order and clarity by it, becomes communicable, like a currency valued everywhere and which everyone can make use of; this thus takes on an international significance, it no longer belongs to us – that's French influence." In a subsequent article for *American Legion Magazine*, he reiterated this point with specific reference to the Académie française: "Thus the Frenchman respects intellectually only that which is clear, free from confusion ... That is why, I think, [he] takes such a passionate interest in anything which concerns his language." Only by ensuring the latter's vitality and clarity – the work of the Académie – could France hold true to preserving key principles, such as faith in the individual, amid growing pressures for conformity.[61]

French status and identity remained key concerns as Siegfried travelled to San Francisco in the spring of 1945 as a member of his country's delegation to the United Nations Conference. The group had to contend with a widespread perception of French, and more generally European, dilapidation, as expressed by the Canadian diplomat Charles Ritchie. "The French delegation here seems to reinforce the painful impression that I formed in Paris – they seem to be *détraqués* ... They have no one who is a connecting link with the past and who still retains faith and vitality ... They seem just a collection of clever, amiable, young Frenchmen – and old Paul-Boncour is too old and tired – so is André Siegfried."[62] There were also problems of a more concrete nature. France had not participated in the drafting of a proposed UN charter at Dumbarton Oaks in 1944 or in the Yalta Conference of February 1945. De Gaulle had retaliated against being excluded from the latter by refusing to participate in organizing the San Francisco conference. France had thus been on the margins of the planning process, and there was some concern that it would be a spoiler during the deliberations. But once the conference got underway, the French delegation was integrated into the proceedings, French became a working language at the sessions, and France became a permanent member of the Security Council. Though some modifications were made to the Dumbarton Oaks proposals, the UN Charter approved at the conference largely reflected great-power concerns.[63] Siegfried was primarily involved in discussions about economic, social, and intellectual cooperation, which culminated in the formation of the UN's Economic and Social Council. He also participated in committees that dealt with trusteeships and drafting the preamble to the Charter.[64]

Attending the conference also gave Siegfried the opportunity to reconnect with North America. Having last visited the United States in September 1939 when it had yet to recover fully from the ravages of the Great Depression, he observed in *Le Figaro* that as their wartime economy boomed Americans had recovered the buoyant optimism of the 1920s. There were concerns about the possibility of a postwar recession but the overall contrast with the situation in Europe was enormous. "American Western humanity has become habituated to a way of life that Europe can no longer equal ... America looks to the future – as for us, we think of paradise lost." Canada's economy had also expanded greatly, though Siegfried worried about the implications of modernization. Visiting a "modern," fully mechanized farm near Regina, Saskatchewan, he noted uneasily that "[t]he farmer is above all a mechanic ... It remains to be seen whether people can detach themselves from the land, treating it no longer as a nourishing earth to be conserved but as raw material that is manufactured, without serious harm."[65]

Siegfried also analyzed the workings of the San Francisco conference, in the process making the case for France's continued international relevance. He could not deny that the global power structure had fundamentally changed: the fact that the gathering was taking place on the Pacific Coast of the United States shows "that the world's centre of gravity has shifted." If the United States and Russia had fully cooperated, they would have utterly dominated the proceedings. But this was far from being the case, for there was a great deal of anxiety surrounding Russian goals and conduct. Such divisions gave Britain and France some leverage. They were now secondary powers but were still capable of exercising influence, especially if they worked together. Though concerned about anti-colonial sentiment in the United States and convinced that China was in the American orbit, Siegfried noted approvingly the persistence of cultural ties between France and Latin America and pointed out that Britain still exercised influence there as well as with Canada, Australia, and New Zealand, even though these countries now looked to the US for security. He was also delighted that Foreign Minister Georges Bidault had ensured that French was adopted as a working language; it signalled, he suggested with a touch of bravado, that "French influence remains vast: from the cultural point of view, it extends over all the earth."[66]

Reflecting on the significance of the conference, Siegfried highlighted Franklin Roosevelt as the chief architect of the gathering, even though he had not lived to see what it wrought. The Security Council was intended to resolve the tension between international cooperation and great-power sovereignty, but it involved a delicate balancing act and Siegfried doubted that Harry Truman had the capacity to uphold Roosevelt's achievements. Competing impulses were also at play in the foreign policies of the other great powers. The Soviet Union, while possessing a revolutionary vision, also clung to a narrower, territorial conception of security that it would not allow abstract principles of international cooperation to jeopardize. As for Britain, its foreign policy could focus either on closer links to Europe or engaging, in association with the United States, on a broader international scale. Challenges to its status, and that of France, as colonial powers lay ahead since both leading world powers were harsh critics of imperialism, and both were seeking to extend their influence.[67] Such problems were greatly magnified by the intensification of anti-colonial sentiment, which Siegfried documented and criticized as he resumed his global travels.

### THE WEST AND AN UNSETTLED WORLD

Some of these concerns first became apparent when he visited Latin America in the summer and autumn of 1946. Siegfried had less to say about the tenacity of Indigenous cultures than he had in the 1930s; this may have had something to do with the fact that he spent much of his time in Argentina and Chile, states where the Indigenous populations were proportionately smaller than those in Bolivia or Peru.[68] What struck him most immediately was the rapid growth these countries were experiencing. Buenos Aires, he observed, had expanded dramatically since the 1930s, and as a whole Argentina was in the throes of a major industrial expansion and enjoying greater financial stability as it entered the stage of economic "maturity." What disturbed Siegfried was the extent to which the capital had become "Americanized" at the expense of its Spanish character. Moreover, the political situation was also fraught. Peron's regime deployed some leftist vocabulary and social policies – which to Siegfried recalled the propaganda of the French Communist Party – but it also relied upon the military and Catholic Church for support. In addition, there was a trade union base that had been incorporated into the state along fascist lines. In all, Argentinian developments illustrated the perils of the region's political traditions; "Machiavelli, who would have loved South America, would have no doubt advised its governments to never interfere, under any pretext, with their police or armies."[69]

Chile offered some contrasts. Though it was indubitably a "New World" country in its geography, Siegfried felt that its cities retained more of a Latin character than did Buenos Aires, though he balked at the growing number of skyscrapers in Santiago. Chilean politics also

Facing the Postwar World

seemed to obey more familiar patterns; analyzing its 1946 presidential election campaign, Siegfried found that the various political parties bore considerable similarity to their French counterparts. They included a Socialist party that was slowly drifting toward the centre, a right that was resolutely anti-modern, and centrists who wanted to conserve the essentials of the system.[70] Privately, though, Siegfried's views were more ambivalent. In a letter to Henri Aubrun, he asserted that Chile's social policies were worthy of further study, and he was pleased that French was widely spoken among the elite. But, to an extent that he did not in *Le Figaro*, he expressed dismay about growing American influence. "Many young people, seduced by American prestige, are going to New York rather than Paris. The United States is not liked, but it is admired and imitated. The cinema has played a decisive role in this respect." Moreover, the Chilean population had its flaws; Siegfried came to the conclusion that the people harboured elements of American materialism along with vaguely defined "Eastern" influences. "The danger for this country is that its Latin ascendancy, mixed with Indian heritage and not without some Arab influence, renders it a country with an Oriental psychology and atmosphere. Everyone lives beyond their means; anyone paying in cash would be considered a curiosity. Among the people there is also a lack of ambition, the result of which is that as soon as a salary ceases to be simply starvation wages people no longer work, content with the bare minimum."[71]

Similar critiques were on display in Siegfried's assessment of Brazil. In some ways he was dazzled by the country. Rio de Janeiro stood out in part because it retained a quasi-imperial character – Dom Pedro II had only abdicated in 1889 – that set it apart from Buenos Aires and New York. He also found the Amazonian city of Belém a charming blend of Portuguese and tropical influences. Overall, the country impressed because of its vast, often untapped resources, though Siegfried contrasted its farmers' proclivity for exhausting the land and moving on – typical of the Americas – with the more conservationist instincts of the French peasant.[72] However, it was during a visit to the northwestern Sertão region, which he likened to the American far west, when his views of the Brazilian people emerged most clearly. He argued in *Le Figaro* that, under the auspices of the Brazil Foundation, civilization was gradually being brought to this remote area. This entailed establishing peaceful relations with Indigenous populations that had hitherto lived in complete isolation. In describing this encounter,

Siegfried was struck by the ethnic complexity of the Brazilian colonizers, whom he praised with condescension; "[A]s we are in a Latin country these pioneering adventurers, whether white, Indian, or black, are pleased to hear us tell them that in their modest and useful way they are working for civilization." The main contrast between them and the Indigenous people was in fact temporal, he claimed; "[C]ontact is not so much between peoples of different ethnic origin as between men of different eras, who are not contemporaries."[73]

Siegfried admired the efforts of the Brazil Foundation, though he hinted that relations between its personnel and the Indigenous population were not always peaceful. This spoke to, he contended, the complexity of colonizing a national territory as well as the composition of the Brazilian people. "[T]he challenge of colonization is not the same as for our colonial empires; it is a matter of peaceful conquest and the Indian himself, even if he ends up being absorbed, will have also left something of his presence and traditions. It is there, perhaps, that one can see the profound and original spirit of the Brazilian nation."[74] Exploring the Brazilian population in a separate article, he reaffirmed that pure races did not exist, but moved on to differentiate between the Portuguese and other European immigrants to the country, and its large Indigenous and African communities. "Indians," he claimed, were "economically useless." Afro-Brazilians could master certain trades but were unlikely to be highly productive; "[I]f two days a week of work gives them enough for a living, they do not work anymore." All Brazilians enjoyed the same rights and opportunities, Siegfried claimed, but "the man of colour is naturally content with humble or inferior situations." In some ways, he concluded, the Brazilian approach was admirable; following the Latin tradition, the Portuguese had apparently eschewed racialist sentiments and embraced ethnic mixing, though perhaps with an eye to eventually absorbing the African population, which he approved of. "If that is the case," he concluded, "Brazil will have peacefully resolved the terrible problem that has blocked the future of the United States with a sinister screen." Nevertheless, he added, tolerance had its costs: "The price paid – informed Brazilians do not overlook it – is the handicap [imposed by] this exotic presence, a source of indolence, superstition, and slackening in economic efficiency."[75]

Siegfried's professed uneasiness with explicitly institutionalized racism, but above all his abiding belief in the inferiority of Africans, resurfaced when he visited the Congo, South Africa, and Rhodesia in 1948. He relayed his impressions in a series of articles for *Le Figaro* that were published as *Afrique du Sud: Notes de voyage* in 1949 and appeared in English translation the following year. This journey, Siegfried informed his readers, had been fifty years in the making. As a young man, he had hoped to meet Cecil Rhodes and witness the mining boom in the region. Instead, he now settled for a visit to Rhodes's tomb, which he characterized, quoting Maurice Barrès, as one of those "places of deep significance for the soul of man." Siegfried praised Rhodes's achievements but conceded that they also "contain[ed] the germs of a crisis."[76] There were hints of it in the Congo, he believed. Glossing over the horrors of the Congo Free State before 1908 – he suggested that the territory was depopulated because of the slave trade, disease, and undernourishment rather than King Leopold II's rapacious polices – he praised the Belgian ruler as "a great man of affairs of the nineteenth century, a builder and, in the last resort, an idealist ready to sacrifice his personal fortune to his great project." Leopold's successors had carried on with a paternalist approach, training the "natives" to become skilled workers while Christian missions provided essential social services and helped to rebuild the population. Such methods remained "well suited to the existing circumstances." But eventually the Black population would seek to better itself; though the African "is racially still a child ... a sort of familiar and affectionate younger brother," eventually he would seek "to raise himself to the level of the white." If this occurred precipitously, "then a crisis arises, sudden and terrible, and affection can then change abruptly to hate."[77]

Siegfried discerned similar patterns elsewhere on the continent. In the case of Rhodesia, he argued for "some form of administrative tutelage" for the time being, lest its white minority be overwhelmed by the granting of rights to the Black majority. The situation in South Africa was even more volatile. Though it lacked rich soil, the country's economy had been transformed by the discovery of gold and diamonds; its leaders now promoted industrialization to ensure that prosperity continued. "But this sudden upsurge," Siegfried continued, "reminiscent of a wild-cat oil gusher, has produced more problems than it is able to solve." While the white minority had a massive, cheap African labour force at its disposal, this was not an unalloyed benefit. Many whites were no longer accustomed to manual labour; indeed, Siegfried implied that many of them were no longer used to really working, even as their trade unions did their utmost to prevent Blacks

216    France in the World

from acquiring skills that would entitle them to higher wages. As for the African majority, many lived in poverty on the fringes of Johannesburg and other cities, where they became "de-tribalized" and grew susceptible to "Communist, or simply anti-white" propaganda. Even though Siegfried believed that Africans were inherently more accustomed to difficult conditions, he also noted that a growing number of them aspired to better education and living standards. Echoing his comments on race relations in the United States in the 1920s, Siegfried concluded that "[t]o look at the colour problem in South Africa is very much like looking over the edge of an abyss."[78]

Assessing the segregationist policies being implemented by the Nationalist Party, he judged them "fundamentally reasonable because neither the white man nor the coloured man really wishes to live together with the other race," but doubted whether the Black majority could be subjugated indefinitely. "The natives are four times as numerous as the Whites in South Africa, hence the somber fear of the future felt by the Boers. That obsession explains, if it does not justify, their intransigence." Regarding racist segregation in South Africa, he expressed distaste for apartheid, but made clear his sympathy for South African whites:

> World opinion is harsh ... too harsh in my opinion. Not that I approve – and who could approve? – of the utterly uncharitable attitude of the South Africans towards the coloured people. But to the Americans who protest I am tempted to say: 'He that is without sin among you, let him cast the first stone,' and to Europeans I would say: 'You know nothing about the daily problem of colour.' The extenuating circumstance lies in the fact that these whites represent an outpost of our race and our civilization which is being compelled to defend itself.[79]

Other aspects of South Africa's racial problems, Siegfried predicted, would intensify as European imperialism waned. The country's Indian minority, concentrated in Natal, was not "primitive" but it was problematic. For the time being, Indians had to endure the colour bar but there was likely trouble ahead as a newly independent India took notice of their difficulties; "[I]f India became an effective political power capable of expansion and intervention then the problem would change in character and become extremely disturbing for a country like South Africa with a population of only two and a half million whites, a small European island in a rising sea of colour." There was also a "coloured" population, particularly visible in Cape Town, which was largely the result of an earlier stage of colonization "when colour prejudice, a comparatively recent notion, either did not yet exist or was by no means so strong as it has since become." These people, he observed, often distanced themselves from Africans but still endured restrictions reminiscent of the Jim Crow system in the southern United States. About this, Siegfried expressed some reservations, but he saw the solution as the effective erasure of African heritage, rather than a change in laws. As in America, he noted, some South Africans of mixed ancestry could "pass" as white; this was a "happy" solution "because it permits the acceptance of human beings who deserve to be accepted and otherwise would not be accepted."[80]

Acute though its problems were, South Africa was but one site in a broader clash of civilizations and races. Siegfried closed by lamenting the general retreat of Western power. He argued that this was partly the result of degeneration, involving a loss of moral vigour and capacity for hard work that left whites unable to compete with other races, notably Asians. But above all, it was because the West had begun "to doubt the validity of our moral rights." The Soviet Union was utterly opposed to such rights while the United States, "brutally intransigent in ethnic matters at home," was undermining the European presence in Asia. There needed to be more understanding for those who lived on the frontiers of the West, in South Africa, Australia, and the southern US; "[W]ithout being a racial fanatic I must insist that it is upon the white race, and on it alone, that the responsibility for Western civilization rests ... I have witnessed a retreat of civilization comparable to that of the Roman Empire when it found itself forced to defend itself on all sides against the rising tide of barbarism which threatened to engulf it."[81]

Two years later, Siegfried visited India and Pakistan, writing another series of articles for *Le Figaro*, which were subsequently published by Armand Colin. In these pieces, he displayed slightly more respect for the local populations, but there was still a strong tone of disdain. He had last travelled to India during his world tour as a young man and found it to be a supremely "spiritual" place. A half century later, he suggested, independence and partition had radically altered the political context and the desire to modernize was now prevalent. Siegfried professed to respect both Pakistan's and India's Western-educated leaders, whom he met in person. Liaquat Ali Khan, educated in Britain and a veteran of pre-independence politics, was "a prime minister of quality"; his Indian counterpart, Jawaharlal Nehru, was "in today's world one of the dominant figures in international politics," who combined keen political skills with a quasi-mystical idealism that reminded Siegfried of the French Socialist leader Léon Blum. Yet both leaders faced major obstacles. Siegfried judged that Ali Khan had only a few capable subordinates and noted that Nehru's Congress Party was highly diverse in outlook, with many of its members holding more conservative views than their leader.[82] More generally, Pakistan had agricultural resources and a rich elite, but Siegfried wondered how much progress there would be now that Western influence was receding. "One would have to return in ten, then twenty years to see what this country, responsible for itself for the first time, makes of itself." As for India, it had a significant industrial base, and Indians could be highly effective in running smaller-scale enterprises. But once larger-scale operations were involved, Siegfried invoked his long-standing conviction that true administrative genius was the preserve of Westerners; in particular, India lacked a cohort of capable middle managers. "The efficiency of a civilization is not measured by the quality of its heads, but by its average level and above all the quality of its deputies [sous-officiers]." At a deeper level, despite prolonged British rule Indian civilization continued to differ from the West in its refusal to distinguish between reason and spirituality. "For the Indians, perhaps as for the first Greeks, there is still a similarity between mathematics and poetry, confusion between the arguments of science and the emotions of lyricism."[83]

Assessing South Asia in a geopolitical context, Siegfried foresaw plenty of trouble. Indian claims of sovereignty over French Pondichéry and Portuguese Goa, both of which he regarded as positive examples of what lasting Western contact could achieve, were bothersome. In the former case, Siegfried argued that a referendum should be held, suggesting that the results might well favour France. As for Goa, for him it confirmed his view that "everywhere the Portuguese flag flies, reigns that extraordinary, paradoxical thing: ethnic peace – there is no superior or inferior race."[84] India's quest to acquire these territories, for him, betrayed a lack of comprehension of Western principles, methods, and achievements. Sadly, the problems associated with South Asian independence went well beyond these specific disputes. At this juncture, Siegfried was not much concerned by a revolutionary threat; both Pakistan and India were anti-communist in their domestic politics, and although Nehru was impressed by aspects of the Soviet economic model, he sought neutrality in the Cold War. The problem that loomed was a clash of cultures. Increasingly assertive Asian nations were now taking advantage of Western weakness. Britain had preserved good relations with both India and Pakistan, but the power vacuum in the Indian Ocean was being filled in an alarming way; "[T]he atmosphere of the countries of the Indian Ocean is hostile to Western civilization and the men of the white race who represent it." What would happen to countries such as Australia and South Africa if China and India sought new outlets for their populations, and the forces of Britain and the United States were no longer able to intervene? "Dark clouds are thus gathering on the horizon. This ocean, until recently so calm, risks becoming a storm center in its turn."[85]

In sum, Europe was on the defensive in Asia, under pressure from a USSR that stoked the flames of revolution, American anti-colonialism, and above all "Asiatics [a term that Siegfried was aware had grown unpopular but persisted in using] themselves in the name of their superiority in the spiritual domain." Ultimately, he reiterated, this situation derived from a lack of Western self-confidence. "Asia, formerly passive, is awakening; it is also revolting against Western domination, less through its own strength than because of our weakness, or rather our abdication." Siegfried conceded that Europeans could not claim superiority when it came to culture – "many Asiatics are more cultivated and refined than us" – and that it was possible for non-Westerners to acquire advanced technology. But the West remained supreme when it came to organization and administration, and probably always would. "If the administration of the world, or certain parts of the world, is passing into hands other than ours – which is in the midst of occurring – there will not necessarily be a collapse, but a decline is likely." Moreover, notwithstanding Eastern spiritual superiority, when it came to social amenities and progress the West stood out; "Thus I do not believe that the attitude of excuse and humility, too often adopted by us, is justified."[86]

As he had done in earlier works, such as his 1935 *La crise de l'Europe*, Siegfried had often generalized about the West in relation to other cultures in his early postwar writings. In 1950, he explored the contrasts that existed between the different components of Western civilization in *L'âme des peuples*. Here too, the tone was often gloomy, though when it came to the Latin nations and France, Siegfried detected some signs of hope. Latinity, he conceded, currently faced the future with a sense of uncertainty. The product of many different racial groups, the Mediterranean climate, and the Roman heritage, the Latin culture was "clearly defined, local and diverse ... the antithesis of a mass-production civilization." It was also a mature culture with deep roots in the past and a well-informed sense of history. This promoted qualities of realism, intelligence, and clarity of thought and expression. There were negatives – lacking the civic-mindedness of Anglo-Saxons, Latins tended to regard the state as something either to be resisted or used "as an instrument of domination." The Latin was also an individualist, which could lead to excesses; "proud and vain ... he desires to shine." Profoundly attached to their families, Latins were skilled in business, but their societies were not at the forefront of current economic growth. Their individualism and maturity were still crucial to Europe, however. Even if the continent's "modern sources of efficiency no longer principally derive from Latin influence," the latter "represents an indispensable factor of our civilization, and it is perhaps with its assistance that we can obtain the highest and most disinterested level of culture, a culture of quality and refinement of spirit, and more literary than scientific."[87]

As for France, it was at the pinnacle of Western values: "[A]mongst the peoples of Europe there is none which has gone further, I will not say with the fusion, but with what one can nevertheless call the synthesis of historical contributions from all points on the compass. Eighteen hundred years of history in an uninterrupted stream have made us into the most highly developed of the Western peoples and, as we have suggested, the most adult." Siegfried did not deny that there were national character flaws, or that in some respects France was less than ideally suited to face contemporary problems. The universalism of its people, combined with a very practical approach to personal affairs, made for a "curious mixture of idealism and shabbiness." Though the French were good at invention, they were less capable of capitalizing upon what they had discovered. Their innate individualism tended to encourage inefficiency, if not chaos. "The familiar humorous definition is not lacking in point: One Frenchman, an intelligent man; two Frenchmen, a great deal of talk; three Frenchmen, utter disorder." But these shortcomings hardly negated France's status as a crossroads of civilization. Blending Western, Continental, and Mediterranean influences, it enjoyed a "unique equilibrium ... [t]here is no country which is at the same time more daring in its ideas and more fixed in its habits." Its people blessed with an unmatched clarity of thought, France championed the rights of man and the freedom of intellectual contemplation.[88]

By contrast, while "Anglo-Saxons" seemed better suited to contemporary demands, they lacked intellectual and spiritual depth. The "English" had profoundly shaped the nineteenth century in a liberal direction, but despite their commercial and political prowess, they remained somewhat insular. Mentally, they were much "younger" than their counterparts across the Channel, to the point of being childlike at times. Siegfried recalled that during the First World War, French soldiers would spend their leisure time reading history or philosophy; in contrast, "my British general occupied his time with a detective story." Siegfried was uncertain whether the country's tradition of "muddling through" could still suffice, though he rejected the notion that unavoidable decline had set in, citing Britain's capacity for adaptation. As for the United States, it was currently at the peak of its powers, serving as the "guarantor" of Western values and providing an imposing political and economic model in global terms. Given their vast resources and recent achievements, it was hardly surprising that Americans felt extremely confident. But for all that, Siegfried remarked, "perhaps America has reached a turning-point." A cavalier attitude toward nature, in contrast to the wisdom of the French peasant, had recently led to problems such as soil erosion. The country's population had lost coherence, with its Anglo-Saxon core diluted by waves of Southern and Eastern European migrants. Americans were less eccentric and adventurous than they had been fifty years ago, having grown more accepting of government intervention in their lives. In this increasingly uniform and conformist society, "the critical spirit" was endangered. "The greatest danger may still be in the future when the organization finally gets the upper hand of the individual."[89]

Despite their shortcomings, for Siegfried Britain was indisputably part of Western civilization; so was the United States, but its status was more tentative as, in some ways, it had departed from its European roots. By contrast, in his estimation, Germany's connections to the West were tenuous. Siegfried's attitude toward Germany thus remained quite negative, though compared with the views he expressed in 1945 his analysis of its national psychology was a little more nuanced and took Cold War dynamics into account. Germany's Rhenish region, he explained, was closely tied to Western Europe but the East seemed like a semi-Asiatic frontier: "[O]ne suddenly has the impression of having just crossed a frontier into the Asia of steppes and forests: immense and monotonous, flat and melancholy." Lacking a tradition of Roman settlement and deep-rooted Christian mores, the East also had little sense of itself. "The historic past of France might be compared to a deep ocean and that of East Prussia to a shallow lake." Influenced by Jacques Rivière's *L'Allemagne*, Siegfried elaborated on the fragility of German identity. Notwithstanding the industriousness and culture of the German people, "they remain tentative, open to all possibilities, disposable and essentially malleable" and thus susceptible to authoritarianism, a tradition that dated back to Martin Luther. "In Germany, the chaos is internal, and discipline can come only from outside."[90]

As for Russia – the country with which Siegfried was the least familiar – he saw it as an "amorphous immensity without a true frontier"; its people were the product of disparate waves of settlement and invasion. Citing authorities such as Luc Durtain, the Marquis de Custine, Charles Seignobos, and the Russian philosopher Nikolai Berdyaev, Siegfried emphasized that despite centuries of emulating Europe and current Soviet confidence in the future, "barbarism is just under the surface all the time as though the assimilation had not been complete or had been periodically arrested by a return to primitive origins." Despite the strength of Russian national sentiment and the real talents of the Russian people, there was, as with Germany, an enduring instability in the national character.[91]

In the conclusion of *L'âme des peuples*, Siegfried emphasized his relief that Nazism had been vanquished – a victorious Hitler, he surmised, would have corrupted European values in a way akin to how eastward expansion had caused the ancient Greeks to lose their "purity." But in many ways, his pessimism about current affairs ran deep; among its many challenges, the West now had to contend with a Soviet Union whose combination of "technique and social mysticism" posed an existential threat to classical beliefs in "the individual as an independent spiritual being."[92] For all their commercial prowess, these were not values that the Anglo-Saxon countries were best positioned to defend, given Britain's current difficulties and the possibility that the United States – which had already moved far from some key Western precepts – may already have reached its full economic and social potential and now risked drifting into conformism. Though the prevailing currents of modernization did not work in their favour, Latin, and especially French qualities, despite their limitations, were at the core of Western uniqueness, and, ultimately, supremacy. Such declarations sound brash given the devastating losses experienced by France during the war, but were certainly in keeping with Siegfried's long-term views.

— * —

Siegfried's activities during the immediate postwar era reflect his belief in France's unique cultural and spiritual contribution to Western civilization, as well as his desire to see his country stabilized as a moderate republic that avoided problematic immigrants. France's international standing could be revived through its cultural influence, judicious alliances, and an economic revitalization that resisted excessive statism. Siegfried's efforts provide a prominent example of how conservative French elites parried what they saw as the threat of left-wing Resistance-inspired reform, instead substituting a more constrained series of changes.[93] In the international sphere, his responses to the Cold War and decolonization are also suggestive. While Siegfried's antipathy to Communism was deep-rooted, to his mind there were other pressing concerns. He had no doubt that France should align with the United States politically, but this never dispelled his worries about the long-term implications of American influence, or American hostility to European colonialism. On the latter, Siegfried's frequent and forceful articulation of concerns about the rise of anti-colonial nationalism and its threat to Western supremacy can help us to understand better the insecurities and belligerence displayed by elements of the early postwar French elite and public when faced with challenges to the country's colonial empire, and international standing more generally.[94]

# 7

# Final Years

Until the final months of his life, Siegfried maintained a very busy schedule. Paule and he did not travel quite as broadly as they had in the early postwar years, but there were still two extended stays in the United States, first in 1951 and then again in 1955; that same year, when André turned eighty, they also visited the Algerian Sahara. Thereafter, their travels were restricted to Western Europe, with the last trip, to West Germany, taking place in October 1958. In France, the couple continued to divide their time between the Rue de Courty and the summer home in Vence; sometimes they escaped from the bustle of Paris to the Hôtel Trianon Palace in Versailles, to allow André to concentrate on his work.[1] Still teaching at Sciences Po, leading the Musée social, and an active member of the Académie française, Siegfried continued to give lectures, contribute to *Le Figaro*, and steadily produce books and articles.

Though he was acutely aware that during these years France's international standing was being battered by destructive colonial wars in Indochina and Algeria, domestically Siegfried's writing focused primarily on the degeneration of Fourth Republic politics, which he attributed mainly to the left. His advocacy of a liberal-conservative regime persisted, though he ultimately condoned de Gaulle's return to power in 1958. Internationally, he remained heavily focused on the United States – his return visit in 1951 included significant new research, though in many respects his views remained the same. America continued to be an imposing but highly problematic social model, a situation exacerbated by its increasingly strident anti-imperialism. That threatened to undermine Western unity, as the Suez Crisis of 1956 painfully illustrated for Siegfried. France's path, he concluded, lay domestically with cautious modernization while preserving the humanist values that made it so special, and internationally with renewed European partnerships. At times, Siegfried proclaimed confidence in such a future, but the undeniable advance of anti-colonial nationalism was to his mind now cause for despair.

There is some evidence that Siegfried's prestige declined in these years. This was most clearly the case in the United States, where his views on race and ethnicity, which had changed little despite the caesura of the Second World War, drew increasing criticism. The American historian H. Stuart Hughes, who at the time was married to a cousin of Siegfried's, described him as a "a waning asset" in French intellectual life.[2] But his continued determination to chronicle and prescribe a path for his country's politics and society, and to delimit the boundaries of and threats to Western civilization, is evident. Nor should the reach of his ideas, or their resonance among French elites at the time, be discounted.

### CLOSING ENGAGEMENTS

Sciences Po remained dear to Siegfried's heart; he taught there until 1957 and remained president of the FNSP until his death, with Jacques Chapsal overseeing its daily operations. Siegfried's letters to Chapsal during his sojourns in the United States shed light on some of his preoccupations during these years. For example, in the fall of 1951 the two discussed efforts to have another member of the Sciences Po faculty, the jurist and historian of political ideas Jean-Jacques Chevallier, elected to a chair in political science at the Collège de France, even though Siegfried was no longer a voting member of the Assembly of Professors. Siegfried saw Chevallier's candidacy as an opportunity to promote "our political science association," though the bid ultimately proved unsuccessful.[3] Four years later, during Siegfried's term as a visiting professor at Harvard, he and Chapsal responded to an entreaty from the Ford Foundation concerning the creation of an "international study group for European problems." Chapsal found the proposal vague, a view that Siegfried shared; he was concerned that the new body would be regarded as a tool of American policy and insisted that it must be genuinely international, though he believed that it was prudent to maintain "a cordial contact." The fate of the proposal is uncertain, but it may have been the first incarnation of what eventually became Raymond Aron's Institute of

European Sociology, for Chapsal had suggested that the Foundation intended Aron to play a leading role.[4]

The correspondence between the two also sheds light on Siegfried's sojourn as a visiting professor at Harvard in 1955. He enjoyed giving his course on French politics, praised the university's business and law faculties, and was impressed by faculty members such as Arthur Schlesinger Sr and Jr, as well as his former student Stanley Hoffmann. But he found Cambridge unattractive, and though he appreciated the beauty of a New England autumn he recalled with fondness the colours of the Midi and observed that "my mental heart is always at the Rue St. Guillaume."[5] This deep attachment to Sciences Po was fully reciprocated; senior colleagues continued to laud his accomplishments while junior ones appreciated his patronage. Jean Gottmann, who began teaching economic geography at the FNSP in 1948 and served as Siegfried's assistant until 1955, found him to be both supportive and open-minded, helping him to create a new seminar in his subject and encouraging him to follow his own path. A note from Siegfried in response to the celebration of his eightieth birthday captures his deep bond with the institution, which he regarded very much as a continuation of the École libre: "The Foundation goes back ten years, but my association with the School (which lives on under the Foundation) is infinitely older and my attachment, if I may say so, is proportional to this number of years, which I dare to count with difficulty."[6]

Siegfried also continued to devote significant time and energy to the Musée social. The minutes of the Musée's *comité de direction* for the 1950s are not very detailed, but they do suggest that he was a conscientious president, chairing meetings and providing oversight while Henri Aubrun continued as director.[7] Siegfried took a particular interest in the psychology and prevention of workplace accidents in the early 1950s, writing a preface for the book *Échec au risque* written by Pierre Caloni, director of the Syndicat générale du garantie des chambres syndicales du bâtiment et travaux publics. Siegfried endorsed Caloni's analysis, which highlighted that the workers most likely to fall victim to accidents were either, on the one hand, very inexperienced ones, or, on the other, seasoned veterans who had grown overconfident. He also seconded Caloni's emphasis on educational initiatives, such as the creation of a Coupe nationale de sécurité. Caloni's book inspired Siegfried to have the Musée's Section des études sociales and Section d'hygiène et d'urbanisme examine the issue further, the results of which

# Final Years    227

appeared in its *Cahiers* in 1953.[8] In his introduction, Siegfried conceded that educational efforts could be helpful in reducing accidents, but, predictably, stressed the geographic and ethnic dimensions of the problem: "[A] sort of psychological geography of prevention emerges: Anglo-Saxons and the men of Central Europe, less brilliant but more disciplined, are less subject to accidents, while the Latin is too artistic, or at the other extreme the African still rough. In France itself (it would be very interesting to map this statistically) the psychology of accidents is not the same in Alsace, the Parisian suburbs, the mines of the Nord, or on the Mediterranean coast."[9]

The Musée also afforded Siegfried opportunities to express misgivings about the cultural implications of contemporary technological change. Hints of this appear in his preface to the economist Jean Fourastié's 1949 book *Le grand espoir du XX$^e$ siècle*, where he wondered what the results of an unceasing emphasis on growth and innovation would be.[10] These concerns soon deepened: addressing the Section des études sociales of the Musée in January 1954, Siegfried posited that a West that was excessively oriented toward technology would lose sight of its Greco-Latin and Christian roots. The Section endorsed this position by passing a motion that admitted the benefits of change, but also expressed concern that Western societies had become too narrowly focused; "Technology, which is only a means, must not be thought of as a goal. The goal must remain man himself, made capable of exercising his critical spirit, thinking and expressing himself with clarity; this is the classical notion of the honourable man, but adapted to a century transformed by the Industrial Revolution."[11] At Siegfried's behest, the Musée's stance on social change had taken on a more explicitly skeptical tone.

At the Académie française, Siegfried became involved in two controversies. The first of these concerned the election of the Catholic historian Henri Daniel-Rops to the institution in 1955, with his formal reception taking place in March 1956. Following protocol, Daniel-Rops was to give an address about the academician whose death had vacated the seat he was to fill, in this case the mathematician and philosopher Édouard Le Roy.[12] Daniel-Rops was then to be received into the Académie with an address, which was assigned to Siegfried. Initially, the process unfolded smoothly, but Siegfried engaged in criticism of the incoming member's work to an unusual degree. He began by praising Daniel-Rops for his productivity and success in reaching a wide audience, and his capacity to evoke intimacy in his writings; the latter gift was the result of Daniel-Rops's powerful faith, Siegfried believed. He also stressed the overarching unity of Daniel-Rops's work, another product of his Catholicism. But this strength, Siegfried continued, was a limitation as well. "The Church's viewpoint, which you adopt, is not necessarily acceptable for all, and in particular you cannot be surprised that the Protestant reader does not follow you."[13] Siegfried closed his address in a relatively conciliatory fashion, but his comments had struck a nerve, occasioning complaints from some Catholics in letters to *Le Figaro* and to Siegfried, while Protestant supporters came to his defence.[14]

A second controversy surrounded the effort to prevent the writer Paul Morand from joining the "Immortals" in 1958. Morand, who had achieved literary fame during the interwar years, had supported Vichy after the defeat of 1940. He had eschewed full-blown collaborationism but served as head of the regime's Commission de censure cinématographique, then as its representative to Romania, and finally, Switzerland. Banned from government service after the war, Morand remained in Switzerland until 1953.[15] Thereafter, a campaign got underway to have him elected to the Académie, which quickly reignited old animosities. Siegfried was an admirer of Morand's work, regularly quoting him in his own publications, but he now joined other Academicians in opposing Morand's candidacy. His reasons for doing so are hinted at in an article he very likely wrote for the *Revue française de science politique* that appeared in September 1958.[16] The article depicts the controversy over Morand's election in terms of a struggle between the academic right and left. The academic right, while not necessarily being royalist or clerical, strongly identified with authority and tradition; its supporters had been on the defensive since the end of the war, but were now seeking to reassert themselves. As for the academic left, its supporters were not necessarily left-wing in political terms, but their outlook was marked by "a kind of humanist liberalism, derived from the Renaissance and the eighteenth-century Enlightenment thinkers." Interestingly, the article did not see Morand as "at heart a man of the right," and took care to emphasize that his talent and personable nature were widely respected.[17] Nevertheless, the academic left strongly believed that electing a figure so clearly tied to the Occupation would be divisive. In their view, Morand's candidacy was the work of the "Vichyist party" within the Académie – the article suggested that Jacques de Lacretelle, Pierre Benoit, and Henri Daniel-Rops had played key roles. Efforts to find a compelling

Final Years 229

"left-wing" candidate, followed by a public appeal by the writer Jules Romains to Morand to withdraw for the sake of the unity of the Académie, were to no avail. But in the end, Morand's supporters were stymied by the continuing opposition of the "left," which included Siegfried. Morand's failure – he would not be elected to the Académie until 1968 – signified, the article concluded, a thwarting of "this old spirit of the right."[18]

Apart from the Collège de France, from which he had been required to retire, Siegfried thus remained fully engaged with the institutions that had defined his career, consistently promoting the continuation of a liberal republican outlook within them. Hence his rejection of Morand on political grounds, his public reservations about Daniel-Rops's Catholic convictions, and his desire to see the FNSP and Musée social reflect his values.

## THE DECLINE OF THE FOURTH REPUBLIC

As discussed in chapter 6, Siegfried hoped that following the victory of a centre-right coalition over the Communists and de Gaulle's RPF in the 1951 legislative elections, the Fourth Republic might stabilize around an "intelligent" conservatism that defended the rights of the individual and private property against leftist collectivism, upholding the legacy of the "governmental republicans" of the late nineteenth century. But as it turned out, establishing a stable centre-right government after the 1951 elections proved to be difficult, as René Pleven presided over a short-lived ministry and Edgar Faure an even shorter one. Antoine Pinay's government was more durable, lasting for most of 1952. Siegfried broadly approved of Pinay's "conservative liberal" economic policies but drew attention to a potential left-wing surge in response.[19] Pinay's fall and the instability that ensued – it took weeks for Joseph Laniel to form a government in the spring of 1953 – led Siegfried to observe that the Fourth Republic had become even more unstable than the Third. Saying little about the effect of the war in Indochina, he maintained that the regime's inability to gain a firm footing was the result of the parties exercising too much control over their deputies and treating governments as a delegation of the Chamber. There were echoes of the 1790s here, he warned: "[I]t is the conception of an assembly absorbing the executive which must be condemned and corrected, if one does not wish the country to slip into anarchy leading to dictatorship or to revolution."[20] Constitutional reforms facilitating the dissolution of parliament were in order, as were changes to the electoral system.

Siegfried was not alone in thinking this: indeed, in September 1952 he was approached by President Vincent Auriol to promote such reforms in *Le Figaro*; he followed through with three articles, but without success.[21] The following year, Siegfried tried to sound hopeful as he lauded the election of the moderate conservative René Coty as the new president of the Republic, suggesting that the latter's qualities as a fellow Norman from the "land of liberalism, moderation, and fidelity," would help to unite and stabilize France. This claim, however, was belied by the fact that it had taken thirteen ballots to elect Coty.[22]

Siegfried remained in touch with Coty during his time in office, occasionally reminiscing about past glories.[23] But he became increasingly skeptical that a liberal, moderate solution to the Fourth Republic's problems would emerge. Commenting on the government of Pierre Mendès France (1954–55) after its fall, Siegfried conceded that it had some accomplishments to its credit but saw the centre-left coalition supporting Mendès France as incoherent and concluded that his government had left many problems unresolved.[24] A translation of this analysis appeared in the *Yale Review* and upset Mendès France to the point where he wrote to Siegfried – who had taught him at Sciences Po – to dispute his conclusions. Mendès France took exception to Siegfried's characterization of him as seeking "peace at any price" when it came to ending the war in Indochina, and for his handling of the European Defence Community (EDC) controversy. The former prime minister also objected to Siegfried's suggestions that he might revive the Popular Front and secure Communist support to realize his program. More generally, Mendès France was upset that Siegfried had criticized his government in a foreign publication: "[I]t is from you that I learned, when I took your courses, the requirements for a proper parliamentary and democratic life. Thus, I must say that I did not expect to find in an article by you, allegations or assertions likely to prejudice the effort at renovation that I am undertaking in and for our country."[25]

Replying after several weeks, Siegfried denied any malevolent intent, stating that he had intended simply to provide an "objective" account of what happened; he also denied being aware of the publication of his essay in the *Yale Review*. Though acknowledging his former student's patriotism, as evidenced by his wartime record, Siegfried held to the central points of his interpretation. Mendès France was

Final Years 231

somewhat mollified by this response, but still objected to Siegfried's characterizations of how he had handled the war in Indochina, the EDC, and his relations with the Communist party. The exchange ended with Siegfried declaring his respect for Mendès France's decisiveness, noting that his efforts to keep NATO intact earned him admiration across the Atlantic. "As a result of this, I note, you remained popular in the United States, and perhaps also because Americans like personality."[26]

It seems clear that Siegfried regarded Mendès France as talented, but disagreed with him profoundly on the best way forward for the country, all the while insisting that his coverage had been fair. One also gets the sense that he disapproved of Mendès France's supposedly "American" approach to politics; his parting compliment to the former prime minister is at best backhanded. In some ways, Siegfried's criticisms were predictable, given *Le Figaro's* editorial stance; neither Brisson nor Siegfried were ever likely to support a left-leaning government.[27] Nevertheless, the episode suggests that Siegfried's opposition to the centre-left had intensified, and provides another example of his firm belief in his own objectivity.

At this time, he was also preparing what became his most thorough study of postwar French politics, *De la IIIe à la IVe République*, which appeared at the end of 1956. The book developed his criticisms of the Fourth Republic in depth while also situating the regime in a longer-term context. Siegfried believed that the Third Republic would probably have endured had the catastrophic defeat of 1940 not intervened. To be sure, the regime had structural problems, but it featured many talented politicians and had substantial achievements to its credit before the First World War; from the perspective of 1918, it was arguably a glorious success. But the collapse of 1940 highlighted the failings of the interwar years. The Radicals' displacement of moderate republicans as the pivot of parliamentary coalitions, he believed, was a major problem. So was the rise of the SFIO, which did not have a deep commitment to the regime; the role of the PCF, he continued, was even more nefarious. The quality of politicians and popular sentiment had also deteriorated: "[T]here was no more statesman of first rank" after Raymond Poincaré, he asserted. "Popular conviction still remains sincerely republican but with an increasingly social dimension, primarily serving working-class interests, entailing class struggle, and the Communists are openly supported by a foreign power, whose directives they blindly accept."[28]

232 France in the World

Evidently, Siegfried saw the parties of the left as bearing heavy responsibility for the dysfunction of the late Third Republic, though he differentiated between their programs. His conviction that governments of the centre-right had played the most constructive role was accompanied by a strong emphasis on the baleful effect of the reactionary right. Movements such as the Action française and other leagues had contributed powerfully to the ferment of the 1930s; key elements of the administration had also lost faith in the system. The far right, of course, reached the apogee of its influence under the Vichy regime. In his analysis of the État français, Siegfried distinguished between the policies of Marshal Pétain and Pierre Laval; in doing so, he reinforced the growing consensus of the time that collaboration with Germany was primarily the work of Laval.[29] He also noted the ideological complexity of the Vichy regime, outlining the contributions of Maurrassians, Catholics, technocrats, and members of the intelligentsia to the National Revolution, and acknowledged that Vichy's anti-Semitism had roots in the Catholic-nationalist tradition, rather than simply being the result of German pressure. However, Siegfried went on to characterize wartime French anti-Semitism as a reaction to Jewish influence during the late Third Republic and differentiated between the supposedly traditional anti-Semitism of Pétain and that of Laval, "more similar to Hitlerian anti-Semitism." In the end, Siegfried judged Vichy to be of the "pure right, within the strictly reactionary framework of a demand for pure authority," which had gained power under unprecedented circumstances, attracting "adventurers of the worst sort" as well as "ideologues and fanatics."[30]

He then turned to discussing the Resistance, stressing its ideological diversity as he traced the vagaries of French political life from the Liberation to the establishment of the Fourth Republic. A key theme in these chapters was the revolutionary atmosphere of the time and the fateful role of the left in shaping the new regime's constitution. The PCF, and to a lesser extent the SFIO, wanted a system dominated by a single assembly; fortunately, Siegfried observed, the 1945 draft constitution was rejected in a referendum, though the revised constitution that was approved the following year still delegated too much power to the legislature. Thereafter, he recounted the different stages of the Fourth Republic's political evolution. Given the powerful opposition to the system emanating from the PCF and de Gaulle's RPF, he observed, it was not surprising that deadlock had ensued, and that subsequent governments were often fragile. Echoing his recent dispute with Mendès France, Siegfried credited the former prime minister with attempting bold changes, but reiterated his view that Mendès France had relied on an unstable coalition and accumulated a wide range of enemies. He also depicted the former prime minister as thin-skinned: "Despite his incontestable qualities M. Mendès France did not know how to eliminate his personal susceptibilities from the political game: those who were not with him were against him, feeling any dissidence to be a wound to his pride, a confidence betrayed."[31]

The national elections of 1956 did little to improve the situation, as the resulting constellation of parties and factional divisions made a coherent government of the centre-right impossible. With the Radical Party now split between left and right-leaning factions – a development he traced back to Mendès France – Siegfried surmised, correctly, that the new government would be led by a socialist. If it pursued "national" policies, he concluded, it could draw upon diverse support; but if it pursued left-wing measures, it could only hope for "a Popular Front majority," which was tricky given the narrow margin of votes and hostility between the PCF and SFIO.[32]

Overall, Siegfried's hopes for postwar politics had not materialized. In contrast to the situation in the English-speaking nations, powerful political forces – de Gaulle's RPF and the Communists – disputed the very system in which they operated. Meanwhile, the parties that accepted it were internally divided or ideologically incoherent. In particular, Siegfried struggled with the notion that the MRP could be moulded by Catholic values yet be left-leaning on some social issues. To these problems he added what he described as long-established French traditions, such as a proclivity for authoritarianism in the state administration, and the simultaneous holding of local and national offices. But for all that, Siegfried refused to believe that the Fourth Republic was doomed, suggesting that criticisms of the regime ignored continuities in personnel and the deep commitment of much of the public to a republican system. While the country had not yet "resolved the problem of [achieving] authority in a democracy," it possessed a powerful capacity for self-correction: "As a boat tossed about by waves rights itself, the country seems to instinctively set on the right and the left, limits that it will not exceed. Only in a catastrophe does it defy them."[33]

Such a catastrophe was in fact unfolding. Siegfried did not immediately discern its gravity, but in fairness, neither did most other commentators. The Republican Front government of SFIO leader

Guy Mollet had to address many issues, but the most pressing of them was the war in Algeria, which the government escalated substantially. Siegfried acknowledged the effect of the conflict but said little more about it in his analysis of the events of 1956 in *L'année politique*, instead focusing on the surprising longevity of the Mollet administration. He attributed this to a lack of alternatives and suggested that the SFIO was successfully placing its supporters in key posts. Another factor was public opinion, which, surprisingly, supported Mollet's escalation in Algeria; this was possibly due to unprecedented economic prosperity, at least until the Suez Crisis affected oil supplies. A mix of contentment and apathy, then, helped to explain the relative stability of the regime amid "an internationally tragic year."[34]

But in 1957, domestic polarization over Algeria increased. Growing evidence of the widespread use of torture by the security forces led to opposition from a variety of quarters, ranging from Jean-Paul Sartre on the left to Catholic publications such as *Témoignage chrétien*. As for *Le Figaro*, while individual columnists such as Raymond Aron believed that it was time for France to disengage from Algeria, in general the paper's editorial line called for reform rather than a complete break.[35] Siegfried continued to express support for France's colonial future, though in a 1958 lecture he briefly referenced the question of torture, denouncing "these so-called 'psychological' operations of re-education, de-fanaticising and readaptation which are the shame of our century," and adding that "it would be most reassuring to know that it is not practiced in North Africa."[36] But his focus remained primarily on metropolitan politics; when Mollet's government fell in June, Siegfried suggested in *L'année politique* that it was due to growing opposition to its *dirigiste* economics rather than colonial and diplomatic crises. It proved impossible to form a stable successor administration, but Siegfried contended that "contrary to what is often written abroad, it does not seem that the Fourth Republic is in peril, not because it is loved, but no other system of government is preferred to it, especially if it originates from the Right."[37]

He also tried to draw attention to more positive developments, notably France's entry into the European Economic Community. This, he conceded, would be disruptive in the short term, but entry should be regarded as "a crisis of growth, or rather adaptation, from which the country will emerge stronger and better armed." Moreover, while France had lost its possessions in Asia and faced major challenges in Africa, including "an Algerian crisis with no end in sight," the

Final Years 235

discovery of petroleum in the Sahara "is opening a new domain to technological expansion by a younger generation of the French, for whom, a century later, aspirations that Jules Verne had not disowned will be realized."[38]

As late as April 1958, Siegfried suggested that the Fourth Republic might continue to muddle through, but in May what turned out to be the final crisis of the regime erupted as elements of the military and Algerian settler community rebelled against the government in Paris. De Gaulle's return to power was soon bruited as a solution to the impasse. Given the failings of its constitution and the solipsistic outlook of most deputies, Siegfried now concluded that the injection of disruption from across the Mediterranean – "a political climate quite different from the metropolitan one" – constituted a body blow to the regime.[39] As the Republic came undone and President Coty named Charles de Gaulle as prime minister – who would bring in a new constitution and replace Coty within months – Pierre Brisson had to define *Le Figaro's* response to a rapidly shifting situation.[40] For years, the paper had expressed reservations about de Gaulle; according to his fellow columnist Raymond Aron, Siegfried had encouraged Brisson in this direction, insisting that "[t]he General's return to power means the end of the Atlantic Alliance," a claim that Aron himself disputed.[41] But by 1958, the paper began altering course on de Gaulle; Siegfried contributed to this by endorsing the necessity for change. Though he had some concerns about de Gaulle's desire to expand executive power, about which he corresponded with a like-minded Jean Monnet, he had long believed that the Fourth Republic was too weak in that regard and suggested that the general's politics had moderated since the days of the RPF. Provided some limits were placed upon the executive, Siegfried believed that the new institutions were acceptable and called upon voters to support them, which, overwhelmingly, they did.[42]

Siegfried's analysis of the emergence and decline of the Fourth Republic was profoundly shaped by his established views on French political culture, though he had paid close attention to the course of events as well. His views on the shortcomings and merits of the regime proved influential, with his insights echoing in subsequent French- and English-language scholarship.[43] There were critics; the far-right former politician Xavier Vallat predictably took issue with Siegfried's commitment to the Republic, while the left-wing journalist Alexander Werth found his perspective quite conservative.[44] But other, key contemporaries were quite respectful. Upon receiving a copy of *De la IIIe à la*

*IVe République*, President Coty commented that "[n]ot content to understand, you make [events] understood; old and faithful memories prove it to me." De Gaulle himself did not share all of Siegfried's judgments but conceded that, "in your way, primarily wishing to be lucid, you have clarified the mass of events, looked for constants and linkages, and set out a philosophy of political history."[45]

Similar patterns emerge in the responses to Siegfried's final book on French politics, *De la IVe à la Ve République*, which appeared in 1958 and collected his prefaces for *L'année politique* and various articles on domestic politics written for *Le Figaro*. Once again, the far right reciprocated Siegfried's disdain for its supporters; reviews in *La Nation française* and *Écrits de Paris* discerned contradictions in his analysis and asserted that the Republican system had been fatally flawed since its inception.[46] But other commentators stressed that while the book was a collection of essays often composed in the heat of the moment, it still offered perceptive analysis. Thierry Maulnier, who had transitioned from the interwar far right to a more respectable postwar conservatism, believed that Siegfried rightly emphasized Communist influence as a key weakness of the regime. Raymond Aron offered praise as well, highlighting Siegfried's "unquestioned fidelity with respect to republican ideas, those of the founders of the Third Republic."[47] Siegfried might have sometimes presented himself as a dispassionate observer, but his personal convictions about the merits of a liberal-conservative brand of Republicanism were clear.

## AMERICA REVISITED

Since his 1945 visit, Siegfried had been transfixed by the United States' wartime recovery from the Great Depression and the unmatched level of prosperity that it now enjoyed. Though holding to his reticence about American materialism and the tenuous nature of the country's links to Western values, he nevertheless supported US leadership in the Cold War and continued to see himself as promoting mutual understanding between the two countries. In a May 1950 talk delivered at the American Library in Paris, he depicted Franco-American relations as "an enduring but delicate plant," outlining the strengths of both nations. He lauded American productivity and the freshness of American literature. More generally, he noted, American optimism, confidence, and simplicity could be a tonic. Yet France still had much to offer. It had inherited the best of the Mediterranean intellectual

Final Years 237

tradition, fortified "by a contribution from the North," enabling it to make a "crucial contribution ... in the domain of the mind, in the method of thinking."[48] At a 1950 colloquium devoted to France held at Princeton University, he placed a greater emphasis on contrasts, contending that US was "largely a creation of the twentieth century," while France was, somehow, "a finished product by the end of the eighteenth century."[49] Overall, he was reportedly pleased with the level of goodwill toward France expressed at the conference, but in a letter to Chapsal he noted with some disquiet that "a single report, read by a woman, was polemical; it will not surprise you that it concerned the colonies."[50] This concern about American anti-colonialism would soon be reinforced.

In 1951, he returned to the United States for an extended stay that lasted several months, including five weeks as a visiting professor associated with the University of Chicago's Committee on Social Thought. This had been arranged by the Committee's founder, the American economic historian John Ulrich Nef. Nef had first met Siegfried in 1926; while he did not fully share the latter's pessimism about American culture, he believed that Siegfried was doing Americans a service by helping them to understand themselves.[51] Siegfried now sought to update his understanding of American life. He relied on magazines ranging from *The Nation* to *Fortune* for information and met with various individuals. He also received support from French diplomats in his endeavours; Roger Seydoux, now the French consul in New York, hosted a meeting with African American leaders to discuss race relations, and the French embassy later sent him data about the US economy.[52]

During his stay, Siegfried took note of a growing divergence in American and French approaches to pressing issues. Writing to Chapsal, he detected widespread ignorance about conditions in Europe and lack of awareness about the huge material advances that the United States enjoyed. Indeed, "[the Americans] are so rich that they can wage war in Korea and keep the entire world at arm's length almost without realizing it. This war is a colonial war, and we know what that means; it also means that they speak lightly of war, period." Having implied that the United States was not really qualified to criticize French colonialism, he also disapproved of the intensity of American anticommunism, noting how difficult it was for some European scholars to obtain visas. However, both he and his host Nef opposed a suggestion by the demographer Alfred Sauvy that French intellectuals should protest; Siegfried feared that Communists were already exploiting the situation to gain publicity.[53]

After returning to France, Siegfried presented his updated views on America in the pages of *Le Figaro* and in a new course given at the IEP. He also gave a strong endorsement to a translation of Frederick Lewis Allen's *The Big Change,* a popular history of the first half of the twentieth century in the United States, which, as its title suggests, underscored the profundity of recent social transformation in the country. In his comments, Siegfried noted themes – the notion that America was experiencing a "crisis of growth," the country's changing demography and racial tensions, and its complex role as the leader of Western civilization even as it opposed European imperialism – that were fully elaborated in his 1954 work *Le Tableau des Étas-Unis.*[54] This book sought to come to grips with the alterations in American society that had taken place since the 1920s but it soon became evident that Siegfried's conclusions were framed by enduring assumptions and anxieties.

In his analysis of the American economy, for instance, he combined an acknowledgement of vast shifts with persistent concern about the effect of mass production. The postwar era of "neo-capitalist" prosperity was characterized by a superhuman scale, massive reliance on new equipment, and an outlook characterized by greater technocracy and emphasis on public relations. Siegfried seemed resigned about many of these developments, as well as the expansion of the welfare state. He regretted that many European industrialists had not yet embraced the Fordist model of applying "democracy to purchasing power," though he asserted that French employers cared more about their workers than their US counterparts did. But in his view, mechanization and technocracy had deleterious effects: "The American's vitality is linked with nervous instability, his attention is easily distracted ... in the long run the perfection of modern machinery will engender in him a certain mental sloth because of his excessive respect for technical achievements and the opinion of experts."[55]

Nor was he reassured by the composition of the US population. "The cessation of immigration since World War I has had the result of speeding up unification, but the general effect is still far from homogenous. This has resulted in a somewhat exotic impression as compared with the European nations racially blended at an earlier date." Siegfried took issue with assumptions of Anglo-Saxon superiority, suggesting that some Slavic and Latin newcomers were "more creative artistically or scientifically than the Nordic peoples," but also believed that diverse immigration had many negative results: "[T]here are currents of English or Scandinavian civic spirit, of German solidarity, of Dutch seriousness, but in this main stream there also flow the unstable geniality of the Irish, typically Jewish reactions, and oriental customs and influences which belong to the Mediterranean lands."[56] Given Siegfried's growing emphasis on the Mediterranean as the core of Western values in these years, the latter remark seems more than a little contradictory. But in the context of the book, that was not a major concern; he was most interested in, and pessimistic about, the status of two minorities.

Notwithstanding his meeting with civil rights leaders in 1951, Siegfried was skeptical about the long-term prospects for African Americans. Though aware of the reforms achieved during and after the Second World War, and complimentary of the efforts of individual activists, he stressed the general "passiveness and resignation" of the Black community. He conceded that US courts were now more critical of segregation but doubted "whether a colored man will ever be treated as an equal, except so far as his legal position is concerned."[57] In his discussion of American Jews, Siegfried largely persisted in views he had first advanced in the 1920s, despite the enormity of recent events in Europe. He conceded that Nazi and then Soviet persecution had led to a new wave of sometimes distinguished Jewish migrants reaching the United States, though "crypto-Communists and spies also appear to have crept in." But the paradox of Jewish life in America remained the same; while "the bearded Jew from some eastern European ghetto seems to become American, so to speak, at the end of an extremely short course ... the soul of the Jew cannot be tamed, it remains at the bottom of the melting pot as a residue incapable of fusion." This led him to the provocative conclusion that the "Jewish problem" in the United States, while "less virulent" than in Germany, was "more acute than in the other countries of Western Europe."[58]

In the end, Siegfried described the US as a "country of vast possibilities, of complete good will and intense sincerity," but believed that it would benefit from imbibing more of the classical heritage transmitted from Europe. He gave some credit to American nationalism – "the United States owes much to their boosting, and other countries might well envy them for it" – though, despite his own hostility to the PCF, he now found American anticommunism disturbing, because it encouraged the belief that "liberty may be permitted only within the strictly limited framework of American institutions."[59] America's deeply

Protestant outlook, notwithstanding a growing acceptance of Catholics, meant that the country "is genuinely anxious to improve the moral destiny of mankind," but this would be achieved primarily in material terms. This combination of moralizing with economic self-interest had unfortunate results, notably in foreign affairs. While America's own westward expansion had been a form of colonialism, its revolutionary tradition led it to condemn the imperialism of others despite the hypocrisy of such a position. "To Americans Algeria is 'colonial,' but neither Texas nor California is." Siegfried closed by despairing for Europe's humanist traditions in the face of quickening Americanization; "[T]his civilization inherited from Europe will shed on the way shreds of contemplative spirit, something of the critical spirit of the individual, as it moves toward a new conception of human dignity, which is more social. The essential element will be preserved and it will always remain a Western civilization, but it will no longer be European."[60]

Many French commentators broadly concurred. Writing from Washington, Roger Seydoux validated his former teacher's criticisms of American anti-colonialism by ruminating about the current lack of US support for its European allies in Asia. Though some colleagues disputed points of emphasis or detail – Jacques Bardoux, for instance, gently suggested that Siegfried had not given enough attention to the role of American women – the consensus seemed to be that he remained an acute observer.[61] Raymond Aron dissented from some of Siegfried's observations on the American economy but described the book as "brilliant." Reviewing for *L'Intransigeant*, Jacques Chastenet observed that "M. Siegfried rightly points out that this civilization, because it has technology as its base, is strangely drawing closer to the one that the Soviet world aspires to."[62]

In the US, however, the response was decidedly mixed. There was praise from some quarters; the *Atlantic Monthly* argued that the book "is written with a degree of detachment which no American could possibly achieve, and with a good-tempered objectivity which few foreigners have succeeded in achieving."[63] But other reactions were more guarded. *Time's* reviewer, referring to Siegfried as "France's No. 1 living authority on the US," was positive in some respects but added that the author's observations "on American economics seem obvious or dated; his discourses on politics are marred by errors of a sort that never appeared in *America Comes of Age*."[64] Historian Crane Brinton, writing in *The New York Herald Tribune*, was scathing, contending that Siegfried's new work was "completely rewritten but fundamentally the same book [as the one published in 1927]."[65] The political scientist David McLellan concluded that Siegfried "has been something of a national force in shaping the contemporary image of America," which he believed was most unfortunate because it encouraged Gallic anti-Americanism.[66] Such responses focused on specific shortcomings in the book, but also arguably reflected growing American frustration with a Cold War ally whose elites were deemed inimical to change – a view that Siegfried's emphasis on European cultural superiority may have reinforced.[67]

However, at a time when a growing number of American intellectuals rejected racism, it was Siegfried's comments about ethnicity that elicited the most pointed objections.[68] Signs of friction on this issue had emerged near the end of the Second World War. In 1945, excerpts from *America Comes of Age* featured in correspondence courses intended for American military and naval personnel, but they included anti-Semitic phrases and were withdrawn. Contacted by the Jewish Telegraphic Agency (JTA) about what had happened, Siegfried denied he was anti-Jewish, suggesting that the excerpts that had been used distorted what he was trying to say; the JTA does not appear to have found his response convincing. An intervention from the JTA also, it seems, led the Red Cross to cancel a talk to be given by Siegfried to US personnel in Paris in July 1945.[69] Nearly a decade later, Siegfried's new book on the United States occasioned a dispute over anti-Semitism before it appeared in translation. Both the British Jewish translator initially assigned to the book, Rita Barisse, as well as its American publisher, Harcourt Brace, expressed reservations about some of the language used to refer to Jews. Siegfried responded by denying that he was an anti-Semite and insisted that he was simply providing an objective analysis; Barisse was replaced as the translator and the US edition featured only minor alterations.[70] Barisse's warning that the book might offend readers was correct; historian Oscar Handlin deemed Siegfried's comments about the supposedly declining ethnic quality of the US population and the inability of Jews to truly assimilate disturbing: "The volume before us shows clearly the pernicious character of Siegfried's influence, especially as it concerns the image of the United States held by many Europeans."[71] Arthur Schlesinger Jr, writing in the *New York Times*, concurred, concluding that "M. Siegfried's rehash of familiar population statistics and outmoded racial theories" was of little value.[72] Perhaps most damning of all, Mercer Cook of Howard University, writing in *The Journal of Negro History*, saw the book as reflecting a broader system of racial thought.

Cook judged Siegfried "in most respects ... admirably prepared for the delicate task of interpreting the United States," but this was compromised by his racism; "[W]hether or not he realizes it, M. Siegfried is himself to some extent a disciple of Gobineau. This reviewer recalls a public lecture, 'Negroes in the World,' delivered by the author at the Salle Gaveau in Paris three years ago. On that occasion, the distinguished Frenchman echoed the familiar stereotypes that revealed his deep conviction of the Negro's inherent inferiority."[73]

Despite these criticisms, Siegfried returned to the US in autumn 1955 as a visiting professor at Harvard. He found the students able and sympathetic, and he and Paule appear to have been popular socially, but in intellectual terms he was somewhat isolated. While his former student Stanley Hoffmann later suggested that *Les États-Unis d'aujourd'hui* grasped essential dynamics of American society, another, Laurence Wylie, noted that at Harvard Siegfried's American colleagues were skeptical about what they saw as his outmoded portrait of their society, characterizing his approach as marred by "an irritating determinism."[74] For his part, in subsequent publications Siegfried continued to bemoan America's growing conformity; intense anticommunism encouraged a mood that was "no longer welcoming, nor liberal, nor tolerant."[75]

US intervention against France, Britain, and Israel in the Suez Crisis of 1956 was a turning point for him. Following the Egyptian leader Gamal Nasser's nationalization of the canal, François Charles-Roux, head of the governing board for the Suez Canal Company, wrote to Siegfried imploring him to exercise his influence, particularly with the Americans, to ensure the company's continued operation of the canal. Siegfried duly published an article in *Le Figaro* criticizing the takeover but was soon bitterly disappointed by persisting US anti-colonial attitudes as the crisis unfolded. In an article published in the *Revue de Paris* later that year, he questioned the US commitment to its allies and Western values. "For a long time, we believed we could appeal to the conscience of a common civilization to be defended, to the solidarity of the white race, to the duty of maintaining Europe's achievement in the world. It must be said, as the Suez Crisis has just clearly shown, that such reasoning does not seriously move American sensibilities."[76]

Worries about the implications of America's growing power, and its attenuated ties to Europe, had long been a hallmark of Siegfried's thinking. The country's increasingly manifest intolerance for conventional

# Final Years 243

European imperialism did not lead him to openly question the Cold War alliance, but it did sharpen his conviction that the United States was increasingly alien and materialist, and thus a social model to avoid emulating. Developing alternatives to an American-inspired modernity became a major concern for him.

## THE PERILS OF MODERNITY

Indeed, for some time Siegfried had reached out to business audiences to convince them of the need to defend humanist values. In 1952 he became vice-president of the Conseil national de l'organisation française (CNOF), a management and counselling service established during the interwar years. Former CNOF president Henri Toulouse later recalled how Siegfried encouraged the organization to commit to "finding the difficult balance between the rigorous application of method and the subtlety required to allow intelligence the possibility of manifesting itself at all times."[77] Siegfried also became president of the Institut du transport aérien; the organization felt that it would benefit from his prominence and Siegfried, an enthusiast for air travel, gladly took on the post.[78] However, in May 1954 he delivered an address in Rome to the Institut's Italian counterpart which sounded notes of caution. In a talk entitled "The 20th Century as an Age of Speed," Siegfried argued that the human ability to enhance speed had outpaced traditional sensibilities with destabilizing effects, though he added that in the age of mass bureaucracy new obstacles to freedom of movement had arisen that might prove to be a blessing in disguise.[79]

These interests culminated in the 1954 book *Aspects du XXe siècle*, Siegfried's fullest exploration of the cultural implications of technology. It was structured around the contention that the twentieth century was characterized by "a struggle" between "the traditional conception of a civilization, Mediterranean, Greek, and Christian in origin, and a new mechanical technique, perhaps incompatible with the legacies of the past." Both the state and business were being transformed in a collectivist age, threatening the humanist tradition and thus the sources of Western supremacy itself. In response, Siegfried invoked, once again, Maurice Barrès to emphasize that white leadership was rooted in organizational ability rather than simple technological prowess: "In one of his last *Cahiers* Barrès firmly expressed this idea that the notion of order, originating from Greece and Rome, is the source of all administration."[80]

Siegfried went on to explore the influx of technology and mass organization, frequently bearing an American imprint, into virtually every aspect of daily life. Discussing the role of mostly female secretaries in the context of changing office routines, he endorsed the French engineer and business guru Auguste Detoeuf's emphasis on their invaluable contributions. However, he continued, these women risked being marginalized in an age of bureaucratization, and American secretaries set a problematic example. Though many had perfected routines to such a level that "one is tempted to establish them as prototypes," they tended to marry, and presumably stop working, more often than their French counterparts. Siegfried also believed that the relentless advance of publicity into every walk of life posed long-term problems. While essential to modern business, it was employed in other sectors as well, notably evangelical religion in the United States, and this alarmed him: "[W]hat shocks me about religious publicity is when the spirit is treated as an item capable of responding to the laws of mass production and distribution: one ends up judging the means more interesting and important than the goal!"[81]

Mass-oriented business approaches had also spread beyond the office. The growing availability of household technologies and easy-to-prepare meals had accelerated the demise of domestic service and reduced women's workloads, but also detracted from the individual personality of the household. Moreover, while women now had more time to engage in education and careers, Siegfried questioned whether, at least in the French case, they were truly ready to accept these changes: "[F]or us, at least, maternal sensibilities have not evolved on a par with domestic technology: how many French women would want to have a personal life, a profession and children without giving up being the real daily caretakers and educators of the latter?" When families went on holiday, their experiences were now defined by the practices of mass tourism; the influence of Thomas Cook, the British pioneer of tours for the masses, had eclipsed that of the elegant hotelier Charles Ritz. Siegfried conceded that the American-style hotels springing up around the globe offered useful conveniences, but hoped that the traditional European hotel might survive, "in the interest of the highest civilization."[82]

In subsequent chapters, Siegfried widened his gaze. His discussion of "The Age of Speed," building on his 1954 Rome lecture, stressed the collapse of distance and traditional notions of time in an era where records were broken so frequently that there was little point keeping

Final Years 245

track of them. Speed had become an addiction. Raoul Dautry, a key figure in promoting modern French technocracy, had ensured that clocks for French trains now counted seconds: the goal was to have employees of the state railways think in shorter time frames. "Have they become wiser for it?" wondered Siegfried. Enhanced speed also erased the distances between continents, a trend that not even the expansion of customs and immigration bureaucracy, while having some effect, could reverse. Traditional geographic scales no longer applied: to thrive in the modern world, nations needed to be enormous, a trend that favoured countries such as the United States and Soviet Union. Notions of what constituted art were also being destabilized as people came to believe that reproductions – be they prints or recordings – were as good as the real thing, and where the laws of marketing trumped original creation. The result was publications such as *Reader's Digest*, which could be well-crafted and engaging but lacked depth and promoted standardization. "The danger," Siegfried concluded, was that "technology is absorbing culture, that the means, as is so often the case, becomes the goal."[83]

*Aspects du XXe siècle* is permeated by a tone of resignation. A new age in history was unfolding: "[T]he common thread that links us to the Mediterranean tradition tends to slacken and it could break, especially if Americans or Asians take the lead." The current democratic era was in some ways inimical to culture. Perhaps anticipating charges of elitism, Siegfried tried to suggest that a person need not be formally educated or wealthy to be cultivated. There were artisans and farmers who knew their métier exceedingly well and understood their place in the order of things; what was required was time for leisure and reflection, and the realization that technology was a means, not an end. However, Siegfried went on to reaffirm the need to defend traditional "high culture" lest the Greco-Roman intellectual tradition and the "very personality of our traditional European civilization" be consigned to history.[84]

Several of Siegfried's contributions to *Le Figaro* during this also period addressed these issues; there were plans to incorporate them into a book tentatively entitled "Au balcon du XXe siècle" with a preface by Pierre Brisson, but the project was never completed.[85] He nevertheless continued his efforts to shape future elites by ensuring that young cadres who had technical training also received cultural education. For example, in a talk delivered to members of the Fédération nationale des syndicats d'ingénieurs et cadres supérieurs,

Siegfried emphasized how important it was that "technology remains in the service of knowledge and that knowledge and technology remain at the service of the individual ... in a nation where technology and culture are in their place these two forms of civilization, far from opposing each other, will combine for the greatest benefit of humanity."[86]

Siegfried also developed an association with the educator Henri Hartung, who had been decorated for valour as a member of the Free French and served as an aide to de Gaulle. After the war, Hartung had embarked upon a complex intellectual and spiritual journey, completing a doctorate in geography, travelling to India, and developing an association with René Guénon, the founder of the Traditionalist movement. With Guénon's support, Hartung converted to Islam in 1949, and later established the École supérieure d'orientation, a night school intended to give lycée graduates a rounded education – including instruction in the "human sciences" – to enable them to succeed in elite postsecondary institutions.[87] Exactly how well Siegfried knew Hartung or of his commitment to Islam (which was a generally kept secret) is uncertain, but in the mid-1950s he became a supporter of Hartung's initiatives to preserve humanist education in a technocratic age. In 1955, Siegfried hosted a meeting of industrial executives, calling on them to support the development of a new section of the École supérieure aimed at junior *cadres*, headed by Hartung, which would imbue students with "a general culture." This endorsement was seconded by Jacques Warnier, president of the Centre des recherches et d'études des chefs d'entreprise, and by the Comte de Paris, who noted that he had asked Hartung to educate his own son Henri. Hartung outlined the kind of education that he sought to provide in terms reminiscent of Siegfried's views: "[W]e must seek to create and develop man's sense of equilibrium and spiritual and moral dignity."[88]

In 1956, Hartung relaunched the section as a separate entity, the Institut des sciences et techniques humains (ISTH); Siegfried joined its steering committee and helped to publicize it, arguing that in an age of increasing specialization it was vital that employers possess the tools of culture. The latter, contrary to popular belief, "[were] not exclusively literary" – they consisted of the ability to situate oneself within an organization, identify problems, formulate logical solutions, and communicate effectively. Siegfried was also asked to prepare an article for *Le Figaro* showcasing the ISTH in the fall of 1957.[89] In the years that followed, the Institut became quite successful, attracting clients such as IBM, Air France, Crédit Lyonnais, and Shell. Hartung himself became a well-known orator, though after the upheavals of 1968 he moved in a more radical direction, denouncing technology for creating a "slave society" and launching a Centre des rencontres spirituelles et de meditation.[90]

But those changes lay years in the future; during Hartung's association with Siegfried, the latter continued to write about the perils of technophilia.[91] Thus, in his preface to the French translation of *The Dignity of Man* by Russell Davenport, the recently deceased editor of *Fortune* magazine, Siegfried proclaimed that the author understood the dangers of excessive faith in technology. On this occasion, in contrast to many of his other publications, Siegfried suggested that both the "Old" and "New" worlds faced parallel challenges: "Let us not deceive ourselves, our civilization, to which Europeans and Americans are so profoundly attached, will falter if we seek its essential foundations outside of humanism."[92]

It appears that Siegfried's views made an impression on members of France's economic elite; at the very least, they felt the need to endorse them after his passing. In an homage published by the ISTH in 1959, various business leaders praised Siegfried's work and seconded his call for a broader conception of education. Hartung compared him to one of France's great empire-builders: "He was, with Lyautey, a technician of general ideas, the master of a method of thought and work." Georges Villiers, president of the Conseil national du patronat français, observed: "For many of us, tyrannized by the immediate demands of our professions, through his books, articles, and lectures he gave us the opportunity to situate our actions in a wider framework." Christian de Waldner, the head of IBM France, noted that Siegfried had praised his firm as "l'anti-Taylor" during a visit to its factory in Essonne, calling the American engineer and management consultant "a technical genius but also a social brute."[93]

## FRANCE, "THE WEST," AND A DECOLONIZING WORLD

During this period, Siegfried also published several works that were more personal. He lectured and wrote about the geography and psychology of Normandy; in an address to the Association Études normandes in Rouen, he stressed the importance of race, in the form of Scandinavian settlement, in shaping the distinctive Norman outlook. The latter, in his view, was an admirable mixture of liberalism, a disdain for extremes and respect for order, a degree of egalitarianism, and a capacity for understatement that contrasted with much of the French population. His conclusion no doubt delighted his audience: "I rejoice that there are Normans, but I am sorry for France that there are not more of them."[94] Siegfried also revisited his family and childhood, reflecting further on his father's career and publishing a memoir of his youth.[95]

But while the personal became more prevalent in Siegfried's writing during these years, his desire to promote France publicly remained strong. In 1953, he gave a thorough statement of his views in the keynote address for a wide-ranging conference on "aspects of French society." Siegfried's portrait of the French included some criticisms; their individualism was both "splendid and pathological," ensuring intellectual freedom but sometimes threatening to descend into anarchy. They displayed creative genius but struggled with applying it, posed profound political questions but found it difficult to articulate workable solutions. For all that, Siegfried praised France as a synthesis of geographic and racial influences, endowing its people with a true "maturity of spirit" and the assets of frugality and devotion to family. The age of mechanization posed a serious challenge to a people with proud artisanal traditions, yet the potential to thrive was there. He stated his views more concisely in a special issue of the women's magazine *Le nouveau femina*. Stressing the country's rapid recovery from wartime devastation, Siegfried hoped that it could hold true to its traditions while thriving in the modern world: "If we find the way to do it, in a world where individuality is increasingly rare but is shown to be increasingly necessary, we could be unmatched. We must refuse to think that this is impossible."[96]

As an academician, for Siegfried promoting the national language would be an essential part of this process. In 1952, he supplied a preface to a book by the poet and essayist Louis Piéchaud entitled *Questions de langage*, in which he underscored the singular qualities of French; the typical reader of the London *Times*, he suggested, was more interested in "biblical controversy and zoological anecdotes ... the German, in all sincerity, thinks that in pursuing the truth one must sink into obscurity, as in the depths of a forest; he distrusts clarity, which he judges to be superficial. For his part, the Frenchman trusts that, in the domain of thought, light is preferable to night." Moreover, unlike some (unspecified) Asian languages, which differentiated between the educated elite and the masses, the beauty and precision of the French language was available to all.[97] Three years later, when Siegfried

Final Years 249

participated in a colloquium on the French language sponsored by the Fondation Singer-Polignac and overseen by the Romanist and medieval scholar Mario Roques, his tone was more defensive.[98] He now contended that the integrity of the French language might be incompatible with the conditions of the modern world. The role of the masses in shaping usage threatened to corrupt it, depriving a major carrier of the Greco-Roman tradition of both precision and elegance. He tried to close on a more positive note but also stressed the challenges ahead: "I do not think that France will renounce the human tradition and the language that expresses it. Is adaptation to the necessities of a new civilization possible? I think so, but the task is arduous."[99]

Whom should France seek out as partners in its quest to thrive in the modern world? As we have seen, by the late 1950s Siegfried was gloomier than ever about the United States; Britain seemed somewhat more promising. For the fiftieth anniversary of the Entente Cordiale, he gave a lecture at the Sorbonne emphasizing the depth of Britain's and France's contributions, different though they were, to European civilization. He made similar points in a talk delivered to the Association France–Grande Bretagne that same year, though conceding that the British had a long tradition of avoiding formal treaties. In a 1957 lecture delivered at the École de guerre, he noted that while British power may have diminished, the Commonwealth remained an "adaptable confederation, necessary for the world's equilibrium," providing a link between Europe, Africa, the Americas, and Asia; the British had also managed to preserve London's status as a financial centre.[100]

Siegfried also became more involved in promoting European unity; in this regard, his suspicions of West Germany subsided to an extent over the course of the 1950s, though he still characterized the German people as obscure in their thinking and overly attached to the state. His preface to a 1952 study of the Soviet zone of Eastern Germany suggests that the circumstances of the Cold War played a key role in this changing outlook. Siegfried observed that Germany's current division into East and West was "the most tragic" event in a long history of misfortune. Another preface, prepared for a study of the West German economy written by André Piettre, dean of the faculty of law and political science at the University of Strasbourg – and a former student of Siegfried's at Sciences Po – ended on a more hopeful note. Though still wondering whether the German people would be able to transcend their troubled legacy, Siegfried noted Piettre's conclusion that the Federal Republic was more "Western" than its predecessors, and suggested that new approaches to old problems were possible. It is noteworthy that his final journey outside France was to West Germany; his itinerary included a conference on Franco-German relations attended by FRG president Theodor Heuss and French-born Carlo Schmid, at the time the SPD's vice-president in the Bundestag.[101] In line with his softening attitude toward Germany, Siegfried supported the efforts of his colleague Édouard Bonnefous to promote "the realization and constitution of a Europe equipped with the means to live, survive and play its role in the world." He also saw the merits of creating a European Defense Community. Following the signing of the Treaty of Rome in 1957, Siegfried presided over a meeting of eighty business leaders, politicians, and journalists to discuss how to promote integration and productivity to the general European public. In his remarks, he underscored the need for both national and continental perspectives, adding that enhanced cooperation presented great opportunities for France. Several weeks later, at a roundtable sponsored by the Institut international d'études humanistes, he opined that a "new Europe" was emerging, rooted in the defence of Greco-Latin and biblical traditions and "a creative spirit doubled by critical spirit."[102]

These efforts in defining European civilization had a practical bent, but Siegfried's more scholarly interests in exploring its roots and features also persisted. In 1958, he published *Les voies d'Israël*, which traced the evolution of Judaism, with a focus on the causes and consequences of its split with Christianity. In a sweeping synthesis that drew upon the insights of older studies by Ernest Renan and Israel Zangwill, along with more recent works, such as Henri Barbusse's *Jésus* (1927) and Edmond Fleg's *Jésus raconté par le juif errant* (1933), he acknowledged Western civilization's debt to Judaism, but argued that the latter had ultimately settled upon a path of conservation rather than development and expansion. From the time of Abraham's covenant through the Babylonian captivity, Judaism had been characterized by an "intransigent" deism that, he claimed, "only Islam subsequently recaptured to the same degree." Siegfried acknowledged diversity within Judaism, between a focus on consolidation and state-building, and a more spiritual current that prefigured Christianity but also reflected "a deviation from the original creed, at the price of a weakening of the uncompromising demand for justice in this world." Jesus was undeniably following in the Jewish tradition, but his criticisms of legal formalism aroused suspicion and the claims of divinity that surrounded him were especially shocking to Jews. The evangelism of the apostle Paul, who "was simultaneously Jewish, Greek, and Roman" led to an irrevocable break: "The [Jewish people] conserved God and the Law according to the original source, but it is the [Christian] embranchment, having become the main river, which brought about the entire course of the future."[103]

The final chapters of *Les voies d'Israël* conceded variation in the subsequent history of Judaism but held to this overarching interpretation. Siegfried drew attention to the powerful legacy of the debates that shaped the Talmud and noted the philosophical and mystical currents over the centuries, as well as the rise of Reform Judaism and Zionism. He recalled how strong differences of opinion over the latter emerged between "four notable Jews" who were invited to a luncheon that he had hosted in 1932. But in the book's conclusion, he returned to what he regarded as the enduring features of Judaism: "The Jew is an optimist for himself, his race, and social progress. But he is also a pessimist, especially regarding the societies where his destiny is experienced. Through a kind of intellectual dissociation, he knows how to judge them with the cold lucidity of the foreigner." Significant numbers of Jews might be tempted by secular visions of social revolution and nation-building, but Siegfried did not think that they could dispose of centuries of tradition. The new "Palestinian" state professed to be secular, but in truth, he argued, Judaism struggled to separate civil and religious affairs, a key characteristic that distinguished the East from the West. "The sense of God in the Jewish soul is permanent."[104]

*Les voies d'Israël* represented the culmination of Siegfried's longstanding interest in the place of Jews in Western societies. Compared with earlier writings, in which he emphasized the inability of Jews to truly assimilate, in 1958 he tried harder to understand the diversity of Judaism. In this sense, it is difficult to see the book as simply rehashing his old views, as Birnbaum suggests. Indeed, Sanguin contends that the book represents an homage to Judaism, noting that both the Grand Rabbi of France and the Israeli ambassador received their complimentary copies warmly.[105] That they did, but while Siegfried's tone is sometimes more respectful compared with his comments on Jewish immigration in his 1927 and 1954 books on the United States, he still portrayed Jews as an inherently unsettling presence. Perhaps recalling earlier controversies, he endeavoured to explore the "Jewish question" in a more nuanced manner, but his conclusions still often distanced Judaism from what he regarded as the essentials of Western civilization.

As for the latter, Siegfried continued to celebrate it, but in an increasingly nostalgic way. In 1951, he collaborated with Jérôme and Jean Tharaud in producing an illustrated volume, *Le centenaire des services des Messageries Maritimes*, which hailed the achievements of an institution that had asserted a Western and more specifically French presence in the East.[106] The following year, he published *Géographie poetique des cinq continents*, which revisited his many travels from an aesthetic standpoint, evoking the sights, sounds, and significance of places that had especially moved him, hoping to showcase geography's full potential as a discipline.[107] Beginning with an exploration of France that reaffirmed its great diversity and role as a repository of classical tradition, he then ranged through Europe, the Americas, Africa, and Asia. The book blended vivid descriptions, interesting parallels – between economic conditions in Sweden and North America, for example – and some curious observations. Siegfried claimed, for instance, that London was not an international capital in the same way that Paris or New York was. He also drew attention to the decline of Indigenous populations across the globe, regarding the trend as somewhat regrettable on aesthetic grounds, but also inevitable. Cultural hybrids resulting from Western contact distressed him, as the following contrast between his view of Samoa when he first visited in 1899, and then during a 1918 return trip, makes clear: "Goodbye to the innocent nudity of the *Voyage de Bougainville*! Henceforth these magnificent bodies no longer show themselves freely: the women wear ridiculous pink, green, or blue shirts, to unfortunate effect. The landscape is still that of Gauguin, splendid, like a plaque on the horizon, but his human models can no longer be found there."[108] At times he seemed to approve of the mingling of cultures, but only within the context of confirming stereotypes; for instance, he described Afro-Brazilians in Rio as follows: "[H]ere are prolific black families who seem to overrun their houses. In this respect Rio recalls New Orleans, but a New Orleans where the Negros would not be unhappy." Elsewhere, he stressed the need for barriers: "*White Australia* must be defended against the Far Eastern flood with the same vigilance of a Holland against marine breaches ... the silence of the Australian countryside perhaps only suggests to me this impression of subtle anguish because I vaguely sense all of that."[109]

Challenges to Western civilization from nonwhites thus remained much on Siegfried's mind. In the spring and summer of 1952, he published a series of articles in *Les annales conferencia* dealing with "peoples of colour"; there were plans to publish them as a book intended to complement the Western-focused *L'âme des peoples*, but they never came to fruition.[110] The articles updated Siegfried's views of other cultures in light of recent global developments and professed to acknowledge the virtues of nonwhites, but his belief in Western superiority remained very much at the fore. Africans were judged to be intelligent in certain contexts and possessed artistic flair, but notwithstanding individual cases of assimilation, white management and supervision were still needed, since Africans remained "in a decisive state of inferiority." Turning his attention to the Indigenous peoples of the Americas, Siegfried endorsed what he claimed was the widely held view that in North America "the 'Red-Skin' no longer counts," but added that the situation in Latin America was very different. While its civilizations of the distant past had become sclerotic and fallen to Western domination, he suggested that its Indigenous peoples were now experiencing a revival that could potentially contest the Western way of life, especially in countries such as Mexico where they were, ironically, more exposed to Western influence. Even though Siegfried believed that, like Africans, "Indians" still lacked Western conceptions of work and production, their elites sought modernization and posed a potential political threat: "[I]t can be said that among the Indian masses there exists an Indian nationalism, which is anti-American but hitherto has not taken on a Communist or Soviet form, but in some cases resembles the policies adopted by a Tito."[111]

Anti-Western assertiveness was even stronger in Asia. Discussing India, Siegfried compared his impressions from his first visit in 1900 with those of 1950, stressing a transformation from a supremely spiritual culture to an intensely politicized one. In recent conversations with intellectuals and students, he found that modernization was the central concern. But he insisted that while Indians possessed formidable commercial skills, they still lacked the Western capacity for large-scale production; the existence of enormous numbers of artisans and peasants was another major barrier to prosperity. Siegfried also worried that India would adopt the Soviet model, stifling the potential for a liberal order to emerge. Pan-Asian nationalism was another potent and troubling influence, which had already led to Indian criticisms of French policy in Indochina and US policy in Korea.

254    France in the World

Siegfried was less concerned about Communist rule in China at the time; to his mind, the country – more properly termed a civilization, he asserted – posed a long-term cultural and economic, rather than specifically political, challenge. To be sure, it had fallen far behind technologically and formidable challenges to modernization lay ahead; he went so far as to claim that "the Chinese do not know Western reasoning and do not have a sufficiently precise language to practice it." But they were resilient and possessed strong agricultural and artisanal traditions as well as great commercial talent. "We conclude that the Chinese remains the great Asian. It may appear today that he is the student of the Russians, as he was the student of the Europeans and Americans yesterday. Let us not deceive ourselves. In the end he will always be himself, capable of maintaining his place in the world. What is of great importance to us is knowing how he will make use of it."[112]

A more broadly defined Asian threat also surfaced in Siegfried's final book, *Itinéraires de contagion*, which was published post-humously in 1960. Based on a 1958 lecture prepared at the request of his fellow Academician, Pasteur Vallery-Radot, for a course on contemporary medicine, the brief volume explored the dissemination of infectious diseases, aiming to illustrate the connections between scientific and social-scientific disciplines in the process. While the book featured a familiar emphasis on the West's leading role in ensuring medical progress, stable administration, and advances in hygiene, Asia remained a major potential source of disease, with the Mediterranean serving as a kind of "antechamber" to a vulnerable Europe.[113] More generally, Siegfried argued in the *Revue de Paris* in October 1958, rising Asian power revealed that the West's moral leadership was in profound crisis, and perhaps reaching its end. Here he confessed that the Western presence in Asia had too often been associated with military force, and the quest for economic gain, for missionaries to have sufficient spiritual impact. The result was that the masses of Asia clung to their traditions, even as their leaders now aimed to reproduce Western prosperity while disdaining the modes of thinking and values that had made it possible. "In the end Asia is a milieu where our modes of reasoning are not valued, that Greek methods of thought have not penetrated." The current situation was thus partly the fault of the West, but Siegfried emphasized the failure of "Orientals" to grasp fully the spiritual values that had inspired Western technical achievements. East and West thus remained far apart, and the only short-term prospects for reconciliation seemed to lie in adopting a revolutionary political path, one that he abhorred. "Wouldn't it be tragic if the [East-West] encounter took place at the inferior stage of technology, inimical to the spirit, according to the precepts of communist materialism?"[114]

— ❋ —

Surveying Siegfried's final years, one is struck by his continuing and variegated engagement and productivity, as he continued to prescribe a course for French politics, society, and culture while also interpreting global developments. He still advocated a moderate conservative approach to politics informed by his liberal values; he did not oppose economic modernization but wanted to ensure that France's individualist traditions remained intact. To be sure, domestic politics unfolded in ways that he found disagreeable; he was dismayed by the staying power of the left in the Fourth Republic and was initially wary of de Gaulle. On the other hand, he took comfort in France's economic growth and deepening connections to Europe, though these developments could not extinguish his anxieties about the preservation of the nation's language and culture. But if Siegfried could not contemplate the future with unshakeable confidence, and his influence may have crested, his interventions still mattered, whether they were directed at fellow academics, politicians, business leaders, or newspaper readers.

In his eyes, world politics, shaped by the dynamics of the Cold War and decolonization, was an increasing cause for pessimism. Though he always remained strongly anticommunist, it was arguably America's foreign policy and sociocultural clout that truly preoccupied him. To his mind, US anti-imperialism had undermined Europe's place in the world, while the "American model" threatened to erode the continent's cultural roots. In an updated version of arguments first advanced in the 1930s, Siegfried believed the American challenge was compounded by increasing self-assertion by other races, with Asia now the most immediate threat. Though he continued to envision ways in which European influence, with French values at its core, might endure, he was increasingly doubtful that the West would meet global challenges in a unified way.

# Epilogue

In September 1958, Siegfried wrote to Henri Aubrun that he felt well rested after his annual stay at Le Mas Saint-Donat and was looking forward to resuming work in the fall.[1] Now eighty-three years old, he still received various requests and sought to maintain an active pace. That same month, Roger Seydoux, now the directeur général des affaires culturelles et techniques at the Quai d'Orsay, wrote to his former mentor and colleague. Following the recommendation of Pierre Brisson, Seydoux requested that Siegfried devote one of his upcoming editorials in *Le Figaro* to the new government's plans for the reform and integration of France's overseas cultural and technical programs, aimed at renewing the country's international stature.[2] Siegfried also received a request from the Ministry of Foreign Affairs to propose candidates for the UN Permanent Court of Arbitration, in conjunction with other members of the French delegation.[3] He proved unable to comply with that request, for by then he was beginning to display the effects of the stomach cancer that would take his life the following spring.

Nevertheless, he remained quite active. Some of his final public interventions were commemorative; among them was an homage to Léon Léal, a high-ranking colonial official and former governor of Martinique, which praised the latter's lifelong devotion to France's "civilizing mission."[4] Siegfried also continued to assess political developments, publishing an article on the advent of the Fifth Republic in *Le Figaro*, in which he expressed satisfaction that in the long struggle between the liberal, constructive tradition of 1789 and that of the revolutionary left, the former had largely prevailed in the new constitution, though he conceded that the new regime also reflected "a plebiscitary complex, not eliminated from our republican heritage."[5]

Just days before this article appeared, he had spoken at the inauguration of new buildings for the city of Rouen's École supérieure de commerce; before doing so, he had sought Aubrun's advice, noting that the invitation had come from a political opponent (of the "clerical right"), Paul Guillard, but the latter had later worked with Jules Siegfried on social initiatives and Siegfried wanted to honour his father.[6] By the time he gave that address, Siegfried appeared quite haggard from weight loss as the cancer took its toll, but he summoned the energy to recount his father's and uncle's success in the cotton business and their subsequent support for commercial education. Such training, he noted, was needed in a world where commerce was ever more international in character, necessitating a greater understanding of "the comparative psychology of peoples"; he also made note of the complications caused by state intervention. Siegfried returned to Le Havre on 13 December, where he presided over the fiftieth anniversary celebration of the Société Havraise de Crédit Immobilier established by his father, marking the importance of private initiative in generating social reform. It was his last public appearance.[7]

In the months that followed, he was increasingly confined to bed and deteriorated rapidly. When his friend Pierre Hamp came to see him early in January 1959, he reportedly weighed only 50 kilograms. The following month, in a letter to Jérôme Carcopino, a fellow Academician, historian of ancient Rome and for a time Vichy's minister of education, Siegfried indicated that he was feeling better, but by mid-March papers such as Brussels' *Le Soir* reported that his condition was worsening. On the morning of 28 March, Pierre Brisson came to see him at his bedside, recalling that "[h]is strength must have been severely undermined for him to remain in bed and tolerate a visitor in such intimacy. His intellect remained sharp but seemed little by little to set itself free from his body. This strange form of relief intensified until the last moments." Siegfried died later that day, following a hemorrhage very similar to the one that killed his father. A later account described his final moments: "'I am dying like my father,' whispered André Siegfried, overcome." The funeral was held at the Rue de Courty residence on 31 March, with Pastor Georges Marchal officiating and only close family, Aubrun, Brisson, and Chapsal in attendance. Siegfried had insisted upon privacy and simplicity: "I do not have the right to take precedence over my faith or my works. Instead, I ask for indulgence, having no illusions about my failings." Some two hundred people attended the interment at Passy Cemetery.[8]

In the weeks that followed, there were many tributes, including an issue of *Le Figaro littéraire* that featured international and French contributors. Jean Desy, a former Canadian ambassador to France, observed that "[Siegfried's] thoughtful remarks were sometimes tinted by a subtle irony and unexpected humour ... *Le Canada, puissance internationale*, is the most comprehensive book written about my country." Abelardo Saenz, Uruguay's ambassador and the doyen of the Latin American diplomatic corps in France, opined that Siegfried was "one of the teachers most beloved and admired by the university students and intellectual elite of the Latin American nations." The British diplomat, politician, and writer Harold Nicolson credited Siegfried with being able to truly understand the British point of view and thus enriched Anglo-French dialogue, avoiding prejudices and polemic. From the United States, John Nef expressed his deep sense of loss, both personally but also "for the entire intellectual world."[9]

French commentators stressed Siegfried's commitment to scientific rigour, graceful expression, and liberal values. Pastor Georges Marchal captured the breadth of his interests as he recounted a recent discussion between the two men in which "the synagogue, messianism, and the moped alternated, in equal parts serious and charming." Édouard Bonnefous, his collaborator on *L'année politique*, emphasized how Siegfried had opened new worlds to generations of students, and prized the preservation of freedom: "Siegfried always remained profoundly attached to liberty. He suffered deeply in his heart from the incessant advances of servitude in the world."[10] This was a central theme in other tributes, notably from fellow Protestants. François Goguel observed that "Beyond his humour and elegance, once you got to know him well you soon discovered his rock-solid liberal principles, his faith in humanity, and his confidence in spirit, which no doubt he owed in large measure to his Protestant heritage." The novelist André Chamson, noting Siegfried's interest in the history of Protestant dissent from the Reformation to the war years, commented: "What he always wanted to uncover, above all and in the final analysis, were the pathways of liberty, the route one must follow to reach it."[11] In a reminiscence entitled "La ligne Siegfried" published the following year, the journalist Louise Weiss made particular note of how deeply Paule had supported André, likening her sacrifices for him to the achievements of Siegfried's mother Julie: "The Siegfried line, so male in its rationalism, courage, and erudition, shone in a way from a feminine halo." In this sense,

Weiss's recollection stood out, but she joined in praising Siegfried's intellectual and moral engagement: "[T]he undefeated Siegfried line represents one of the finest French defenses against everything that is not intellectual wisdom, love for humanity, and dignified conduct in all circumstances, even deadly ones."[12]

An Association des amis d'André Siegfried was soon established and held a commemorative ceremony on 31 May 1960. Among the most probing comments were those by Bonnefous, who reaffirmed that Siegfried was a modern de Tocqueville but also noted that his later years were tinged with gloom: "Though deeply optimistic by nature he experienced sadness during his final years, as he noted the discontent of the masses, and even some elites, with regimes of liberty."[13] Fifteen years later, the centenary of Siegfried's birth was marked in several ways. At the Institut de France, the Académie des sciences morales et politiques highlighted his travels and reportage as well as his political and moral commitments. His contributions as a scholar and teacher were the focus of a colloquium held at the Collège de France. In Le Havre, the French Red Cross, using materials from the previous exhibit, hosted an event in November to mark the issue of a stamp bearing Siegfried's likeness.[14] Today, the Siegfrieds' former home on the Rue du Courty bears a commemorative plaque. Streets in Le Havre and Mont Saint-Aignan, a suburb of Rouen, bear his name, as does a lycée in Haguenau (Bas-Rhin).

Siegfried's intellectual legacy is complex. It has been noted that since he taught outside of the state university system, he did not have the opportunity to train graduate students and thus encourage the formation of a "school." There is perhaps an assumption here that he would have wanted to do so; given his desire to travel and write, even if the circumstances had been more favourable, postgraduate supervision may not have become a high priority for him. Nevertheless, he did have disciples, among the most prominent of whom was Abel Miroglio, whose Institut havrais de sociologie économique et de psychologie des peuples, was, as we have seen, founded with Siegfried's support in December 1937, and became more active after the war. Though he never articulated a theory of the psychology of peoples, Siegfried supported the Institut as its first honorary president, participating in discussions that culminated in its transformation into an affiliated institute of the University of Rouen. Despite his failing health, he also hosted an Institut-sponsored conference held in Paris, at Sciences Po, in December 1958.[15]

But within a decade of Siegfried's passing, the Institut faced major challenges. In its earlier years, it enjoyed the patronage of local political and business elites, and had attracted some prominent lecturers, including Léopold Senghor and Raymond Aron. But by the mid-1960s, the quickening of decolonization, the affirmation of Third World independence, and the advent of Western European integration created an environment in which the study of "national psychologies" seemed outmoded, even problematic.[16] Miroglio did find a successor to take over the Institut when he retired in 1970, but its review was renamed, from the *Revue de psychologie des peuples* to *Ethnopsychologie*, a reflection of shifting times. Before long, the Institut faced funding shortages and had to cease its activities for a time, though it later resurfaced as the Institut de sociologie économique et culturelle. *Ethnopsychologie* was published from 1970 until 1982, then merged with another publication of the Institut into the *Cahiers de sociologie économique et culturelle*, which began appearing in 1984.[17] By then, the field of the psychology of peoples was a thing of the past.

By contrast, Siegfried's influence on the field of geography arguably intensified over time. His former colleague, Jean Gottmann, in works such as *La politique des états et leur géographie* (1952), *Megalopolis* (1961), and *The Significance of Territory* (1973), acknowledged an influence, while avoiding the use of racial language. Various dimensions of Siegfried's geographic studies – particularly those focusing on the diffusion of ideas and practices, as well as the evolution and persistence of local and regional identities – have shaped the evolution of a "French" approach to social geography. Hugh Clout observed that the vast project directed by the French geographer Yves Lacoste, aimed at tracing voting behaviour and electoral traditions throughout all of France, certainly bears traces of Siegfried's earlier efforts.[18]

Above all, Siegfried is best known as a "founding father" of French political science. As we have seen, François Goguel played the key role in this regard, but Siegfried's consecration did not take place in a vacuum, and he was hardly immune from criticism. The influence of American political science, incorporating insights from psychology and polling methods, was growing in France and some of its supporters, such as Georges Dupeux, criticized Siegfried for lacking scholarly rigour. Other scholars, such as Paul Bois in his book *Paysans de l'Ouest*, challenged Siegfried's specific findings. However, Bois was respectful and continued to emphasize the pioneering nature of the *Tableau*, and in the 1960s and 1970s Siegfried's status was cemented with the publication of a new edition of the *Tableau* in 1964, commemoration by Sciences Po, and recognition in subsequent histories of the discipline.[19] As noted by Loïc Blondiaux and Philippe Veitl, since the 1980s the *Tableau* has shifted from being the oft-cited progenitor of an academic field to itself becoming an object of historical study.[20]

So, of course, has Siegfried himself. He does not occupy centre stage in many classic histories of French intellectuals, but he was devoted to the life of the mind, and one of the key themes of this book is that his career sheds considerable light on the workings of influential networks and institutions. Though generally avoiding specialization and theorizing, Siegfried worked to shape French academic, political, and intellectual life in a variety of ways. His life-long associations with Sciences Po and the Musée social had profound implications for both institutions. As he gained prominence and standing within his country's elite institutions, such as the Collège de France and the Académie française, Siegfried's interventions helped to shape their evolution as well. His postwar position as a regular commentator for, and informal advisor to, the editor of *Le Figaro* gave him a platform from which to reach a national audience.

From that platform, he continued to advance a political vision of liberal republicanism, as he had done in preceding years. This comparatively neglected aspect of his oeuvre has been a second unifying theme of this study. Siegfried's vision of France had deep roots, which can be traced back to the moderates of the early Third Republic. Though his own early ambitions for office were unsuccessful, in the classroom, the newspaper column, the learned article, and various books he promoted individual rights and freedom of conscience as being at the heart of what was most valuable in the French Republican tradition. He was also profoundly convinced of the need for minimal state intervention in the workings of the economy. Always skeptical about socialism and deeply hostile to Communism, he was a prominent voice among the chorus stressing that the PCF defied logic, as a foreign intrusion into the French political system. Like many French liberals, Siegfried's views had an elitist bent: he gave a high priority to defending the virtues and status of the bourgeoisie. But while he became more critical of the Third Republic in its later years, he largely avoided the drift of some prominent interwar French liberals toward authoritarian solutions, a path that sometimes led to endorsing the Vichy regime.[21] Though Siegfried's writings from the period 1940–44 indicate adjustments to that regime's prerogatives, there are also declarations of attachment to the Republican tradition and evidence of skepticism about the National Revolution. After the war, he gradually became disillusioned by the Fourth Republic, but his hostility to the nationalist far right as well as the PCF remained intact, and he continued to promote liberal-conservative solutions to France's political and economic dilemmas. He was an advocate for, rather than an original theorist of, French liberalism, which perhaps explains why he is not part of its canon. But he had promoted this political tradition throughout his career; his work serves as a reminder of both its historical potency as well as its serious limitations.

Another overarching theme is Siegfried's complex position when it came to preserving France's social and economic fabric. He has sometimes been presented as a traditionalist, and indeed, in many of his writings he defends the virtues of artisanship, the need for high-quality goods, and a concomitant suspicion about the implications of contemporary social change. But he was not a technophobe: he regularly expressed enthusiasm for new technology and admiration for American-pioneered productivity. What bothered him the most were the implications of growing state intervention and the rise of a mass consumer society. Over time, he grudgingly accepted some expansion of the state, but he never ceased to lament this trend. As for his misgivings about the rise of the consumer society, Siegfried argued that higher standards of living for working-class people were bad for economies, and thus for nations and even workers themselves. As a young man, he had engaged in efforts to promote class harmony through the *universités populaires*, and in his early studies for the Musée social he noted the difficult conditions faced by workers in some nations. Nevertheless, he consistently stressed the negative effect of trade unions and high wages. Whether they raised the costs of mining in turn-of-the-century Australia, supposedly nurtured dissipation among British workers in the 1920s, or discouraged the French from engaging fully in the work of postwar reconstruction, Siegfried was consistently skeptical about the merits of working-class activism in search of material betterment.

Inextricably linked to his criticisms of mass consumer society was the spread of American international influence, a development at the heart of this book's fourth theme: Siegfried's views on shifting international economic, political, and cultural trends. From early in his career, he regarded Americanization as a destabilizing force, soon displaying a propensity for juxtaposing France and the United States as embodiments of two different approaches to Western civilization. The former valued restraint, frugality, and intellect; the latter embraced modernization with admirable verve, but with the concomitant loss of individual freedom and cultural sophistication. A clash was thus overdetermined; Siegfried's first book on Canada, for instance, envisioned Americanization as a potential threat to the French-rooted civilization that had endured there. In the years to come, he would reframe the confrontation as a contest between America and Europe, a collision between Mediterranean traditions and the American model, and as a schism within Western civilization. But in his various discussions of these supranational entities, the threat to quintessentially French values was a crucial continuity. Though he travelled throughout Europe and in doing so observed various contrasts between its constituent states, when it came to developing contrasts with the United States, Siegfried tended to present the continent in unitary terms, with a discernable Gallic inflection. Moreover, the growing reach of the American model imperilled French cultural influence elsewhere, notably in Latin America. As he shifted focus to the Mediterranean in the late 1930s and early 1940s, Siegfried continued to highlight the negative consequences of Americanization, which he believed would distort that region's ancient values. After the Second World War, the United States was a necessary Cold War ally, but economically and culturally it threatened to divide Western civilization and "the white race"; the Suez Crisis was for Siegfried a particularly telling example of American disdain for Europe's international status.

To be fair, during the Depression, Second World War, and Cold War, Siegfried had not ignored the threat of Nazi Germany or the appeal of the Soviet Union, consistently advocating cooperation with the United States. But throughout these years, he also remained fixated on America's supposedly growing differentiation from Europe, and the potentially concomitant erosion of Western high culture. His views have echoed over the years: it is noteworthy that the influential historian Fernand Braudel, in one of his final works, found Siegfried's emphasis on the profound differences between American and European cultures compelling.[22]

If America was a tricky political partner while also an existential challenge, other parts of the world were inferior to Western civilization but were nevertheless a growing threat to its leadership. Siegfried's earliest travels point to concern about growing Asian influence in relation to the West but in his writings the anti-imperial challenge fully emerged in the 1930s. His travels in Latin America and encounters with Indigenous nationalism helped to inspire the broader racial and cultural anxieties expressed in his 1935 book *La crise de l'Europe*. His post-1945 travels only reinforced his concerns about the future of the West and "the white race." He had paid relatively little attention to Sub-Saharan Africa until late in his career, but when he did his writings consistently emphasized the intellectual and moral inferiority of its peoples. He was both dismissive of Indigenous cultures and fearful that they might nurture revolution. The emergence of an independent India and a Communist China posed greater, even more immediate challenges to Western leadership and the security of white people.

How could France, whose power Siegfried did not deny had diminished, flourish in such a challenging environment? Though regularly upholding his nation as the pinnacle of Western intellectual and cultural achievement, Siegfried accepted that partnerships were needed. The American alliance was a necessity, but it was within Europe that France would find its true allies. Exactly who those would be often remained vague in his writing, however. Eastern Europe had been of limited interest to him even before Communist regimes were established there. He sometimes presented himself as an Anglophile – though never an uncritical one – but his efforts to nurture Franco-British ties had limited results. Switzerland, about which he had written an admiring book, could provide a model when it came to rebuilding economies, but Siegfried gradually came to accept that the Federal Republic of Germany would have to be a partner, in conjunction with other Western European states.

In recommending the courses that French politics and diplomacy should follow, Siegfried drew upon a particular conception of the nation's identity. On this point, some of his publications offered a nuanced analysis of regional differences, rooted in social, economic, geographic, ethnic, and religious factors. Such differences meant that the French people themselves were a synthesis, a particularly admirable one in Siegfried's estimation. But while he rejected notions of pure races, Siegfried frequently described the French nation and its qualities in unitary and essentialist terms. He consistently held that the ethnic compound that constituted the French people was only capable of so much variation. In an era where population growth was an imperative for many policy makers, and immigration was a major public issue, Siegfried was among those voices calling for selectivity to ensure the nation's "integrity."

This was certainly the case with Jewish influence upon French society, which Siegfried insisted must be carefully restricted. He consistently denied contemporary suggestions that this view amounted to anti-Semitism, and some scholars have broadly supported this contention. On this point, André-Louis Sanguin argues, Siegfried's attitudes must be distinguished from those of the anti-Semites who promoted hatred, of whom there were many in the 1930s.[23] To be sure, Siegfried did not devote his energies to denouncing Jews in the pages of far-right newspapers; indeed, he professed to value Jewish contributions to French society – but only as long as they remained "proportionate." He can thus be regarded as an important example of the paradoxical connections between philo-Semitism and anti-Semitism, for his writings on the subject are often "expressions of ambivalence towards Jews" that shed light on his broader conceptualization of national and ethnic identities.[24] Siegfried's comments on Jews – which were criticized, and in some cases condemned, by a number of contemporaries, especially in his later years – suggest that he accepted the concept of peoples as being socially constructed entities, but also saw them as constituting deeply rooted, persistent essences that resist modification or acculturation. Ultimately, he was convinced that Jews would remain distinct from French and other Western societies because their values persistently set them apart; most infamously, this led him to join in a chorus of voices condoning exclusionary immigration policies during the Occupation. Overall, Siegfried's decades-long insistence on Jewish "difference" had very troubling implications.

Similar points can be made in assessing his characterizations of Africans, Asians, and Indigenous peoples, situated within broader trends of French thinking about race. For despite long-established perceptions of French republican theory as being rooted in universalism, different strands of racial thought were well-established in France by the beginning of the twentieth century.[25] Siegfried would sometimes invoke republican universalism but then challenge it, suggesting that the ostensible colour-blindness of French revolutionary theory gave it great appeal, but adding that the principle was too ambitious because of the "realities" of racial differences and limitations. He sometimes qualified his analyses by noting that race was not a fixed biological category, but he defended the utility of the concept and frequently asserted a hierarchy of differentiated peoples in his analyses. When it came to asserting why Western civilization was dominant, he invoked technological and organizational superiority, but also stressed that these were the achievements of the European tradition and "the white race."

It might be argued that Siegfried was in essence a nineteenth-century man, coming of age at a time when the language of race and assumptions of European superiority were hegemonic; his use of racial assumptions and language might thus be regarded as an unfortunate persistence of older ways of thinking. Such an argument is a powerful reminder of the importance of contextualization. But the context in which Siegfried operated was hardly static; countervailing attitudes existed during his career, in relation to which his ongoing assertions of racial hierarchies represented a firm conviction rather than just a passive reflex. To be sure, during his formative years a belief in the inequality of peoples, as Reynaud Paligot puts it, "constituted a very large consensus" that was well integrated into mainstream republican ideology, a process greatly facilitated by the fact that it legitimized French imperial expansion. Within this consensus there was a spectrum of opinion ranging from hardline determinists, inclined to apply biological criteria, to those who possessed a more "meliorist" outlook but still denoted unequal mental and moral capacities between different groups of people.[26] Siegfried's expressions of hesitation about rigid biological criteria may situate him more toward the meliorist end of the spectrum, but his lifelong belief in inequality between humans based on supposedly innate characteristics was clearly racist. Nor was this racism an unfortunate appendage to studies largely devoted to other themes; in many of his writings, developing classifications and hierarchies of peoples was an integral part of his approach.

Scholars such as Reynaud Paligot and Conklin have traced the very gradual and uneven growth of anti-racism in France beginning in the 1930s, noting that earlier critics focused on rejections of Nordic racism and anti-Semitism; challenges to mainstream perceptions about the supposed inferiority of colonial populations slowly emerged later.[27] Still, by the 1950s, in large measure responding to the atrocities of the Second World War, organizations such as UNESCO sought to promote anti-racism through various publications. To support those efforts, the prominent *Annales* historian Lucien Febvre and a younger but later prominent colleague, François Crouzet, produced a new history of France that sought to emphasize the role of other nations and cultures in shaping its identity. Their work should not be interpreted anachronistically – Febvre accepted France's colonial project, and it should also be noted that he also admired many of Siegfried's works, praising them in reviews written for *Annales* between the 1930s and 1950s.[28] Febvre's and Crouzet's proposed book, entitled *Nous sommes des sang-mêlés*, also stressed the significance of France's contribution to European and global history, a theme that Siegfried would very likely have found congenial. But the book was notable for its rejection of ethnic and racial hierarchies. As it turned out, UNESCO rejected the manuscript, which then disappeared into obscurity for decades. But its very production – with one of its authors only three years younger than Siegfried – does illustrate how some French scholars participated in a transformation of postwar thinking about difference.[29] Siegfried was acutely aware of the importance of transnational connections and influences, but these were assessed in relation to firm convictions about the supposedly profound disparities between various peoples.

André Siegfried has often been depicted as a cosmopolitan. To be sure, as a member of the Third Republic's elite he took an exceptionally deep interest in other cultures, as well as the complexity of his own country's social dynamics and political traditions. Into middle age, he explored different avenues to prominence, but his passion for travel, observation, and writing remained consistent. Those qualities ultimately made him the most prominent face of an organization that shaped generations of the French establishment and won him recognition through admission to France's leading cultural institutions. At the same time, despite his international interests and reputation, France remained integral to his work. His ambitious goal of mapping his nation's political traditions in the modern era, to which he devoted extensive time and effort, was not fully realized but produced fruitful, influential arguments. His intensive, if relatively neglected, association with the Musée social highlights his ongoing commitment to promoting a liberal framework for socioeconomic relationships, as well as his desire to preserve humanist values in the face of rapid change. His writings on French politics and society were informed by deep knowledge and a consistent vision, as well as a willingness to accept some innovations, but also an exclusionary conception of national identity.

Situating his country in the wider world, Siegfried presented himself as an objective interpreter of other lands, though his belief that France, despite its shortcomings, represented the pinnacle of Western culture could often be discerned. In his travels and writings, he brought readers to various corners of the globe but in doing so systematically highlighted difference and distance. For all its worldly power, the United States could only preserve the materialist elements of Western culture, not its deeper soul. Looking beyond Europe and North America, Siegfried on occasion acknowledged that Western imperialists had given some cause for grievances but believed that in the end they were agents of progress. He held to the view that non-Europeans were, left to their own devices, destined to remain at a lower level of civilization. Siegfried's analyses and eloquence won him considerable respect at home and abroad, but his views also elicited dissent, especially from the United States, in the later stages of his career. While he needs to be situated within the context of his time, in retrospect it seems fair to conclude that, given his substantial talents, he had missed valuable opportunities to promote deeper, more empathetic cross-cultural understanding.

# Notes

### INTRODUCTION

1  AHC 3 SI/16, dossier 8, clipping of Xavier Vallat, "Le fanatique résigné," *Aspects de la France*, 15 February 1957.

2  AHC 13 SI/1, dossier 3, Seydoux to Siegfried, 28 March 1947. Unless otherwise noted, all translations from French are my own.

3  AHC 11 SI/1, dossier 3, Brisson to Siegfried, n.d.

4  Pommier, *Notice sur la vie et les travaux de André Siegfried*, 3; see also *Académie française: Discours prononcés dans la séance privée tenue par L'Académie française pour la reception de M. Henry de Montherlant.*

5  Alexander, "André Siegfried: A Twentieth Century de Tocqueville," 14–27.

6  Siegfried, *Tableau politique*; Siegfried, *Race Question in Canada.* On Underhill, see Dewar, *Frank Underhill*, esp. 71–2, 168.

7  Miroglio, *Un grand Havrais.*

8  Goguel, "André Siegfried," 14–15.

9  See his remarks in *L'oeuvre scientifique d'André Siegfried*, ed. Bonnefous, 123–4.

10  The proceedings were published as a special issue of *Études Normandes* 38, no. 2 (1989); among the contributions focusing most specifically on Siegfried as a geographer are Delvallet, "Les géographes, les élections et la sociologie électorale;" and Claval, "André Siegfried et les démocraties anglo-saxonnes."

11  Bussi, "L'Ouest politique, 75 puis 100 ans après," in *Le* Tableau politique de la France de l'Ouest *d'André Siegfried*, ed. Bussi, Le Digol, and Voilliot, 99.

12  Favre, *Naissances de la science politique en France*; Siegfried, *Tableau politique.* See also Blondiaux and Veitl, "La carrière symbolique d'un père fondateur."

270                    Notes to pages 11–16

13  Bergeron, *Quand Tocqueville et Siegfried nous observaient.*

14  Kuisel, *Seducing the French*, 10–11, 119–20; de Grazia, *Irresistible Empire*, 103–4, 124, 154; Ellwood, *The Shock of America*, 98, 145, 382–3.

15  Birnbaum, *France aux français*, 145–86.

16  Sternhell, *Ni droite ni gauche*, 3rd ed., 23–37, quotation on 36.

17  Noiriel, *Les origines républicaines de Vichy*, 254–60.

18  Roussellier, entry for Siegfried in *Dictionnaire des intellectuels français*, ed. Julliard and Winock, 2nd ed., 1287–9.

19  Epstein, *Les Dreyfusards sous l'Occupation*, 213–15.

20  Reynaud Paligot, "André Siegfried et la question raciale." For an earlier discussion of Siegfried as a founder of *l'étude scientifique de la psychologie des peuples*, see Claret, *La personnalité collective des nations*, 87–101.

21  Buléon, "Siegfried, la Normandie et les temperaments politiques"; Milza, preface to Siegfried, *Tableau politique*, 22–3.

22  Boulet, "André Siegfried," esp. 11–15, 23–4.

23  Fabre, "Le comparatisme d'André Siegfried"; "Un arc transatlantique"; "André Siegfried: Un regard decalé sur le Canada"; "Passeur ou passager?"; *Le pari canadien d'André Siegfried.*

24  Clout, "André Siegfried (1875–1959)," 168.

25  Sanguin, *André Siegfried*, 244, 247.

26  Tillmann, "André Siegfried."

27  Ibid., 419.

28  From the AHC, in addition to Siegfried's personal papers (1–13/SI), this includes records from Sciences Po itself (1 SP); for the Musée Social, it includes personal correspondence from Siegfried held at the AMS, as well as the relevant minutes for its executive committee.

29  A series of cartons (AHC 12SI/5–15) contain albums preserving a great many of Siegfried's newspaper and journal articles dating from 1897 to 1959.

30  There is relevant documentation in SHD Département de l'Armée de la Terre 17N/447; from the MAE there is relevant material in series B, E, and Y; for further information see the relevant references in chapters 2 and 6, and the bibliography.

31  In particular, there are relevant materials from the records of the UK Foreign Office – TNA Fo/371, 395, and 432 – and the archives of the RIIA, specifically 8/46, 8/1603, 8/1095.

32  For the Collège de France, there is ACF dossier C–XII (Siegfried's dossier) and record group G–IV (minutes of the Assemby of Professors); for the AIF there are relevant records from its Section de Morale as well as

Notes to pages 17–26

the Académie française, and the BIF houses correspondence relating to Siegfried. For further information see the bibliography as well as specific references for chapters 3–6.

33 Studies of French intellectual history in this vein include: Winock, *Le siècle des intellectuels*; Leymarie, *Les intellectuels et la politique en France*; and Ory and Sirinelli, *Les intelllectuels en France*. In-depth studies have shown the variegated forms engagement took; see, for example, Laurent, *Daniel Halévy* and Leymarie, *La prevue par deux*.

34 See, for example, Martinez, "Comment les libéraux sont arrivés à Vichy."

35 On the changing connotations of neoliberalism, see Audier, "Is There a French Neoliberalism?"

36 On the liberal revival of the 1980s and 1990s, see Hazareesingh, *How the French Think*, 241–5.

37 For a recent overview, see Behrent, "Liberal Dispositions"; on the contrast between the English and French liberal traditions, see Siedentop, "Two Liberal Traditions."

38 Craiutu, *A Virtue for Courageous Minds*; Craiutu, "Raymond Aron and the Tradition of Political Moderation in France"; on the elitism of French liberals, see Behrent, "Liberal Dispositions," 459.

39 Beale, *Modernist Enterprise*, 165–72; Nord, *France's New Deal*, 145–213, here 209.

40 Clarke, *France in the Age of Organization*, 7–8.

41 On republican racial thinking see Rosenberg, "Albert Sarraut and Republican Racial Thought"; Reynaud Paligot, *La République raciale* and *Races, racisme et antiracisme*.

42 On this theme, see Conklin, *In the Museum of Man*.

CHAPTER ONE

1 This paragraph is based on Siegfried, *Jules Siegfried*, chapter 1. Siegfried first sketched out his thoughts on his father's career in a lecture presented to the Société d'histoire de la Troisième République, which is preserved in AHC 6S1/6, dossier 4, "Jules Siegfried: 50 ans de vie publique sous la IIIème," 4 June 1937.

2 Siegfried, *Jules Siegfried*, 57–8, 60–2; for further context, see Ardaillou, "Les républicains modérés du Havre," 194–7.

3 Siegfried, *Jules Siegfried*, chapter 2 (quotation on 40); Ardaillou, "Les républicains modérés du Havre," 195; AN F/7/16006, commissaire spécial (Le Havre), report, 4 March 1886, attaching clipping from *Le journal du Havre*, 3 March 1886.

272     Notes to pages 27–34

4   Siegfried, *Jules Siegfried*, 97–113.

5   Ardaillou, "Les républicains modérés du Havre," 196–7; Clark, *Prophets and Patrons*, 111–16; Elwitt, *Third Republic Defended*; Nord, *Republican Moment*, 106–7. Jules Siegfried's work with the Musée social is discussed in detail in Horne, *A Social Laboratory for Modern France*.

6   Tillmann, "André Siegfried," 90–1.

7   For press commentary on Jules Siegfried's position, see AN F/7/16006, clippings of *L'Écho de Paris*, 22 January 1900, *Éclair*, 21 April 1900, and *Le Gaulois*, 21 April 1900. On the contentious nature of the amnesty, see Harris, *Man on Devil's Island*, 342–3.

8   Siegfried, *Jules Siegfried*, 121–3.

9   Ibid., 123.

10  Sanguin, *André Siegfried*, 29–30; Hause with Kenney, *Women's Suffrage and Social Politics*, esp. 59, 176; Rupp, *Worlds of Women*, 82, 173; Siegel, *Peace on Our Terms*, 74.

11  Siegfried, preface to Sanua, *Figures féminines*, 1–2; Siegfried, *Jules Siegfried*, 120; Siegfried, *Mes souvenirs de l'enfance*, 80.

12  Siegfried, *Jules Siegfried*, 36–7.

13  Ibid., 141.

14  Sanguin, *André Siegfried*, 33–5; Chevalier, "Siegfried et l'école française de géographie," 19–20.

15  Siegfried, *Mes souvenirs d'enfance*, 85.

16  Siegfried, *Jules Siegfried*, 99–100, 115; *Mes souvenirs d'enfance*, 14–15, 56–8, 78–9.

17  Siegfried, *Mes souvenirs d'enfance*, 32–3.

18  Siegfried, *Jules Siegfried*, 69–74, quotations on 74, 70 respectively.

19  Ibid., 85, 87–9; for some skepticism about the reliability of these recollections, see Goguel, "La politique française," 38.

20  Siegfried, *Jules Siegfried*, 105–6, 115–19.

21  Ibid., 29, 136–7.

22  Siegfried, *Mes souvenirs d'enfance*, 72.

23  Siegfried, *Jules Siegfried*, 140–1.

24  Siegfried, *Mes souvenirs d'enfance*, 49, 51–2; on Izoulet see Siegfried's postwar reflections on his research methodology; AHC 12SI/3, "Cher correspondant inconnu," 3 March 1946.

25  De Traz, "André Siegfried," 313.

26  Siegfried, *Mes souvenirs d'enfance*, 50.

27  Sanguin, *André Siegfried*, 39.

28  De Traz, "André Siegfried," 312–13.

29  Siegfried, "Discours de reception."

Notes to pages 34–9 273

30 Kuisel, *Capitalism and the State in Modern France*, 5–6; Tillmann, "André Siegfried," 215.

31 Nord, *Republican Moment*, 248; see also Clark, *Prophets and Patrons*, 111–17.

32 Roger, *American Enemy*, 209–13.

33 Siegfried, "Discours de reception"; Fabre, *Le pari canadien d'André Siegfried*, 8–10.

34 On these influences, see Fabre, "Passeur ou passager," 213–20. Tillmann, "André Siegfried," 220, stresses Taine's influence in particular.

35 Birnbaum, *La France aux français*, 161–3; Sternhell, *Maurice Barrès et le nationalisme français*, 14–15; Leuillot, "Littérature et histoire: Quatre jours chez M. Barrès," 339–40.

36 Classic studies of Barrès include Soucy, *Fascism in France: The Case of Maurice Barrès*; Doty, *From Cultural Rebellion to Counterrevolution*; and Sternhell, *Maurice Barrès et le nationalisme français*.

37 For a recent case study, see Dard, "Le Barrèsisme d'Henri Massis: Bilan d'un demi-siècle."

38 Leuillot, "Littérature et histoire: Quatre jours chez M. Barrès," 340; AHC 12SI/3, dossier 2, typescript by Siegfried, "Pensées politiques de Barrès," n.d.

39 Churchill, "Unlikely Barrèsian Inheritance."

40 Ibid., 258, 286.

41 AHC 12SI/3, dossier 3, Siegfried, "Cher correspondant inconnu," 3 March 1946.

42 AD Seine-Maritime 1R/2986, service record of André Robert Siegfried; see also Sanguin, *André Siegfried*, 39. I am very grateful to the staff of the Archives départementales de la Seine-Maritime for providing me with a copy of Siegfried's record.

43 AHC 12SI/5, clippings of "Le socialisme d'état en Australie Occidentale," parts 1 and 2, *Le Signal*, 3 and 14 April 1897.

44 AHC 12SI/5, clippings of "La politique russe en Chine," *Le Signal*, 11 February 1897, "Quelques mots sur les Tchècques et la Bohème d'aujourd'hui," *Le Signal*, 16 June 1898.

45 AHC 12SI/5, clippings of "La lutte économique de l'Allemagne et de l'Angleterre," *Le Signal*, 19 March 1897 (first quotation); "Cecil Rhodes et la Chartered," *Le Signal*, 25 February, 3 March 1897 (second quotation).

46 AHC 12SI/5, clipping of "Le Musée social," *Journal des instituteurs*, no. 38 (13 June 1897), 109–13. Scholarship on the Musée includes Elwitt, "Social Reform and Social Order in Late Nineteenth-Century France";

274    Notes to pages 39–43

Chambelland, ed., *Le Musée social en son temps*; Horne, *A Social Laboratory for Modern France*.

47  On Siegfried's long association with the Musée social, see Deroy, "Hommage à la mémoire d'André Siegfried."

48  Martin Siegfried, "La démocratie en Nouvelle-Zélande vue par André Siegfried," 662, suggests that Kahn supported Siegfried's travel; the relevant files are in AN AJ16/7023 but I was unable to locate any file on Siegfried. The comment by the Duc de La Force regarding Jules Siegfried's funding of the journey is quoted in Tillmann, "André Siegfried," 116.

49  AN F/17/3007/1, file on Siegfried's global tour; the correspondence runs from 12 September to 29 October 1898.

50  See Winter, *Dreams of Peace and Freedom*, 15–17; and Tronchet, "Les bourses de voyage 'autour du monde' de la Fondation Albert Kahn (1898–1930)."

51  Brief discussions of the journey are as follows: de Traz, "André Siegfried," 313; Pommier, *Notice sur la vie et les travaux de André Siegfried*, 6; Goguel, "André Siegfried: L'homme et l'oeuvre," 2; Favre, *Naissances de la science politique en France*, 262; Sanguin, *André Siegfried*, 39.

52  AD Seine-Maritime 1R/2986, Siegfried service record; copies of the articles are preserved in AHC 12SI/5; see also "Causerie de M. André Siegfried," *Le mémoral cauchois*, 26 September 1900.

53  AHC 12SI/5, clippings of Siegfried, "Au Canada français: Une visite à Saint-Hyacinthe," *Le Petit Havre*, 23 November 1898, and "La vie politique au Canada," *Revue politique et parlementaire* 19 (January-March 1899), 134–42, quotation from 138. See also, "La colonisation au Canada français," *La quinzaine coloniale*, 25 December 1898 and, in English, "French Canadians under English Rule," *East & West*, January 1902, 250–7.

54  AHC 12SI/5, clipping of "La politique canadienne et la victoire du ministère Laurier," *La Revue et maritime et coloniale*, 1 February 1901, 149–56.

55  Siegfried, "L'enseignement du journalisme aux États-Unis," *Le Temps*, 12 March 1899, 3; "Au jour le jour: Le Musée commercial de Philadelphie," *Le Temps*, 15 June 1899, 2–3.

56  AHC 12SI/4, dossier 3, subdossier a, typescript of "Une promenade dans Chicago," 22 May 1899, published in *Le Petit Havre* on that date.

57  Siegfried, "Nouvelle-Zélande: Une enquête économique et sociale."

58  Ibid., 177 (quotation), 178–80, 687, 689–93, 696.

59  Ibid., 677, 688, 183–4, 193–4, 199–200; see also AHC 12SI/5, clippings of "Les droits politiques des femmes en Nouvelle-Zélande," unidentified

Notes to pages 43–50

journal, 15 August 1900; and "La lutte contre l'alcoolisme en Nouvelle-Zélande," *La Source*, October 1900, 29–33.

60 Siegfried, preface to Raymond Ronze, *Le commonwealth britannique*, x–xi.

61 AHC 12SI/4, dossier 3, subdossier a, typescript, "Manille," 20 August 1899; see also AHC 12SI/4, clippings of *Le Petit Havre*, 7, 18 October 1899.

62 AHC 12SI/4, dossier 3, sub-dossier a, typescript, "Manille," 20 August 1899.

63 AHC 12SI/4, dossier 3, sub-dossier a, typescript, "En Corée," January 1900; see also AHC 12SI/5, "En Corée," *Le Petit Havre*, 1 and 2 January 1900.

64 AHC 12SI/5, clippings of "La question ouvrière et le pauperisme au Japon," *La revue chrétienne*, 1 January 1900, 39–50 (quotation on 49–50); "Causerie de M. André Siegfried," *Le mémorial cauchois*, 26 September 1900; and "Le développement économique et social du Japon," *Musée social (Chronique du Musée social)* 6, no. 3 (1901), 65–83.

65 AHC 12SI/5, clipping of "Causerie de M. André Siegfried," *Le mémorial cauchois*, 26 September 1900.

66 ACH 12SI/5, clippings of *Le Petit Havre*, 3, 4, 7, 13, 16 July 1900, 11, 17 January, 27 February 1901, "La Chine coloniale: Les Chinois de Singapore," *Revue des revues*, 1 October 1903, 79–89; BIF, manuscript 5480, card from Siegfried to Cordier, 20 October 1908.

67 On these developments, see Lake and Reynolds, *Drawing the Global Colour Line*.

### CHAPTER TWO

1 Mercier, "Universités populaires," in *Dictionnaire des intellectuels français*, ed. Julliard and Winock, 1375–8; see also Mercier, *Les universités populaires 1899–1914*.

2 This account derives from two articles published by Siegfried; "La Fondation Universitaire de Belleville (Exercice 1903–1904)" and "La Fondation Universitaire de Belleville: Une expérience de cinq ans."

3 On this issue, see AHC 12SI/5, clipping of English-language article by Siegfried, "Why the French Have No Social Settlements," *The Outlook*, 22 August 1903, 995–7, quotation on 996.

4 Siegfried, "La Fondation Universitaire de Belleville (Exercise 1903–1904)," 181–2.

276                                 Notes to pages 50–7

5  Ibid., 200–2.

6  The different perspectives are outlined in Sanguin, *André Siegfried*, 41–2.

7  Schumberger, comments in Association Andre Siegfried, *Hommage à Andre Siegfried*, 5–7, quotation on 6.

8  Hamp, "In memoriam: André Siegfried."

9  Siegfried, "La Fondation Universitaire de Belleville (Exercice 1903–1904)," 182–4; Sanguin, *André Siegfried*, 41.

10  Sanguin, *André Siegfried*, 43–4; Favre, *Naissances de la science politique*, 263–5; Garrigou, "André Siegfried dans les Basses-Alpes."

11  AN C/7180, Siegfried to President of Chamber of Deputies, 31 May 1902; this document is reproduced in Garrigou, "Un document d'André Siegfried."

12  AN C/7180, letter by Siegfried, 29 June 1902.

13  AN C/7180, "Réponse de M. de Castellane à la protestation de M. Siegfried et Blanc contre l'élection du 27 avril 1902," 5 June 1902.

14  Favre, *Naissances de la science politique*, 264; Garrigou, "L'initiation d'un initiateur," 28–9; AN C/7180, notes by Siegfried, 31 August, 3 November 1902; Garrigou, " Siegfried dans les Basses-Alpes," 37–8.

15  On the early years of the Alliance démocratique, see Sanson, "Centre et gauche (1901–1914)."

16  Favre, *Naissances de la science politique*, 266–7; the election dossier is in AN C/6450.

17  Siegfried, "Les partis politiques en France," 155.

18  The following two paragraphs are based on Favre, *Naissances de la science politique*, 267; Sanguin, *André Siegfried*, 44; and materials on the two elections in AN C/6752 and AN C/6742.

19  Comments in *L'oeuvre scientifique d'André Siegfried*, ed. Bonnefous, 60–1.

20  ACF, dossier C–XII (André Siegfried), clipping of *Le guide protestant de l'édition, bulletin bibliographique trimestriel* no. 5, July 1946, interview of Siegfried by G. Chabrut; comments by Bonnefous in *L'oeuvre scientifique d'André Siegfried*, 61. Tillmann, "André Siegfried," 121, convincingly notes that this later acceptance does not square with Siegfried's repeated efforts to secure a seat.

21  Lancelot, "Les problèmes électoraux," 51; on the decline of clientelism during this period, see Courrière, "Clientélisme, autorité et domination politique dans les Alpes-Maritimes."

22  Sanguin, *André Siegfried*, 46–7; Goguel, "André Siegfried," 3–4.

23  Sanguin, *André Siegfried*, 47–9; Pozzi, *Journal 1913–1934*, 443–5, 449–50, 503, 514–16, 558–61, 587–8, entries for 6, 22 March, 25 April, December 1928, 9 February 1929, 23 February, 6, 9 March, 7 November 1930.

Notes to pages 58–63

24  AHC 13SI/1, dossier 3, clipping of *La Presse*, 7 September 1945.
There is a partial record of their travels together in AHC 12SI/4,
dossier 3, "Voyages de Paule et André Siegfried, 1907–1940"; Leurquin,
"André Siegfried devant ses élèves," 27.

25  AHC 13SI/1, dossier 3, pamphlet by Siegfried for his wife, *Les saisons
et les jours* (Paris: Imprimerie Lahure, 1920).

26  Sanguin, *André Siegfried*, 47–8; AHC 2SI/24, dossier 2, letter from
Claire Siegfried, 13 December 1943.

27  ACF, dossier C–XII (André Siegfried), *Le guide protestant de l'édition,
bulletin bibliographique trimestriel* no. 5, July 1946, interview by
G. Chabrut; Goguel, "André Siegfried," 4, states that the chair was
in economic geography.

28  Sanguin, *André Siegfried*, 142–3; on Paul Leroy-Beaulieu and parallels
between his career and that of Siegfried see Favre, *Naissances de la science
politique*, 271–5.

29  Clippings of articles up to the end of 1908 are preserved in AHC 12SI/5;
those for 1909, along with various journal articles, are preserved in
AHC 12SI/6.

30  AHC 12SI/5, clipping of "The American and French Workingman
Contrasted," *Social Service* (July 1901), 7.

31  On Vidal de la Blache, see Sanguin, *Vidal de la Blache*; on Dubois,
see Clout, "Marcel Dubois," and Broc, "Nationalisme, colonialisme
et géographie."

32  Sanguin, *André Siegfried*, 39–40.

33  Siegfried, *Democracy in New Zealand*, chapters 2–5, quotation on 271.

34  Ibid., 10–12; On the obscuring of the violence of British expansion,
see Tillmann, "André Siegfried," 175.

35  David-Ives, "André Siegfried in New Zealand," 28–31.

36  Siegfried, *Democracy in New Zealand*, chapter 17, quotations on 216,
228.

37  See Piterberg and Veracini, "Wakefield, Marx, and the World turned
Inside Out," 460–3.

38  Siegfried, *Edward Gibbon Wakefield*.

39  AHC 12SI/4, dossier 3, "À l'exposition de Saint-Louis," September 1904;
see also AHC 12SI/5, clippings of *Le Petit Havre*, 21 September, 4, 13,
15 October 1904.

40  Siegfried, *Race Question in Canada*, 27, 82, 186.

41  AHC 4SI/2, dossier 2, "Conférence sur le Canada," Le Havre,
23 November 1906, "Le Canada français et la vieille civilisation française
en Amérique: Conférence pour l'Alsace," January 1910.

278 Notes to pages 63–72

42 AHC 2SI/16, dossier 5, Max Leclerc to Siegfried, 23 January 1906.

43 Siegfried, *Race Question in Canada*, 179–86, 242–3.

44 Ibid., 92, 112, 119.

45 Ibid., 137, 187, 102.

46 Airey, "André Siegfried's Democracy in New Zealand," 41; Leask, "André Siegfried and the Discovery of New Zealand Democracy." I am grateful to the author for providing me with a copy of his essay.

47 For further discussion, see Fabre, *Le pari canadien d'André Siegfried*, 81–7.

48 On reactions to *Le Canada*, see Kennedy, "A Tocqueville for the North," 124; on Underhill and Siegfried, see Dewar, *Frank Underhill*, 71–2, 168.

49 Favre, *Naissances de la science politique*, 236–9.

50 See, for example, materials relating to the Finistère department in AHC 7SI/2. Siegfried also discusses his sources and methodology in *Tableau politique*, appendix A, 605–11.

51 Siegfried, "Le régime et la division de la propriété dans le Pays de Caux," and "Le régime et la division de la propriété dans le Maine et l'Anjou." For meetings with Vidal and Seignobos, see Siegfried, *Cours de geographie economique et politique*, 15.

52 Siegfried, *Tableau politique*, 55.

53 Ibid., 45.

54 Ibid., 40–1, 51–2.

55 Ibid., 136, 87.

56 Ibid., 125, 98 (quotation).

57 Ibid., 178, 180.

58 Ibid., 194, 219, 269, 296.

59 Ibid., 300, 369.

60 Ibid., 389, 396, 416.

61 Ibid., 363–6.

62 Ibid., 598.

63 Favre, *Naissances de la science politique*, 261; Sanguin, "André Siegfried et le *Tableau*," 17–27; Garrigou, "Initiation d'un initiateur," 31–9.

64 Siegfried, *Tableau politique*, 602.

65 Sanguin, *Vidal de la Blache*, 321–35.

66 Siegfried, *Tableau politique*, 448.

67 For criticisms of Siegfried along these lines, see Favre, *Naissances de la science politique*, 245–6 and, more forcefully, Birnbaum, *La France aux français*, 186; for recent evaluations, see Bussi, "L'Ouest politique, 75 puis 100 ans après," and Buléon, "La tentative de Siegfried et sa faille épistémologique."

Notes to pages 72–9

68 Paul Vidal de la Blache, review of *Tableau politique* in *Annales de géographie* 23, no. 129 (1914), 261–4; Pierre Millet, "À la recherche de la vraie France," *Le Temps*, 6 January 1914.

69 Siegfried, *Cours de géographie économique et politique*, 15; Favre, *Naissances de la science politique*, 289–90.

70 Siegfried, *Deux mois en Amérique du Nord*, 10–12, 22.

71 Ibid., 118, 121.

72 For a detailed analysis of French perceptions of the United States during this era, see Portes, *Fascination and Misgivings*.

73 Siegfried, *Deux mois en Amérique du Nord*, 37, 47, 64.

74 Ibid., 4.

75 Ibid., 35, 67, 95.

76 Ibid., 102, 39, 42.

77 Siegfried, *Deux mois en Amérique du Nord*, 131; Portes, *Fascination and Misgivings*, 415.

78 SHD Département de l'Armée de la Terre 17N/447, "Bordereau récapitulatif des états en double expédition faisant ressortir les mutations survenues pendant les mois écoulé dans le personnel de la mission française attachée à l'armée britannique," 1 March 1915; Bureau du Personnel No. 5204 P, order no. 34, July 1915; Chef d'Escadron Jamet, officier de liaison à la 1ère Armée Britannique à Monsieur le Général, chef de la mission française attachée à l'armée britannique, 8 October 1915.

79 MAE, Blocus 361, "Liste du personnel, SFB," 1 March 1918; Blocus 362, "Service blocus financier," note on Siegfried, n.d. but probably spring-summer 1918; on Métin see Favre, *Naissances de la science politique*, 288 n.1.

80 Hamp, "In memoriam: André Siegfried," 17, 19.

81 AHC 2SI/18, dossier 1, Max Leclerc to Siegfried, 16 November 1915; Campbell, *De Verdun aux Vosges*.

82 Siegfried, comments in "France and Her Allies."

83 AHC 13SI/1, dossier 3, sub-dossier c, preface to *Les saisons et les jours* (Paris: Imprimerie Lahure, 1920).

84 Siegfried, comments in "France and Her Allies."

85 MAE, série E (Asie, Océanie, 1918–1940), sous-série Australie, vol. 9, note, "Mission d'Australie," 12 June 1918, Paul Cambon (ambassador in London), 27 July 1918. For further context, see Aldrich, "La mission française en Australie de 1918."

86 MAE, série E, sous-série Australie, vol. 9, telegram from Siegfried to Madame Métin, 21 August 1918; MAE, série E, sous-série Australie,

280                    Notes to pages 79–83

vol. 10, French consul (Sydney) to minister of foreign affairs, 20 December 1918; on the desire to include Bergson, see Alexander, "André Siegfried: A Twentieth Century de Tocqueville," 15.

87 Quoted in MAE, série E, sous-série Australie, vol.11: "Mission française en Australie: rapport," 12.

88 Quoted in MAE, série E, sous-série Australie, vol. 10, French consul (Sydney), 20 December 1918; MAE, série E, sous-série Australie, vol. 11, "Mission française," 395–6.

89 MAE, série E, sous-série Australie, vol. 10, vice-consul (Auckland) to minister of foreign affairs, 1 February 1919.

90 MAE, série E, sous-série Australie, vol. 11, "Mission française," quotations on 83, 380–1.

91 MAE, série SDN 205, minister of finances to président du conseil, 2 March 1920, "Service française de la Société des Nations," 1920. On the creation of these services, see Jeannesson, "Jacques Seydoux et la diplomatie économique," 10–11; for a detailed analysis of French policy during this period, see Jackson, *Beyond the Balance of Power*; he notes the creation of the SFSDN on 373.

92 Walters, *History of the League of Nations*, vol.1, 111–12, 143; for overall French policy at the conference, see Jackson, *Beyond the Balance of Power*, 354.

93 For an overview, see Steiner, *The Lights that Failed*, 211–13; for detailed analysis, see Fink, *The Genoa Conference*.

94 MAE, série SDN, sous-série 1J (questions économiques et financières), vol. 1221, 245–7, Siegfried to Gout, 8 October 1920 (quotation), vol. 1222, 89, Siegfried and Paul West to Gout, 14 October 1920.

95 MAE série SDN, sous-série 1K (communications and transit), vol. 1481, 80–3, Siegfried to Gout, 15 March 1921.

96 MAE série SDN, sous-série 1J (questions économiques et financiers), vol. 1205 (Genoa Conference, 1922), 273–4, 288, Siegfried to Gout, 26 April, 1 May 1922; for his view on French policy toward the USSR, see Hogenhuis-Seliverstoff, "French Plans for the Reconstruction of Russia," 143–4.

97 On the resignation, see MAE-SDN 207, président du conseil/ministre des affaires étrangères, notice, 8 November 1922; Goguel, "André Siegfried," 4; MAE-SDN 205, minutes, 6 September 1922, note, 1 February 1923, Gout, "Note pour m. le président du conseil," 24 February 1923.

98 Goguel, "André Siegfried," 4; Ardaillou, "Les républicains modérés du Havre," 197.

Notes to pages 83–91

99 MAE-SDN 1199, pamphlet, Société des Nations/League of Nations, conférence économique internationale (le 4 Mai 1927)/International Economic Conference (4 May 1927): *Liste des membres de la conférence (revisée): List of Members of the Conference (revised)* (Geneva, 1927).

## CHAPTER THREE

1 École Libre, *Organisation et programme des cours: Année scolaire 1927–1928*, 20–1.
2 Nord, *France's New Deal*, 67–8, 71–2.
3 See his contribution to *Élie Halévy, 6 septembre 1870–21 août 1937*, 11–17; on Halévy, see K. Steven Vincent, *Élie Halévy*.
4 Nord, *France's New Deal*, 68–9, 73.
5 For details, see École Libre, *Organisation et programme des cours: Année scolaire 1927–1928*, 87–8, 119–20, 128–9; *Organisation et programme des cours: Année scolaire 1928–1929*, 77, 148; *Organisation et programme des cours: Année scolaire 1938–1939*, 107, 134; Sanguin, *André Siegfried*, 143–4.
6 AHC 4SI/4, dossier 2, "Décrire les caracteristiques du commerce extérieur d'un pays neuf et d'un vieux pays," December 1932; "Dangers économiques qui menacent éventuellement les pays industrialisés à l'excès comme l'Angleterre et l'Allemagne," n.d.
7 AHC 4SI/4, dossier 2, "Les peuples dépensier et les peuples frugaux," n.d.
8 AHC 4SI/4, dossier 4, "Le péril jaune," n.d.
9 AHC 4SI/2, dossier 2, "Conférence de préparation au Quai d'Orsay – leçon d'introduction (1922–23)"; dossier 3, "Rapport à M. le directeur sur la conférence de géographie économique, 1924–1925."
10 Roger Seydoux, "Le mecredi, André Siegfried monte en chaire aux Sciences Po," *Le Figaro littéraire*, 6 May 1950, quoted in Sanguin, *André Siegfried*, 147.
11 Des Portes, *L'atmosphère des Sciences Po*, 52–4.
12 Wylie, "André Siegfried à Harvard," 67–8.
13 Scot, "Sciences Po et les femmes: 140 ans d'histoire."
14 AHC 4SI/2, dossier 3, "Rapport à M. le directeur sur la conférence de géographie économique, 1924–1925."
15 Siegfried, preface to des Portes, *L'atmosphère des Sciences Po*, 7–11.
16 Nord, *France's New Deal*, 73–81; see also Charle, "Savoir durer," 99–105.
17 AHC 1SP/52, dossier 3, clipping, "Un foyer de rayonnement français," *Le petit Parisien*, 14 February 1938.
18 For details of this process, see Nord, *France's New Deal*, 75–86.

282                                Notes to pages 92–100

19 On the postwar decline in Anglo-French relations, see Boyce, "Behind the façade of the *Entente cordiale* after the Great War" and Cairns, "A Nation of Shopkeepers in Search of a Suitable France."

20 AMS, folder, "André Siegfried et le Musée Social: lettres," Siegfried to Risler, 18 November 1923.

21 AMS, Siegfried to Risler, 18 November 1923.

22 Siegfried, *Post-War Britain*, 19–43.

23 Ibid., 273.

24 Ibid., 249.

25 Ibid., 298.

26 Ibid., 99.

27 Ibid., *Post-War Britain*, 227.

28 Ibid., 308, 314.

29 AHC 2SI/18, dossier 4, Attaché financier, ambassade de France à Londres to Siegfried, 24 May 1924; Joseph Aynard, review of *L'Angleterre d'aujourd'hui, Journal des débats*, 20 April 1924; on the Association France–Grande Bretagne commissioning this review, see AHC 2SI/18, dossier 4, letter to Siegfried, 15 May 1924.

30 AHC 2SI/18, dossier 4, Lionel Curtis to Siegfried, 15 January 1925, Leo Amery to Siegfried, 14 July 1924.

31 R.H. Tawney, "A Frenchman on England," *The New Republic*, 18 February 1925, 347–8.

32 AHC 13SI/4, dossier 1, Siegfried to Chapsal, 30 November 1927.

33 Siegfried, "A Frenchman on Britain: Breaking with the Past," *The Times*, 1, 2 February 1928; Siegfried, "The Passing of England's Economic Hegemony."

34 Siegfried, "Passing of England's Economic Hegemony," 540.

35 Siegfried, "Dark Hours in England," *The Nation & Athenaeum*, 26 July 1930, 524–5.

36 Siegfried, *England's Crisis*. For the five excerpts see "M. Siegfried on England," *The Times*, 9–13 March 1931.

37 Siegfried, *England's Crisis*, 72.

38 Ibid., 150–4.

39 Ibid., 179, 222, 250.

40 Ibid., 251, 145, 147, 109.

41 Siegfried, "La crise de l'industrie britannique"; for British government reactions, see TNA, FO 371/15641, W1145/56/17, Tyrrell to Henderson, 28 January 1931, W1296/56/17, C. Howard Smith to Secretary of the Treasury, 13 February 1931.

42 Layton, "La situation économique de l'Angleterre."

Notes to pages 100–6 283

43 "Siegfried's England," *The New Statesman and Nation*, 8 May 1931, 396.

44 "Economic Future of Britain: Sir Walter Layton's Analysis," *The Times*, 31 March 1931, 13; Alfred Zimmern, "England's Crisis," *The Spectator* 146 (11 April 1931), 588–9; Harold J. Laski, "Siegfried Looks at England," *The Saturday Review of Literature* 7 (13 June 1931), 892.

45 J.L. Garvin, review of *England's Crisis* in *The Observer*, 12 April 1931, 16; AHC 2SI/22bis, dossier 1, Siegfried to Garvin, 22 April 1931, Garvin to Siegfried, 28 April 1931.

46 "Since the Crisis: M. Siegfried on England," *The Times*, 14 October 1933, 11; see also J. de V. Loder, review of 1933 edition of *England's Crisis* in *International Affairs* 13, no. 2 (March-April 1934), 286–7.

47 TNA FO 432/4, part 9 (January-June 1938), doc. no. 4, C 102/102/17, Phipps to Chamberlain, 6 January 1938, enclosing "Report on Leading Personalities in France for 1937," 49–50.

48 AMS, folder, "André Siegfried et la Musée Social: Matériaux," typescript, "André Siegfried," n.d.

49 AHC 2SI/19, dossier 3, Douglas Fairbanks to Siegfried, 13 April 1927.

50 Siegfried, *America Comes of Age*, 9–10, 274.

51 AHC 12SI/4, dossier 3, "Los Angeles, la Nice californienne," September 1925, "El Paso de north," 5 October 1925.

52 AHC 13SI/4, dossier 1, Siegfried to Chapsal, 15 November 1925.

53 Siegfried, *America Comes of Age*, 118; see also AHC 12SI/8, copy of Siegfried, "American Immigration and Eugenics," *Eugenics Review*, October 1926, 3–8.

54 For a comparison, see Rosenberg, "Albert Sarraut and Republican Racial Thought," 37–9, 43–4.

55 Siegfried, *America Comes of Age*, 30, 28, 16.

56 Ibid., 91, 97–9.

57 Ibid., 105, 107–8.

58 Ibid., 35–6, 40.

59 Ibid., 177, 348.

60 Ibid., 69.

61 Ibid., 246, 352.

62 Galloux-Fournier, "Un regard sur l'Amérique," 314; Strauss, *Menace in the West*, 67–9, 71; on the longevity of the book, see Lacorne, *Crise de l'identité américaine*, 151n1.

63 AHC 2SI/20, clippings of Jacques Bainville, "Chronique du jour: Terre de liberté," *La Liberté*, 28 August 1927; Alfred Berl, "Les juifs aux États-Unis," *Paix et droit: Organe de l'Alliance Israélite Universelle* 8, no. 3 (March 1928), 1–3.

284 Notes to pages 106–9

64 For sales figures, see Favre, *Naissances de la science politique*, 289; references to lectures and discussions about the book include the following press clippings: AHC 2SI/21, dossier 1, *New York Times*, 24 April 1927; dossier 5, *The Record* (Greensboro, NC), 24 February 1928, and *The Seattle Post Intelligencer*, 29 April 1928.

65 For an overview of conflicting attitudes toward modernization, as well as the xenophobic sentiments of the era, in the United States, see Dumenil, *Modern Temper*, 145–200, 203–17.

66 AHC 2SI/21, dossier 1, clipping of *The News* (Chicago), 7 April 1927.

67 AHC 2SI/21, dossier 5, clipping of Los Angeles *Record*, 16 April 1927.

68 Charles Beard, "A Frenchman on America," *The New Republic* 51 (8 June 1927): 75–6.

69 Parkhurt Whitney, review of *Les États-Unis d'aujourd'hui* in *Outlook* 146 (21 December 1927): 504.

70 See Jacobson, *Whiteness of a Different Color*, 78–87.

71 AHC 2SI/19, dossier 2, Rebecca Godchaux to Siegfried, 28 March, 19 May 1927.

72 Ernest Boyd, "Readers and Writers," *The Independent*, 30 April 1927, 470.

73 H.L. Mencken, "A Frenchman Takes a Look," *The Nation*, 11 May 1927, 533.

74 AHC 2SI/19, dossier 4, Walter Hart Blumenthal (associate editor of *The American Hebrew*) to Siegfried, 18 May 1927; AHC 12/SI 8, clipping of article on French Jews (title unknown), *The American Hebrew*, 22 November 1929.

75 These articles include "The Gulf Between"; "European Reactions to American Tariff Proposals"; and "Will Europe Be Americanized?"

76 Siegfried, "The Gulf Between," 295.

77 Siegfried, "Will Europe Be Americanized," 442.

78 AHC 12SI/8, "The Yale Review Award: Decision of the Judges," n.d.

79 Siegfried, *Douze lettres des États-Unis*, 33.

80 Siegfried, *États-Unis-Canada–Méxique*, 87–8.

81 Siegfried, *Qu'est-ce que l'Amérique*, 41, 48.

82 Siegfried, "Middletown: Une ville américaine pendant la crise." On the Lynds' work, see Fox, "Epitaph for Middletown."

83 Siegfried, *Qu'est-ce que l'Amérique*, 13, 19, 24–25.

84 AHC 4SI/5, dossier 2, notes for "Cours de politique économique des puissances," lecture: "Les États-Unis, I: Introduction – de l'indépendance à la guerre de sécession," 18 March 1938 (emphasis in original).

Notes to pages 110–17

85  Siegfried, "Franco-American and Franco-British Relations," 226, 229–30, 236. See also Siegfried, "Britain and America through French Eyes," *The Spectator*, 4 February 1928.
86  Siegfried, "French Industry and Mass Production," 1, 9–10.
87  Siegfried, "Psychology of French Political Parties" and *France: A Study in Nationality*. See also Siegfried, "Psychology of French Politics."
88  Siegfried, "The French Mind," 744; *France: A Study in Nationality*, 22–23, "Psychology of French Political Parties," 17.
89  Siegfried, "Psychology of French Politics," 95, *France: A Study in Nationality*, 18.
90  Siegfried, *France: A Study in Nationality*, 80–5, 91–2.
91  Ibid., 59–60, 68, 76, 112.
92  AN 475AP/307, Siegfried to Lyautey, 1 November 1932 (emphasis in original).
93  AHC 2SI/22, dossier 1, Barthelémy to Siegfried, 14 December 1930; Garric to Siegfried, 24 November 1930; Thomas to Siegfried, 15 December 1930.
94  Gottschalk, review of *France: A Study in Nationality* in *The Historical Outlook* 21 (October 1930), 289–90; Hayes, review of *France: A Study in Nationality* in *The Nation*, 18 June 1930, 709–10.
95  Some earlier commentary on Canada appears in Siegfried, *États-Unis–Canada–Méxique*.
96  Siegfried, *Canada*, 27, 294–304. See also the analysis in Bergeron, *Quand Tocqueville et Siegfried nous observaient*, chapter 7.
97  Siegfried, *Canada*, 85.
98  Ibid.; *États-Unis–Canada–Méxique*, 10–11.
99  Siegfried, *Canada*, 118, 77.
100  Ibid., 35, 275.
101  For further analysis of responses throughout Canada, see Fabre, *Le pari canadien d'André Siegfried*, 87–96.
102  AHC 2SI/23, dossier 2, Tweedsmuir to Siegfried, 17 March 1937, Archbishop of Québec to Siegfried, 8 April 1937.
103  AHC 2SI/23, dossier 2, Henri de Lageneste to Siegfried, 14 June 1937; W.M. Conacher, review of *Le Canada*, *Queen's Quarterly* 44, no. 3 (1937), 359–70, quotations on 369, 362.
104  Siegfried, "French Democratic Tradition," 657.
105  AHC 3SI/15, dossier 7, letter by Siegfried, 7 October 1938.
106  Siegfried, presentation in *Office français de renseignements aux États-Unis/French Information Center*, 11–19; Siegfried, "French Democratic Tradition," 658.

## CHAPTER FOUR

1 Siegfried, *Cours de géographie économique et politique*, passim. An outline of this lecture can be found in AHC 4SI/5, dossier 7, and a substantial proportion of the text is reproduced in Sanguin, *André Siegfried*, 156–60.

2 Siegfried, *Cours de géographie économique et politique*, 15–16.

3 AIF, dossier "Élection, 1932: section de morale, fauteuil de M. Auguste Gauvain," rapport de M. le baron Seillière, lu dans la séance du 9 janvier 1932.

4 For an indication of his activities, see AIF, Vol. 2D 17 (minutes of the Académie des Sciences morales et politiques, 1931–38), 386–7, 415–21, 424–5, 490–2, 495–6, meetings of 8 February, 16, 23 May, 6 June 1936, 20 March, 17 April 1937.

5 Bistis, "Managing Bergson's Crowd," 391.

6 See Harvey, "Conservative Crossings."

7 ACF, dossier C-XII, Siegfried to Joseph Bédier, administrator of the Collège de France, 13 November, 20 December 1931; Tillmann, "André Siegfried," 270 quotes the letter in full.

8 Will, *Unlikely Collaboration*, 61–5.

9 Sanguin, *André Siegfried*, 154–5; see also ACF, minutes of the professors' assemblies, box GIV k 1–27, folder GIV-k 14, "Assemblée du 8 Janvier 1933."

10 ACF, dossier C-XII, *arrête* by minister of national education, direction de l'enseignement supérieur, 30 July 1945.

11 ACF, dossier C-XII, dossier on Siegfried, n.d, 2–3, "Hommage à André Siegfried, 31 mai 1960: allocution de M. Marcel Bataillon, administrateur [originally delivered 26 April 1959]."

12 ACF, minutes of the professors' assemblies, box GIV k1–27, folder GIV-k 21, "Assemblée du 13 Janvier 1935, " box GIV k 28–53, folder GIV k– 29, "Assemblée du 29 mars 1936."

13 BIF, manuscrit 6160, pièce 19, Siegfried to Roques, 17 March 1937; ACF, minutes of the professors' assemblies, box GIV k 28–53, folder GIV k 39, "Assemblée du 28 novembre 1937," citing Siegfried to Faral, 13 October 1937.

14 Siegfried, "Collège de France," 513, 515, 520.

15 On the formation of the discipline in Germany and its reception in France, see Klautke, "The French Reception of *Völkerpsychologie*"; on the interwar context see Reynaud Paligot, *Races, racisme et antiracisme*, 61–87 and "La psychologie des peuples et ses applications."

Notes to pages 123–31     287

16 AHC 2SI/22bis, dossier 1, Le Bon to Siegfried, 22 April 1931. For evidence of earlier contact see AHC 2SI/19, dossier 1, Le Bon to Siegfried, 10 March 1927.

17 AHC 5SI/2, dossier 2, "Le contraste du continent Europe et du continent Amérique," conférence aux Annales, 18 November 1936.

18 The notes are in AHC 13SI/1, dossier 1.

19 Claret, *Personnalité collective des nations*, 107–13. The postwar evolution of the Institut is discussed in the epilogue.

20 Reynaud Paligot, "Les *Annales* de Lucien Febvre à Fernand Braudel," 129–30; for an example of a lecture to the Annales group, see AHC 5SI/2, dossier 2, "Le contraste du continent Europe et du continent Amérique."

21 Nord, *France's New Deal*, 25–49, and Clarke, *France in the Age of Organization*. On Coutrot, see also Clarke, "Engineering a New Order in the 1930s."

22 Nord, *France's New Deal*, 55–7.

23 See his comments in Siegfried et al., eds., *L'économie dirigée*, 71–2.

24 The text of the talk was reproduced as Siegfried, "La révolution industrielle et ses répercussions," quotations on 43–4.

25 Nord, *France's New Deal*, 57–62; for a full-length study, see Reggiani, *God's Eugenicist*.

26 AHC 3SI/15, dossier 7, letter by Siegfried, 10 August 1936.

27 See Behrent, "Justifying Capitalism in an Age of Uncertainty," 177–8 and Denord, "Aux origines du néo-libéralisme en France."

28 AHC 12SI/4, dossier 1, manuscript, "Quelques domaines encore mal explorés de la géographie," 24 February 1935.

29 See, for example, AHC 7SI/40, dossier 3, Henri Bunle, statisticien à la direction de la statistique générale et de la documentation, to Siegfried, 29 March 1938.

30 AHC 3SI/15, dossier 7, letters by Siegfried, 10 August, 3 September 1936.

31 AHC 3SI/15, dossier 7, letter by Siegfried, 7 October 1938.

32 AHC 12SI/10, copy of Siegfried, "Évolution politique d'un département," 164–5.

33 Ibid., 165–6.

34 Ibid., 166–7.

35 AHC 8SI/5, dossier 1, "Géographie de l'opinion politique en France: Le Midi, cours d'introduction," Collège de France, 8 January 1935.

36 AHC 8SI/5, dossier 2, lecture notes, "Conclusion sur la repartition géographique de l'opinion publique," Collège de France, 25 March 1935.

37 AHC 8SI/5, dossier 1, "Géographie de l'opinion politique en France: Le Midi, cours d'introduction," Collège de France, 8 January 1935.

288  Notes to pages 131–41

38  AHC 6s1/6, dossier 2, "Allocution à l'Assemblée du Dessert,"
3 September 1933.

39  AHC 13s1/1, dossier 1, letter by Siegfried, 4 October 1936.

40  AHC 12s1/8, clipping of article from *The American Hebrew*,
22 November 1929, n.p.

41  Siegfried, *Le rôle moral et social d'Israel dans les démocraties
contemporaines*, quotations on 18–19, 23–24, 27, 29–30. On Zangwill's
*Melting Pot*, see Rochelson, *A Jew in the Public Arena*, 17, 180–7.

42  AHC 3s1/15, dossier 7, letters by Siegfried, 10 August 1936,
7 October 1938.

43  AHC 6s1/6, dossier 4, "Jules Siegfried: 50 ans de vie publique
sous la IIIème," Société d'histoire de la IIIème, 4 June 1937.

44  AHC 12s1/9, clipping of Siegfried interview for *La revue illustrée de
l'Amérique latine*, April 1932, 18; for an example of the lectures, see
AHC 12s1/9, copy of Siegfried, *Les principaux courants de la pensée
réligieuse en France*.

45  ACF, dossier C-XII, annex to Bernard Hardion, chargé d'affaires
de France au Méxique, to Minister of Foreign Affairs, 5 October 1935.

46  AHC 12s1/4, dossier 3, "Voyages de Paule et d'Andre Siegfried
1907–1940," n.d.

47  Siegfried, *Impressions of South America*. A part of the translation
appeared as Siegfried, "Letters from South America."

48  Siegfried, *Amérique latine*; *États-Unis–Canada–Méxique*, 41–60;
*Impressions du Brésil*; *Suez and Panama*.

49  Siegfried, *Impressions of South America*, 15.

50  Siegfried, *Amérique latine*, 9, 22, 25.

51  Ibid., chapter 2; *Impressions of South America*, 63.

52  Siegfried, *Impressions of South America*, 55, 79, 100–1.

53  Ibid., 41; *Amérique latine*, chapter 3, quotation on 106.

54  Siegfried, *Amérique latine*, 164; *Impressions of South America*, 125–7.

55  On this point, see Tillmann, "André Siegfried," 288.

56  TNA FO 395/448, P1681/3/150, minute appended to report by Bentinck
(Lima), 9 June 1931.

57  La Llosa, "La réception de l'oeuvre d'André Siegfried," 116–18.

58  La Llosa, "L'Indien et le crocodile," 207–9.

59  La Llosa, "La réception de l'oeuvre d'André Siegfried," 119–23.

60  AHC 5s1/5, dossier 1, "Quelques figures d'hommes politiques français,"
Mexico, 11 September 1935; ACF, dossier C-XII, chargé d'affaires
to minister of foreign affairs, 5 October 1935.

61  Siegfried, *États-Unis–Canada–Méxique*, 41; AHC 13s1/4, dossier 1,
Siegfried to Chapsal, 4 November 1935.

Notes to pages 141–56

62 Siegfried, *États-Unis–Canada–Méxique*, 60.

63 La Llosa, "L'Indien et le crocodile," 206–7.

64 Siegfried, "Brazil and Its People"; see also AMS, folder "André Siegfried et le Musée Social: lettres," Siegfried to Risler, 4 August 1937.

65 Siegfried, *Vue générale de la Colombie*, 12–13, 25.

66 Giladi, "Rayonnement et propaganda culturels français."

67 AHC 12SI/4, dossier 3, "Impressions de Berlin," 5 June 1928, clippings; "Impressions de Berlin," May 1930; "Allemagne," April 1932; "Impressions de l'Europe Sud-Orientale," n.d. but probably 1932.

68 Siegfried, "L'occident et la direction spirituelle du monde"; *Europe's Crisis*. This book was also excerpted in the *Revue de Paris* 15 December 1934, 1, 15 January 1935, 757–80, 59–81, 241–62.

69 Siegfried, "L'occident et la direction spirituelle du monde," 6–8; *Europe's Crisis*, 45, 25; see also Siegfried, "The Clash of Continents."

70 Siegfried, *Europe's Crisis*, 61, 65.

71 Ibid., 66, 75.

72 Ibid., 70, 68.

73 Ibid., 101, 121, 124.

74 Ibid., 126–7.

75 Ibid., 128.

76 Siegfried, preface to Henri Decugis, *Le destin des races blanches*.

77 Siegfried, *Autour de la route de Suez*, 17, 25.

78 Ibid., 37, 41, 45.

79 Ibid., 43, 62, 77.

80 Siegfried, *Suez and Panama*, 73–74, 60.

81 Ibid., 103, 201.

82 Ibid., 315, 303–4.

83 Ibid., 176, 388–90.

84 See Bonnett, "From White to Western."

CHAPTER FIVE

1 Siegfried, "French Democratic Tradition"; on the journal's support for Britain and France, see Young, *Marketing Marianne*, 156.

2 Siegfried, "French Democratic Tradition," 650, 653.

3 Ibid., 655, 658, 661–2.

4 Ibid., 656, 657–8.

5 AHC 12SI/4, dossier 3, "Voyages de Paule et André Siegfried, 1907–1940"; AHC 2SI/24, dossier 1, M.G. Puaux to Siegfried, 21 April 1940; AHC 4SI/10, dossier 2, "Voyage en Méditerranée orientale (Mars 1940)"; Siegfried, "L'Europe et l'Amérique."

290 Notes to pages 156–62

6  AHC 4SI/10, dossier 2, "Voyage en Méditerranée orientale (Mars 1940)";
  Siegfried, "L'Europe et L'Amérique," 219–22.

7  AHC 4SI/11, dossier 1, Collège de France lectures, "Situer la géographie
  économique dans la géographie générale," 9 January 1940, "Notes à
  divers pays," 9 February 1940.

8  AHC 5SI/5, dossier 5, "Comment l'Angleterre est gouvernée," lectures
  for Radio-Paris, 22 November, 6, 27 December 1939.

9  Siegfried, *What the British Empire Means to Western Civilization*, 4,
  16, 27.

10  For further details, see Noël, "Le projet d'union franco-britannique,
  juin 1940;" and Beloff, *Intellectual in Politics*, chapter 14, esp. 173–7.

11  AIF, Fonds André Mazon, manuscrit 6784, pièces 39–56,
  "Organisation internationale et fédération franco-anglaise:
  Communication de M. André Siegfried au Centre d'études de politique
  étrangère le 13 février 1940."

12  For a detailed account, see Beloff, *Intellectual in Politics*, 180–99.

13  Siegfried, "Politique extérieure des États-Unis," 771, 775–6.

14  Siegfried, "Contribution de la France, de l'Angleterre et des États-Unis,"
  382–3.

15  Ibid., 385–8; see also Siegfried, "War for Our World," 417.

16  Siegfried, "Contribution de la France, de l'Angleterre et des États-Unis,"
  390; "War for Our World," 417–18.

17  Siegfried, "War for Our World," 419, 421, 423.

18  ACF, dossier C–XII, Edmond Faral to directeur de l'enseignement
  supérieur, 3 October 1939, ministre de l'éducation nationale to Farral,
  7 October 1939, Siegfried to Farral, 20 November 1939. On Hyde
  see Young, *Marketing Marianne*, 51, 87, 105.

19  ACF, dossier C–XII, note by Commandant Faral, Secrétariat
  général du Conseil supérieur de la défense nationale chargé de
  l'administration du Collège de France, 24 May 1940, Faral to ministère
  de l'éducation nationale, 7 August 1940, ministère de l'éducation
  nationale, directeur de l'enseignement supérieur to Faral,
  21 August 1940.

20  The various criticisms are summarized in Young, *Marketing Marianne*,
  140–53.

21  Young, *Marketing Marianne*, 153–64.

22  On class distinctions during the *exode*, see Diamond, *Fleeing Hitler*,
  chapter 2.

23  ACF, dossier C–XII, Siegfried to Faral, 27 May, 9, 21 July 1940.

24  Hamp, "In Memoriam: André Siegfried."

Notes to pages 162–6 291

25 AIF, Vol. 2D18 (minutes of the Académie des Sciences morales et politiques, 1939–1947), 126–7, 161–2, 175–6, 185, 187–8; minutes for 8 September 1940, 19 April, 28 June, 11 October, 8 November 1941.

26 Burrin, *France à l'heure allemande*, 312–13.

27 ACF, minutes of the Assemblies of Professors, Box GIV 1, 1–18 (minutes for 1941–44), assemblies of 14 March, 7 November 1943.

28 ACF, dossier C-XII, note on Siegfried, "Cours professés au Collège de France."

29 Nord, *France's New Deal*, 132–3; for earlier accounts of the École libre during the war see Rain, *École libre*, 109–18 and Vincent, *Sciences-Po*, 106–9.

30 Nord, *France's New Deal*, 133–5.

31 École libre, *Organisation et programmes des cours: Année scolaire 1942–43*, 24, 92, 111–12, 127; on the Lyon courses, see Rain, *École Libre*, 110.

32 AHC 5S1/2, dossier 2, lecture notes, "Les relations anglo-américains," Lyon, 9 May 1941; AHC 1SP/64, dossier 5, course notes for Siegfried's "Les États-Unis et la civilisation américaine" (ELSP, 1941–42), 369–76.

33 AHC 8S1/3, dossier 5, "Cours sur la géographie de l'opinion politique dans le Midi, 1942–1943; Tableau politique du Languedoc Méditerranéen sous la IIIème, introduction."

34 Tillmann, "André Siegfried," 347–8; Birnbaum, *France aux français*, 171–3.

35 AHC 1SP/79, "Rapport présenté par le président du Comité des études, à M. le président du Conseil d'Administration, sur la réorganisation générale du programme des cours," July 1941.

36 For the rationale behind the Comité's decision, see AHC 1SP/79, Comité d'études, "Rapport du Comité d'études sur l'organisation d'une première année d'études à l'École," n.d; for the new regulations, see École Libre, *Organisation et programme des cours: Année scolaire 1943–44*, 1–3.

37 AN F17/13358, "Corps enseignant de l'École Libre des Sciences Politiques," n.d.

38 On Siegfried's nomination see Boegner, ed., *Carnets du Pasteur Boegner*, 71, entry for 25 January 1941; Boulet, "André Siegfried," 14; and Cabanel, *De la paix aux résistances*, 132–3.

39 Cointet, *Conseil National de Vichy*, 183–222, esp. 206; Barral, "Idéal et pratique du régionalisme," 918–19; Tillmann, "André Siegfried," 335–6; AHC 13S1/1, dossier 3, Siegfried to Admiral Fernet, 1941.

40 Nord, *France's New Deal*, 136–7; Baruch, *Servir l'État français*, 174–6; for some of the Comité d'étude's proposals, see AHC 1SP/79, folder,

292        Notes to pages 167–71

"Comité d'études pour la France." On Siegfried's participation in what became the Comité général d'études, see Bellescize, *Neuf sages de la Résistance*, 33–4; on working with de Traz see Kuisel, *Ernest Mercier*, 150.

41  Boegner, ed., *Carnets du Pasteur Boegner*, 178–9, entry for 7 May 1942; Roussel, *Charles de Gaulle*, 294–5.

42  AN F7/15529, clipping of *Les Lettres françaises*, 24 January 1946. The journal cited *The New York Herald Tribune* as its source. On the journal, see Gisèle Sapiro, "*Lettres françaises (Les)*," in *Dictionnaire des intellectuels français*, ed. Julliard and Winock, 849–50.

43  Barthélemy, *Ministre de Justice*, 303–4n6 , 409.

44  Nord, *France's New Deal*, 137–9; Rain, *École libre*, 112–14.

45  For interwar trends, see Naviaux, "Le Musée social," 117–19; on the aspects of the Musée's history that remain to be explored, see *Le Musée social en son temps*, ed. Chambelland, 365–72.

46  AMS, Procés-verbaux du comité de direction, vol. 7 (du 16-1–29 au 26-2–63), no pagination, minutes for 12 March, 30 May, 8 October 1941; on the Institut, see Kaplan, "Un laboratoire de la doctrine corporatiste."

47  AMS, Procés-verbaux du comité de direction, vol. 7, minutes of 4 February, 25 March, 8 July, 28 October, 22 December 1942; AHC 12S1/8, "Allocution de M. André Siegfried à la première séance de la Section d'études sociales." These remarks subsequently appeared in the *Cahiers du Musée social* 2 (1943), 67–75.

48  AMS, Procés-verbaux du comité de direction, vol. 7, minutes of 28 October 1943, 3 March, 6 July 1944.

49  AMS, Procés-verbaux du comité de direction, vol. 7, minutes of 28 October 1943, 3 March, 6 July 1944; AHC 6S1/6, dossier 3, "Grand conseil du Musée social," 9 December 1943, report by Siegfried, "L'activité du Musée social en 1943: Travaux des sections."

50  Siegfried, "La défense sanitaire de l'occident."

51  AHC 12S1/8, "L'éducation sociale du Français: Compte-rendu de la conference presentée le 6 avril 1944 devant la Section d'études sociales du Musée social."

52  AHC 12S1/8, "Allocution de M. André Siegfried à la première séance de la Section d'études sociales."

53  AHC 6S1/6, dossier 3, "Le Musée social: Ingénieurs sociaux, le 10 juin 1943."

54  AHC 6S1/6, dossier 3, "Grand conseil du Musée social," 9 December 1943, "Cinquantenaire du Musée social," 21 March 1945.

55  On wartime developments at *Le Figaro*, see Blandin, *Le Figaro*, chapter 6.

# Notes to pages 171–8

56 Siegfried, "Sociologie téléphonique," *Le Figaro*, 9 September 1942.

57 Siegfried, "Le service de l'état et l'intérêt general," *Le Temps*, 19 June 1941.

58 Siegfried, "Examen de conscience," *Le Figaro*, 7 August 1942, "Encore la question de l'intelligence," *Le Figaro*, 23 October 1942. On some parallels between Vichy and Resistance thought, see Shennan, *Rethinking France*.

59 Siegfried, "Le sport et la vie politique," *Le Figaro*, 10 October 1941; "La France change," *Le Temps*, 22 October 1941.

60 Siegfried, "Un esprit libre (Lyautey)," *Le Figaro*, 24 July 1941; "Pour réussir," *Le Figaro*, 18 December 1941.

61 Siegfried, "Souvenirs sur mon père," *Le Figaro*, 25, 28 October 1941; "Charles Seignobos," *Le Figaro*, 1 June 1942.

62 Siegfried, "L'Atlantique nord," *Le Temps*, 26 July 1941; "L'Amérique des isthmus," *Le Temps*, 6 September 1941; "Insularité anglaise, isolement américain?" *Le Temps*, 12 November 1941.

63 Siegfried, "Les routes maritimes du Pacifique," *Le Temps*, 19 August 1941, "Les routes de terre vers l'Inde et l'Asie centrale," *Le Temps*, 27/28 September 1941; comments by Odile Rudelle at "Normandie constitutionnelle: séminaire André Siegfried," 11 February 2004, quoting *Le Figaro*, 10 September 1941. I downloaded these comments from the Sciences Po website in 2006; they have since been removed.

64 Siegfried, "L'océan indien," *Le Figaro*, 20 February 1942.

65 Siegfried, "La civilisation occidentale," 130–3.

66 Ibid., 136, 146.

67 Ibid., 147–8.

68 Bruneteau, *"L'Europe nouvelle" de Hitler*, 127–30.

69 Siegfried, "Le problème de l'assimilation des immigrants," *Le Temps*, 6/7 December 1941.

70 Fabre-Luce, *Anthologie de la nouvelle Europe*, i–xlv, 271–5.

71 AN 472AP/2, Siegfried to Fabre-Luce, 26 February 1942; Cantier, *Lire sous l'Occupation*, 204.

72 Siegfried, "Le New Deal et la guerre aux États-Unis," *Le Figaro*, 9 June 1942.

73 Birnbaum, *France aux français*, 146–7; Marrus and Paxton, *Vichy France and the Jews*, 188–9.

74 AHC 6s1/6, dossier 4, "Jules Siegfried: 50 ans de vie publique sous la IIIème," Société d'histoire de la IIIème, 4 June 1937. This lecture is discussed in chapter 4.

75 Siegfried, *Jules Siegfried*, 28–9.

76 Ibid., 53–4, 100, 139.

294 Notes to pages 178–86

77 Ibid., 69.
78 Siegfried, *Quelques maximes,* 7–12. The preface was also published in *Le Figaro,* 31 March 1942.
79 Ibid., 22, 24, 30–1.
80 Ibid., 38–9, 46.
81 AHC 2SI/24, dossier 2, copy of René Dollot, review of *Jules Siegfried (1837–1922), Revue d'histoire diplomatique* (1942), 9–12. On the book's limited circulation, see the letter from William Halpern of the Institut universitaire de hautes études internationales in Geneva to Siegfried, 2 June 1943, in the same folder.
82 AHC 4SI/10, dossier 1, "Vue générale de la Méditerranée," Collège de France, 5 December 1941.
83 Siegfried, *Vue générale de la Méditerranée,* 92, 100; for an analysis that draws attention to the poetic qualities of the book, see Cabanel, "André Siegfried et la Méditeranée."
84 Siegfried, *Vue générale de la Méditerranée,* 188.
85 Ibid., 68–9,73, 82; Birnbaum, *France aux français,* 171–4; on Haddon, see Conklin, *In the Museum of Man,* 166–7.
86 Siegfried, *Vue générale de la Méditerranée,* 78–80.
87 AHC 2SI/24, dossier 2, clippings of Claude Bied-Charreton, review in *La cité nouvelle,* January 1944, 113–15; Georges Albertini, review in *L'Atelier,* 20 November 1943.
88 Siegfried, preface to *Mon village,* quotation on 12.
89 AHC 6SI/6, dossier 2, text of Siegfried's address to the 79th Assemblée de la Société de l'Histoire du Protestantisme Français (commemoration du bicentaire de la naissance de Rabaut Saint–Étienne), Paris, 7 May 1944.
90 AHC 13SI/1, dossier 3, typescript, "Journal d'une quinzaine (du 7 au 27 août 1944)."
91 Toynbee, *Acquaintances,* 144–5.
92 "La reconstruction de l'occident," *Le Figaro,* 28 August 1944, reprinted in Siegfried, *France, Angleterre, États-Unis, Canada,* 13–16.
93 Roussel, *Charles de Gaulle,* 294–5, 461–2; TNA, FO 371/42082, z6458/5766/17, minute by Holman, 26 September 1944, comments by Cooper, 27 September and Toynbee, 4 October.
94 AHC 12SI/1, dossier 2, "Entretien avec le Général de Gaulle (le 5 Septembre 1944)."
95 Ibid.
96 "Ceux qui on su dire: non," "Le rayonnement de la France," *Le Figaro,* 5, 21 September 1944, reprinted in Siegfried, *France, Angleterre, États-Unis, Canada,* 9–12, 7–21.

Notes to pages 187–93    295

97 "La crise de la bourgeoisie," "Les conditions de la reconstruction économique de la France (I)," "Les conditions de la reconstruction économique de la France (II)," *Le Figaro*, 31 October, 21, 22 November 1944, reprinted in *France, Angleterre, États-Unis, Canada*, 22–5, 26–35.

98 AHC 12SI/10, Mendès France to Siegfried, 28 November 1944.

99 TNA, FO 371/41900, Z5901/68/17, Holman to Harvey, 6 September 1944, minute by Speaight, 15 September, FO 371/42082, Z6458/5766/17, Holman to Harvey, 27 September 1944, minute by Stewart, 11 October. Mathieu-Fréville was an alias for Jacques Lecompte-Boinet, one of the leaders of Ceux de la Résistance, a conservative-leaning resistance organization. See https://www.ordredelaliberation.fr/fr/les-compagnons/560/jacques-lecompte-boinet.

## CHAPTER SIX

1 AHC 13SI/1, dossier 3, clipping of *La Presse*, 7 September 1945.

2 See Sapiro, *La guerre des écrivains*, 280–315, 640.

3 AIF, procès-verbaux des séances de l'Académie française, vol. 2B20 (novembre 1941–novembre 1951) 114–16, session of 12 October 1944. On the significance of the cross on the ballots, see Sapiro, *La guerre des écrivains*, 303.

4 Sapiro, *La guerre des écrivains*, 257n22, 265, 314, 642–3; Siegfried, "Les élections à l'Académie française," 646–8; though the author of the article did not provide their name, Sapiro convincingly attributes the authorship to Siegfried.

5 On Faÿ's fate see Will, *Unlikely Collaboration*, chapter 5.

6 ACF, minutes of the Assembly of Professors, Box G IV l, 19–31 (1945–47), folder 126, assembly of 23 June 1946; dossier C-XII, "Rapport de M. André Siegfried sur la proposition de nomination par le Collège de France de M. Marcel Giraud à une Chaire d'Histoire de la Civilisation de l'Amérique du Nord," 23 December 1946.

7 ACF, dossier C-XII, "Assemblée du 27 novembre 1949, proposition pour une chaire de psychologie des arts plastiques par M. Siegfried."

8 Sanguin, *André Siegfried*, 171–2.

9 Nord, "Reform, Conservation, and Adaptation," 138.

10 Ibid., 137, 139–40; Sanguin, *André Siegfried*, 172–3. See also Charle, "Savoir durer," 103–4.

11 AHC 13SI/4, dossier 1, "Note sur l'audience accordée par le Général de Gaulle à MM. André Siegfried et Roger Seydoux le 20 Juin [1945] à 16h."

12 Nord, "Reform, Conservation, and Adaptation," 140–1; Sanguin, *André Siegfried*, 173–4.

13 AHC 6S1/7, dossier 8, lecture notes, "L'Institut d'Études Politiques à Paris," 5 April 1952.

14 Nord, "Reform, Conservation, and Adaptation," 142–4.

15 AHC 13S1/1, dossier 3, Seydoux to Siegfried, 28 March 1947; Seydoux, *Le Figaro littéraire*, 4 April 1959, quoted in Sanguin, *André Siegfried*, 176.

16 Nemni, *Trudeau Transformed*, 62–3, 352–3; see also English, *Citizen of the World*, chapter 3.

17 Kaplan, *Dreaming in French*, 24.

18 Interview quoted in Vincent, *Sciences Po*, 359.

19 Siegfried, "Discours d'André Siegfried," 164.

20 Ibid., 170–2.

21 AMS, Procés-verbaux du comité de direction, vol. 7, minutes of 26 September 1944; Siegfried, "Discours d'André Siegfried," 166.

22 AMS, Procés-verbaux du comité de direction, vol. 7, minutes of 10 July, 22 October 1945, 19 February 1946, 21 February, 22 December 1947, 15 February, 23 June 1949, 11 July 1950.

23 AMS, Procés-verbaux du comité de direction, vol. 7, minutes of 27 March 1947; AMS, folder, "André Siegfried et le Musée social: Lettres," Siegfried to Aubrun, 8 April 1949.

24 See, for example, Siegfried, "Un monde nouveau" and "Les problèmes ethniques de l'Afrique du Sud."

25 Siegfried, "La culture populaire"; "La crise de l'ouvrier qualifié"; "Introduction à l'étude du rôle de l'ouvrier qualifié dans l'industrie."

26 Siegfried, "Le rôle de l'épargne dans le développement européen."

27 Siegfried, "La France et les problèmes de l'immigration et de l'émigration," 72–5.

28 Siegfried, "Le groupe protestant cévenol," 45. On Siegfried and the role of religion, see also Cabanel, *Protestants et la République*, 117–19.

29 Siegfried, *Géographie électorale de l'Ardèche*, 51. My reading of this work has been influenced by Cabanel, *Protestants et la République*, 123–4 and Michel Bussi, "L'Ouest politique, 75 ans puis 100 ans après," 97–9.

30 Siegfried, *Géographie électorale de l'Ardèche*, 70–2, 92–3.

31 Ibid., preface.

32 Favre, *Naissances de la science politique*, 301–4; Blondiaux and Veitl, "La carrière symbolique d'un père fondateur," 4–14.

33 Blandin, *Le Figaro*, 182, 188; Aron, *Memoirs*, 162–4.

34 Siegfried explained his role in the preface to the first volume; see *L'année politique 1944–45*, i–iii.

35 "La leçon des ruines," *Le Figaro*, 26 December 1944, reprinted in Siegfried, *France, Angleterre, États-Unis, Canada*, 46–8.

36 *Le Figaro* articles: "Définitions," 24 February 1945; "La France vue des dehors," 3 July 1945; "Il y a pour l'état une morale économique," 31 July 1945; "Ressaisissons-nous," 7 August 1945, reprinted in Siegfried, *France, Angleterre, États-Unis, Canada*, 57–60, 66–9, 74–82, quotation on 69.

37 *Le Figaro* articles: "Pour une consultation sans equivoque," 12 July 1945; "La droite et la gauche," 13 November 1945; "Que veulent les français?" 18 January 1946, reprinted in Siegfried, *France, Angleterre, États-Unis, Canada*, 70–3, 88–91, 101–5, quotation on 104.

38 AHC 12SI/1, Minister of Finances to Siegfried, 21 January 1946.

39 Smith, "*Sénat ou pas Sénat?* The 'First' Council of the Republic," 43.

40 Siegfried, preface for *L'année politique 1946*, viii.

41 Siegfried, preface to *L'année politique 1948*, ix.

42 Siegfried, preface to *L'année politique 1947*, x–xi.

43 Siegfried, preface to *L'année politique 1948*, ix–x.

44 See Vinen, *Bourgeois Politics in France*.

45 Siegfried, preface to *L'année politique 1948*, x–xi.

46 Siegfried, *Switzerland*, 11.

47 Ibid., 44–8, 63–4.

48 Ibid., 135, 73, 87.

49 Ibid., 200–1.

50 Siegfried, *Savoir parler en public*, 55.

51 Siegfried, *La Fontaine*, 15–17, 87–91.

52 Siegfried, *Géographie humoristique de Paris*, 149.

53 Ibid., 161, 168.

54 Prefaces for the 1949 and 1950 volumes of *L'année politique*, reprinted in Siegfried, *De la IVe à la Ve République*, 39–46 and 47–55 respectively.

55 Siegfried, "L'instabilité ministerielle," *Le Figaro*, 10 March 1951.

56 Siegfried, "Pourquoi ils croient que ...," *Le Figaro*, 25/26 August 1951, and "Pour une droite intelligente," *Le Figaro*, 23 July 1951.

57 This and the next paragraph are based on the following: AHC 4SI/11, dossier 2, "Cours: Caractères et limites de la civilisation occidentale," Collège de France, December 1944–January 1945; lecture notes for 14 December 1944, 19 January 1945; Siegfried, *Civilisation occidentale*, esp. 19–21.

58 Siegfried, "Les parrainages de la France dévastée"; RIIA 8/1095, "Record of General Meeting Held at Chatham House on 27 February 1945: A French View of Post-War Reconstruction in Europe," comments by Siegfried, 1.

298 Notes to pages 209–13

59 TNA FO 371/40956, UE 2145/226/53, minute by Colson, 31 October 1944, UE 2539/226/53, Scarlett to Coulson, 3 December 1944; RIIA 8/1095, "Record of General Meeting Held at Chatham House on 27 February 1945," 13–14.

60 RIIA 8/1095, "Record of General Meeting Held at Chatham House on 27 February 1945," 10–13, and comments by Siegfried in ensuing discussion.

61 "Le rayonnement de la France," *Le Figaro*, 21 September 1944, reprinted in Siegfried, *France, Angleterre, États-Unis, Canada*, 17–21; AHC 7S1/42, "Le rayonnement Français," lecture delivered at the Salle du Théâtre des Champs-Elysées, 14 January 1945; AHC 12S1/8, copy of Siegfried, "French: The Language of Human Thought," 475, 481.

62 Ritchie, *Siren Years*, 220.

63 For the French Foreign Ministry perspective; see MAE Série Y (Internationale 1944–1949), no. 125, circular by Minister of Foreign Affairs, "La Conférence de San Francisco – Le Charte des Nations Unies," 30 July 1945; on the San Francisco Conference, see MacKenzie, *World Beyond Borders*, 39–41 and Luard, *History of the United Nations*, vol. 1, 37–68.

64 MAE NUOI (Secretariat des Conférences, 1944–49), box 3, folder 2, "Délégués français dans les diverses commissions et comités," 2 May 1945; "Délégués français dans les comités," 9 May 1945.

65 "Mes premières impressions des États-Unis," *Le Figaro*, 28 April 1945; and "Fermiers 1945," *Le Figaro*, 10 September 1945, reprinted in *France, Angleterre, États-Unis, Canada*, 155, 233–4.

66 "Topographie morale de la conférence de San-Francisco," *Le Figaro* 2 May 1945; "Une victoire française à San-Francisco," *Le Figaro* 11 May 1945, reprinted in Siegfried, *France, Angleterre, États-Unis, Canada*, 157, 170.

67 Siegfried, "La signification de la conférence de San-Francisco (I): Le point de vue des États-Unis," *Le Figaro*, 19 May 1945; "La signification de la conférence de San-Francisco (II): Le point de vue de la Russie et de l'Angleterre," *Le Figaro*, 20/21 May 1945.

68 Siegfried did note a significant Indigenous presence in the Argentinian city of Cordoba; see "Paysages et villes d'Argentine et du Chili," *Le Figaro*, 17 September 1946.

69 Siegfried, "Buenos-Aires 1946," "Regards sur la nouvelle Argentine," and "Le régime du general Peron," *Le Figaro*, 4/5, 8 August, 7 September 1946.

70 Siegfried, "Traversée des Andes," "Élections présidentielles au Chili," and "Paysages et villes d'Argentine et du Chili," *Le Figaro*, 27 August, 4, 17 September 1946.

Notes to pages 213–25

71 AMS, folder, "André Siegfried et le Musée social – lettres," Siegfried to Aubrun, 14 August 1946.

72 Siegfried, "Une des merveilles du monde: Rio de Janeiro," "Les lois de l'immensité," "Aux bouches de l'Amazone," *Le Figaro*, 22/23 September, 20/21, 27/28 October 1946.

73 Siegfried, "Aux confins de la civilisation: dans le Sertão bréslien," "Aux confins de la civilisation (II): chez les chavantes, Indiens indomptés," *Le Figaro*, 5, 6/7 October 1946.

74 Siegfried, "Au confins de la civilisation (II)," *Le Figaro*, 6/7 October 1946.

75 Siegfried, "Le peuple brésilien et la nation brésilienne," *Le Figaro*, 17 October 1946.

76 Siegfried, *African Journey*, 12–13, 129–33.

77 Ibid., 29–31.

78 Ibid., 41, 73–4.

79 Ibid., 139, 145.

80 Ibid., 80, 91, 96.

81 Ibid., 155, 157–9.

82 Siegfried, *Voyage aux Indes*, 23–4, 62–6.

83 Ibid., 32, 123–4, 159.

84 Ibid., 96–100, 130–6.

85 Ibid., 144, 149.

86 Ibid., 144, 150–2, 154.

87 Siegfried, *Character of Peoples*, 34–7, 39, 43–4.

88 Ibid., 69, 52, 65, 45–6.

89 Ibid., 75, 141, 159–60.

90 Ibid., 98, 100, 109, 115.

91 Ibid., 121, 126.

92 Ibid., 189–90.

93 Vinen, *Bourgeois Politics in France*, 1–20; for a perspective that focuses less on party politics, see Chapman, *France's Long Reconstruction*.

94 For a recent comparative analysis of French decolonization, see Thomas, *Fight or Flight*.

CHAPTER SEVEN

1 AHC 13SI/4, dossier 1, "Voyages de M. André Siegfried," n.d.; Sanguin, *André Siegfried*, 125, 223–4.

2 Hughes, *Gentleman Rebel*, 219–21.

3 AHC 13SI/4, dossier 1, Siegfried to Chapsal, 6 October 1951, Chapsal to Siegfried 11, 16 October 1951, Siegfried to Chapsal, 23 October 1951

300 Notes to pages 226–9

(quotation), Chapsal to Siegfried, 5 November 1951, Siegfried to Chapsal, 9 November 1951, Chapsal to Siegfried, 27 November 1951.

4 AHC 13s1/4, dossier 1, Siegfried to Chapsal, 14 October, 4 November 1955, Chapsal to Siegfried, 7 November, 15 December 1955, Siegfried to Chapsal, 18 December 1955 (quotation); Berghahn, *America and the Intellectual Cold Wars*, 207–8.

5 AHC 13s1/4, dossier 1, Siegfried to Chapsal, 14 October 1955.

6 Quoted in Sanguin, *André Siegfried*, 149–52. On Gottmann, see now Ferraz de Oliveira, "Territory and Theory in Political Geography."

7 AMS, procès-verbaux du comité de direction, vol. 7, minutes from 10 January 1952 to 2 December 1958 (the last meeting over which Siegfried presided); Siegfried to Aubrun, 11 September 1953, 6 April, 10 October, 21 December 1955, 4 October 1957, 16 September 1958.

8 Siegfried, "Le prévention des accidents du travail" and "Les causes psychologiques de l'accident du travail."

9 Siegfried, "Le prévention des accidents du travail," 137.

10 Siegfried, preface to Fourastié, *Le grand espoir du XX^e siècle*, ix–xv. Other explorations of this theme include AHC 6s1/5, dossier 6, "Technique et culture dans la civilisation moderne," Comité Protestant des Amitiés Françaises à l'Étranger le 27 février 1948" and AHC 6s1/7, dossier 3, "L'age administratif," Chicago, 1 November 1951.

11 Siegfried, "Technique et culture."

12 Daniel-Rops's real name was Henri Petiot; for an overview of his career, see Jean-Louis Loubet del Bayle, "Daniel-Rops (Henri) [Henri Petiot], 1901–1965," in *Dictionnaire des intellectuels français*, ed. Julliard and Winock, 394–5; for his comments on Le Roy, see *Académie française: Discours prononcés dans la séance publique tenue par l'Académie française pour la reception de M. Daniel-Rops.*

13 For Siegfried's commentary, see *Académie française: Discours prononcés pour la reception de M. Daniel-Rops*, 29–46, quotations on 42 and 44.

14 For the dispute see Sanguin, *André Siegfried*, 195–6.

15 Marc Dambre, "Morand, Paul (1888–1976)," in *Dictionnaire des intellectuels français*, ed. Julliard and Winock, 977–9.

16 Sapiro, *La guerre des écrivains*, 265–6, 644–5.

17 [Siegfried], "Les élections à l'Académie française," 648–9.

18 Ibid., 647, 651–4.

19 Preface to *L'année politique 1952*, reprinted in Siegfried, *De la IVe à la Ve République*, 66–77.

20 Ibid., 78–87, quotation on 83.

Notes to pages 230–5

21 Vincent Auriol to Siegfried, 10 September 1952, in Auriol, *Journal du Septennat*, Vol. 6, 549–51; Siegfried, "La revision de la constitution [parts 1–3]," *Le Figaro*, 8, 9, 10 September 1952.

22 "René Coty citoyen du Havre," *Le Figaro*, 24 December 1953, reprinted in Siegfried, *De la IVe à la Ve République*, 203–5, quotation on 203–4.

23 See, for example, AN 452AP/1, Coty to Siegfried, n.d. but from 1950s.

24 Prefaces to *L'année politique 1954* and *L'année politique 1955*, reprinted in Siegfried, *De la IVe à la Ve République*, 88–98, 99–114.

25 AHC 12SI/1, dossier 2, Mendès France to Siegfried, 27 July 1955; the exchange of letters is reproduced in full in Sanguin, *André Siegfried*, 198–209.

26 AHC 12SI/1, dossier 2, Siegfried to Mendès France, 13 August 1955; Mendès-France to Siegfried, 9 September 1955; Siegfried to Mendès France, 8 October 1955.

27 For an overview of the newspaper in the 1950s, see Blandin, *Le Figaro*, chapter 7.

28 Siegfried, *De la IIIe à la IVe République*, 61.

29 Chapter 6 of the book was also published as Siegfried, "Le Vichy de Pétain, le Vichy de Laval." On the historiography of Vichy, see Jackson, *France: The Dark Years*, 9.

30 Siegfried, *De la IIIe à la IVe République*, 85–7, 101–2, 105.

31 Ibid., 173.

32 Ibid., 185.

33 Ibid., 236–7, 252, 267.

34 Preface to *L'année politique 1956*, reprinted in Siegfried, *De la IVe à la Ve République*, 115–25, quotation on 124.

35 For an overview, see Goetschel and Toucheboeuf, *La IVe République*, 448–89; for French intellectuals and the war, see Schalk, *War and the Ivory Tower*, 61–111; on *Le Figaro's* stance Blandin, *Le Figaro*, 188.

36 The lecture was later published as Siegfried, *Routes of Contagion*, quotation on 93.

37 Siegfried, preface to *L'année politique 1957*, reprinted in *De la IVe à la Ve République*, 126–45. When the preface was republished in 1958, Siegfried added a footnote (see 140) stating "J'avoue ici m'être trompé. Je croyais que la IVe République se serait ou aurait été défendue."

38 Ibid., 144–5.

39 "Analyse d'une chute," *Le Figaro*, 11 June 1958, reprinted in Siegfried, *De la IVe à la Ve*, 261–5, quotation on 264.

302 Notes to pages 235–9

40 For an overview of de Gaulle's return to power, see Goetschel and Toucheboeuf, *La IVe République*, 489–505; for *Le Figaro*'s editorial line, see Blandin, *Le Figaro*, 186–8.

41 Aron, *Memoirs*, 286.

42 AHC 11SI/1, dossier 2, Monnet to Siegfried, 4 September 1958; "Devant la choix," *Le Figaro*, 6/7 September 1958, reprinted in Siegfried, *De la IVe à la Ve République*, 294–7.

43 See, for example; Goguel, *France under the Fourth Republic*, preface; Elgey, *Histoire de la IVe République*, vol. 1, 227–8, 412; Williams, *Crisis and Compromise*, 10; MacRae, *Parliament, Parties, and Society in France*, 64; Rioux, *The Fourth Republic, 1944–1958*, 249, 409.

44 AHC 3SI/16, dossier 7, clipping of *Aspects de la France*, 15 January 1957; Werth, *France 1940–1955*, 317–18.

45 AHC 3SI/16, dossier 7, Coty to Siegfried, n.d., de Gaulle to Siegfried, 17 January 1957; see also the letter by Michel Debré, dated 11 January 1957; the last two letters are also reproduced in Sanguin, *André Siegfried*, 100–1.

46 AHC 11SI/1, dossier 2, clippings of *La Nation française*, 21 January 1959 and the lengthy review by Pierre Dominique in *Écrits de Paris*, February 1959, 53–56.

47 AHC 11SI/1, dossier 2, clippings of reviews by Maulnier in *Le Figaro*, 5 February 1959 and Aron in *Le Figaro littéraire* 18/19 April 1959.

48 AHC 5SI/2, dossier 1, "L'échange intellectuel franco-américain," Bibliothèque américaine, 13 May 1950.

49 Siegfried, "Approaches to an Understanding of Modern France," 5.

50 AHC 13SI/4, dossier 1, Siegfried to Chapsal, 5, 13 February 1950.

51 AMS, copy of L'Association André Siegfried, *Hommage*, comments by Nef on 35–9; for details on Nef, see his obituary in *The New York Times*, 27 December 1988.

52 AHC 1SI/14, dossier 2, Ivy to Siegfried, 21 December 1951; AHC 1SI/15, dossier 6, note from French embassy, "Évolution des prix et de la situation économique aux États-Unis, août-septembre 1953," n.d.

53 AHC 13 SI/4, dossier 1, Siegfried to Chapsal, 6, 23 October (quotation), 9 November 1951.

54 Siegfried, "Où en sont les États-Unis?," *Le Figaro*, 2, 3, 4, 5/6, 7, 8, 9, 10 January 1952; AHC 6SI/1, "Cours sur les États-Unis et la civilisation américaine," dossier 8, "Conclusion générale du cours," 8 March 1953; Siegfried, preface to *Le grand changement*.

55 Siegfried, *America at Mid-Century*, 160, 150–1.

56 Ibid., 27, 61, 42.

Notes to pages 239–41

57 Ibid., 73–4, 80–1.

58 Ibid., 103, 106–7.

59 Ibid., 356, 240, 247.

60 Ibid., 240, 336, 357.

61 AHC 3 SI/16, dossier 4, Seydoux to Siegfried, 9 June 1954, Bardoux to Siegfried, 14 June 1954.

62 AHC 3 SI/16, dossier 6, review of *Tableau des États-Unis* by Raymond Aron, *Le Figaro*, 20 May 1954; review by Jacques Chastenet, *L'Instransigeant*, 20 April 1954. Other clippings in this file from the French press suggest a generally positive reception.

63 AHC 3 SI/16, dossier 6, clippings of *Chicago Sun-Times*, 19 June 1955 and *The Christian Science Monitor*, 1 July 1954 (the latter is a review of the original French edition); Charles Rolo, review in *The Atlantic Monthly*, July 1955, 181–2.

64 Clarke Irwin, review of *America at Mid-Century*, *Time*, 13 June 1955, 100.

65 Crane Brinton, "Looking at the USA with Eyes of 1927," *New York Herald Tribune Books*, 12 June 1955, 5; Henry Popkin, "As a Frenchman Sees Us," *Commonweal*, 8 July 1955, 356–7.

66 David McLellan, "Two French Views of America," *American Quarterly* 7, no. 1 (1955), 58, 65.

67 On this trend, see Kuisel, "American Historians in Search of France," 308–10.

68 On this shift, see Jacobson, *Whiteness of a Different Color*, 96–135; Barkan, *Retreat of Scientific Racism*; and King, *Race, Culture, and the Intellectuals*.

69 AN F7/15529, clipping of *Les Lettres françaises*, 24 January 1946; JTA *Daily News Bulletin* 12, no. 171 (27 July 1945), accessed at https://www.jta.org/archive/andre-siegfried-denies-he-is-anti-jewish-author-says-his-writings-have-been-distorted, and https://www.jta.org/archive/siegfried-will-not-speak-to-american-servicemen-at-red-cross-club.

70 AHC 3 SI/16, dossier 5, Rita Barisse to Siegfried, 7 March 1954; Michael Howard (of Jonathan Cape) to Siegfried, 13 January 1955, "Note à M. Siegfried," n.d.; the incident is also discussed in detail in Birnbaum, *France aux français*, 156–9.

71 Oscar Handlin, "Dangerous Friend," *Commentary* 21, no. 3 (1956), 290–1.

72 Schlesinger, "M. Siegfried Looks at Us Again," *New York Times Book Review*, 12 June 1955, 3, 16.

73 Mercer Cook, review of *America at Mid-Century*, *Journal of Negro History* 40 (October 1955), 372–3. On Cook, see Germain, "Mercer Cook and the Origins of Black French Studies."

74 AHC 13S1/4, dossier 1, Siegfried to Chapsal, 14 October, 4 November 1955; Wylie, "André Siegfried à Harvard," 81–5.

75 Siegfried, "Un dictionnaire américain," 18; see also Siegfried, "États-Unis 1956."

76 Sanguin, *André Siegfried*, 210–14; Siegfried, "L'anticolonialisme américain," 16.

77 AMS, copy of Institut des Sciences et Techniques Humaines, *Un homme*, n.p., comments by Toulouse. On the CNOF see Ehrmann, *Organized Business in France*, 203.

78 AMS, Institut du Transport Aérien, obituary of Siegfried, 31 March 1959.

79 Centro per lo Sviluppo dei Trasporti Aerei, *Le XXème siècle*, 4–7; the lecture was given and published in French.

80 Siegfried, *Aspects du XXe siècle* (Paris: Hachette, 1955), 8, 17; available online at http:// classiques.uqac.ca/classiques/siegfried_andre/aspects_XXe_siecle/aspects_XXe_siecle.html.

81 Ibid., 52, 88–9.

82 Ibid., 100–1, 148. On Siegfried as an elitist critic of mass tourism, see Furlough, "Making Mass Vacations," 247–8.

83 Siegfried, *Aspects du XXe siècle*, 160, 208.

84 Ibid., 213–14, 222.

85 AHC 11S1/1, dossier 3, materials for "Au balcon du XXe siècle," including draft preface by Brisson, n.d.

86 Siegfried, "La technique et la culture," 39, 43.

87 On Hartung, see Sedgwick, *Against the Modern World*, 103–4, 196; he does not discuss the connection with Siegfried.

88 For a list of the participants and record of the meeting, see AHC 6S1/7, dossier 6, "Liste des personnalités devant assister à la réunion du 28 juin 1955 présidée par M. André Siegfried" and "Compte rendu de la réunion du 28 juin 1955."

89 AHC 6S1/7, dossier 6, Siegfried, "Institut des Sciences et Techniques Humaines," 9 May 1956; "Note communiquée à M. André Siegfried le 4 juillet 1957 et accompagnant un dossier sur le ISTH en vue de la rédaction d'une article dans *Le Figaro*, fin sept.-début oct. 1957."

90 Sedgwick, *Against the Modern World*, 196–200, 210–12.

91 Siegfried, "L'oeuvre technique de l'homme," 257–60.

92 Siegfried, preface to *La dignité humain*, 10.

Notes to pages 247–52 305

93 For these reminiscences, see AMS, copy of Institut des sciences et techniques humaines, *Un homme*, no pagination.

94 AHC 12S1/1, dossier 3, Siegfried, "La psychologie du normand"; for other reflections on Normandy, including his family life, see his preface to *Normandie* and AHC 13S1/1, dossier 3, clipping of *Le Havre libre*, 15 December 1958.

95 AHC 13S1/1, dossier 3, clipping for *Le Havre libre*, 15 December 1958; Siegfried, *Mes souvenirs d'enfance*; for further discussion of this book, see chapter 1.

96 Preface to Siegfried, ed., *Aspects de la société française*, 12–15; AHC 12 S1/4, clipping of "Qu'est-ce qui va bien en France?" *Le Nouveau Fémina*, September 1954, 34–35.

97 Siegfried, preface to Piéchaud, *Questions de langage*, 3–4.

98 Fondation Singer-Polignac, *Cinq propos sur la langue française*; for Siegfried's previous contacts with Roques, see their correspondence in BIF, ms 6160.

99 Siegfried, "La langue française et les conditions de la vie moderne," in Fondation Singer-Polignac, *Cinq propos de la langue française*, 66.

100 AHC 5S1/5, dossier 5, "Cinquantenaire de l'Entente Cordiale," Sorbonne, 21 May 1954; AHC 12S1/4, clipping of "Hommage à la Grande-Bretagne" (summer 1954), 9; AHC 5S1/5, dossier 7, lecture notes, "Commonwealth," École de Guerre, 15 February 1957; Siegfried, preface to de Sailly, *La zone sterling*.

101 Siegfried, preface to Agourtine, *Géographie économique de l'Allemagne Orientale*; Siegfried, preface to Piettre, *L'économie allemande contemporaine*; Sanguin, *André Siegfried*, 221–2.

102 Siegfried, preface to Bonnefous, *L'Europe en face de son destin*, 9; AHC 6S1/2, dossier 6, "Les rélations publiques au service de la Communauté Économique Européenne: Journée d'études du 4 mars 1958," and clipping of "L'Europe definie par André Siegfried, Gabriel Marcel et Denis Rougement," *Combat*, 26 March 1958.

103 Siegfried, *Les voies d'Israël*, 20, 99, 119.

104 Ibid., 159–60, 167–8, 173.

105 Birnbaum, *La France aux français*, 159–60; Sanguin, *André Siegfried*, 243.

106 Siegfried with Jérôme and Jean Tharaud, *Le centenaire des services des Messageries Maritimes*, 12.

107 Siegfried, *Géographie poétique des cinq continents*, 11–12, 19–23.

108 Ibid., 71–2, 74, 95–6, 109–12, 332.

109 Ibid., 234, 238, 325.

110 Clippings of the articles are preserved in AHC 12SI/3; for the book manuscript, see AHC 11SI/2, dossier 1, Siegfried, "Peuples de couleur." Exactly when the manuscript was prepared is uncertain but the most recent annotated revision dates from 30 June 1953 (chapter 4, "Les Chinois," 4). Subsequent references will be to the individual chapters and respective page numbers of this manuscript.

111 AHC 11SI/2, dossier 1, Siegfried, "Peuples de couleur," chapter 1, "Les Noirs dans le monde," 5; chapter 2, "Les Indiens d'Amérique," 1, 12.

112 Ibid., chapter 3, "Les Hindous," 27; chapter 4, "Le Chinois," 13, 15.

113 Siegfried, *Routes of Contagion*, 18, 92–3, 98.

114 Siegfried, "L'occident et la direction spirituelle," 6, 12.

## EPILOGUE

1 AMS, Siegfried to Aubrun, 16 September 1958.

2 AHC 12SI/1, dossier 1, Seydoux to Siegfried, 18 September 1958.

3 AHC 13SI/1, dossier 3, Ministère des Affaires Étrangères, Nations Unies et Organisations Internationales to Siegfried, 21 November 1958.

4 AHC 12SI/5, copy of Siegfried, "Hommage à Gouverneur Léon Léal," *Résonances*, fall 1958, n.p.

5 "Regard d'ensemble sur la IVe," *Le Figaro*, 20 November 1958, reprinted in Siegfried, *De la IVe à la Ve République*, 313–17, quotation on 317.

6 AMS, Siegfried to Aubrun, 16 September 1958.

7 Sanguin, *André Siegfried*, 224–8, quotation on 226.

8 Sanguin, *André Siegfried*, 228–9; BIF, Manuscrit 7168, ff. 290, Siegfried to Carcopino, 10 February 1959; ACF, dossier C-XII, clipping of *Le Havre presse*, 21 April 1975, article by F. Tardif.

9 Jean Desy, "L'ami du Canada"; Abelardo Saenz, "L'un des maîtres les plus admirés dans les pays de l'Amérique latine"; Harold Nicolson, "Trois hommes dans le même homme"; and "Voix d'Angleterre et des États-Unis," all from *Le Figaro littéraire*, 4 April 1959.

10 Pasteur Georges Marchal, "Toujours, grâce à lui, l'échange des idées prenait grand air"; Édouard Bonnefous, "Il était de ceux, de plus en plus rares qui font la sythèse," *Le Figaro littéraire*, 4 April 1959.

11 François Goguel, "Le roc solide du libéralisme et de la foi en homme"; André Chamson, "Une grande leçon de libéralisme," *Le Figaro littéraire*, 4 April 1959; for details on Chamson,, see Gisèle Sapiro, "Chamson (André), 1900–1983," in *Dictionnaire des intellectuels français*, ed. Julliard and Winock, 294–5.

Notes to pages 259–67

12 Weiss, "La ligne Siegfried"; on Weiss see Laurence Klejman and Florence Rochefort, "Weiss (Louise), 1893–1983," in *Dictionnaire des intellectuels français*, ed. Julliard and Winock, 1429–30.

13 See AHC 13SI/14, dossiers 3 and 4; the reminiscences given in the memorial are reprinted in Association André Siegfried, *Hommage*; for the comments by Bonnefous see 20–5.

14 Blondiaux and Veitl, "La carrière symbolique d'un père fondateur," 17. There are photographs of the displays in AHC 10SI, dossier 1; for the exhibition hosted by the Red Cross in Le Havre, see AHC 10SI, dossier 4, R. Loisel to Madame Bourdin, 17 November 1975, and a copy of the handbill for the event.

15 Miroglio, *Un grand havrais*, 20. On Miroglio, see Claret, *Personnalité collective des nations*, 107–11.

16 Carbonel, "Création et essor de l'Institut Havrais de Sociologie Économique et de Psychologie des Peuples," 8–15.

17 Gueissaz, "André Nicolaï et l'Institut Havrais," 53–6, 61–2; Carbonel, "Origines et développement de l'Institut Havrais," 81.

18 Sanguin, *André Siegfried*, 245–6; Clout, "André Siegfried," 167; Ferraz de Oliveira, "Territory and Theory in Political Geography," 564–6.

19 Blondiaux and Veitl, "La carrière symbolique d'un père fondateur," 14–20; Bois, *Paysans de l'Ouest*. For a discussion of Bois and other scholars' revisions of Siegfried, see also Zeldin, *France 1848–1945*, vol. 1, 366–79.

20 Blondiaux and Veitl, "La carrière symbolique d'un père fondateur," 20–6.

21 For a prominent example of such a trend, see Laurent, *Daniel Halévy*.

22 Braudel, *History of Civilizations*, 497.

23 Sanguin, *André Siegfried*, 240–4.

24 On this issue, see Kalman, *Rethinking Antisemitism*, 9.

25 For context, see Chapman and Frader, "Introduction: Race in France," esp. 1–8.

26 Reynaud Paligot, *République raciale*, 317–26, quotation on 319.

27 Reynaud Paligot, *Races, racisme et antiracisme*; Conklin, *In the Museum of Man*.

28 Reynaud Paligot, "Les *Annales* de Lucien Febvre à Fernand Braudel," 129–31.

29 Conklin, *In the Museum of Man*, 326–31; Febvre and Crouzet, *Nous sommes des sang-mêlés*.

# Bibliography

## ARCHIVAL SOURCES

### Archives du Collége de France

Dossier André Siegfried (C-XII)
GIV (minutes of the Assembly of Professors)

### Archives départementales de la Seine-Maritime

1R/2986 (service record of André Siegfried)

### Archives d'Histoire Contemporaine, Centre d'histoire Sciences Po

Archives de l'École libre des sciences politiques (ISP)
Fonds André Siegfried (1–13SI)

### Archives de l'Institut de France

Académie française: Dossier on André Siegfried; 2B20 (minutes of
the Académie française, November 1941–November 1951, session
of 12 October 1944)
Section de Morale: Élection 1932, fauteuil de M. Auguste Gauvain;
2D17 (minutes of the Académie des sciences morales et politiques,
1931–1938); 2D18 (minutes of the Académie des sciences morales
et politiques, 1939–1947)

310 Bibliography

## Archives du Ministère des Affaires étrangères

Series B (Commercial and International Relations, 1920–1929), sub-series blockade 1914–1920, boxes 361–3 (personnel)

Series E (Asia-Oceania, 1918–1940), sub-series for Australia, vols. 9–11: French mission to Australia and New Zealand, 1918–1920

Series Y (International, 1918–1940), League of Nations series, SDN 205 (organization and personnel); sub-series 1J (economic and financial issues), vol. 1221 (Brussels Conference, 1920), vol. 1205 (Genoa Conference, 1922); sub-series 1K (communications and transit), vol. 1481 (Barcelona Conference, 1921)

Series Y (International, 1944–49), NUOI sub-series (conferences secretariat, 1944–49), boxes 3–4 (San Francisco Conference, 1945)

## Archives du Musée social

Folder, "André Siegfried et le Musée social: Lettres"
Folder, "André Siegfried et le Musée social: Matériaux"
Folder, "André Siegfried: Textes"
Minutes of the Comité de Direction, vol. 7 (16 January 1929 to 26 February 1963)

## Archives nationales

452AP/1 Fonds René Coty (correspondence with André Siegfried)
472AP/2 Fonds Alfred Fabre-Luce (correspondence with André Siegfried)
475AP/307 Fonds Hubert Lyautey (correspondence with André Siegfried)
AJ16/7023 Albert Kahn Scholarships
C/7180 (1902 election, Basses-Alpes)
C/6450 (1906 election, Le Havre, 2nd district)
C/6752 (1910 elections, Le Havre, 2nd district)
F7/15529 dossier on André Siegfried, 1945–58
F7/16006 Prefecture of Police, dossier on Jules Siegfried
F17/3007/1 dossier on André Siegfried's global tour, 1898
F17/13358 Cabinet du Ministre de l'Éducation nationale

## Archives of the Royal Institute of International Affairs

RIIA 8/46, 8/1603, 8/1095: presentations by André Siegfried

# Bibliography

## Bibliothèque de l'Institut de France

Manuscripts 5480 (correspondence with Henri Cordier), 6160 (correspondence with Mario Roques), 6784 (Fonds André Mazon), 7168 (correspondence with Jérôme Carcopino)

## Bibliothèque nationale de France

Annuaire du Collège de France (8R 17917)

## Service historique de la défense

Département de l'Armée de la Terre 17N/447

## UK National Archives

FO 371, 395, 432

### PUBLISHED SOURCES

*Note:* Citations of individual newspaper and magazine articles by André Siegfried, as well as individual reviews of his work, are indicated in the endnotes.

*Académie française: Discours prononcés dans la séance privée tenue par L'Académie française pour la réception de M. Henry de Montherlant le jeudi 20 Juin 1963.* Paris: Firmon-Didot, 1963.

*Académie française: Discours prononcés dans la séance publique tenue par l'Académie française pour la reception de M. Daniel-Rops le jeudi 22 mars 1956.* Paris: Firmin-Didot, 1956.

Airey, Willis. "André Siegfried's Democracy in New Zealand: Fifty Years After." *Political Science* 6, no. 2 (1954): 33–51.

Aldrich, Robert. "La mission française en Australie de 1918: l'Australie et les relations franco-australiennes au lendemain de la guerre." In *Les Français et l'Australie: Voyages de découverte et missions scientifiques de 1756 à nos jours,* edited by André Dommergues and Maryvonne Nedeljkovic, 295–305. Paris: Université de Paris X Nanterre, 1989.

Alexander, Fred. "André Siegfried: A Twentieth Century de Tocqueville." *Australian Journal of Politics and History* 6, no. 1 (1960): 14–27.

Allen, Donald Roy. *French Views of America in the 1930s.* New York: Garland Press, 1979.

Bibliography

Ardaillou, Pierre. "Les républicains modérés du Havre de Jules Siegfried à René Coty." In *Les modérés dans la vie politique française (1870–1965)*, edited by François Roth with Laurent Bigorgne, 193–208. Nancy: Presses universitaires de Nancy, 2000.

Armus, Seth. *French Anti-Americanism (1930–1948): Critical Moments in a Complex History.* Lanham: Lexington Books, 2007.

Aron, Raymond. *Memoirs: Fifty Years of Political Reflection.* Translated by George Holoch. New York: Holmes & Meier, 1990. Originally published as *Mémoires* (Paris: Julliard, 1983).

Association André Siegfried. *Hommage à André Siegfried.* Paris: Association Andre Siegfried, 1961.

Audier, Serge. "Is There a French Neoliberalism?" In *French Liberalism from Montesquieu to the Present Day*, 208–29, edited by Raf Geenens and Helena Rosenblatt. Cambridge: Cambridge University Press, 2012.

Auriol, Vincent. *Journal du septennat 1947–1954.* Vol. 6, *1952.* Edited by Dominique Boché. Paris: Armand Colin, 1978.

Barkan, Elazar. *The Retreat of Scientific Racism: Changing Concepts of Race in Britain and the United States between the World Wars.* Cambridge: Cambridge University Press, 1992.

Barral, Pierre. "Idéal et pratique du régionalisme dans le régime de Vichy." *Revue française de science politique* 24, no. 5 (1974): 911–39.

Barthélemy, Joseph. *Ministre de la Justice: Mémoire.* Paris: Pygmalion, 1989.

Baruch, Marc Olivier. *Servir l'État français: L'administration en France de 1940 à 1944.* Paris: Fayard, 1997.

Beale, Marjorie A. *The Modernist Enterprise: French Elites and the Threat of Modernity, 1900–1940.* Stanford: Stanford University Press, 2000.

Behrent, Michael C. "Justifying Capitalism in an Age of Uncertainty: L'Association pour la liberté économique et le progrès social, 1969–73." In *France since the 1970s: History, Politics and Memory in an Age of Uncertainty*, 175–98, edited by Emile Chabal. London: Bloomsbury Academic, 2015.

– "Liberal Dispositions: Recent Scholarship on French Liberalism." *Modern Intellectual History* 13, no. 2 (2016), 447–77.

Beloff, Max. *The Intellectual in Politics and Other Essays.* New York: Library Press, 1971.

Bell, Philip. *France and Britain, 1900–1940: Entente and Estrangement.* London: Longman, 1996.

Bellescize, Diane de. *Les neuf sages de la Résistance: Le Comité général d'études dans la clandestinité.* Paris: Plon, 1979.

# Bibliography

Bergeron, Gérard. *Quand Tocqueville et Siegfried nous observaient.* Sillery: Presses de l'Université du Québec, 1990.

Berghahn, Volker. *America and the Intellectual Cold Wars in Europe.* Princeton: Princeton University Press, 2001.

Birnbaum, Pierre. *"La France aux français": Histoire des haines nationalistes.* Paris: Seuil, 1993.

Bistis, Marguerite. "Managing Bergson's Crowd: Professionalism and the *Mondain* at the Collège de France." *Historical Reflections* 22, no. 2 (1996): 389–406.

Blandin, Claire. *Le Figaro: Deux siècles d'histoire.* Paris: Armand Colin, 2007.

Blondiaux, Loïc, and Philippe Veitl. "La carrière symbolique d'un père fondateur: André Siegfried et la science politique française après 1945." *Genèses: Sciences sociales et histoire* no. 37 (1999): 4–26.

Boegner, Marc, and André Siegfried, eds. *Protestantisme français.* Paris: Plon, 1945.

Boegner, Philippe, ed. *Carnets de Pasteur Boegner 1940–1945.* Paris: Fayard, 1992.

Bois, Paul. *Paysans de l'Ouest: De structures économiques et sociales aux options politiques depuis l'époque révolutionnaire dans la Sarthe.* Paris: Flammarion, 1971 (1960).

Bonnefous, Édouard, ed. *L'oeuvre scientifique d'André Siegfried.* Paris: Presses de la Fondation Nationale des Sciences Politiques, 1977.

Bonnett, Alastair. "From White to Western: 'Racial Decline' and the Idea of the West in Britain, 1890–1930." *Journal of Historical Sociology* 16, no. 3 (2003): 320–47.

Boulet, François. "André Siegfried (1875–1959): Un maître à penser au XXe siècle." Manuscript deposited at the Fondation Nationale des Sciences Politiques, Paris, 2001.

Boyce, Robert. "Behind the Façade of the *Entente Cordiale* after the Great War." In *Britain, France, and the Entente Cordiale since 1904,* edited by Antoine Capet, 41–63. Houndmills: Palgrave Macmillan, 2006.

Braudel, Fernand. *A History of Civilizations.* Translated by Richard Mayne. New York: Allen Lane, 1994. Originally published as *Grammaire des civilisations* (Paris: Arthaud, 1993).

Broc, Numa. "Nationalisme, colonialisme et géographie: Marcel Dubois (1856–1916)." *Annales de géographie* 87, no. 481 (1978): 326–33.

Bruneteau, Bernard. *"L'Europe nouvelle" de Hitler: Une illusion des intellectuels de la France de Vichy.* Monaco: Éditions du Rocher, 2003.

Buléon, Pascal. "Siegfried, la Normandie et les temperaments politiques: Quelques raisons d'une redécouverte." *Études normandes* 38, no. 2 (1989): 69–84.

– "La tentative de Siegfried et sa faille épistomélogique, tempérament et âme du people." In *Le* Tableau politique de la France de l'Ouest *d'André Siegfried 100 ans après: Héritages et posterités*, 131–47, edited by Michel Bussi, Christophe Le Digol, and Christophe Voillot. Rennes: Presses Universitaires de Rennes, 2016.

Burke, Peter. *The French Historical Revolution: The Annales School 1929–1989.* Stanford: Stanford University Press, 1990.

Burrin, Philippe. *La France à l'heure allemande 1940–1944.* Paris: Seuil, 1995.

Bussi, Michel. "L'Ouest politique, 75 puis 100 ans après." In *Le* Tableau politique de la France de l'Ouest *d'André Siegfried 100 ans après: Héritages et posterités*, 91–100, edited by Michel Bussi, Christophe Le Digol, and Christophe Voillot. Rennes: Presses Universitaires de Rennes, 2016.

Cabanel, Patrick. "André Siegfried et la Méditerranée: Le travail empaysagé et le chasseur des frontières," in *Regards sur la Méditerranée: Actes du 7ème colloque de la Villa Kérylos à Beaulieu-sur-Mer les 4 & 5 octobre 1996*, 175–92. Paris: Académie des Inscriptions et Belles-Lettres, 1997.

– *De la paix aux résistances: Les protestants français de 1930 à 1945.* Paris: Fayard, 2015.

– *Les protestants et la République: De 1870 à nos jours.* Brussels: Éditions Complexe, 2000.

Cairns, John C. "A Nation of Shopkeepers in Search of a Suitable France: 1919–1940." *American Historical Review* 79, no. 3 (1974): 710–43.

Campbell, Gerard. *De Verdun aux Vosges: Impressions de guerre (septembre 1914 à janvier 1915).* Translated by André Siegfried. Paris: Armand Colin, 1916.

Cantier, Jacques. *Lire sous l'Occupation: Livres, lecteurs, lectures, 1939–1944.* Paris: CNRS Éditions, 2019.

Carbonel, Frédéric. "Création et essor de l'Institut Havrais de Sociologie économique et de Psychologie des Peuples de l'hiver 1937 aux années 1970." 2006. HAL open archives, https://halshs.archives-ouvertes.fr/halshs-00090431.

– "Origines et développement de l'Institut Havrais de Sociologie économique et de Psychologie des Peuples." *Cahiers internationaux de psychologie sociale* 77 (2008): 69–86.

# Bibliography

Centro per lo Sviluppo dei Trasporti Aerei. *Le XXe siècle, âge de la vitesse; Conferenza tenuta ai membri del Centro per lo Sviluppo dei Trasporti Aerei dall'Accademico di Francia André Siegfried, Presidente dell'Institut français du transport aérien.* Rome, 5 May 1954.

Chambelland, Colette, ed. *Le Musée social en son temps.* Paris: Presses de l'École normale supérieure, 1998.

Chapman, Herrick. *France's Long Reconstruction: In Search of the Modern Republic.* Cambridge: Harvard University Press, 2018.

Chapman, Herrick, and Laura L. Frader. "Introduction: Race in France." In *Race in France: Interdisciplinary Perspectives on the Politics of Difference,* 1–19, edited by Herrick Chapman and Laura L. Frader. New York: Berghahn Books, 2004.

Charle, Christophe. "Savoir durer: La nationalisation de l'École libre des sciences politiques, 1936–1945." *Actes de la recherché en sciences sociales,* nos. 86–87 (1991): 99–105.

Chevalier, Michel. "Siegfried et l'école française de géographie: Un problème de sociologie." *Études normandes* 38, no. 2 (1989): 17–23.

Churchill, Christopher. "The Unlikely Barrèsian Inheritance of Albert Camus." *Journal of the Canadian Historical Association* 23, no. 2 (2012): 251–97.

Claret, Philippe. *La personnalité collective des nations: Théories anglo-saxonnes et conceptions françaises du caractère national.* Brussels: Établissements Émile Bruylant, 1998.

Clark, Terry Nichols. *Prophets and Patrons: The French University and the Emergence of the Social Sciences.* Cambridge, MA: Harvard University Press, 1973.

Clarke, Jackie. "Engineering a New Order in the 1930s: The Case of Jean Coutrot." *French Historical Studies* 24, no. 1 (2001), 63–86.

– *France in the Age of Organization: Factory, Home and Nation from the 1920s to Vichy.* New York: Berghahn Books, 2011.

Claval, Paul. "André Siegfried et les démocraties anglo-saxonnes." *Études normandes* 38, no. 2 (1989): 121–35.

Clout, Hugh. "André Siegfried, 1875–1959." In *Geographers: Biobibliographical Studies,* vol. 30, edited by Hayden Lorimer and Charles W.J. Withers, 152–74. London: Bloomsbury Academic, 2011.

– "Marcel Dubois, 1856–1916." In *Geographers: Biobibliographical Studies,* vol. 30, edited by Hayden Lorimer and Charles W.J. Withers, 134–51. London: Bloomsbury Academic, 2011.

Cointet, Michèle. *Le Conseil National de Vichy: Vie politique et réforme d'état en régime autoritaire.* Paris: Aux Amateurs de Livres, 1989.

Conklin, Alice. *In the Museum of Man: Race, Anthropology, and Empire in France, 1850–1950*. Ithaca: Cornell University Press, 2013.

Craiutu, Aurelien. "Raymond Aron and the Tradition of Political Moderation in France." In *French Liberalism from Montesquieu to the Present Day*, edited by Raf Geenens and Helena Rosenblatt, 271–90. Cambridge: Cambridge University Press, 2012.

– *A Virtue for Courageous Minds: Moderation in French Political Thought, 1748–1830*. Princeton: Princeton University Press, 2012.

Creswell, Michael. *A Question of Balance: How France and the United States Created Cold War Europe*. Cambridge: Harvard University Press, 2006.

Dard, Olivier. "Le Barrèsisme d'Henri Massis: Bilan d'un demi-siècle." In *Maurice Barrès, la Lorraine, la France et l'étranger*, edited by Olivier Dard, Michel Grunwald, Michel Leymarie et Jean-Michel Wittmann, 183–98. Bern: Peter Lang, 2011.

David-Ives, Corinne. "André Siegfried in New Zealand: A Racialist Vision of Social Progress." *Journal of New Zealand and Pacific Studies* 3, no. 1 (2015): 25–37.

De Grazia, Victoria. *Irresistible Empire: America's Advance Through 20th-Century Europe*. Cambridge, MA: Harvard University Press, 2005.

Denord, François. "Aux origines du néo-libéralisme en France: Louis Rougier et le Colloque Walter Lippmann de 1938." *Le Mouvement Social*, no. 195 (2001): 9–34.

Deroy, Henri. "Hommage à la mémoire d'André Siegfried." *Cahiers du Musée social*, no. 2 (March-April 1959): 51–5.

Des Portes, Claude. *L'atmosphère des Sciences Po*. Paris: Éditions SPES, 1935.

Dewar, Kenneth C. *Frank Underhill and the Politics of Ideas*. Montreal and Kingston: McGill-Queen's University Press, 2015.

Diamond, Hannah. *Fleeing Hitler: France 1940*. Oxford: Oxford University Press, 2007.

Doty, C. Stewart. *From Cultural Rebellion to Counterrevolution: The Politics of Maurice Barrès*. Athens: Ohio University Press, 1976.

Courrière, Henri. "Clientélisme, autorité et domination politique dans les Alpes-Maritimes." In *Qu'est-ce que l'autorité? France-Allemagne(s), XIXe–XXe siècles*, edited by Emmanuel Droit and Pierre Karila-Cohen, 161–81. Paris: Éditions de la Maison des sciences de l'homme, 2016.

Dumenil, Lynn. *Modern Temper: American Culture and Society in the 1920s*. New York: Hill and Wang, 1995.

École libre des sciences politiques. *Élie Halévy: 6 septembre 1870–21 août 1937*. Paris: École libre des sciences politiques, 1938.

## Bibliography

- *Organisation et programme des cours: Année scolaire 1927–1928.* Paris: Librairie Vuibert, 1927.
- *Organisation et programme des cours: Année scolaire 1938–1939.* Paris: Librairie Vuibert, 1938.
- *Organisation et programme des cours: Année scolaire 1942–43.* Paris: Librairie Vuibert, 1942.
- *Organisation et programme des cours: Année scolaire 1943–44.* Paris: Librairie Vuibert, 1943.

Ehrmann, Henry W. *Organized Business in France.* Princeton: Princeton University Press, 1957.

Elgey, Georgette. *Histoire de la IVe République.* Vol. 1. Paris: Fayard, 1965.

Elwitt, Sanford. "Social Reform and Social Order in Late Nineteenth-Century France: The Musée Social and Its Friends." *French Historical Studies* 11, no. 3 (1980): 431–51.

- *The Third Republic Defended: Bourgeois Reform in France, 1880–1914.* Baton Rouge: Louisiana State University Press, 1986.

Ellwood, David W. *The Shock of America: Europe and the Challenge of the Century.* Oxford: Oxford University Press, 2012.

English, John. *Citizen of the World: The Life of Pierre Elliott Trudeau.* Vol. 1, *1919–1968.* Toronto: Alfred A. Knopf Canada, 2006.

Epstein, Simon. *Les Dreyfusards sous l'Occupation.* Paris: Albin Michel, 2001.

Fabre, Gérard. "André Siegfried: Un regard decalé sur le Canada." *Textual Studies in Canada,* no. 17 (2004): 131–48.

- "Un arc transatlantique et sa tangente ou comment se dessine un réseau intellectuel franco-québécois?" *Revue internationale d'études québécoises* 7, no. 1 (2004): 43–78.
- "Le comparatisme d'André Siegfried." *Recherches sociographiques* 43, no. 1 (2002): 111–31.
- *Le pari canadien d'André Siegfried.* Québec: Presses de l'Université Laval, 2021.
- "Passeur ou passager? Idéologie et connaissance de l'internationale dans les travaux nord-amércains d'André Siegfried (1906–1937)." *Sociologie et société* 37, no. 2 (2005): 209–34.

Fabre-Luce, Alfred, ed. *Anthologie de la nouvelle Europe.* Paris: Librairie Plon, 1942.

Favre, Pierre. *Naissances de la science politique en France 1870–1914.* Paris: Fayard, 1989.

Febvre, Lucien, and François Crouzet. *Nous sommes des sang-mêlés: Manuel d'histoire de la civilisation française.* Introduction and epilogue by Denis and Élisabeth Crouzet. Paris: Albin Michel, 2012.

Ferraz de Oliveira, António. "Territory and Theory in Political Geography, c. 1970s–90s: Jean Gottmann's *The Signficance of Territory.*" *Territory, Politics, Governance* 9:4 (2021): 553–70.

Fink, Carole. *The Genoa Conference: European Diplomacy, 1921–1922.* Chapel Hill: University of North Carolina Press, 1984.

Fondation Singer-Polignac. *Cinq propos sur la langue française.* Paris: Fondation Singer-Polignac, 1955.

Fox, Richard Wightman. "Epitaph for Middletown." In *The Culture of Consumption: Critical Essays in American History, 1880–1980*, edited by Richard Wightman Fox and T.J. Jackson Lears, 103–41. New York: Pantheon Books, 1983.

Furlough, Ellen. "Making Mass Vacations: Tourism and Consumer Culture in France, 1930s to 1970s." *Comparative Studies in Society and History* 40, no. 2 (1998): 247–86.

Gagnon, Paul. "French Views of the Second American Revolution." *French Historical Studies* 2, no. 4 (1962): 430–49.

Galloux-Fournier, Bernadette. "Un regard sur l'Amérique: Voyageurs français aux États-Unis, 1919–1939." *Revue d'histoire moderne et contemporaine* 37, no. 2 (1990): 308–23.

Garrigou, Alain. "André Siegfried dans les Basses-Alpes: 'Des leçons à l'humanité à 1000 francs le cachet.'" In *Le Tableau politique de la France de l'Ouest d'André Siegfried 100 ans après: Héritages et posterités*, edited by Michel Bussi, Christophe Le Digol, and Christophe Voilliot, 29–41. Rennes: Presses Universitaires de Rennes, 2016.

– "Un document d'André Siegfried." *Cahiers de sociologie politique de Nanterre*, accessed 24 July 2018, http://www.gap-nanterre.org/spip.php?article6.

– "L'initiation d'un initiateur: André Siegfried et le *Tableau politique de la France de l'Ouest.*" *Actes de la recherche en sciences sociales* 1–2, nos. 106–7 (1995): 27–41.

Germain, Félix. "Mercer Cook and the Origins of Black French Studies." *French Politics, Culture & Society* 34, no. 1 (2016): 63–81.

Giblin-Delvallet, Béatrice. "Les géographes, les élections et la sociologie électorale." *Études normandes* 38, no. 2 (1989): 51–8.

Giladi, Amotz. "Rayonnement et propaganda culturels français autour de la "panlatinité": Les échanges entre intellectuels français et hispano-américains au début du vingtième siècle." *French Politics, Culture & Society* 31, no. 3 (2013): 93–113.

Goetschel, Pascale, and Bénédicte Toucheboeuf. *La IVe République: La France de la Libération à 1958.* Paris: Librairie Générale Française, 2004.

Goguel, François. "André Siegfried: L'homme et l'oeuvre, 1875–1959." *Bulletin de la Société de l'histoire du protestantisme français* 121, no. 2 (1975): 1–15.

– *France under the Fourth Republic.* Translated by Roy Pierce. New York: Russell and Russell, 1971 (1952).

– "La politique française." In *L'oeuvre scientifique d'André Siegfried,* 37–47, edited by Édouard Bonnefous. Paris: Presses de la Fondation Nationale des Sciences Politiques, 1977.

Gueissaz, Albert. "André Nicolaï et l'Institut Havrais de Sociologie économique et de Psychologie des Peuples." *Cahiers de sociologie économique et culturelle: Ethnopsychologie* no. 57 (2014): 51–65.

Hamp, Pierre. "In Memoriam: André Siegfried." *Économie contemporaine,* 29 March 1960: 19–21.

Harris, Ruth. *The Man on Devil's Island: Alfred Dreyfus and the Affair that Divided France.* London: Allen Lane, 2010.

Harvey, John L. "Conservative Crossings: Bernard Faÿ and the Rise of American Studies in Third-Republic France." *Historical Reflections* 36, no. 1 (2010): 95–124.

Hause, Steven C., with Anne R. Kenney. *Women's Suffrage and Social Politics in the French Third Republic.* Princeton: Princeton University Press, 1984.

Hazareesingh, Sudhir. *How the French Think: An Affectionate Portrait of an Intellectual People.* London: Allen Lane, 2015.

Hitchcock, William I. *France Restored: Cold War Diplomacy and the Quest for Leadership in Europe, 1944–1954.* Chapel Hill: University of North Carolina Press, 1998.

Hogenhuis-Seliverstoff, Anne. "French Plans for the Reconstruction of Russia." In *Genoa, Rapallo, and European Reconstruction in 1922,* edited by Carole Fink, Axel Frohn, and Jürgen Heideking, 131–48. Cambridge: Cambridge University Press, 1991.

Horne, Janet. *A Social Laboratory for Modern France: The Musée Social and the Rise of the Welfare State.* Durham: Duke University Press, 2002.

Hughes, H. Stuart. *Gentleman Rebel: The Memoirs of H. Stuart Hughes.* New York: Ticknor and Fields, 1990.

Institut sciences et techniques humaines. *Un homme ... un enseignement: Hommage à André Siegfried*. Les Lilas: SEPI, 1959.

Jackson, Julian. *France: The Dark Years, 1940–1944*. Oxford: Oxford University Press, 2001.

Jackson, Peter. *Beyond the Balance of Power: France and the Politics of National Security in the Era of the First World War*. Cambridge: Cambridge University Press, 2013.

Jacobson, Matthew Frye. *Whiteness of a Different Color: European Immigrants and the Alchemy of Race*. Cambridge: Harvard University Press, 1998.

Jeannesson, Stanislas. "Jacques Seydoux et la diplomatie économique dans la France de l'après-guerre." *Relations internationales* no. 121 (2005): 9–24.

Julliard, Jacques, and Michel Winock, eds. *Dictionnaire des intellectuels français*. 2nd ed. Paris: Seuil, 2002.

Kalman, Julie. *Rethinking Antisemitism in Nineteenth-Century France*. New York: Cambridge University Press, 2010.

Kaplan, Alice. *Dreaming in French: The Paris Years of Jacqueline Bouvier Kennedy, Susan Sontag, and Angela Davis*. Chicago: University of Chicago Press, 2012.

Kaplan, Steven L. "Un laboratoire de la doctrine corporatiste sous le régime de Vichy: L'Institut d'Études Corporatives et Sociales." *Le Mouvement Social*, no. 195 (2001): 35–77.

Kennedy, Sean. "André Siegfried and the Complexities of French Anti-Americanism." *French Politics, Culture & Society* 27, no. 2 (2009): 1–22.

– "Situating France: The Career of André Siegfried, 1900–40." *Historical Reflections* 30, no. 2 (2004): 179–203.

– "A Tocqueville for the North? André Siegfried and Canada." *Journal of the Canadian Historical Association* 14, no. 1 (2003): 117–36.

King, Richard H. *Race, Culture, and the Intellectuals, 1940–1970*. Baltimore: Johns Hopkins University Press, 2004.

Klautke, Egbert. "The French Reception of *Völkerpsychologie* and the Origins of the Social Sciences." *Modern Intellectual History* 10, no. 2 (2013): 293–316.

Kuisel, Richard. "American Historians in Search of France: Perceptions and Misperceptions." *French Historical Studies* 19, no. 2 (1995): 307–19.

– *Capitalism and the State in Modern France*. Cambridge: Cambridge University Press, 1981.

# Bibliography

- *Ernest Mercier: French Technocrat.* Berkeley: University of California Press, 1967.
- *Seducing the French: The Dilemma of Americanization.* Berkeley: University of California Press, 1993.

La Llosa, Alvar de. "L'Indien et le crocodile: André Siegfried, une vision de l'Amérique latine." *Crisol* no. 10 (2006): 183–221.

- "La réception de l'oeuvre d'André Siegfried en Amérique latine: Impacts, rejets et intérêt de la part des élites locales, une traduction oubliée de Luis Alberto Sánchez." In *Hommes de science et intellectuels européens en Amérique latine (XIXe–XXe siècles),* edited by Joseph Farré, Françoise Martinez, and Itamar Olivares, 113–27. Paris: Éditions Le Manuscrit, 2005.

Lacorne, Denis. *La crise de l'identité américaine: Du melting-pot au multiculturalisme.* Paris: Fayard, 1997.

Lacorne, Denis, Jacques Rupnik, and Marie-France Toinet, eds. *The Rise and Fall of Anti-Americanism: A Century of French Perceptions.* Translated by Gerry Turner. New York: St Martin's Press, 1990. Originally published as *L'Amérique dans les têtes: Un siècle de fascinations et d'adversions* (Paris: Hachette, 1986).

Lake, Marilyn, and Henry Reynolds. *Drawing the Global Colour Line: White Men's Countries and the International Challenge of Racial Equality.* Cambridge: Cambridge University Press, 2008.

Lancelot, Alain. "Les problèmes électoraux." In *L'oeuvre scientifique d'André Siegfried,* edited by Édouard Bonnefous, 48–55. Paris: Presses de la fondation nationale des sciences politiques, 1977.

Latreille, André, and André Siegfried, eds. *Les forces religieuses et la vie politique: Le catholicisime et le protestantisme.* Paris: Armand Colin, 1951.

Laurent, Sébastien. *Daniel Halévy: Du libéralisme au traditionalisme.* Paris: Bernard Grasset, 2001.

Layton, Walter. "La situation économique de l'Angleterre." *Revue de Paris* 38, nos. 3–4 (1931): 556–85.

Leask, Rognvald. "André Siegfried and the Discovery of New Zealand Democracy." Unpublished paper, 2005.

Lebovics, Herman. *True France: The Wars over Cultural Identity, 1900–1945.* Ithaca: Cornell University Press, 1992.

Leuilliot, Paul. "Littérature et histoire: Quatre jours chez M. Barrès." *Annales: Histoire, sciences sociales* 18, no. 2 (1963): 332–45.

Leurquin, Xavier. "André Siegfried devant ses élèves." *Économie contemporaine,* 29 March 1960: 27–8.

Leymarie, Michel. *Les intellectuels et la politique en France.* Paris: Presses Universitaires de France, 2001.

– *La preuve par deux: Jérôme et Jean Tharaud.* Paris: CNRS Éditions, 2014.

Luard, Evan. *A History of the United Nations.* Vol. 1, *The Years of Western Domination, 1945–1955.* London: Macmillan, 1982.

MacKenzie, David. *A World beyond Borders: An Introduction to the History of International Organizations.* Toronto: Canadian Historical Association/University of Toronto Press, 2011.

MacRae, Duncan. *Parliament, Parties, and Society in France 1946–1958.* New York: St Martin's Press, 1967.

Marrus, Michael, and Paxton, Robert O. *Vichy France and the Jews.* 2nd ed. Stanford: Stanford University Press, 1995.

Martin-Siegfried, Alfred. "La démocratie en Nouvelle-Zélande vue par André Siegfried en 1900 puis par Fernand Braudel en 1986." *Mondes et cultures* 48, no. 4 (1988): 662–74.

Martinez, Gilles. "Comment les libéraux sont arrivés à Vichy: Étude d'un parcours paradoxal." *Revue d'histoire moderne et contemporaine* 46, no. 3 (1999): 571–90.

Mercier, Lucien. *Les universités populaires 1899–1914: Éducation populaire et mouvement ouvrier au début du siècle.* Paris: Les Éditions Ouvrières, 1986.

Miroglio, Abel. *Un grand Havrais: André Siegfried.* Le Havre: *Bulletin maritime du Havre,* 1971.

– "L'oeuvre sociologique de M. André Siegfried." *Revue de métaphysique et de morale* 50, no. 4 (1945): 272–302.

Naviaux, Jean-Hubert. "Le Musée social au lendemain de la première guerre mondiale et dans l'entre-deux-guerres: Permanences et mutations." Mémoire de maîtrise, Université de Paris X – Nanterre, 1986.

Nemni, Max, and Monique Nemni. *Trudeau Transformed: The Shaping of a Statesman 1944–1965.* Translated by George Tombs. Toronto: McClelland and Stewart, 2011. Originally published as *Trudeau, fils du Québec, père du Canada,* tome 2, *La formation d'un homme d'état* (Montreal: Les Éditions de l'Homme, 2011).

Noël, Léon. "Le projet d'union franco-britannique, juin 1940." *Revue d'histoire de la deuxième guerre mondiale* 6, no. 21 (1956): 22–37.

Noiriel, Gérard. *Les origines républicaines de Vichy.* Paris: Hachette, 1999.

Nord, Philip. *France's New Deal: From the Thirties to the Postwar Era.* Princeton: Princeton University Press, 2010.

# Bibliography

- "Reform, Conservation, and Adaptation: Sciences-Po, from the Popular Front to the Liberation." In *The Jacobin Legacy in Modern France: Essays in Honour of Vincent Wright*, edited by Sudhir Hazareesingh, 115–46. Oxford: Oxford University Press, 2002.
- *The Republican Moment: Struggles for Democracy in Nineteenth-Century France*. Cambridge: Harvard University Press, 1995.

Office français de renseignements aux États-Unis/French Information Center: *Assemblée générale annuelle du 23 février 1939*. Paris: E. Desfossés, 1939.

Ory, Pascal, and Jean-François Sirinelli. *Les intellectuels en France, de l'affaire Dreyfus à nos jours*. 3rd ed. Paris: Armand Colin, 2002.

Panchasi, Roxanne. *Future Tense: The Culture of Anticipation in France between the Wars*. Ithaca: Cornell University Press, 2009.

Piterberg, Gabriel, and Lorenzo Veracini. "Wakefield, Marx, and the World Turned Inside Out." *Journal of Global History* 10, no. 3 (2015): 457–78.

Pommier, Jean. *Notice sur la vie et les travaux de André Siegfried (1875–1959)*. Paris: Firmin-Didot, 1961.

Portes, Jacques. *Fascination and Misgivings: The United States in French Opinion, 1870–1914*. Translated by Elborg Forster. Cambridge: Cambridge University Press, 2000. Originally published as *Une fascination réticente: Les États-Unis dans l'opinion française, 1870–1914* (Nancy: Presses universitaires de Nancy, 1990).

Pozzi, Catherine. *Journal: 1913–1934*. New edition by Claire Paulhan with Éric Dussert. Preface by Lawrence Joseph. Paris: Editions Phébus, 2005 (1997).

Rain, Pierre. *L'École libre des sciences politiques*. Paris: FNSP, 1963.

Reggiani, Andrés Horacio. *God's Eugenicist: Alexis Carrel and the Sociobiology of Decline*. New York: Berghahn Books, 2007.

Reynaud Paligot, Carole. "André Siegfried et la question raciale." *Sociétés et représentations* 20, no. 2 (2005): 268–85.

- "Les *Annales* de Lucien Febvre à Fernand Braudel: Entre epopée coloniale et opposition orient/occident." *French Historical Studies* 32, no. 1 (2009): 121–44.
- "La psychologie des peuples et ses applications durant l'entre-deux-guerres." *Revue de synthèse* 129, no. 1 (2008): 125–46.
- *Races, racisme et antiracisme dans les années 1930*. Paris: Presses universitaires de France, 2007.
- *La République raciale: Paradigme racial et idéologie républicaine (1860–1930)*. Paris: Presses universitaires de France, 2006.

Rioux, Jean-Pierre. *The Fourth Republic, 1944–1958*. Translated by Godfrey Rogers. Cambridge: Cambridge University Press, 1987. Originally published as *La France de la Quatrième République*, 2 vols. (Paris: Seuil, 1980–83).

Ritchie, Charles. *The Siren Years: A Canadian Diplomat Abroad 1937–1945*. Toronto: McClelland and Stewart, 2001 (1974).

Rochelson, Meri-Jane. *A Jew in the Public Arena: The Career of Israel Zangwill*. Detroit: Wayne State University Press, 2008.

Roger, Philippe. *The American Enemy: The History of French Anti-Americanism*. Translated by Sharon Bowman. Chicago: University of Chicago Press, 2005. Originally published as *L'ennemi américain: Généologie de l'antiaméricanisme français* (Paris: Seuil, 2002).

Rosenberg, Clifford. "Albert Sarraut and Republican Racial Thought." In *Race in France: Interdisciplinary Perspectives*, edited by Herrick Chapman and Laura L. Frader, 36–53. New York: Berghahn Books, 2004.

Roussel, Éric. *Charles de Gaulle*. Paris: Gallimard, 2002.

Rupp, Leila J. *Worlds of Women: The Making of an International Women's Movement*. Princeton: Princeton University Press, 1997.

Sanguin, André-Louis. "André Siegfried et le *Tableau*." In *Le* Tableau politique de la France de l'Ouest *d'André Siegfried*, edited by Michel Bussi, Christophe Le Digol, and Christophe Voilliot, 17–27. Rennes: Presses Universitaires de Rennes, 2016.

– *André Siegfried: Un visionnaire humaniste entre géographie et politique*. Paris: L'Harmattan, 2010.

– *Vidal de la Blache (1845–1918): Un génie de la géographie*. Paris: Éditions Belin, 1993.

Sanson, Rosemonde. "Centre et gauche (1901–1914): L'Alliance Républicaine Démocratique et le Parti Radical-Socialiste." *Revue d'histoire moderne et contemporaine* 39, no. 3 (1992): 493–512.

Sapiro, Gisèle. *La guerre des écrivains 1940–1953*. Paris: Fayard, 1999.

Schalk, David. *War and the Ivory Tower: Algeria and Vietnam*. New York: Oxford University Press, 1991.

Scot, Marie. "Sciences Po et les femmes: 140 ans d'histoire." *Émile*, 28 November 2019, https://www.emilemagazine.fr/article/2019/11/28/sciences-po-et-les-femmes-140-ans-dhistoire.

Sedgwick, Mark. *Against the Modern World: Traditionalism and the Secret Intellectual History of the Twentieth Century*. New York: Oxford University Press, 2004.

Shennan, Andrew. *Rethinking France: Plans for Renewal, 1940–1946*. Oxford: Clarendon Press, 1989.

# Bibliography

Siedentop, Larry. "Two Liberal Traditions." In *French Liberalism from Montesquieu to the Present Day*, edited by Raf Geenens and Helena Rosenblatt, 15–35. Cambridge: Cambridge University Press, 2012.

Siegel, Mona L. *Peace on Our Terms: The Global Battle for Women's Rights After the First World War*. New York: Columbia University Press, 2020.

Siegfried, André. *African Journey*. Translated by Edward Fitzgerald. London: Jonathan Cape, 1950. Originally published as *Afrique du Sud: Notes de voyage* (Paris: Armand Colin, 1949).

– "Allocution de M. André Siegfried à la première séance de la Section d'études sociales, le mercredi 25 November 1942." *Cahiers du Musée social* no. 2 (1943): 67–75.

– *America at Mid-Century*. Translated by Margaret Ledésert. New York: Harcourt, Brace and Company, 1955. Originally published as *Tableau des États-Unis* (Paris: Armand Colin, 1954).

– *America Comes of Age: A French Analysis*. Translated by H.H. Hemming and Doris Hemming. London: Jonathan Cape, 1927. Originally published as *Les États-Unis d'aujourd'hui* (Paris: Armand Colin, 1927).

– *Amérique latine*. Paris: Armand Colin, 1934.

– "L'anticolonialisme américain." *Revue de Paris* 64 (September 1957): 3–16.

– "Approaches to an Understanding of Modern France." In *Modern France: Problems of the Third and Fourth Republics*, edited by Edward Mead Earle, 3–16. Princeton: Princeton University Press, 1951.

– ed. *Aspects de la société française*. Paris: Librairie général de droit et de jurisprudence, 1954.

– *Aspects du vingtième siècle*. Paris: Hachette, 1955.

– *Autour de la route de Suez: Articles parus dans* Le Petit Havre *d'Octobre 1937 à Janvier 1938*. Le Havre: Imprimerie du Journal *Le Petit Havre*, 1938.

– "Brazil and Its People." *The Economist* 130 (12 March 1938): 550–2.

– *Canada: An International Power*. Translated by Doris Hemming. London: Jonathan Cape, 1937. Originally published as *Le Canada, puissance internationale* (Paris: Armand Colin, 1937).

– "Les causes psychologiques de l'accident du travail." *Cahiers du Musée social*, no. 3 (1953): 51–8.

– *The Character of Peoples*. Translated by Edward Fitzgerald. London: Jonathan Cape, 1952. Originally published as *L'âme des peuples* (Paris: Hachette, 1949).

– "La Chine coloniale: Les Chinois de Singapore." *Revue des revues*, 1 October 1903: 79–89.

# Bibliography

- "La civilisation occidentale." *Revue des deux mondes* 111, no. 65 (15 September 1941): 129–48.
- *La civilisation occidentale: The Romanes Lecture, Delivered in the Sheldonian Theatre, 5 June 1945.* Oxford: Clarendon Press, 1945.
- "The Clash of Continents." *Current History* 42, no. 1 (April 1935): 1–8.
- "Le Collège de France." *Revue de Paris* 45, no. 23 (1 December 1938): 510–21.
- "La contribution de la France, de l'Angleterre et des États-Unis à la civilisation occidentale." *Revue de Paris* 47, no. 3 (1 February 1940): 381–92.
- *Cours de géographie économique et politique (leçon d'ouverture, faite le 28 avril 1933 au Collège de France).* Paris: Boivin & Cie, 1933.
- "La crise de l'industrie britannique." *Revue de Paris* 38, nos. 1–2 (January-February 1931): 509–42.
- "La crise de l'ouvrier qualifié." *Cahiers du Musée social*, no. 1 (1948): 3–5.
- "La culture populaire." *Cahiers du Musée social*, nos. 5–6 (1947): 143–5.
- *De la IIIe à la IVe République.* Paris: Bernard Grasset, 1956.
- *De la IVe à la Ve République au jour le jour.* Paris: Bernard Grasset, 1958.
- "La défense sanitaire de l'Occident." *Cahiers du Musée social*, no. 1 (1943): 5–12.
- *Democracy in New Zealand.* Translated by E.V. Burns. London: G. Bell and Sons, 1914. Originally published as *La Démocratie en Nouvelle-Zélande* (Paris: Armand Colin, 1904).
- *Deux mois en Amérique du Nord à la veille de la guerre: Juin-juillet 1914.* Paris: Armand Colin, 1916.
- "The Development of French Tariff Policy after the War." In *A Picture of World Economic Conditions at the Beginning of 1929.* New York: National Industrial Conference Board, 1929.
- "Le développement économique et social du Japan." *Musée social (Chronique du Musée social)* 6, no. 3 (1901): 65–83.
- "Un dictionnaire américain des idées reçues." *Revue de Paris* 62, no. 1 (January 1955): 5–18.
- "Discours d'André Siegfried." *Cahiers du Musée social*, no. 3 (1945): 157–74.
- "Discours de reception." Académie française, 21 June 1945, http://www.academie-francaise.fr/discours-de-reception-dandre-siegfried.

# Bibliography

- *Douze lettres des États-Unis parues dans* Le Petit Havre *de septembre 1929 à janvier 1930.* Le Havre: *Le Petit Havre,* 1930.
- *Edward Gibbon Wakefield et sa doctrine de la colonisation systématique.* Paris: Armand Colin, 1904.
- [unsigned]. "Les élections à l'Académie Française, analyse d'un scrutin significatif: L'échec de M. Paul Morand." *Revue française de science politique* 8, no. 3 (1958): 646–54.
- *England's Crisis.* Translated by H.H. Hemming and Doris Hemming. London: Jonathan Cape, 1931. Originally published as *La crise britannique au vingtième siècle* (Paris: Armand Colin, 1931).
- "États-Unis 1956." *Revue de Paris* 63, no. 5 (May 1956): 3–18.
- *États-Unis–Canada–Méxique: Lettres de voyage écrites au* Petit Havre. Le Havre: *Le Petit Havre,* 1936.
- "L'Europe et l'Amérique," Lecture delivered at Istanbul University, 22 March 1940. *Üniversitesi ⊠kisat Fakültesi Mecmuasi* 1, https://dergipark.org.tr/en/download/article-file/8801.
- "European Reactions to American Tariff Proposals." *Foreign Affairs* 8, no. 1 (October 1929): 13–19.
- *Europe's Crisis.* Translated by H.H. Hemming and Doris Hemming. London: Jonathan Cape, 1935. Originally published as *La crise de l'Europe* (Paris: Calmann-Lévy, 1935).
- "Évolution politique d'un département sous la troisième République: L'Aude:" *Société d'histoire de la Troisième République* 20 (March 1939): 164–7.
- "La Fondation Universitaire de Belleville (Exercice 1903–1904)." *Le Musée social: Mémoires et documents,* 1904: 181–206.
- "La Fondation Universitaire de Belleville: Une expérience de cinq ans." *Revue politique et parlementaire* 11, no. 41 (September 1904): 573–85.
- *La Fontaine, Machiavel français.* Paris: Éditions Fragrance, 1950.
- *France: A Study in Nationality.* No translator identified. New Haven: Yale University Press, 1930. Originally published as *Tableau des partis en France* (Paris: Bernard Grasset, 1930).
- "France and Her Allies: Addresses by General Paul Pau and M. André Siegfried." *The Empire Club of Canada Addresses,* 25 February 1919, 138–48, http://speeches.empireclub.org/62503/data?n=1.
- *France, Angleterre, États-Unis, Canada: Articles parus dans* Le Figaro *depuis la Libération jusqu'au début de 1946.* Paris: Émile-Paul, 1946.
- "La France et les problèmes de l'immigration et de l'émigration." *Cahiers du Musée social,* nos. 2–3 (1946): 59–75.

## Bibliography

- "Franco-American and Franco-British Relations." *Journal of the Royal Institute of International Affairs* 5, no. 5 (September 1926): 225–38.
- "The French Democratic Tradition." *Foreign Affairs* 17, no. 4 (July 1939): 649–62.
- "French Industry and Mass Production." *Harvard Business Review* 6, no. 1 (October 1927): 1–10.
- "The French Mind." *Atlantic Monthly* 144 (December 1929): 744–54.
- "French: The Language of Human Thought." *The American Legion of Honor Magazine* 40 (Autumn 1946): 469–81.
- *Géographie électorale de l'Ardèche sous la Troisième République.* Paris: Armand Colin, 1949.
- *Géographie humoristique de Paris.* Paris: La Passerelle, 1951.
- *Géographie poétique des cinq continents.* Paris: La Passerelle, 1952.
- "Le groupe protestant cévenol sous la IIIe République." In *Protestantisme français*, 23–55, edited by Marc Boegner and André Siegfried. Paris: Plon, 1945.
- "The Gulf Between." *Atlantic Monthly* 141 (March 1928): 289–95.
- *Impressions du Brésil: Articles parus dans* Le Petit Havre *du 5 au 19 septembre 1937.* Le Havre: *Le Petit Havre*, 1937.
- *Impressions of South America.* Translated by H.H. Hemming and Doris Hemming. London: Jonathan Cape, 1933. Originally published as *En Amérique du Sud: Articles parus dans* Le Petit Havre *de juillet à décembre 1931* (Le Havre: *Le Petit Havre*, 1932).
- "Introduction à l'étude du rôle de l'ouvrier qualifié dans l'industrie." *Cahiers du Musée social*, no. 1 (1949): 3–6.
- *Jules Siegfried: 1837–1922.* Paris: Firmin-Didot, 1942. Republished as *Mes souvenirs de la Troisième République: Mon père et son temps, Jules Siegfried, 1836–1922.* Paris: Éditions du Grand Siècle, 1946.
- "Letters from South America." *Fortnightly Review*, 1 February 1933: 137–57.
- *Mes souvenirs d'enfance.* Bourges: Imprimerie Tardy, 1957.
- "Middletown: Une ville américaine pendant la crise." *Revue de Paris* 47, no. 8 (15 April 1940): 553–80.
- "Un monde nouveau." *Cahiers du Musée social*, no. 1 (1947): 3–14.
- "Nouvelle-Zélande: Une enquête économique et sociale." *Revue politique et parlementaire* 7, no. 23 (January-March 1900): 173–99, 677–99.
- "L'occident et la direction spirituelle du monde." *La Cause*, November 1932: 5–19.
- "L'oeuvre technique de l'homme et la géographie." *Les études philosophiques* new series, 12, no. 3 (July-September 1957): 257–60.

- "Les parrainages de la France dévastée." *Addresses Delivered at the Reception of the Allied and Foreign Press, on the 30th January 1945*, 9–16. Fontenay-aux-Roses: Imprimeries Bellenand, 1945.
- "Les partis politiques en France." *The University Magazine* 7, no. 1 (1908): 153–68.
- "The Passing of England's Economic Hegemony." *Foreign Affairs* 6, no. 4 (July 1928): 525–40.
- "La politique extérieure des États-Unis." *Revue de Paris* 46, no. 22 (15 November 1939): 757–76.
- *Post-War Britain.* Translated by H.H. Hemming. London: Jonathan Cape, 1924. Originally published as *L'Angleterre d'aujourd'hui: Son évolution économique et politique* (Paris: G. Crès, 1924).
- Preface to *Figures féminines mil neuf cent neuf – mil neuf cent trente-neuf: Billets du samedi*, by Louli Sanua, 1–2. Paris: Beaufils, 1946.
- Preface to *Géographie économique de l'Allemagne Orientale, zone soviètique d'occupation*, by Léon Agourtine. Berlin: Haut Commissariat de la République Française en Allemagne, 1952.
- Preface to *L'économie allemande contemporaine (Allemagne Occidentale) 1945–1952*, by André Piettre, vii–vx. Paris: Éditions M. Th. Genin, 1952.
- Preface to *L'Europe en face de son destin*, by Édouard Bonnefous, 9–20. Paris: Presses universitaires de France, 1955 (1952).
- Preface to *La dignité humain*, by Russell Davenport, 7–10. Paris: Nouvelles Éditions Latines, 1958.
- Preface to *La zone sterling*, by Jean de Sailly, xiii–xviii. Paris: Armand Colin, 1957.
- Preface to *Le commonwealth britannique et le monde anglo-saxon*, by Raymond Ronze, ix–vi. Monaco: Éditions du Rocher, 1947.
- Preface to *Le destin des races blanches*, by Henri Decugis, i–vii. Paris: Félix Alcan, 1935.
- Preface to *Le grand changement de l'Amérique (1900–1950)*, by Frederick Lewis Allen, 7–10. Paris: Amiot-Dumont, 1953.
- Preface to *Le grand espoir du XXe siècle*, by Jean Fourastié, ix–xv. Paris: Presses universitaires de France, 1949.
- Preface to *Mon village: Ses hommes, ses routes, son école*, by Roger Thabault, 7–15. 10th ed. Paris: Presses de la Fondation Nationale des Sciences Politiques, 1993 (1944).
- Preface to *Normandie*, with photographs by Noel Le Boyer and captions by Georges Monmarché, 5–31. Paris: Librairie Hachette, 1957.
- Preface to *Questions de langage*, by Louis Piéchaud, 1–7. Paris: Éditions du Lys, 1952.

330          Bibliography

- "La prévention des accidents du travail: lettre préface." *Cahiers du Musée Social*, nos. 5–6 (1952), 135–7.
- *Les principaux courants de la pensée réligieuse en France: Conférence prononcée à l'Hotel Majestic, à Buenos-Ayres le 17 Septembre 1931.* Buenos Aires: Comite Pro-Église Évangelique de Langue Française, n.d.
- "Les problèmes ethniques de l'Afrique du Sud." *Cahiers du Musée social*, no. 4 (1949): 123–38.
- "La psychologie du Normand." *Études normandes* 15, no. 2 (1955): 233–44.
- "The Psychology of French Political Parties." *Journal of the Royal Institute of International Affairs* 7, no. 1 (February 1928): 12–28.
- "The Psychology of French Politics." *Atlantic Monthly* 143 (January 1930): 87–96.
- *Quelques maximes.* Paris: J. Haumont, 1943.
- *Qu'est-ce que l'Amérique?* Paris: Flammarion, 1937.
- *The Race Question in Canada.* Translator not identified. Toronto: McClelland and Stewart, 1966 (1907). Originally published as *Le Canada, les deux races: Problèmes politiques contemporains* (Paris: Armand Colin, 1906).
- "Le régime et la division de la propriété dans le Maine et l'Anjou." *Le Musée social: Mémoires et documents* (1911): 197–215.
- "Le régime et la division de la propriété dans le Pays de Caux." *Le Musée social: Mémoires et documents* (1909): 221–35.
- "La révolution industrielle et ses répercussions sur les problèmes de notre temps." *Le Musée social* 46, no. 2 (February 1939): 30–44.
- "Le rôle de l'épargne dans le développement européen." *Cahiers du Musée social*, no. 4 (1950): 105–9.
- *Le rôle moral et social d'Israel dans les démocraties contemporains: Conférénce faite le 13 mai 1930 au Cercle d'Études Juives* (Paris: Cahiers d'études juives, 3 February 1932).
- *Routes of Contagion.* Translated by Jean Henderson and Mercedes Clarasó. New York: Harcourt, Brace & World, 1965. Originally published as *Itinéraires de contagions: Épidémies et ideologies* (Paris: Armand Colin, 1960).
- *Savoir parler en publique.* Paris: Albin Michel, 1950.
- *Suez and Panama.* Translated by H.H. Hemming and Doris Hemming. London: Jonathan Cape, 1940. Originally published as *Suez, Panama et les routes maritimes mondiales* (Paris: Armand Colin, 1940).
- "The Suez: International Roadway." *Foreign Affairs* 31, no. 4 (1953): 605–18.

# Bibliography

331

- *Switzerland: A Democratic Way of Life*. Translated by Edward Fitzgerald. London: Jonathan Cape, 1950. Originally published as *La Suisse, démocratie-témoin*. Neufchâtel: Éditions de la Baconnière, 1948.
- *Tableau politique de la France de l'Ouest sous la Troisième République*. Preface by Pierre Milza. Paris: Imprimerie national Éditions, 1995 (1913).
- "Technique et culture." *Cahiers du Musée social*, nos. 1–2 (1954): 3–5.
- "La technique et la culture dans une civilisation moderne." *Bulletin technique de la Suisse romande* 81, no. 2 (1955): 37–43.
- "Le Vichy de Pétain, le Vichy de Laval." *Revue française de science politique* 6, no. 4 (1956): 737–49.
- *Les voies d'Israël: Essai d'interprétation de la religion juive*. Paris: Hachette, 1958.
- *Voyage aux Indes*. Paris: Armand Colin, 1951.
- *Vue générale de la Colombie*. Paris: Éditions France-Amérique, 1939.
- *Vue générale de la Méditerranée*. Paris: Gallimard, 1943.
- "War for Our World." *Foreign Affairs* 18, no. 3 (April 1940): 413–23.
- *What the British Empire Means to Western Civilization*. Translated by George M. Wrong. Toronto: Oxford University Press, 1940.
- "Will Europe Be Americanized?" *Yale Review* 19 (March 1930): 433–46.

Siegfried, André, Jérôme Tharaud, and Jean Tharaud. *Le centenaire des Services des Messageries Maritimes (1851–1951)*. Engravings by Patrick de Manceau. Paris: Imprimerie Ettighoffer et Raynaud, 1952.

Siegfried, André, et al., eds. *L'économie dirigée: Conférences organisées par la Société des anciens élèves de l'École libre des sciences politiques*. Paris: Librairie Félix Alcan, 1934.

Sirinelli, Jean-François. *Intellectuels et passions françaises: Manifestes et pétitions au vingtième siècle*. Paris: Fayard, 1990.

Smith, Paul. "*Sénat ou pas Sénat*? The 'First' Council of the Republic." In *The Uncertain Foundation: France at the Liberation, 1944–1947*, edited by Andrew Knapp, 41–56. Houndmills: Palgrave Macmillan, 2007.

Soucy, Robert. *Fascism in France: The Case of Maurice Barrès*. Berkeley: University of California Press, 1972.

Steiner, Zara. *The Lights that Failed: European International History 1919–1933*. Oxford: Oxford University Press, 2005.

Sternhell, Zeev. *Maurice Barrès et le nationalisme français*. 2nd ed. Paris: Arthème Fayard, 2000.

- *Ni droite ni gauche: L'idéologie fasciste en France*. 3rd ed. Brussels: Éditions Complexe, 2000.

Strauss, David. *Menace in the West: The Rise of French Anti-Americanism in Modern Times*. Westport: Greenwood Press, 1978.

Thomas, Martin. *Fight or Flight: Britain, France, and Their Roads from Empire*. Oxford: Oxford University Press, 2014.

Tillmann, Serge. "André Siegfried, l'odyssée de l'occident: La construction d'une histoire des identités." Thèse de doctorat, Normandie Université, 2018.

Toynbee, Arthur J. *Acquaintances*. London: Oxford University Press, 1967.

Traz, Robert de. "André Siegfried." *Revue de Paris* 45, no. 2 (15 January 1938): 311–30.

Tronchet, Guillaume. "Les bourses de voyage 'autour du monde' de la Fondation Albert Kahn (1898–1930)." In *La vie intellectuelle en France*, vol. 1, *Des lendemains de la Révolution à 1914*, edited by Christophe Charle and Laurent Jeanpierre, 618–20. Paris: Éditions du Seuil, 2016.

Vincent, Gérard. *Sciences-Po: Histoire d'une réussite*. Paris: Olivier Orban, 1987.

Vincent, K. Steven. *Élie Halévy: Republican Liberalism Confronts the Era of Tyranny*. Philadelphia: University of Pennsylvania Press, 2020.

Vinen, Richard. *Bourgeois Politics in France, 1945–1951*. Cambridge: Cambridge University Press, 1995.

Walters, F.P. *A History of the League of Nations*. 2 vols. London: Oxford University Press, 1952.

Weiss, Louise. "La ligne Siegfried." *Économie contemporaine*, 29 March 1960: 11–14.

Werth, Alexander. *France 1940–1955*. Boston: Beacon Press, 1966.

Will, Barbara. *Unlikely Collaboration: Gertrude Stein, Bernard Faÿ, and the Vichy Dilemma*. New York: Columbia University Press, 2011.

Williams, Philip M. *Crisis and Compromise: Politics in the Fourth Republic*. 3rd ed. London: Longman, 1964.

Winock, Michel. *Le siècle des intellectuels*. Paris: Seuil, 1997.

Winter, Jay. *Dreams of Peace and Freedom: Utopian Moments in the 20th Century*. New Haven: Yale University Press, 2006.

Wylie, Laurence. "André Siegfried à Harvard." In *L'oeuvre scientifique d'André Siegfried*, edited by Édouard Bonnefous, 67–88. Paris: Presses de la Fondation nationale des sciences politiques, 1977.

Young, Robert J. *Marketing Marianne: French Propaganda in America, 1900–1940*. New Brunswick: Rutgers University Press, 2004.

Zeldin, Theodore. *France 1848–1945*. Vol. 1. Oxford: Oxford University Press, 1975.

# Index

Académie des sciences morales et politiques, 7, 16, 119–20, 125, 162, 259
Académie française, 8, 16, 190–1, 227–9
administrative age, 196. *See also* modernity
Africa, 21, 214–17, 264
*Afrique du Sud, L'*, 215–17
Algerian War, 234–5, 240
*âme des peoples, L'*, 219–23
Americanization, 3, 37, 64, 72, 84, 115, 116, 119, 143, 144, 147, 151, 175, 240, 262, 263
*Amérique latine*, 135, 137–9
*Angleterre d'aujourd'hui, L'*, 7, 93–6
Anglo-Saxons. *See* Australia; Canada; Great Britain; New Zealand; United States of America
Annales School, 121, 124
*année politique, L'*, 200, 202, 234
antisemitism, 11, 103–4, 132–3, 176–7, 232, 241, 265. *See also* Jewish People
Argentina, 134, 136, 17, 212

Aron, Raymond, 10, 200, 225, 235, 236, 240
Asia, 44–6, 253–5. *See also* China; Korea; Philippines
*Aspects du XXe siècle*, 243–5
Aubrun, Henri, 197, 213, 226, 256–7
Auriol, Vincent, 206, 230
Australia, 37, 79–80

Barrès, Maurice, 11, 35–7, 71–2, 131, 183, 243
Barthelémy, Joseph, 86, 113, 163, 167
Birnbaum, Pierre, 11, 22, 177, 180, 251, 278n67
Bloch, Marc, 121, 124
Blum, Léon, 91, 129, 133
Boegner, Marc, 166, 198
Bonnard, Abel, 165, 167, 169, 190
Bonnefous, Édouard, 55, 200, 250, 258, 259
Boutmy, Émile, 34–5, 58, 123
Brazil, 141–2, 213–14
Brisson, Pierre, 8, 200, 235, 245, 256, 257

334 Index

Canada, 20, 40, 62–4, 72–4, 114–16

*Canada. Les deux races, Le,* 9, 63–4

*Canada, puissance international, Le,* 114–16

Carrel, Alexis, 18, 126

Castellane, Boniface de, 51–3

Catholicism, 24, 26, 34, 40, 54, 63, 64, 67, 70, 112, 115, 130–1, 137–8, 154, 169, 199, 203, 228, 232, 233. *See also* Protestantism

*centenaire des services des Messageries Maritimes, Le,* 252

Centre international d'études pour le renoveau du libéralisme (CIRL), 126–7

Centre polytechnicien d'études économiques, 124–5

Chapsal, Jacques, 96, 102–3, 140, 197, 225–6, 237, 257

Chatham House. *See* Royal Institute of International Affairs

Chile, 212–13

China, 37, 45–6, 87, 112, 211, 219, 254, 264

class relations, 30, 33, 50–1, 59, 69–70, 98, 186–7, 197, 205–6, 262

Collège de France, 7, 9, 16, 120–2, 156, 160, 161–3, 191–2, 207, 259

Colloque Lippmann. *See* Centre international d'études pour le renoveau du libéralisme (CIRL)

Colombia, 142–3

Communism, 137, 153, 155, 183, 207, 238. *See also* Parti communiste français (PCF); socialism; Soviet Union

Congo, 215

Conservatism. *See* right-wing politics (France)

Cot, Pierre, 134, 193

Coty, René, 83, 230, 235, 236

Coutrot, Jean, 125–6

*crise britannique aux XXe siècle, La,* 97–101

*crise de l'Europe, La,* 144–8, 175, 176, 219, 264

Daniel-Rops, Henri, 227–8, 300n12

Dautry, Raoul, 200–1, 245

Debré, Michel, 167, 193

de Gaulle, Charles, 57, 167, 184–6, 191, 193–4, 201, 203, 206, 210, 224, 229, 232, 233, 235, 236

*De la IIIe à la IVe République,* 231–3, 235–6

*De la IVe à la Vème République,* 236

democracy, 26, 30, 69, 112–13, 137–8, 154–6, 186, 233

*démocratie en Nouvelle-Zélande, La,* 35, 60–1, 64

*Deux mois en Amérique du Nord,* 72–6

Dubois, Marcel, 59–60

Duhamel, Georges, 190, 191, 193

École libre des sciences politiques (Sciences Po), 5, 6, 7, 15, 34–5, 85–92, 163–5, 167–8, 192–5, 225–6

École nationale d'administration (ENA), 193–4

Egypt, 148–50

*En Amérique du Sud,* 135–9

*États-Unis d'aujourd'hui, Les,* 7, 101–7

# Index

Fabre, Gérard, 12–13
Faral, Edmond, 162
Faÿ, Bernard, 120, 191–2
Febvre, Lucien, 121, 124, 192, 266–7
*Figaro*, 8, 16, 17, 162, 171, 177, 184, 186, 200, 206, 210, 213, 217, 228, 230–1, 234–5, 238, 245, 246, 256, 292n55, 301n27, 301n35, 302n40
Fondation nationale des sciences politiques (FNSP), 9, 194, 196–7, 226
Fondation universitaire de Belleville. See *universités populaires*
*Foreign Affairs*, 154, 159
Foreign Office (United Kingdom), 99, 101
Fourth Republic (French), 200–7, 224, 229–43
France: centrality to Western civilization, 14, 23, 78–9, 220–1, 263, 264, 267; compared to English-speaking nations, 20, 110–11, 113–14, 116–17, 154–5, 159–60, 179, 221, 236–7, 263; cultural status, 209–10, 248–9; identity of, 264; impact of Second World War on, 208
Franco-Prussian War, 5, 25, 34, 134
French Antilles, 134–5
French Communist Party. See Parti communiste français (PCF)
French Indochina (war in), 224, 229, 230, 231, 233
French Socialist Party. See Section française de l'internationale ouvrière (SFIO)

*Géographie électorale de l'Ardèche*, 199
*Géographie humoristique de Paris*, 205
*Géographie poétique des cinq continents*, 205 .
Germany, 21, 147, 156–7, 182, 209, 221–2, 249–50, 264.
See also Nazism
Gobineau, Arthur de, 149, 242
Goguel, François, 9, 10, 83, 199–200, 258, 260, 272n19
Gottmann, Jean, 226, 260, 300n6
Great Britain, 19, 38, 92–101, 156–8, 208–9, 221–2, 249, 264

Halévy, Daniel, 51, 130
Halévy, Élie, 86, 145
Hamp, Pierre, 51, 77, 161–2, 257
Hartung, Henri, 246–7
Hoffmann, Stanley, 10, 226, 242

immigration, 18, 42–3, 44, 61, 64, 74–5, 80, 88, 103–4, 107, 109, 115, 136, 175–7, 195, 198, 214, 238–9, 264, 265
India, 217–19, 253, 264
Institut de France, 34, 119, 259
Institut d'études politiques (IEP), 162, 194
Institut Havrais de Sociologie économique et de Psychologie des Peoples, 123–4, 259–60
*Itinéraires de contagion*, 254

Japan, 44–5, 87, 130, 149, 159, 173
Jewish People, 18–19, 33, 103–4, 107; 131–3, 156, 173–5, 232, 239, 241, 250–2, 265

336 Index

*Jules Siegfried*, 177–8, 179

Korea, 44, 237, 253

*La Fontaine: Machiavel français*, 205

Latin America, 20–1, 134–44, 212–14

Laurier, Wilfrid, 41, 63, 73

League of Nations, 82–3

Le Havre, 5, 6, 9, 25, 32, 40, 48, 54, 56, 69, 71, 83, 200, 257, 259

liberalism, 17–18, 37, 43, 53, 108, 122, 126–7, 154, 157, 160, 170, 179, 185, 187, 190–1, 196–7, 202, 229, 261–2

Lloyd George, David, 81, 82, 94

Lyautey, Hubert (Marshal), 113, 172

Madariaga, Salvador de, 123

Māori, 42, 60–1

Marxism. *See* Communism; socialism

Mediterranean, 21, 148–50, 155–6, 180–2, 245, 263

Mendès France, Pierre, 187, 230–1, 233

Métin, Albert, 64, 79

Mexico, 135, 140–1, 253

Midi (France), 21, 118, 127–30, 170, 199, 226

Ministry of Foreign Affairs (France), 49, 83, 86, 140, 256

Miroglio, Abel, 9, 123–4, 259–60

modernity, 19–20, 105–6, 108, 243–7, 262. *See also* Americanization; technology

Montandon, Georges, 164–5, 181

Morand, Paul, 35, 112, 228–9

Mouvement républicain populaire (MRP), 203

Musée social, 6, 7, 15–16, 20, 38–9, 168–70, 196–8, 226–7, 273–4n46

National Revolution, 17, 171–2, 178, 186, 232. *See also* Vichy regime

Nazism, 155, 157, 175, 207, 222, 263. *See also* Germany

Nef, John U., 237, 258, 302n51

New Zealand, 42–3, 60–1, 80

Normandy, 30, 56, 67, 69–70, 166, 247–8, 303n94

Pakistan, 217–19

Palestine, 148, 156

Panama, 150–1

Panama Canal, 148, 150, 169, 173

Parti communiste français (PCF), 18, 183, 192, 201–2, 206, 231–3, 261. *See also* Communism

Peru, 139–40

*Petit Havre*, 40, 46, 59, 72, 81, 135, 140, 148, 149

Philippines, 44

Poincaré, Raymond, 17, 113, 133, 140, 205, 231

Popular Front (France), 91, 133–4, 206, 230

Pozzi, Catherine, 57

Protestantism, 9, 33, 56, 57, 63, 95, 104–5, 119, 130–1, 132, 144, 159, 169, 172, 183, 198–9. *See also* Catholicism; Siegfried family

*Quelques maximes*, 178–9

racism, 18, 20, 21–2, 46–7, 61, 87, 103–4, 116–17, 164–5, 174–5, 180–1, 198, 214, 215–17, 218–19, 239, 241–2, 252–3, 265–6

Radicalism (France), 128–9, 130, 199, 233

Rassemblement du peuple français (RPF), 203, 206, 231, 232

religion. *See* Catholicism; Jewish People; Protestantism

*Revue de Paris*, 33, 99, 122, 158–9, 242, 254

Reynaud Paligot, Carole, 12, 123, 265

Rhodesia, 214, 215

right-wing politics (France), 17, 18, 26, 46, 48, 53, 54, 67, 70–1, 112–13, 129–30, 131, 133, 185, 199, 203, 206–7, 232, 236, 262

Risler, Georges, 92, 95, 142, 168

Romania, 144

Roques, Mario, 121, 149

Royal Institute of International Affairs (Chatham House), 96, 110, 158, 208

Rueff, Jacques, 98, 163

rural life, 182. *See also* modernity.

Russia. *See* Soviet Union

Sanguin, André-Louis, 13, 22, 58, 71, 251, 265

Sapiro, Gisèle, 191, 295n4

*Savoir parler en publique*, 205

Schlesinger, Arthur, Jr, 226, 241

Schlumberger, Jean, 57

Sciences Po. *See* École libre des sciences politiques

Section française de l'internationale ouvrière (SFIO), 185, 201–3, 231–4, 261. *See also* socialism

Seignobos, Charles, 35, 60, 65, 172, 222

Service français de la Société des Nations (SFSDN), 81–2

Seydoux, Roger, 8, 86, 88, 163, 167, 193–5, 200, 237, 240, 256

Siegfried, André: appointment to Sciences Po, 58; death, 256–7; decision to remain in France (1940), 160–2; education, 33–4; election to Académie des sciences morales et politiques (1932), 119–20; election to Académie française (1944), 190–1; election to Collège de France (1933), 120–1; electoral campaigns, 51–6; family and upbringing, 28–32; First World War, 76–9; intellectual influences, 34–7; and League of Nations, 81–3; and liberation of Paris, 183–4; marriage and family life, 56–8; military service, 37; Phony War (1939–40), 154–61; president of Musée social, 168–70, 196–8; San Francisco Conference (1945), 210–12; Suez Crisis 1956, 21–2, 242; teaching at Collège de France, 121–2, 156, 162, 195–6; teaching at Harvard University (1955), 225–6; teaching at Sciences Po, 85–9, 164

Siegfried, André, views on: Americanization, 138–9, 143–4, 146–7, 175, 180, 213, 180, 207–8, 240, 262–3; anti-Black racism, 62, 74, 136, 142, 214–17, 227, 239, 253; anticolonialism, 218, 237–8, 254–5, 264; Czechoslovak Crisis (1938), 116, 134; Europe, 20, 144–8, 174–6, 208, 242, 250; France, 14, 65–72, 110–14, 130, 179; French Revolution, 14–15, 116–17, 153–5, 166, 183, 265; geography as a discipline, 30, 33, 35, 59, 71, 118, 127, 252, 260; Indigenous Peoples, racism toward, 136, 140, 253, 264, 298n68; Latinity, 14, 141, 143, 219–20; New Deal, 106, 170, 176; psychology of peoples, 9, 12, 123–4, 257, 260, 270n20

Siegfried, Jules, 5, 6, 25–7, 31–2, 39, 51–2, 82, 134, 172, 177–8, 271n1, 272n5

Siegfried, Julie (née Puaux), 5, 28–9, 31–2, 82

Siegfried, Paule (née Laroche), 6, 56–8, 78, 140, 189, 242, 258

Siegfried family: Claire (daughter), 57–8, 184, 189; Ernest (brother), 29; Jacques (uncle), 29; and Liberation of Paris (1944), 183; relocation to Brittany (1940), 161; Robert (brother), 7, 29

socialism, 3, 6, 26, 55, 68–9, 70, 71, 110, 261. *See also* Section française de l'internationale ouvrière (SFIO)

social reform, 26, 46, 169–70, 226–7, 254. *See also* Musée social

Société d'histoire de la Troisième République, 129, 134

South Africa, 215, 216–17

South Asia, 21, 217–19. *See also* India; Pakistan

Soviet Union, 155, 156, 212, 222, 263

Sternhell, Zeev, 11–12, 22, 35

Stoddard, Lothrop, 145, 152

Suez Canal, 148–50, 169

*Suez, Panama et les routes maritimes mondiales,* 149–51

*Suisse, démocratie témoin, La,* 203–5

Switzerland, 203–5, 264

*Tableau des États-Unis,* 238–42

*Tableau des partis en France,* 111–14

*Tableau politique de la France de l'Ouest,* 6, 9, 10–11, 17, 65–72, 199–200, 260–1

Taine, Hippolyte, 35, 123

Tardieu, André, 106, 120

technology, 227, 243–7. *See also* modernity

*Temps, Le,* 9, 16, 162, 171, 177

Third Republic (French), 17, 111–13, 134, 170, 199, 202, 203, 205, 231

Tillmann, Serge, 13, 22, 164, 273n34, 276n20, 277n34

Tocqueville, Alexis de, 9, 35, 259

Toynbee, Arnold, 152, 158, 184, 185

Trudeau, Pierre, 195

Turkey, 156

Underhill, Frank, 9, 64

United States of America, 14–15, 19–21, 41, 62, 74–6, 101–9, 158–60, 174–5, 211–12, 221–2, 236–43 *universités populaires*, 49–51, 98, 262

Valéry, Paul, 35, 190
Vallat, Xavier, 8, 235
Vichy regime, 17, 166, 171–2, 232, 261–2. *See also* National Revolution
Vidal de la Blache, Paul, 35, 59, 65, 66, 71–2, 118
*voies d'Israël, Les*, 250–2
*Vue générale de la Méditerranée*, 21, 178–80, 294n83

Wakefield, Edward Gibbon, 61–2
Weiss, Louise, 57, 258

Western Civilization, 4, 13, 15, 21, 23, 37, 74, 85, 139, 145, 147, 151–2, 156, 157, 159, 160, 163, 173–5, 182 186, 207–8, 209, 217, 218–19, 225, 240, 252–3, 263
women, 44–5, 78, 89, 98, 102, 104, 163, 244
Wylie, Laurence, 10, 89, 242

X-Crise. *See* Centre polytechnicien d'études économiques

Zangwill, Israel, 133, 250
Zay, Jean, 91